EIGHTEENTH CENTURY SHAKESPEARE

No. 26

General Editor : Professor Arthur Freeman, Boston University

I0591896

A

Supplemental Apology

FOR

THE BELIEVERS

IN THE

Shakspeare-Papers

A complete list of titles in this series
is included at the end of this volume.

A

SUPPLEMENTAL APOLOGY

FOR

THE BELIEVERS

IN THE

Shakspeare-Papers

BEING A REPLY

To Mr. Malone's Answer

Which was Early Announced, but never Published

BY

George Chalmers

Routledge

Taylor & Francis Group

LONDON AND NEW YORK

First published 1971 by
FRANK CASS AND COMPANY LIMITED

Published 2013 by Routledge
2 Park Square, Milton Park, Abingdon, Oxfordshire OX14 4RN
711 Third Avenue, New York, NY 10017

First issued in paperback 2016

Routledge is an imprint of the Taylor and Francis Group,
an informa business

Publisher's Note
The publisher has gone to great lengths to
ensure the quality of this reprint but points out that
some imperfections in the original may be apparent

ISBN 13: 978-1-138-98338-0 (pbk)
ISBN 13: 978-0-7146-2536-2 (hbk)

PREFACE

At the time of the appearance of George Chalmers *Apology* (1797) it was rumoured that Malone intended a full reply; but whether tired of the controversy, unable to make enough capital of the defects in the *Apology*, or simply discreet, no such answer forthcame from the author of *An Inquiry*. Steevens, however, reviewed the *Apology* without any attenuation of the peremptory if righteous condescension Chalmers had censured in the work under notice. Ignoring the bulk of Chalmers' disputation, Steevens concentrates upon the apparent truism that 'when men confess themselves knaves, there is an end of Detection'.

Quite sensibly Chalmers abandoned that sunken ship. *A Supplemental Apology* has little if anything to add to the Ireland controversy; it is instead an extension of the more general methodological principles set out in *An Apology*, carrying forth the investigation into miscellaneous new areas of antiquarian research. As satirist Chalmers is not always deft, but the mock dedication to Steevens is a successful beginning to a book rerely querelous, and rarely foolish or arbitrary. If Chalmers' contribution to the progress of scholarly method (as opposed to antiquarian discovery or editorial service) is ever to be reassessed, the *Supplemental Apology* no less than the earlier *Apology* will independently stand among his most estimable achievements, perhaps eclipsing *Caledonia* and the bulk of his 'indefatigable' output of tracts and pamphlets on no end of topics over fifty years of productivity.

An Appendix to the 'Supplemental Apology', being the Documents for the Opinion that Hugh Boyd wrote Junius's 'Letters' appeared later in the same year, another massive but less successful assembly of fact and extrapolation, again independent and quite unrelated to Shakespearean affairs. The present reprint of *A Supplemental Apology* is prepared from an uncut presentation copy (to Sir John Scott, probably Lord Eldon) in the possession of the Publishers, dismantled by the General Editor, and compared with copies in the British Museum and at Harvard. It collates ^{4}A–Z^{8}Aa–Tt^{8}, with no cancels, Tt^{8} containing the errata both for *An Apology* and for the present volume.

December, 1970   A. F.

A

SUPPLEMENTAL APOLOGY

FOR

THE BELIEVERS

IN THE

SHAKSPEARE - PAPERS:

BEING

A REPLY

TO MR. MALONE'S ANSWER,

WHICH WAS EARLY ANNOUNCED, BUT NEVER PUBLISHED:

WITH

A DEDICATION

TO GEORGE STEEVENS, F. R. S. S. A.

AND

A POSTSCRIPT

TO T. J. MATHIAS, F. R. S. S. A.

THE AUTHOR OF THE PURSUITS OF LITERATURE.

By GEORGE CHALMERS, F. R. S. S. A.

LONDON:
Printed for THOMAS EGERTON, Whitehall.

1799.

To GEORGE STEEVENS, F. R. S. S. A.

SIR,

I COULD not dedicate this work, which has for its principal objects *the Studies of* SHAKSPEARE, the Chronology of his Dramas, the Hiftory of the Stage, during his age, and of the Office of the Mafter of the Revels, to any one fo fitly as to you, who are the oldeft, I was going to fay, the beft, though not the *immaculate,* Editor of *the* PLAYS of our immortal Dramatift. For dedicating this work to you, I have another reafon, which may be deemed rather *undedicatory :* While I was writing my APOLOGY, you often declared, " that I " could not poffibly know any thing of Shakfpeare."

I was in the act of thanking you, for fome communications, when I was affured, that you daily made fuch declarations, with threats of chaftifement. You admitted, indeed, that the object of your obloquy was a good fort of a man; but you, conftantly, afked, what can he know about Shakfpeare? He has written very able *Tracts upon Trade* ; but, what can he know about Shakfpeare? He has written an elaborate book of *Political Annals*; but, what can he know about Shakfpeare? He has written feveral *Lives*, with knowledge, and elegance; but, what can he know about Shakfpeare? In all his writings, he, certainly, gives us fomething new; new facts, and new principles; but, what can he

a 2   know

know about Shakſpeare? WE are, however, prepared for him; we have our bliſtering plaſters ready ; and WE will make him ſore: we will teach him, by our Paragraphs, our Eſſays, our Epigrams, and our Reviews, what it is to write about what he cannot know.

But, you did not conſider, that the man, whom you thus threatened, had been bred in the School of Adverſity, and was not ſo eaſily to be made ſore ; that he had written much, without the vain incitement of praiſe, or the empty hope of profit; and had become callous to monthly criticiſms, weekly eſſays, and daily paragraphs; becauſe he was no ſtranger to the motives of thoſe, who penned them. You did not recollect, what Johnſon had taught you, that an Author may write himſelf down, but cannot be written down by others, unleſs he be wanting to himſelf. He who endeavours well, and is, at the ſame time, indifferent alike to cenſure, or praiſe, needs not fear ſuch *cantharides* as your ſhop ſupplies.

When I was told of your daily talk, I made, in my Apology, a few remarks on your Shakſpeare, by way of intimation to your ſhrewdneſs, that I had heard of your threats, without being frightened from my purpoſe: But, I truſted to a ſagacity, which I ſoon perceived you did not poſſeſs. And, I have been thus obliged to addreſs much of this Supplement to you, as an apology, for preſuming, like ſome of the Editors of Shakſpeare, to write upon that immortal poet, without much knowledge of the ſubject ; a ſubject, which few have made any pretenſions to underſtand, without incurring reproach. You have lived to enjoy the conſolation of perceiving, that every conteſt about Shakſpeare has left the readers of

that

that great poet, better inftructed, in the nature of his
ftudies, more filled with admiration at the extent of his
genius, and better difpofed to cultivate the rich garden
of his poetry.   Whatever there may be in this truth, I
have no intention, I affure you, to interrupt any biographer's purpofe of publifhing a new life of Shakfpeare ;
to inflame, by my labours, any Editor's jealoufy ; to
roufe envy, by anticipating difcovery ; or to provoke
malignity, by fuccefsful perfeverance, in making good
my points, to renew infidious attacks againft me ;

" ———— Maugre what might hap
" Of heavier on himfelf."————

G. C.

The ADVERTISEMENT.

THE APOLOGY, to which this work is a SUPPLEMENT, had not been long publifhed, when an anfwer, a *full* anfwer, was announced by Mr. Malone's authority. Yet, wife men faid. that a book of documents, and facts, could not be anfwered, though it might be mifconceived, and mifreprefented; though the miftakes of hafte might be noted, and the petty errors of the eye, rather than the underftanding, might be magnified into bulk :

" As things feem large, which we through mifts defcry;
" *Dulnefs* is ever apt to magnify."

What was thus forefeen has actually happened. At the end of two years, no anfwer has appeared, though a kind of *bufh-fighting* has been kept up againft the apologift, by news-paper paragraphs, magazine effays, and monthly criticifms Knowing that my refutation of Mr. Malone's inquiry could not be fhaken, by diftant fkirmifh-ing, I never heeded this infidious warfare.

At length, Mr. Malone has become fenfible of what others could have told him, that as a general he had pufhed his army too far into the enemy's territories; and had expofed himfelf to be attacked with advantage, in front, in flank, and in rear. He was thus attacked. And he filently retreated from a country, where he found, that he could neither maintain an inch of ground, nor acquire an atom of glory. Knowing the motives of

his

his retreat, I have chofen to adopt the policy of the Conftable Montmorencie, who erected a golden bridge, for the retiring foe, rather than to imitate the imprudence of Gafton de Foix, who continued to purfue, till he fell in the field: Influenced by *the Conftable's* policy, I have, in this Supplement, accordingly, turned afide, from Mr. Malone, to fome of thofe, who have fince come into the field, not fo much to cover his retreat, as to annoy his antagonift.

Mean while, Mr. Steevens, who had difavowed any purpofe of interfering, chofe rather to lend his aid to the management of ambufcade, than to ufe the open hoftilities of magnanimous war. The repulfes, which I have herein given to his attacks, may perhaps induce him to think, in the end, that *honefty is the beft policy.*

The meddler, Mathias, muft mingle too in the fray, without any pretence of paft injury, or motive of future good: His petulance has provoked me to let fall **my** *leaden mace* upon him; as, I truft, he will feel in my *poftfcript.*

But, although I may have repulfed all thofe aggreffors; although I may have confuted the enquirer himfelf, ftill the *Mifcellaneous Papers,* which gave rife to this controverfy, remain unfupported by me. At the time I wrote my Apology, I had *particular reafons*, for thinking them to *be fuppofititious :* Nay, *I exprefsly acknowledged them to be fpurious*, by my prefatory advertifement. A criminal may be guilty ; yet, the proofs, which are brought by the profecutor, may be defective in their forms, and inconclufive in their inferences.

I have

I have tried, in this *Supplement*, to ftrengthen what is weak, to correct what is erroneous, and to fupply what is defective, in my *Apology*. The admirers of Shakfpeare, I truft, will find, that fomething has been added, while nothing has been taken away : The biographer of the poet, the commentator on his writings, the hiftorian of the ftage, will all be fupplied with dates, and details, and facts, which will facilitate the further cultivation of a field, which was ere while over run by the briers of falfe criticifm, and obftructed by the weeds of wild conjecture.

I now retire from a controverfy, which was rather provoked by others, than fought by me ; leaving the *biographer* to publifh the promifed life of Shakfpeare ; the *commentator* to amend his own errors ; and the *lampooner* to feed upon his appropriate malignity : I leave them all to gratify their feveral purfuits, without any further interruption from me.

G. C.

*** The ornament of the title page is the Creft of Shakfpeare ; the *tail-piece* is his Arms ; and they were both emblazoned by the fkilful hand of Francis Townfend, the Windfor Herald, from the Declaration of Arms, which was given to the Poet's Father in 1599.

A

SUPPLEMENTAL APOLOGY

FOR THE

BELIEVERS

IN THE

SUPPOSITITIOUS SHAKSPEARE-PAPERS.

———

THE INTRODUCTION.

WHILST Mr. Malone was bufily employed, in trying to difcover, by means
of his friends, thofe of the Believers, who
were moft likely to anfwer his *Enquiry*, I often
faid, that, feeble as his powers were, he would
eafily overcome the opponent of whatever talents, who fhould attempt to vindicate the
genuinenefs of the Shakfpeare-papers; becaufe,
falfehood, however fupported, cannot ftand
with truth.

But, it was equally apparent, that Mr. Malone's *Enquiry*, as it partook much of the qualities of the *fuppofititious-papers*, was equally
with thofe papers, fubject to confutation, by
oppofing facts to fictions. So often did I re-

B   peat

peat this fentiment, that I found myfelf, at
length, in fome manner pledged to anfwer what
was deemed by the fuperficial, to be decifive,
and by the thoughtlefs, to be unanfwerable.
In accomplifhing this objeɗ, I feized upon the
ftrong ground of an explicit avowal, that *The
Mifcellaneous Papers*, which had been exhibited as Shakfpeare's, *were fpurious* (*a*).   By
this *explicit avowal*, that *the exhibition* of thofe
Mifcellanies was *a cheat*, Mr. Malone was deprived of his ftrength, like Antæus of other
times, who was no longer ftrong, than while
he could touch his mother earth.   From that
vantage ground, it was not difficult to expofe
the Enquirer's petulance, and to confute his
fiɗions ; to vindicate our Archaiology from his
mifreprefentations, and to defend the independence of the Republic of Letters againft
his attacks (*b*).

Such

(*a*) See the Prefatory advertifement to *The Apology*, which
was written for this very purpofe.

(*b*) Mɾ. Malone lays it down as a *fixed principle*, " that
" the authenticity, or fpurioufnefs, of the poems attributed
" to Rowley cannot be decided by any perfon who has not
" a tafte for Englifh poetry, and, a moderate, at leaft, if
" not a critical, knowledge of the compofitions of moft of
" our poets, from the time of Chaucer to that of Pope.
" Such *a* [an] one is, in my opinion, a competent judge of
" this matter ; and were a jury of twelve fuch perfons empan-
" nelled

Such were the important objects, which remained to be accomplished, after the *Miscellaneous Papers* had been, positively, acknowledged to be spurious : and, those objects will be for ever interesting to liberal minds, so long as personal character shall be deemed worthy of defence ; as literary questions remain to be answered ; and whilst the independence of the learned world shall be thought equally entitled to support, as freedom is, in political society. All these points may be fairly discussed, without much recollection of an *exploded cheat,* whilst, at the same time, the character of Shakspeare may be, incidentally, vindicated, his writings elucidated, and his fame extended ; which are all subjects, not only very interesting in themselves, but are also connected, intimately, with our national character.

" nelled to try the question, I have not the smallest doubt " what would be their almost instantaneous decision." [See his Cursory Observations on the poems attributed to Thomas Rowley, 1782. p. 2.] Such is the spirit of domination, which is assumed as a principle over all persons, except the chosen few, who have a fancied taste ; and who alone, in the opinion of Mr. Malone, are qualified to decide a question of fact, like other facts of full as much importance. That spirit is still stalking abroad, in the learned world ; frightening all, who are to be frightened by spirits ; and insulting all, who are supposed to be unable to resist attack, or unwilling to resent injury. I allude, here, to Thomas James Mathias, with *his Pursuits of Literature.*

B 2 § I. The

—— § I. ——

The GENERAL ARGUMENT.

Thoufands there are, indeed, who, with fome pretenfions to fcience, and many attainments in literature, neither trouble themfelves about Shakfpeare, nor much care for our Archaiology: They have a privilege in their indifference; a title to their own purfuits; and a kind of charter, for the freedom of enjoying thefe rights, fafe from the ftroke of fatire, and free from the fneer of reprehenfion. But, whether the admirers of Shakfpeare be *chartered libertines*; whether our poet's editors, be entitled to thofe immunities of indifference, may admit of fome doubt. It can admit of no doubt, however, whether an editor of that illuftrious dramatift, " who had announced a " Life of Shakfpeare, either in folio, quarto, or " octavo;" who had offered a frefh edition of his Dramas, in fifteen volumes, royal quarto, after fo many other editions had been publifhed, with a greater, or lefs, fuccefs, during the laft thirty years, may hear of Shakfpeare with indifference; or fit down, heedlefsly, when new Songs of *Avon's Swan* are propofed to be carolled, to liftening ears. If fuch an editor fhould *attempt to teach what he has never learned himfelf*, the indifference, which was

innocent

innocent in others, becomes criminal in him.
With fuch an editor,

> " Indiff'rence, clad in Wifdom's guife,
> All fortitude of mind fupplies."

But, when indifference, clad in the difguife
of wifdom, comes out upon the ftage to hifs
at curiofity, to defpife inquiry, and to lampoon
character, it then becomes an object, for
fcorn to point at, a mark, for ridicule to expofe,
and for reprehenfion to chaftife: and, when it is
confidered, that the fame affected indifference
had already roufed curiofity, with regard to
Shakfpeare, and urged refearch to inquire for
Shakfpearean *treafure trove*, its fcoffs, and its
fcepticifm, muft be left for difdain to deride, as
the tricks of a zany, rather than for philofophy
to hold up to contempt as the follies of a critic.   During the infancy of criticifm, far different was the critical philofophy of Spenfer,
which he inculcated, in 1590, when anfwering,
by *anticipation*, our Enquirer's objections:

> " But, let that man with better fenfe advife,
> That of the world leaft part to us is *red :*
> And daily how, throw hardy enterprize,
> Many great regions, are difcovered,
> Which, to late age, were never mentioned.
> Who ever heard of the Indian Peru ?
> Or who in ventrous veffel meafured
> The *Amazons* huge river now found true ?
> Or fruitfulleft *Virginia* who did ever view ?

B 3

Yet

Yet all thefe were, when no man did them know;
Yet have from wifeft ages hidden been:
And later times more unknown things fhall fhow.
Why, then, *fhould* WITLESS *man fo much mif-ween.*
That nothing is, but that which he hath feen?
What if within the moon's fair fhining fpheare,
What if in every ftar unfeen,
Of other worlds he happily fhould hear?
He wonder would much more, yet, *fuch to fome appear.* (*c*)"

Thus are we taught, in charming poetry, to
expect every thing from *hardy enterprize.* and
to contemn the *witlefs man,* who fhould conceive, that *nothing is, but that which he hath
feen:* And thus doth the feer foretel, how, later
times more unknown things fhall fhow. What
incitements have we here to anfwer every inquiry by the inveftigation of facts, rather than
by the inculcation of theory. Yet, ages elapfed
before the true mode of criticifing Shakfpeare
was either practifed or acknowledged: And,
in our own days, an attempt has been made
to draw the life, and character, of a moft illuftrious poet, from his writings, rather than
from documents *(d).*

Far

(*c*) See the proem to the Second Book of the Faerie Queen,
which was firft publifhed, in 1590.

(*d*) As an example how much more is to be obtained, by
collecting facts, than by dwelling on theories, I beg leave
to lay before the reader an unedited Proclamation about
MILTON:

*

By

Far different were the principle, and practice
of the Believers, from the fcepticifm, and inac-
tivity

By the King.

A Proclamation for calling in and fuppreffing of two
Books written by John Milton, the one intituled,
Johannis Miltoni Angli pro Populo Anglicano Defenfio contra Claudii Anonymi alias Salmasii, Defenfionem Regiam ; And the other in anfwer to a Book
intituled, The Pourtraicture of His Sacred Majeftie in
His Solitudes and Sufferings: And alfo a Third Book,
intituled, The obftructers of Juftice, written by John
Goodwin.

Charles R

Whereas John Milton late of Weftminfter, in the County
of Middlefex, hath publifhed in print two feveral Books,
the one intituled, Johannis Miltoni Angli pro Populo Anglicano Defenfio, contra Claudii Anonymi alias Salmasii,
Defenfionem Regiam : And the other in anfwer to a Book,
intituled, The Pourtraicture of His facred Majeftie in His
Solitudes and Sufferings.   In both which are contained fundry treafonable paffages againft Vs and Our Government,
and moft impious endeavours to juftifie the horrid and un-
matchable Murder of Our late dear Father of glorious Memory.

   And whereas John Goodwin, late of Coleman-ftreet
London, Clerk, hath alfo publifhed in print, a Book, intituled, The obftructers of Juftice, written in defence of the
Traiterous fentence againft His late Majefty.   And whereas
the faid John Milton and John Goodwin are both fled, or
fo obfcure themfelves, that no endeavours ufed for their ap-
prehenfion can take effect, whereby they might be brought
to legal Tryal, and defervedly receive condign punifhment
for their Treafons and Offences: Now to the end that Our
good fubjects may not be corrupted in their judgments with

B 4   fuch

tivity of the *witlefs man :* They aſſumed experience, for their principle ; and adopted enterprize,

ſuch wicked and Traiterous principles, as are diſperſed and
ſcattered throughout the before mentioned Books; We,
upon the motion of the Commons in Parliament now aſ-
ſembled do hereby ſtrictly charge and command all and
every perſon and perſons whatſoever, who live in any City,
Borough, or Town Incorporate within this our Kingdom of
England, the Dominion of Wales, and Town of Berwick
upon Tweed, in whoſe hands any of thoſe Books are or hereafter ſhall be, That they, upon pain of our high diſpleaſure,
and the conſequence thereof; do forthwith upon publication
of this Our command or within Ten dayes immediately following, deliver, or cauſe the ſame to be delivered, to the
Mayor, Bailiffs, or other Chief Officer or Magiſtrate in any
of the ſaid Cities, Boroughs, or Towns Incorporate, where
ſuch perſon or perſons ſo live ; or, if living out of any City,
Borough, or Town Incorporate, then to the next Juſtice of
Peace adjoining to his or their dwelling or place of aboJe; or
if living in either of Our Univerſities then to the Vice-
Chancellor of that Univerſity where he or they do reſide.

And in default of ſuch voluntary delivery, which We do
expect in obſervance of our ſaid Command, That then and
after the time before limited expired, the ſaid Chief Magiſtrate of all every the ſaid Cities, Boroughs, or Towns Incorporate, the Juſtices of the Peace in their ſeveral Counties,
and the Vice-Chancellors of Our ſaid Univerſities reſpec-
tively, are hereby Commanded to ſeize and take all and every
the Books aforeſaid, in whoſe hands or poſſeſſion ſoever they
ſhall be found, and certifie the names of the offenders unto
Our Privy-Council

And we do hereby alſo give ſpecial charge and command
to the ſaid Chief Magiſtrates, Juſtices of the Peace, and Vice-
Chancellors,

terprize, for their practice. They knew, from
" lefs reading than makes felons 'fcape," that
almoft

Chancellors, refpectively, That they caufe the faid Books
which fhall be fo brought unto any of their hands, or feized,
or taken as aforefaid, by vertue of this Our Proclamation,
to be delivered to the refpective Sheriffs of thofe Counties
where they refpectively live, the firft and next Affizes that
fhall after happen. And the faid Sheriffs are hereby alfo
required, in time of holding fuch Affizes, to caufe the fame
to be publickly burnt by the hands of the Common Hang-
man.

And we do further ftrieghtly charge and Command, That
no Man hereafter prefume to Print, Vend, Sel, or Difperfe
any the aforefaid Books, upon pain of Our heavy difplea-
fure, and of fuch further punifhment, as for their prefumption, in that behalf may any way be inflicted upon them by
the Laws of this Realm.

Given at Our Court at Whitehall the 13th of Auguft,
in the Twelfth Year of Our Reign, 1660.

Burnet fuppofes, that Milton was forgotten, at the Refto-
ration : Johnfon fays, that he was ordered to be profecuted,
though perhaps not very diligently purfued. It appears from
the Commons' Journal 8 vol. p. 66. that the King was addreffed to iffue his Proclamation, for calling in Milton's two
Pamphlets ; that the Attorney General was ordered by the
Commons to caufe *effectual proceedings* to be had againft
John Milton ; it was refolved by the Houfe, that Mr. Milton
be fent for in Cuftody by the Serjeant at Arms.—I have lodg-
ed the *original* Proclamation, which was founded on the Re-
folves of Parliament, in the Britifh Mufeum, for the benefit
of the public. I will only add, for removing all fufpicion,
that it was republifhed in the News-papers of thofe times :
I have a Copy of it, which was reprinted in *Mercurius Pub-*
licus,

almoft every notice about Shakfpeare had
been difcovered by inveftigation, rather than
found by intuition. They had been taught,
by Mr. Malone himfelf, that many documents, with regard to the illuftrious bard,
were yet to be difclofed by time. They faw
with *fond* eyes, perhaps, difcoveries daily made,
in refpect to to his Life, and Writings, which
did not gratify curiofity, fo much as animate
hope. And they inferred from experience, that
what had often happened might again happen;
that, as difcoveries generally reproduce difcoveries, they were as much led by expectation,
as induced by reafon, to conclude, that the announced books, Dramas, and papers, of the
exhibiter, were the " expected fragments,"
which had been foretold by *our Seer :*

"——— Expectation was almoft ready to faint;
" Longing for what it had not."

Whatever might be the expectation of fome
of the Believers, or the hope of others, they
all applied the fame rules of inveftigation to
thofe books, and Dramas, papers, and paint-
ings, which direct them in the ordinary affairs
of life. They made ufe of the evidence of their

licus, from Wednefday Auguft 15th to Wednefday Auguft
22d 1660. Why will not biographers fearch for fuch documents ? We want more facts ; not more theories, and declamations ! !

fenfes.

senses, which affift them in matters of more intereft; fome of them, indeed, with greater difcernment, and circumfpection, and fome of them, with lefs. It was fufficient for them, that they had, on their fide, " Probability, " which, bifhop Butler had affured them," is the very guide of *Life (e)*. They examined the evidence, *external,* and *internal,* which was laid before them *(f)* : And, on the

---

(*e*) Bifhop Halifax's Edition of *The Analogy,* p. 3.

(*f*) Amidft a million of miftakes, Mr. Malone confounded the nature of *external,* and *internal,* evidence, [See his Enquiry, p. 17, and the Apology for the Believers, 22-3.] From our Critic's practice, very differently taught the Diplomatifts of the Benedictin Congregation of S. Maur. In treating of the characters of Charters, *extrinfic* and *intrinfic,* Dom. de Vaines fays, that, " Les Characteres extrinse- " ques des Chartes font, les figures des lettres qui y font " employées, la forme & la matiere des Sceaux qui y font " appofés, and les matieres fur lefquelle & avec lefquelles " on a écrit les diplomes ou actes quelconques, ce qui com- " prend inftrument dont on s'eft fervi pour ecrire, la li- " queur q'on a employée pour faire fortir les lettres, & " la matiere fubjective de l'ecriture :—Les characteres in- " trinseques qui font des fignes fi évidents de fuppofition " ou de vérité, d'authenticité ou de fufpicion, font, le ftyle " propre aux chartes, les différentes manières fucceffives " d'orthographier le langage employe dans les chartes, les " differentes epoques de l'ufage de pluriels & des fingu- " liers, les titres d'honneur pris & donnés dans le foufcrip- " tions des chartes les noms & furnoms & le nombre dif- " tinctif

the whole examination, the Believers were
induced, by what they had feen, to conclude,
with Bifhop Butler, "that in queftions of dif-
" ficulty, or fuch as are thought fo, where
" more fatisfactory evidence cannot be had,
" or is not feen ; if the refult of examination
" be, that there appears upon the whole, any
" the loweft prefumption, on the one fide,
" and none, on the other, or a greater pre-
" fumption, on one fide, though in the loweft
" degree greater; this determines the quef-
" tion, even in matters of fpeculation ; and in
" matters of practice, will lay us under an ab-
" folute and formal obligation, in point of
" prudence and of intereft, to act upon that
" prefumption or low probability, though it
" be fo low as to leave the mind in very great
" doubt which is the truth *(g)*." Thus argued
Bifhop

" tinctif des Princes de même nom les diverfes invocations
" tant explicites que cachées les addreffes, les débuts, les pré-
" ambules avec leurs claufes, tant dérogatoires que commina-
" toires, les falutations ou l'adieu final, les formules générales,
" les annonces de précaution, les dates, les fignatures, &c.
" &c. &c." [See *Dictionnaire Raifonné de Diplomatique :*
Tome Premier, p. 257.]

(*g*) Bifhop Butler's Analogy, which was republifhed by
Bifhop Halifax, p. 3.—Yet, is it faid, in oppofition to thofe
great authorities, by an anonymous writer in a monthly mif-
cellany, called *The Britifh Critic* [vol. ix. p. 514.] " When
" Mr.

Bifhop Butler, when fupporting *Religion* ;
thus reafoned Mr. Locke, when inveftigating
the

" Mr. C. puts the *probabilities* on which thefe *paltry papers*
" were believed *by a few*, on the footiug with thofe which
" regulate juftice, and form the foundation of religious
" faith, WE *ſtand aſtoniſhed at his indiſcretion*." Since
this attack on me, on the fcore of religion, I have read
Butler's *Analogy*, and Locke on *The Underſtanding*, which
before I had never read : I am more confirmed in my judgment, that I was perfectly correct, in my principle of reafoning, and perfectly prudent, in my application of it. I
will repeat from *Wilkins*, that, " Things of feveral kinds
" may admit, and require feveral forts of proofs, all which
" may be good in their kinds : and, therefore, nothing can
" be more irrational, than for a man to doubt of, or to deny,
" the truth of any thing ; becaufe it cannot be made out,
" by fuch kind of proofs, of which the nature of fuch thing
" is not capable." Thus reafoned Wilkins ! And I was,
by his argument, induced to add : " Thefe reafonings apply
" more forcibly to Religion than to Law : The leading
" articles of our faith do not admit of rigid demonſtration :
" rational probability is, in thefe, the ſtrongeſt proof, which
" can be given to induce belief, without deluding our un-
" derſtandings with the fuggeſtions of *poſſibility*, or entan-
" gling our convictions with the *fophiſms of infidelity*." [Apo-
logy, 19, 20.] I will, moreover, repeat, that the faid Anonymous Critic, no doubt, thinks, that he can argue about religion more rationally than Tillotfon and Wilkins, than
Butler and Halifax. But, a Law Lord is quoted, as reafoning differently from me, about the rules of evidence. Is
there any Law Lord, who demands *demonſtration* in the
adminiſtration of Juftice ; or any other evidence than the
nature of the cafe allows ; who *preſumes fraud*, in the firſt
inſtance ;

the philofophy of the Underftanding *(h)* ; and, thus taught Chief Baron Gilbert, when laying down the law of Evidence *(i)*.

It was, however, referved for Mr. Malone, and for thofe, who fupport his fcepticifm, by their paragraphs, their effays, and their reviews, to expect *demonftration* in the affairs of life, and in the hiftory of *facts*, before they give any judgment about the facts themfelves ! Yes; the Believers were ultimately deceived in their object, by their own energies, and difappointed, in their reafonable hopes, by *fallible proofs*; as other men are fometimes deceived in their judgments, by their fenfes, and difappointed often in their projects, by their reafonings : Yet, mankind muft, in the affairs of life, truft to the evidence of their fenfes; and, in their judgment about facts, muft rely on their powers of ratiocination;

inftance; who forms his judgment, upon the point in queftion, like the Commentators, and Critics, without any inquiry at all; or who, like them, prefers fecond rate evidence, to firft rate; or who like them too, would rather liften to *hearfay* witneffes, than truft to the examination of his own fenfes?

(h) See *Locke* concerning the *Human Underftanding*, the 20th Edition, the Chapter " of *Probability*; which is the *appearance* of *agreement* upon *fallible proofs*."

(i) The Treatife on the Law of Evidence, p. 1-5.

though

though difappointment be the reward of their efforts; and though *fcepticifm* may refufe to act, or to think; becaufe he may fail in his fteps, or be deceived in his opinion. Geographers long expected the difcovery of the *Southern Continent*, which our great navigator, Cooke, failed to difcover, notwithftanding his confummate fkill, and obftinate perfeverance: But, neither philofophy, nor prefumption, though difappointed in finding what was not to be found, ever objected to the propriety of the trial, or to the efforts of perfeverance, when conducted both by prudence, and fcience. Yet, active curiofity may difcover fomething in the poffibilities of time, place, and circumftance; but, heedlefs inaction can find nothing, while *wifdom is confumed in confidence*. The Believers were accordingly right, in their mode of inquiry, and were only led into error, by their fyftematic principles: Their opponents, the Sceptics, were only right by accident: If fortui ous events furnifh a rational principle, for conducting daily affairs;—

" Then, any thing might come from any thing :
" For, how from chance can conftant order fpring ?"

—— § II. ——

QUEEN ELIZABETH; AND HER LETTER.

The obftinacy of dogmatifm is fuch, that confutation cannot convince it: Of Queen Elizabeth,

Elizabeth, conceitednefs often remarked, with the confidence of certainty, that, fuch was her loftinefs, *fhe difdained to correfpond with much greater men than Shakfpeare.* This objection was even repeated by felf-fufficient folly, after it had been proved, by a thoufand documents, that fhe correfponded, conftantly, with her male fervants, and goffiped, familiarly, with her female attendants ; that fhe perfonally thanked Lambard, for his book ; and penfioned Spenfer, for his flatteries : Yet, are there Critics, who declare, " that I have not fully " proved it *probable*, that a letter might be " written by that Sovereign to Shakfpeare !" I know not, if this confidence can be fhamed into filence, by a letter from her Secretary, Sir Robert Cecil, to Sir John Harrington ; which fays, " that the bleffed Queen was more than " a man, and, in troth, fometimes lefs than a " woman *(k)*." The character of that extraordinary princefs will continue to be difcuffed, long after her notorious epiftle to Shakfpeare fhall be ranked with the figments of her flatterers ; and fhall be juftly condemned, with the other forgeries of her reign.

(*k*) See this very curious epiftle, which is dated the 29th May 1603, in the *Nugæ Antiquæ*, Edit. 1779, vol. ii. p. 263.

Of

Of that accomplifhed Statefman, who knew her perfectly, it was faid, (*l*) that if he were born in 1550, he was not a *youth*, in 1602. This remark was thus doubtfully expreffed, from the avowal of a late Biographer, that he could never difcover, when Sir Robert Cecil was born (*m*). What the Biographer's diligence could not find, my perfeverance has traced : Burleigh, amidft all his cares for the ftate, left behind him a ftatement of the dates, when his wife was delivered of all her children, which Strype has preferved; and which fhows, that the birth of his Son Robert, was on the 1ft of June 1563 (*n*). What a refplendent period ! Spencer was born in 1553; Bacon, Lord Verulam, was born in 1562; Cecil, Lord Salifbury, in 1563; and Shakfpeare in 1564. Every notice, about thofe extraordinary men, is fo interwoven with the ftory of that great Queen, as to form an interefting portion of her character. Of Eliza-

(*l*) The Apology, 38.

(*m*) Dr. Kippis, in the New Biog. Brit. vol. iii. p. 404.

(*n*) Strype's Annals, 4 vol. 338. This date proves, that Mr. Secretary Cecil was ftill under *fortv*, in September 1602; and was even yet an object of Elizabeth's jealoufy. See a very remarkable fpecimen of the Queen's *jealoufy*, and *frolicfomenefs* in The *Apology*, 37.

C   beth

beth it has been, truly, faid, that fhe wrote, when fhe was young, a fine print-like hand; that fhe greatly enlarged her writing, as fhe grew older: But, it has not yet been fhown, that fhe could not write, legibly, when fhe became aged; owing to the failure of her nerves; a diforder, which carried her to the grave. The fame Secretary of State has furnifhed a proof of that curious particular, when he wrote to Lord Mountjoy, the Lord Deputy of Ireland, in July 1602; faying in his poftfcript: " Becaufe I am not fure, whether you " can perfectly reade her Majeftie's hande, I " fend you the fame in a coppy, *the latter part* " whereof, being futeable to the former ftile " of favour, that was wont to paffe betweene " you, grew by the occafion of your owne Poft- " fcript, when you wrote to the Treafurer " that you had been a good while in O'Neil's " kitchen, which you meant to warm fo well, " as he fhould keep the worfe fiers ever " after (*o*)." The *latter part* of the Queen's Letter to the Lord Deputy, before referred to, contains the odd expreffions following : " We have forgotten to praife your humility, " that after having beene a *Queene's kitchen*

(*o*) Moryfon's Itinerary, 1617, p. 230.

" *maide,*

" *maide,* you have not difdained to be a *trai-*
" *tor's Skullion.*   God bleffe you with perfe-
" verance.—Your Soveraigne, E. R. (*p*)."
We may herein fee, as in a mirror, how Elizabeth could condefcend, even to buffoonery.
In a former letter to the fame great Officer,
fhe had written full as familiarly, but not fo
unintelligibly, as to require a Commentator :—
" My *faithful George,* If ever more fervice of
" worth were performed in fhorter fpace then
" you have done, we are deceived among many
" eye witneffes : We have received the fruit
" thereof, and bid you faithfully credit, that
" that what fo wit, courage, or care may do,
" we truly find, they have all been thoroughly
" acted in all your charge.   And for the fame
" beleeve, that it fhall neither be unremem-
" bered, nor unrewarded, and in mean while
" beleeve my help nor prayers fhall never fail
" you.—Your Soveraigne that beft regards
" you, E. R. (*q*)."   In return, the Lord Deputy fhewed Elizabeth, that he could not
only perform great actions, for her fervice, but
could fpeak fugred words, for her gratification.
He wrote her *facred Majeflie,* who was then

(*p*) Moryfon's Itinerary, 1617, p. 228.
(*q*) Ib. 133.

C 2   fixty-

fixty-eight :—" When I have done all that I
" can, the uttermoft effects of my labours doe
" appeare fo little to my owne zeale to doe
" more, that I am often afhamed to prefent
" them unto your *faire*, and royall, *eyes.*—I
" befeeche your Majeftie to thinke, that in a
" matter of fo great importance, my affection
" will not fuffer me to commit fo groffe a fault
" againft your fervice, as to doe any thing, for
" the which I am not able to give you a very
" good account, the which above all things,
" I defire to do at your *owne royall feete*, and
" that your fervice here, may give me leave to
" *fill my eyes* with their onely *deare* and *defired*
" *object*. I befeech God confound all your
" enemies and unfaithful fubjects, and make
" my hand as happy, as my heart is zealous to
" doe you fervice.—Your Majeftie's trueft
" fervant, Mountjoy."(*r*) Thefe letters, with
the illuftrations of them, which have paffed into
hiftory, indeed, would, alone, exhibit the true
character of Elizabeth, although our anecdote-
writers do not fee, either her genuine portrait, or
the vivid lights, wherein it was placed. What

(*r*) Moryfon's Itenerary, 1617, p. 233.—It is to be
remembered, that this *love-letter* of Lord Deputy Mountjoy was addreffed to Queen Elizabeth, at the Age of *Sixty-
eight.*.

blindnefs

blindnefs could not fee, nor folly comprehend,
is now apparent to the world, viz. that Elizabeth, who *was often more than a man*, and
fometimes lefs than a woman, could be very
familiar at times; and had a voracious appetite
for praife, which all her Servants, and Stran-
gers, were ftudious to gratify, by the moft
fervile adulation : Yet, this is the Queen,
who, as we are told by the Commentators,
would not condefcend to write to Shakfpeare!

Among the adulators of Elizabeth, Spenfer, and Shakfpeare, appear to have known
her character, fully, and to have gratified,
fuccefsfully, her defire of commendation.
As thefe firft-rate poets will ere long be
brought nearer to each other, than has yet
been done by Critics, it will be neceffary to
dwell a little upon the life, and writings, of
Spenfer ; as they will exhibit Shakfpeare
under a new afpect. I mean to prove 1ft,
that Spenfer addreffed his *Amoretti* to Elizabeth ; 2dly, that Shakfpeare was ambitious of
emulating Spenfer; and 3dly, that Shakfpeare
was thus induced to addrefs *his Sonnets* to the
fame Queen.

The life of Spenfer has been often written,
but never with much effort, and always with

many

many mifreprefentations. That this great Poet was born in London has been generally afferted, without contradiction; yet, I have not been able, by the offer of a reward, which was deemed fufficiently liberal by the parifh-clerks, to trace his baptifm in the parochial (*s*) regifters of London. He was, probably, born about the year 1553: For, his *Amoretti*, which were certainly publifhed, in 1595, and probably written, in 1593, fpeak, in the fixtieth Sonnet, of the year of writing them being longer, ——

" Than all thofe *forty*, which my life outwent.

The poet's frequent boafts of the refpectability of his family have induced Biographers to regard him, as a Scion of the ancient ftem in Northamptonfhire; yet, I could not find, by my fearches in the College of Arms, though I was obligingly affifted by the very intelligent, Francis Townfend, Windfor-Herald, that any of the Pedigrees of the Spenfers recognize every body's Spenfer, as connected with them (*t*): From the filence about Spenfer,

(*s*) The Parifh Regifters of the City of about the period of Spenfer's birth have generally difappeared; owing to various caufes; as I was told by the Parifh-Clerks.

(*t*) Speaking, in his Colin Clout, of the three daughters of Sir John Spenfer of Althorpe; namely, Elizabeth, Lady Cary,

9

ser, which the Herald's books preserve, I suspect, that his father must have died before the Son had risen to eminence, by the products of his genius. Neither do the records of the University contain any notice of his parentage; though they indicate, that his father was not opulent, when they record the matriculation of Spenser as a *Sizer*. He entered at Pembroke Hall, Cambridge, in 1569; he proceeded batchelor of Arts, in 1572; and master of Arts, in 1576 (*u*). It was at the University, that he became acquainted with Gabriel Harvey, who introduced him to Sir Philip Sydney; and by the recommendation

Cary, Anne, Lady Compton, and Alice, Lady Strange, he says:—

> " Ne less praise worthy are the Sister's thrae,
> " The honour of the noble familie,
> " *Of which, I meanest,* boast myself to be
> " And most, that unto them, I am so nigh."

(*u*) The Register of Pembroke Hall does not go further back than 1620; But, having engaged an accurate friend to search the University record, He found, that Edmond Spencer [The name is also spelt Spenser] was entered a Sizer of Pembroke Hall, on the 20th of May 1569; received his degree of Batchelor of Arts on the 16th of January $157\frac{2}{3}$; and his Master of Arts Degree, on the 26th of June 1576. There are in Pembroke Hall two pictures of Spenser: yet, is he almost forgotten there, as an *alumnus*.

of this univerſal patron of genius (*v*), Spenſer was received into the family, and ſervice of the Earl of Leiceſter, by whom he was appointed his Agent in foreign Countries, during the year 1579. It was in this year, that he firſt ſhewed the world his powers of poetry, by the publication of his *Shepherd's Calendar* (*w*). He appears to have even then formed the plan, and to have compoſed part of *The faerie Queene.*

At what time of his life he married, or whom he married, cannot be aſcertained, though he has told us himſelf, in 1595, that his wife's name was Elizabeth, as his mother's name had been.

When he left the houſe of the Earl of Leiceſter, in 1580, he became private Secretary to Lord Grey of Wilton, on his appointment to the high office, of Lord Deputy of Ire-

(*v*) In his Dedication of his *Ruins of Time*, in 1591, " Sithens his late coming into England, to the celebrated Counteſs of Pembroke, Spenſer, ſays that Sir Philip Sydney, her brother, " was *the patron of my Young Muſes.*"

(*w*) On the 5th of December 1579 was entered in the Stationers' Regiſters, for Hugh Singelton, " The Shep- " perd's Calendar Conteyninge xii eclogs, proportionable " to the xii Monethes." It was aſſigned to John Harriſon, junior, on the 18th of October 1580.

land.

land.   Spenfer afterwards fpoke of Lord
Grey, as *the patron of his Mufe's pupillage*;
as *the pillar of his life*.   Lord Grey was fucceeded by Sir John Perrot in 1583 : Yet,
Spenfer feems to have kept up his connection with Ireland ; having obtained, in
1586 (*x*), in conjunction with Raleigh, and
other adventurers, a Grant of three thoufand
acres of forfeited lands, with the Caftle of
Kilcolman, which had belonged to the attainted
Earl of Defmond.

In the Caftle of Kilcolman, Spenfer probably fettled, like other married men, in a
family way ; and, in this retreat, he certainly
finifhed his *Faerie Queene*; as he fpeaks, in
his Sonnet to Lord Grey, of his

> " Rude rymes, the which a *ruftic Mufe* did weave,
> In *Salvage Soil, far from Parnaffo Mount.*

At the end of ten years, appeared, in 1590 (*y*),

(*x*) At the Conclufion of Gabriel Harvey's *Four proper
Letters* there is a Sonnet by Spenfer to Harvey, dated at
Dublin, the 18th of July, 1586, which has never been re-
printed till now.

(*y*) On the 1ft of December 1589 ; was entered in
the Stationers' Regifters for Mr. Ponfonbye, " The *fay-*
" *rye Queene* dyfpofed into xii books ;" being licenfed
by the Archbifhop of Canterbury, and both the Wardens.

the

the three firſt books of the never to be forgotten *Faerie Queene* :—

——————— "Nature here
Wantons, as in her prime, and plays at will
Her Virgin fancies, pouring forth more ſweets ;
Wild above rule, or art, enormous bliſs !"

Amidſt this *enormous bliſs*, Queen Elizabeth
was celebrated, in the Introduction to each
book, with ſuch encomiaſtic enthuſiaſm, as
the eloquent pen of ſuch a poet could en-
dite. Her principal Courtiers were alſo
praiſed in prefatory Sonnets. It was an age
of adulation ; and we may eaſily ſuppoſe, that
the poet, who greatly excelled in the powers
of panegyrick, would be ſuitably rewarded :
In fact, a penſion was conferred on Spenſer, in
February 1590, of fifty pounds, a year, for
life, without any official duty (z). The publication of this immortal poem enabled him
to renew his old friendſhips in England ;

(z) The world is indebted to the diligence of Mr. Malone for the diſcovery of this important fact in the Pat. Roll
of the 33d Elizabeth p. 3. I ſay *important fact* ; becauſe it
eſtabliſhes truth, in oppoſition to falſehood ; it frees the
memory of Burleigh from much obloquy ; it ſhows, that
Spenſer never could have been in great want : For fifty
pounds a year went far in the affairs of life, during thoſe
frugal times : But, he never was poet Laureat, as the Biographers aſſert, though he talks, in his *Amoretti*, of having
the Laurel.

though

though his home was in Ireland. In 1591, was publifhed by Ponfonbie a mifcellaneous collection of poems, which he entitled *Complaints* (*a*), while the Poet was on his *voyage beyond Sea :* And whilft the impreffion of his favourable reception in England was yet ftrong on his fpirits, he wrote his *Colin Clouts come home again* (*b*); wherein he praifes Raleigh for his " fingular favours," and celebrates Elizabeth's bounty; " *Great Cynthia's* good-" neffe, and high grace." Indeed, *Great Cynthia* feems to have been always uppermoft in his mind : Whatever he publifhed, fhe never

(*a*) Ponfonbie, the Bookfeller, fays in the Preface, that fince the Faerie Queene had found a *favourable paffage*, he had endeavoured, by all good means, to get into his hands fuch fmall poemes of the fame author's, as he had heard were difperfed abroad in fundrie hands, and not eafie to be come by, by himfelf; fome of them having bene purloyned from him, *fince his departure beyond Sea.* This expreffion fhows, that Spenfer returned to Ireland, early in 1591. Ponfonbie begged the gentle Reader " graciouflie to entertaine *the* " *new Poet.*" In one of thofe Poems, *The Ruines of Time*, he fpoke of Camden, as *the nourice of antiquitie* ;
" Camden, though time all moniments obfcure,
" Yet, thy juft labours ever fhall endure."
(*b*) Spenfer dated his epiftle dedicatorie to Raleigh " from my houfe of Kilcolman, the 27th of December 1591 :" Yet, the book was not publifhed till 1595. He thanked Raleigh " for his fingular favours, and fundry good turnes, fhewed to him, at his *late being in England.*"

failed

failed to come in for a full fhare of celebration. This great poet now fat down to finifh the fecond part of *The Faerie Queene,* and to en-dite his *Amoretti* (*c*) : The firft, compre-hending the fourth, fifth, and fixth books, was publifhed, in 1596 (*d*) ; the fecond confifting of his Sonnets, were printed in 1595.

Much

(*c*) On the 19th of November 1594, was entered for William Ponfonbye in the Stationers' Regifters, a poem, entitled, *Amoretti* and Epithalamion, written *not long fince* by Edmond Spencer : on the 20th January 1595-6, was entered for the fame bookfeller the fecond parte of the *Faery Queene,* containing the 4th, 5th, and 6th books.

(*d*) Of this great performance, he fpeaks feelingly in Sonnet LXXX : —

" After fo long a race as I have run,

" Through *Faerie Land,* which thofe *fix books* compile,

" Give leave to reft me, being *half foredun,*

" And *gather to myfelf new breath* a while.

" Then, as a fteed refrefhed after toil,

" Out of my prifon, I will break anew,

" And ftouty will *that fecond Work* affoil,

" With ftrong endeavour and attention due.

" Till then, give leave to me, in pleafant mew

" To fport my mufe, and fing *my love's* fweet praife;

" The contemplation of whofe *heavenly hew,*

" My fpirit to an higher pitch will raife :

" But, let her praifes yet be low and mean,

" Fit for the handmaid of the *Faerie Queene.*

We may, herein, fee how Spenfer was fatigued with the long race through *Faerie Land !* And, we may thence in-fer,

Much of myftery has always been connected with the *Amoretti* of Spenfer.   When they
were printed; on what occafion they were
written; and to whom they were addreffed;
are queftions, which have never been fatisfactorily anfwered.   The Biographers, who appear neither to have feen the entry of it in
the Stationers' Regifters, nor the book, fpeak
of its having been publifhed, in 1592; but the
Stationers' Regifters, the *title page*, and the
coincidence of circumftances, prove, that it was
publifhed in 1595 (*e*).   The biographers affume

fer, that he never wrote that *fecond work* which was to confift of fix additional books in continuance : He never wrote
more on this *faerie* theme, I think, than the *two Cantos* of
Mutability which were afterwards printed, as a *Seventh*
book.   He wrote, as is fuppofed, his *View of the State of
Ireland*, in 1596; when, he appears to have been in England.   The opening of his *View of Ireland*, fpeaks of
it as the Country, " Whence *you* [himfelf] *lately came.*"
He foon after publifhed his *Four Hymns*, which he
dedicated to Margaret, the Countefs of Cumberland,
and to Mary, the Countefs of Warwick, in an Epiftle,
that he dated from Greenwich, on the 1ft September
1596.

(*e*) Herb. Typ. An. 2 v. p. 1275.   I have a Copy of
the *Amoretti*, which I bought at the late Doctor Farmer's
Sale; and on which, he has beftowed a MS Note; in order
to prove that this Copy [1595] was the *firft* Edition, in
oppofition

fume ftill more, when they fpeak of the occafion, which gave rife to the *Amoretti*; viz.
that the poet, having loft his firft Wife, fell
in love a fecond time with a Lady, who was
as cruel, as fhe was fair; that he tried to foften
her obduracy by every topic of praife (*f*):
But, it appears diftinctly to me, who pay little regard to affumptions without authority

oppofition to Mr. Ball and others. It appears from Ponfonbie, the bookfeller's, dedication to Sir Robert Needham,
who had brought the Manufcript from Ireland, that it was
printed in *the abfence* of the Author. The book is a very
fmall volume in 12° with only one Sonnet printed on each
page. This dedication is not prefixed to my Copy; but,
Doctor Farmer quotes the Dedication of a Copy in the library of Emanuel College, *Emmanuel*, I fhould have
faid.

(*f*) Nothing can be fo illogical, as affumptions againft probability. That Spenfer left a Son, named, *Sylvanus*, who inherited his Irifh Eftate, is a fact, which proves, that he had
been married; and had a Son, who was born in the *Woods*
of Kilcolman. Tradition tells, what probability indeed
would fhow, that his wife was driven away from Kilcolman with him by the Irifh rebellion, in 1598. It is a fact,
as he himfelf avowed, that Spenfer was abafhed, when he
looked forward to the *twelve* books of the *Faerie Queene*,
as Pope was frightened, when he began to tranflate *The
Iliad:* And, of confequence, Spenfer was too much occupied,
and too much fatigued, to write fuch a poem as the *Amoretti*; but, on fome great occafion. It would have coft the
Poet his penfion, if he had addreffed fuch love Verfes to
any other Nymph, than great *Cynthia* herfelf.

that

that the *Amoretti* were written, as an apology
for the delay of the *Faerie Queene*; as memorials, that the author was ftill alive, and was
fomewhat apprehenfive of being forgotten, or
of being involved in the difgrace of his friend
Sir Walter Raleigh. It is fo extremely improbable, that Spenfer, living with his Wife,
and family, at Kilcolman; and writing the
Faerie Queene in *Salvage Soyle*, far from *Par-
naffo Mount*, fhould have addreffed fuch a body
of Amatory Sonnets to a private Woman,
whom to addrefs in fuch encomiaftic ftrains
would have been dangerous in him and un-
fafe in her, that it requires the ftrongeft proof,
to eftablifh a pofition of fuch irrational unlikelihood, as approaches, according to Mr.
Locke's doctrine, even to *the confines of im-
poffibility.*

The objects, which the Poet had obvioufly
in view, point out the perfonage, to whom
the poem was addreffed. And every reader
of difcernment, who recollects Elizabeth's
character; her eagernefs of praife, her keen-
nefs of jealoufy, the blandifhments, which fhe
allowed, and the flatteries, which fhe courted;
muft be of opinion, that each Sonnet, indivi-
dually, and all the Sonnets, conjointly, prove

fatissatisfactorily, the *Amoretti* of Spenfer to have been addreffed to *the faireft proud:*

" The *Soveraign* beauty, which I do admire,
" Witnefs *The world* how worthy to be prais'd;
" The light whereof hath kindled heavenly fire
" In my frail fpirit, *by her from bafenefs rais'd (g).*

After fmoothing the ruggednefs of Elizabeth, by his *Amoretti,* and panegerifing her

(g) In his firft Sonnet the Poet fpeaks of her *Angel's bleffed look*; in S. 2. he calls her *that faireft proud*; in S. 3. he admires her as *the Soveraign beauty*; in S. 5. he talks of her *portly pride*, which he often diverfifies into *high look* [S. 10.] *proud port*, [S. 12.] awful Majefty [Ib]; in S. 15. he defcribes *her looks* as *fineft gold on ground, her mind* as adorned *with virtues manifold*; in S. 17. he defpairs of being able to paint

" The *glorious pourtract* of that *angel's face*,
   Made to *amaze weak men's confufed fkill.*

But, he comes, at length, in S. 33, and 34 to the *two great* objects of his *Amoretti:*

Great wrong I do, I can it not deny
To that moft *facred Emprefs*, my *dear dread*,
Not finifhing her Queene of Faerie
That mote [might] enlarge her living praifes, dead:
But, Lodowick, this of grace to me aread;
Do you not think th' accomplifhment of it,
Sufficient work for one man's fimple head,
All were it, as the reft, but rudely writ.
How then fhould I, without an other wit,
Should ever to endure fuch tedious toil?
Sith that this one is toft with troublous fit
Of a *proud love,* that doth my fpirit fpoil:

Ceafe,

her beauty and her virtues, by the Faerie Queene, the Poet returned to Kilcolman, at

> Ceafe, then, till *fhe* vouchfafe to grant me reft,
> Or lend you me another living breft.

> Like as a fhip, that through the Ocean wide,
> By conduct of fome ftar doth make her way,
> When as a ftorm hath dim'd her trufty guide
> Out of her courfe doth wander far aftray !
> So I, whofe *ftar*, that wont with *her bright ray*,
> Me to direct, with clouds is over caft,
> Do wander now in darknefs and difmay,
> Through hidden perils round about me plaft :
> Yet, hope I well, that when this ftorm is paft,
> My Helice, the load ftar of my life,
> Will fhine again, and look on me at laft,
> With lovely light to clear my cloudy grief.
> Till then I wander careful, comfortlefs,
> In fecret forrow, and fad penfivenefs.

I faid above, that the two great objects of the *Amoretti* were, an Apology for not proceeding with the *Faerie Queene*, and an attempt to clear himfelf from the *cloud*, under which he wandered in darknefs, and difmay. The two Sonnets, which have juft been quoted, are the moft pofitive proofs of both my affertions. Add to thefe, S. 74. in which he mentions Elizabeth by name, and S. 80, wherein he again apologifes for the detention of the *Faerie Queene*, and pro - mifes the more vigorous profecution of the whole work. Now; what woman, but Queen Elizabeth, who had a *patent* of *monopoly* for that poem, had any connection with the *Faerie Queene?* The anfwer muft be, that the Sonnets had been impertinent, if applied to any other fair one : And, fee S. 86, wherein he imprecates, in a ftrain of fublime of Poetry, *the horrid pains of bell,* on the *venomous tongue,* that with

D *falfe*

at the end of the year 1596. But, the patron-
age, and the power, of Elizabeth, were infufficient to avert the fate, which unhappily
awaited Spenfer. The clouds, which had
been long collecting in the South of Ireland,
burft forth into a ftorm, in October 1598 ;
and, the Irifh of Munfter, rifing univerfally in
rebellion, laid wafte the Country, and expelled
the Englifh : Neither Kilcolman, nor Spenfer
were fpared (*h*). He was thus conftrained to
return with his Wife, and family, to England ; but in ruined circumftances. Spenfer
died in London, during the year 1599 (*i*) ;
leaving a Son, called Sylvanus, who inherited
his Eftate, without the poet's genius, talents,
or fame ; and who found it difficult, during
the revolutions of Ireland, and their incidental
forfeitures,

falfe forged lies, in his *true love* did *ftir up coals of fire :* and
S. 87, and 88, wherein he deplores his abfence [from Court,
at Kilcolman.]

" Since I did leave the prefence of my love
" Many long weary days I have out worn:
" Since I have lack'd the comfort of that light
" The which was wont to lead my thoughts aftray
" I wander, as in darknefs of the night,
" Affraid of every danger's leaft difmay.

(*h*) Moryfon's Itinerary, p. 25. Smith's Hiftory of Cork,
vol. i. p. 55, 233-6.

(*i*) In oppofition to the monumental infcription in Weftminfter Abbey, I concur with Sir James Ware, and Mr.
Malone.

forfeitures, to tranfmit that eftate to his grand children (*k*).

From

Malone, in faying, that Spenfer died, in 1599, though towards the end, rather than the beginning of that year : For, the preface of *Belvidere*, or *Garden of the Mufes*, which was printed, in 1600, fpeaks of Spenfer as an *extant poet*. My fearches at Doctors Commons difcovered neither any Will of Spenfer, nor adminiftration to his Eftate.

(*k*) As an additional proof how much may be collected by active perfeverance, I beg to lay before the reader *The Cafe of William Spenfer, Grandfon and Heir of Edmond Spenfer the Poet*, which gives a more diftinct account of the Poet's defcendants than has yet been done : I have fent the original to The Britifh Mufeum, for the benefit of the Public : —

The Cafe of William Spencer of Kilcolman in the County of Cork in the Kingdom of Ireland, Efq; Grandfon and Heir to Edmond Spenfer the Poet :—

That Sylvanus Spencer Efq; Father of William, in his life time, in order to prefer his fecond brother Peregrine in marriage ; did give and affign to him part of his Eftate in the faid County of Cork.

Peregrine dies, and that Part of the Eftate that was fettled on him by Silvanus, defcended and came to Hugoline Son of the faid Peregrine.

Hugoline being feized and poffeffed of the faid Eftate, was Outlaw'd for Treafon and Rebellion after the late Revolution.

William Spencer finding Hugoline's Eftate vefted in the King, and being the next proteftant Heir, as alfo Heir at Law to him, that part of the Eftate being formerly vefted in Sylvanus (to whom William was eldeft Son and Heir) did apply himfelf to his Majefty for a grant thereof, and by

From the foregoing documents, I will affume, as a certainty, what I have proved by
evidence,

his petition did fet forth his claim to the faid Eftate, and
alfo his fervices, fufferings, and loffes in the late Rebellion
in Ireland, in behalf of the Government, which are very
well known.

Upon which petition his Majefty was gracioufly pleafed
to refer the fame to the Lords Commiffioners of the Treafury in England, and they were pleafed to refer it further to
the Earls of Montrath, Drogheda, and Galloway, then
Lords Juftices of Ireland, to examin the matter and make
their report.

The Lords Juftices reported it back to the Lords of the
Treafury of England; wherein they recommend the faid
William to His Majefty for his great fervices, fufferings
and loffes in the late Troubles, and that he was next pro-
teftant Heir to Hugoline, and to deferve His Majefty's
Grace and Favour.

His Majefty was thereupon gracioufly pleafed to grant
the faid Hugoline's Eftate, to the faid William, by His
Letters patents bearing date at Dublin the fourteenth day
of June, in the ninth year of His Reign.

That the faid Eftate was then of the yearly value of
fixty-feven pounds feventeen fhillings and fix pence.

That there is a mortgage upon the faid Eftate for five
hundred pounds, which is yet unpaid.

That it coft the faid William, above fix hundred pounds,
the beft part of his fortune, in improving the faid Eftate,
and procuring the faid Grant, and hath received little or no
profit thereof.

For by a late Act of Parliament, all Grants were made
void in Ireland, and the forfeited Eftates were vefted in
Truftees, to be fold for the ufe of the publick, and whilft
that

evidence, which cannot be countervailed, that Spenser addressed his *Amoretti* to Elizabeth.

that Act was in agitation the said William was so disabled by sickness, that he could not apply himself to this Honourable House for a saving clause, whereby the Trustees have dispossessed the said William of the said Estate, without any manner of consideration for his improvements and other charges about the same, to his utter ruin and impoverishment.

That this is conceived to be the only case of this nature in the whole Kingdom of Ireland, he being the next Protestant Heir, and whose Grand-father Edmond Spencer by his Book, entitul', a View of Ireland, modled the settlement of that Kingdom, and these lands were given him by Queen Elizabeth of blessed memory for his Services to the Crown.

That your Petitioner having apply'd himself to this Honourable House last Sessions of Parliament for relief herein.

The Petitioner was refer'd to the Trustees then in England, who reported the same to this Honourable House, and upon further consideration of that Report the same was refer'd to the Trustees in Ireland, who now have made their Report to this effect :

That the Petitioner was very serviceable to the publick, by being a guide to His Majesty's General the Earl of Arthlone, during the late wars in that Kingdom.

That he had 300 Head of black Cattle and 1500 Sheep taken from him, had several Houses burnt: That his family was stript, his house plunder'd, and his only Son had above twenty wounds given him by the Irish Army.

That in consideration of his said services and sufferings, and of his being next Protestant Heir to Hugoline Spencer, Attainted; His Majesty was pleased to Grant the forfeited

D 3   Estate

beth. I will now proceed to fhow, that Shakfpeare wrote his *Sonnets,* in emulation of Spenfer. Like other men of uncommon genius, Shakfpeare was confcious of his own powers, which, he probably perceived, were not always appreciated to the full claim of his pride. He faw Spenfer placed in the foremoft rank of Poets (*l*) : He obferved Spenfer place

Eftate of the faid Hugoline to the Petitioner in 1697, now fet at Sixty pounds per Ann.

That there is a claim heard and allow'd as an Incumbrance of £. 300 abfolute, on the faid Eftate, and £. 200 more in cafe Hugoline who is very old and unmarried, dies without Iffue male.

That the Petitioner has expended near the Sum mention'd in his Petition, in making Jorneys into England to procure his Grant, in paffing his patent in Ireland, and in building a Houfe and planting an Orchard on the premifes, fo that his Grant has hitherto been a charge to him, and not an advantage; All which they fubmit to this Honourable Houfe.

And the Petitioner humbly hopes this Honourable Houfe will be pleafed to take his Cafe into confideration, and re-eftablifh him in his faid Eftate, or otherwife relieve him as to your great wifdom fhall feem meet.

(*l*) Bifhop Hall, in his fourth Satyre, thus breaks out:

" But, let no rebel Satyre dare traduce
" Th' eternal legends of thy *faerie* mufe,
" Renowned Spenfer; whom no earthly wight
" *Dares once* to *emulate*, much lefs dares defpight.
" Saluft of France, and Tufcan Arioft,
" Yield up the laurel Garland ye have loft:

" And

place Alabafter, and Daniel, before him (*m*) :
And he often heard poetafters of very inferior
talents named, as poets, while he was paffed
by, in filence (*n*).   Shakfpeare knew alfo what
all men, foreigners, as well as fubjects, underftood, that Elizabeth delighted in blandifhments, and fawned on flatterers.   And he
was, thus, induced to write his Sonnets, in
emulation of Spenfer's Amoretti : So, he cries
out in his 80th Sonnet :

    " O how I faint, when I of you do write !
    " Knowing *a better fprite* doth ufe your name ;
    " And, in the praife thereof, fpends all his might,
    " To *make me tongue ty'd*, fpeaking of your fame (*o*).

                                  He

    " And let all others, willow wear with me,
    " Or let their undeferving temples bared be.
                [I quote from the Edition 1602.]
  (*m*) In Colin Clout, which though written, in 1591, was
firft publifhed, in 1595 :
    " And there is Alabafter throughly taught,
    " In all this fkill, though knowen yet to few ;
    " Yet were he knowne to *Cynthia*, as he ought,
    " His *Elifeïs* would be redde anew.
    " *Who lives, that can match that heroick Song,*
    " Which he hathe of that mightie Princeffe made ?
Spenfer immediately exclaims ;
    " Then roufe thy feathers quickly *Daniel.*"

  (*n*) Lodge's *Wits Miferie*, 1596, p. 57.

  (*o*) Mr. Malone, indeed, fays. " That Spenfer, who was
then in the Zenith of his reputation, was the perfon here alluded to [Sup. vol. i. p. 645.] But, Dr. Sewell, who *revifed*,
               D 4   and

He artfully endeavours, in his 83d Sonnet, to raife himfelf to a level with his opponent, by telling the objeƈt of his adoration :—

" There lives more life, in one of *your fair eyes,*
" Than *Both* your poets can, in praife devife."

Shakfpeare's emulation again breaks out, in his 85th Sonnet :—

" My tongue-ty'd mufe, in manners, holds her ftill
" While comments of your praife, richly compil'd,
" Referve their charaƈter with golden quill,
" And precious phrafe, by all the Mufes fil'd.

" I think

---

and *correƈted,* an Edition of Shakfpeare's *Works,* for the Book-fellers, in 1728, preceded Mr. Malone, in this remark, and went beyond him far, in the argument, whereby he fupported his pofition, that *Shakfpeare emulated Spenfer :* " We find,
" to wander no farther, that Spenfer, Cowley, and many
" others, paid their firft fruits of poetry to a real, or an
" imaginary Lady. Upon this occafion, I conjeƈture, that
" Shakfpeare took fire on reading our admirable Spenfer,
" who went but juft before him in the line of life, and was
" in all probability the Poet moft in vogue, at that time.
" To make this argument the ftronger, Spenfer is taken
" notice of in one of thefe little pieces [The Paffionate
" Pilgrim] as a favourite of our Author's. He alludes
" certainly to the *Fairy Queen,* when he mentions his
" *Deep Conceit;* that Poem being entirely allegorical. It
" has been remarked, that more Poets have fprung from
" Spenfer, than all our other Englifh Writers ; to which
" let me add an obfervation of the late Dr. Garth, That
" moft of our late ones [Poets] have been fpoiled by too
" early an admiration of Milton. Be it to Spenfer, then,
" that we owe Shakfpeare,
         " The faireft Scyon of the faireft tree !"
[vol. x. pref. vii,]

" I think good thoughts, whilft others write good words,
" And, like unletter'd Clerk, ftill cry *Amen*
" To every hymn, that *able fprite* affords,
" In polifh'd form of well refined pen :
" Hearing you prais'd, I fay, '*tis fo*, '*tis true*.

In his 86th Sonnet, Shakfpeare's pride of
genius tries to rife above his rival :—

" Was it the proudful Sail of *his great Verfe*,
" Bound for the prize of *all-too-precious you*,
" That did my ripe thoughts in my brain inhearfe,
" Making their tomb, the womb wherein they grew?
" Was it *his fpirit* by *fpirits taught* to *write*
" *Above* a *mortal pitch*, that ftruck me dead ?
" No ; neither he, nor his Compeers, by night,
" Giving him aid, my verfe aftonifhed.

—————   —————   —————

" But, when your countenance fil'd up his line;
" Then, lack'd I matter, that enfeebl'd mine.

Add to thofe proofs, that Shakfpeare was
a deligent reader of Spenfer, and an avowed
admirer of his *deep conceit* (*p*).   Spenfer appears

(*p*) In Colin Clout, 1595. Sign, C. 2. Spenfer fays :—
" And, there, *though laft not leaft*, is Action."
" *Though laft, not leaft* in love, your's good Trebonius."
                    [Shak. Jul. Cæf.]
Shakfpeare avows his admiration of Spenfer in the *Paf-
fionate Pilgrim*, though Spenfer had not efpied the merits of
Shakfpeare :—
    " Spenfer to me, whofe *deep conceit* is fuch
    " As paffing all conceit, needs no defence."
    This, fays Mr. Malone, as Dr. Sewell had faid before nim,
" feems to allude to the *Faerie Queene*.   If fo, the Sonnets
were not written till after 1590, when the firft three books
                                                    of

pears to have been plainly in the mind of Shakfpeare, during the year 1596. Now; if it be true, as I have fhown, that Spenfer addreffed his *Amoretti* to Elizabeth; if it be true, as I have proved, that Shakfpeare wrote his *Sonnets,* in emulation of Spenfer, and in imitation of the *Amoretti*; this important conclufion will follow, that Shakfpeare alfo addreffed *his Sonnets* to the fame Queen.

Yet, is it faid pretty pofitively by Mr. Malone, that, "Daniel's Sonnets, which were "publifhed, in 1592, appear to have been "the model that Shakfpeare followed (*q*)." Though probability be violated by this affertion, neither argument is brought to juftify its unlikelihood, nor authority to fupport its inference: There is between Daniel's Sonnets

of that poem were publifhed. [Sup. vol. i. 714.] This is the truth; but it is not the whole truth! The *Faerie Queene,* which was completely printed, and re-printed, in 1596, was often alluded to in *The Merry Wives of Windfor,* that was written, in its rude fketch, as I will fhow, in 1596: Miftrefs Page fays, "*My Nan fhall be the Queene of all the Faeries*;—The Amoretti of Spenfer were certainly publifhed, for the firft time, in 1595: The Sonnets of Shakfpeare, as Meres afferts, were handed about, among his private friends, before September 1598: This implies, that they had been recently written: And, I fuppofe, that they were written, partly, in 1596, and partly, in 1597.

(*q*) Sup. vol. i. p. 581.

and

and Shakſpeare's no other Analogy, than the
ſame conſtruction, as Sonnets, and ſimilar
topicks, as amatory Verſes.

But, in the *Amoretti* of Spenſer, and the
Sonnets of Shakſpeare, may be ſeen, not only
the ſame mode of conſtruction, as Sonnets,
the like ſimilarity of topicks, but even a frequent ſameneſs of expreſſion. I will prove
theſe poſitions, by the minute detail of ſtriking
compariſons : Spenſer opens his *Amoretti,* by
dedicating, in his firſt Sonnet, his *leaves,* lines,
and rhimes, to his bleſſed ANGEL, whom he
endeavours alone to gratify :

" Leaves, lines, and rimes, ſeek *her to pleaſe alone,*
" Whom, if ye pleaſe, *I care for other none."*

Shakſpeare opens his amatory ditties, in a
different manner ; and does not avow the *ſame
unity of purpoſe,* till he arrives at his 103d Sonnet, wherein, ſpeaking of his *Argument,* he
cries out, at length :——

" Were it not ſinful, then, ſtriving to mend,
" To mar the ſubject, that before was well !
" For, to *no other paſs my verſes tend,*
" Than of *your graces,* and *your gifts to tell."*

He enlarges on *this purpoſe,* not of one verſe,
but of all his verſes, ſhewing the *unity* of *their
deſign,* in his 105th Sonnet :

" Let not my *love* be called idolatry ;
" Nor *my beloved* as an idol ſhow ;
" Since *all alike my Songs, and praiſes be*
" To *one,* of *one,* ſtill ſuch, and ever ſo :

" Therefore,

" Therefore, *my Verfe* to conftancy confin'd,
" *One thing* expreffing, *leaves out difference.*

Mr. Steevens quotes fome of thefe verfes (*r*),
for the purpofe of fhowing, what they do not
fhow, viz. that Shakfpeare intended fome of
his Sonnets for publication; without perceiving, that the Poet proves, by his expreffions, the *Unity* of *his defign,* and the *conftancy*
of *his application* of *his praifes,* to *one* object.
Mr. Malone, indeed, infifts, this object was
not a *female;* " the majority of them not be-
" ing directed to a female (*s*)." Shakfpeare,
furely,

(*r*) Sup. vol. i. p. 704.
(*s*) Sup. vol. i. 653, 685. Mr. Malone fays, fpecifically, " that one hundred and twenty of the Sonnets are
" addreffed to a man; the remaining twenty-eight are ad-
" dreffed to a Lady" [Ib. 579.] The anonymous Critic
before mentioned [Britifh Critic, vol. 9. p. 515.] remarks;
" Mr. Malone has obferved very juftly, that of the whole
" number of 154 Sonnets, 120 are addreffed to a Man,
" and 28 to a Lady. Here is a manifeft error in the Arith-
" metic, both as written by Mr. Malone, and copied by
" Mr. Chalmers; it fhould be 126 to a male, which is *the*
" *fact,* for the 125th Sonnet begins, *O, thou my lovely*
" *boy.*" But, why queftion the fufficiency of Mr. Malone's
arithmetic, or my little fkill in the common rules of *Addition* and *Subtraction,* to calculate, that 120 and 28 do not
make up the Sum total of 154? He meant merely to give
it as his opinion, that the poet had addreffed 120 Sonnets
to a man, and 28 to a Woman; and I took him, implicitly,
at

furely, knew his own defign: And, having avowed his purpofe, by repeated declarations, of praifing *one*, the contrarieties of Commentators ought to vanifh, as darknefs difappears at the approach of day. When he, who knew beft, has fpoken, pofitively, and may well be believed; whilft they, who know not at all, although the author wrote plainly; and who neverthelefs, talk, contradictorily, may well be difregarded.

Shakfpeare unfolds, at once, his amatory purpofe, by a propofal of marriage to his *faireft creature*:

" Thou that art now *the world's frefh Ornament*,
" And only *herald* to the *gaudy Spring* (*t*)."

---

at his word; knowing, that neither the one pofition, nor the other was right. He left the balance of Six, (as this number had been given neither to man, woman, nor boy) to be addreffed, according to the fublime doctrine of the Commentators, to an *Hermaphrodite.* The Anonymous Critic was quite confiftent, when he was detecting the blunders of Mr. Malone, and Mr. Chalmers, in Arithmetic, to fall into a blunder of ftatement himfelf: It is not the 125th, but the 126th, Sonnet, which, according to Mr. Malone's Edition, Mr. Steevens's Edition, and the original Edition, fpeaks of the " lovely boy."—As to the fophiftry of affuming *the fact*, which is the point to be proved, I will only, here, remark the unfairnefs of it.

(*t*) Shakfpeare, when writing the above Couplet, had probably his eye on the 70th Son. of Spenfer:

" *Frefh Spring*, the *herald* of love's mighty King.

He

He woos her to marriage, becaufe " from
" faireft Creatures we defire increafe," through
feveral Sonnets, by every topick of Courtfhip.
On the contrary, Spenfer poftpones his propofal of marriage till his Sixty-fifth Sonnet ; urging his "*fair love,*"

" That fondly fear to lofe your liberty,
When lofing one, two liberties you gain :
Without conftraint, or dread of any ill,
The gentle bird feels no captivity,
Within her Cage, but *fings*, and feeds her fill.
There pride dare not approach, nor difcord fpill
The league 'twixt them that loyal love hath bound.

Shakfpeare, in his 8th Sonnet, rings all the
changes on the topick of mufic, having in his
eye, no doubt, the Sonnet of Spenfer, which
has juft been quoted.

" If the true *Concord* of well-tuned founds,
" By *Unions married*, do offend thine ear,
" They do but fweetly chide thee, who confounds
" In finglenefs the parts, that thou fhouldft bear.
" Mark how *one ftring*, fweet *hufband* to an other,
" Strikes each in each, by mutual ordering ;
" Refembling Sire, and Child, and happy Mother,
" Who all in *one*, one pleafing *note* do *fing*.

Spenfer urges his fweetheart to take *joyous
time* by the *forelock :*

" Make hafte, therefore, *fweet love*, whilft it is prime ;
" For, none can call again the paffed time.

Shakfpeare, in his 2d, 3d, 5th, and 6th
Sonnets, preffes on his " beauteous niggard"
9   the

the fame topick, from the effluxion of years :

" For, never refting time leads Summer on
" To hideous Winter, and confounds him there.

And, in feveral of the Sonnets, wherein the *dear delight* of both is wooed to wed, by all the blandifhments of poetry, Shakfpeare, not only catches the topicks of Spenfer, but even copies his words (*u*). Spenfer attributes her creation to the hand of nature, and her

(*u*) Compare Spenfer's 3d Son. with Shakfpeare's 5th and 69th. Spenfer's 4th Son. with Shakfpeare's 3d and 21ft. Spenfer fpeaks, in his 5th Son. of her *portly pride*, of HER *lofty looks* ; " threatning rafh *eyes, that gaze on her fo wide :* Shakefpeare in his 5th Son. talks of " The *lovely gaze* where *every eye doth dwell :*" Spenfer in Son. 10, exclaims:

 " Unrighteous *Lord of Love*, what *law is* this
 " That me thou makeft thus tormented be ?
 " See how, the *Tyrannefs* doth joy to fee
 " The huge maffacres, which her eyes do make."

Shakfpeare in his 26th Son. cries out :—

 " *Lord of my Love*, to whom in *Vaffalage*,
 " Thy merit hath my duty ftiongly knit,
 " To thee, I fend this written Embaffage
 " To witnefs duty, not to fhow my wit."

In his 131ft Son. he fays " Thou art as *tyrannous :*" In his 131ft Son. he afks, in the Spirit of Spenfer, " O! " from *what power haft* thou *this powerful might ?*" Spenfer in his 11th Son. alfo fends an "*Embaffage* to fue for peace ; " and to offer hoftages, for his truth." In Son. 41, and 48, Spenfer complains of her Cruelty; Shakfpeare alfo, complains of her cruelty, in his 131ft and 133d Sonnets.

birth

birth to a divine origin (*x*) : Shakſpeare alſo
gives her the ſame origin, and the ſame birth (*y*).
Spenſer likens his Goddeſs to what is moſt
brilliant on earth, ſaphyrs, rubies, pearls, ivory,
gold, and ſilver ſheen (*z*) :

" But, that which faireſt is, and few behold,
" Her *mind adorned is with virtues manifold* :"

Shakſpeare, trying to outdo his rival, compares, obliquely, *his fair* " to thoſe *gold can-*
" *dles* fixed in heaven's air ;" and adds " that
" ſhe is as fair, in *knowledge,* as in hue (*a*)."
Spenſer, praiſes his *divine objeȼt,* by drawing
topicks, from the *Seaſons,* from a *Storm,* from
the *Sky* (*b*) : In the ſame ſtrain, Shakſpeare
derives topicks of commendation from the
Seaſons, from a *Storm,* from the *Stars* (*c*). Spenſer likens the *idol* of *his thought* to a rich laden
bark, with precious *merchandize* (*d*) : Shakſpeare alſo ſends out his " *ſaucy bark,*" laden
with her *worth, wide, as the ocean is* ; and at
laſt exclaims,

" That love is *merchandiz'd,* whoſe rich eſteeming
" The Owner's tongue doth publiſh every where."

Spenſer has a *Dream* of pompous *royalty,* and
of a feaſt, fit to entertain the greateſt *Prince* (*e*) :

(*x*) Son. 17.   (*y*) Son. 20.   (*z*) Son. 15.   (*a*) Son.
21. 85   (*b*) Son. 62. 63. 72.   (*c*) Son. 32, 33, 34, 14.
(*d*) Compare Spen. Son. 81, with Shak. Son. 80. 102.
(*e*) Son. 77.

Shakſpeare

Shakfpeare alfo flatters himfelf with a *dream*, wherein he fancies himfelf, " in " fleep, a king *(f)*." Spenfer goes into *The Theatre*, for diverfities of celebration *(g)*: Shakfpeare finds on the *Stage* dumb prefagers of his fpeaking breaft; and cries out, with a theatrical tone,

" O! learn to read what *filent* love hath writ;
" To *hear* with *eyes* belongs to love's fine wit *(h)*."

Shakfpeare likewife copied Spenfer, in fuppofing, that the fair object of his praife would be immortalized, by his Sonnets: Spenfer defires his *fair proud* to cherifh his *verfes*, that *never fhall expire*, that fhall make *her immortal* (*i*): Shakfpeare is equally confident, as a prophet, that her moft high deferts would live, for ever, in his rhime;—

" But, thy eternal Summer fhall not fade;
" Nor, fhall death brag thou wandreft in his fhade;
" So long as men can breath, or eyes can fee;
" So long *lives this*, and this gives life to thee *(k)*."

Shakfpeare, after fo many imitations, when he comes to his clofe, copies Spenfer's

(f) Son. 87. *(g)* Son. 54. *(h)* Son. 23. *(i)* Son. 27, 69, 75. *(k)* Son. 18, 19, 55.

E,   concluding

concluding ftanzas, about Cupid, and Dian;
and Dian's maid, who ftole his fhafts :
The tautology, the thoughts, the words,
in both the poets, are the fame (*l*). Yet,
Shakfpeare having fome intimation of Spenfer's embarrafsments, which, indeed, are
plainly avowed in his *Amoretti*, feems to
fneer at the penfion of his rival: For, he
fays, " I will not praife, that *purpofe not to*
" *fell*; *who plead for love*, and look *for re-*
" *compence* (*m*)." And, he appears to affect
a fuperior independence; as if he had been
anticipating Pope's petulance, when he defires his love to accept his *oblation*, *poor* but
free (*n*). Spenfer, however, had given him
a fpecimen of this kind of Cant, for imitation :

" *Fondnefs* it were, for any, being *free*,
" To covet fetters, though they golden be (*o*)."

Such are the proofs, which, as I before
propofed, I have now adduced, in fupport
of my pofitions, that Spenfer addreffed his

(*l*) Compare Spenfer's concluding verfes, with
Shakfpeare's two laft Sonnets, 153, and 154.

(*m*) Son. 21, 23. (*n*) Son. 125, 25.

(*o*) Son. 37. *Fondnefs*, in the language of that age,
meant *foolifhnefs*.

Amoretti,

Amoretti, wholly, to Elizabeth; that Shakfpeare, in imitation of Spenfer, addreffed his
Sonnets, entirely, to the fame Queen: But,
there are thofe, who prefer prejudices to
proofs; who reafon from doubtful affumptions, rather than from logical deductions;
and who ftart difficulties, when they ought
to relinquifh prepoffeffion.

I will now proceed to anfwer fuch objections to my refults, as have occurred to my
obfervation.

It has never been fhown, with any precifion, to whom either Spenfer addreffed
his *Amoretti*, or Shakfpeare his *Sonnets*:
There are not, therefore, any perfons in
poffeffion of thofe Amatory Verfes, who
muft be difpoffeffed of their rights, if the title
be adjudged to Elizabeth. To fuppofe, that
Spenfer, and Shakfpeare, in their fituations,
as married men, and in their circumftances,
as to wealth, addreffed fuch Sonnets to ordinary Women, (and much more to ordinary Men,) we muft at once prefume, in
oppofition to *the fact*, that thofe illuftrious
poets were deftitute of common fenfe, and

were

were without any employment for their tranfcendent talents.

It has been conjectured, indeed, that the Sonnets of Shakfpeare, at leaft one hundred and twenty of them, were addreffed to two men, or boys; to W. Hart, or to W. Hughes. Thorpe, the firft publifher of them, dedicated thofe *Amatory* effufions " to the *only* " *begetter* of thefe enfuing Sonnets, Mr. " W. H."—How he was the *begetter* of them, it is not eafy to tell; unlefs we prefume, what is not improbable, that he begot a defire in Shakfpeare to deliver a Copy to the Bookfeller, for publication: W. H. was the *getter* of the manufcript, imperfect as it was, from which the Sonnets were printed inaccurately. Doctor Farmer was thus iduuced, though with little felicity of conjecture, to fuppofe that many of thefe Sonnets were addreffed to the poet's Nephew, William Harte, the Son of his Sifter, Joan: That critic's conjecture, then, is, that an Uncle addreffed one hundred and twenty Amatory Sonnets to his Nephew: But, Mr. Malone confutes Doctor

Doctor Farmer's conjecture, by shewing,
that Joan Harte's children were all young,
in 1616, even twenty years after the writing
of the verses; " Many of them," adds Mr.
Malone, " are written to shew the pro-
" priety of Marriage; and therefore, can-
" not well be supposed to be addressed to a
" *Schoolboy* (*p*)." Yet Mr. Tyrwhit pointed out a line :—

　" A man in *hew* all Hews in his controlling,"
which

(*p*) The before mentioned Anonymous Critic [The
British Critic, vol. ix. p. 516] says " when Mr. C.
" adds, p. 50, to *shew the propriety of Marriage*, we do
" not find that he is warranted by Mr. M. whom he
" *seems* to quote. They were certainly written to shew
" *him* that propriety." I see enough of the British
Critic's meaning to understand, that he designed to
maintain, that Mr. Malone's observation was applied
to a *man*, and not to a *schoolboy*, who had not yet arrived
at the age of puberty. If this were the meaning of
Mr. Malone, he must have equally meant to apply to
his man, the feminine *Epithet*, " *tender churl*," in the
first Sonnet, and the womanish epithets, " unthrifty
" *loveliness*, and *beauteous* niggard," in the fourth sonnet.
If Mr. Malone thought over the sonnets, which he
was to criticise, he must, moreover, have maintained,
when he made Shakspeare persuade a man to marry,

E 3 which

which inclined Mr. Malone to think, " that
" the initials W. H. ftand for W. Hughes."
Our commentator regards this conjecture,
as not " improbable, confidering, that one

which is not a very hard tafk, on moft occafions, that
the Poet faid to this man, in the opening Sonnet,
" from *faireft creatures,* we defire increafe," that
thereby we may have progeny: " But, *thou* [the man
addreffed] contracted to *thine own bright eyes,*" refufeft
to wed; thou [the man addreffed] that art *now* the
" *world's frefh ornament,* and *only herald to the gaudy
fpring,*" art content to remain fingle, without pitying
the world, which has a claim upon thee for Children.
Now, I would afk, was there a *man* in England, who
had fuch *bright eyes,* or could be called *the world's frefh
ornament*; was there a woman in England, whom it
was fit to call, as in the 5th Sonnet," the *lovely gaze,*
where *every eye doth dwell?*" Yes; the fitnefs, and the
fact, properly applied to the *greateft* woman. Shakfpeare
goes on, in the 9th Sonnet, by *a natural collocation,* to
woo *his* fuppofed *man* to wed; and afks, " Is it for fear to
" wet a *widow's* eye, that thou confum'ft thyfelf in
" fingle life?—When every PRIVATE *widow* well may
" keep, by Children's eyes, her hufband's fhape in
" mind."—I never fuppofed, that Mr. Malone was
fo abfurd as to apply fuch perfuafions to a *man.* It is
only the Anonymous *Critic,* who is fo abfurd, as to
apply fuch fentiments, and expreffions, to a *man,* or
indeed to any *woman,* except Elizabeth.

of

" of the Sonnets is formed entirely on a
" play on our author's Chriftian name.(*q*)"

When Shafpeare talked of his love,
" as the *mafter*-miftrefs of his paffion,"
Mr. Steevens exclaimed, " how impoffible
" it is, to read this fulfome panegyric, ad-
" dreffed to a male object, without an
" equal mixture of difguft and indigna-
" tion (*r*)." Such are the avowed opinions
of thofe famous Critics, and celebrated
Commentators !

But, there is a rule in reafoning, which,
amid their fuppofes, conjectures, and in-
dignations, they feem to have entirely forgotten, that in proportion as any affertion
is improbable, ought to be the ftrength of
proof, which is neceffary for its fupport.
Their affumption is, that Shakfpeare, a
hufband, a father, a moral man, addreffed
a hundred and twenty, nay, a hundred and
twenty-fix *Amourous* Sonnets to a *male*
object! And, their proofs confift of fuppofes, without fupport, conjectures, with-

(*q*) Sup. vol. i. 579.   (*r*) Ib. 596.

E 4   out

out conceptions, and of indignation, without propriety.

The fuppofition of Doctor Farmer, of whom, on any other occafion, I would fpeak with praife, may be fafely ranked in the numerous clafs of *bare fuppofes*. Mr. Tyrwhit, whofe learning, and modefty, make him refpectable, even when he is miftaken, might have known, that there was not, among the poets of that age, a more common epithet for *mien*, than *hew*. Sydney, in his *Arcadia*, fpeaks of Mopfa's cheeks of opal *hue:* " What marvel, then, " I take a woman's *hue* (*s*)." Daniel, in his defcription of Beauty, declares:

" That forrow is the *hewe* of fweet delight."

In his Queen's Arcadia, he talks of " a " form, and flattered hew ;" and he at laft cries out;—

" .Then, lovely Venus, in bright majefty,
" Appears with mild afpect, in dove-like hue (*t*)."

(*s*) Arcadia, p. 31, 43.

(*t*) We may thus obferve, in Daniel, this unlucky word, under thefe forms; *hewe, hew,* and *heu :* again, Daniel has " That rofie *Hew*, the glory of the Cheek." [Queen's Arcadia.]

But,

But, it was from Spenfer, that Shakfpeare
borrowed both the word, and the verfe (*u*):
When Shakfpeare wrote his *twentieth Sonnet*,
which Mr. Steevens, particularly, fuppofes
to have been addreffed to a *male objeƈt*, he
had before his imitative eyes the *feventeenth*
Sonnet of Spenfer (*x*), whence our poet
borrowed

(*u*) Spenfer, fpeaking of the *mien* of Elizabeth, has
lovely *hew*, [7th and 31ft Son.] Glorious *hew*,
[79th Son.] celeftial *hew*, [3d and 45th Son.] and heavenly *hew*, [80th Son. Add to all thofe examples, from
Whitney's Emplems, 1586, p. 177, 227.

" The Phœnix rare, with fethers frefh of *hewe*,
" Arabia's righte, and facred to the Sonne :
" Whome, other birdes with wonder feeme to *viewe*;
" Dothe live untill a thoufand years be ronne:
" The one is white, the other, black, of *hewe*."

(*x*) Here is Spenfer's 17th Sonnet :
" The glorious *pourtraiƈt* of that *Angel's face*,
" Made to amaze weak *men's confufed* fkill ;
" And this world's worthlefs glory to embrace,
" What pen, what *pencill*, can exprefs her fill ?
" For though he colours could devife at will
" And eke his learned hand at pleafure guide,
" Leaft trembling, it his workmanfhip may fpill,
" Yet, many wondrous things there are befide ;
" The fweet eye-glances that like arrows glide;
" The charming fmiles, that rob fenfe from the hart,
" The lovely pleafance, and the *lofty pride*;
" Cannot expreffed be by any art.

" A greater

borrowed feveral of the thoughts, and fome of the expreffions ; and if Spenfer drew his *pourtraiét* for Elizabeth, fo Shakfpeare, *with nature's own hand, painted the mafter-miftrefs of his paffion*, by figuring the fame Queen.

The following is Shakfpeare's twentieth Sonnet, which, I maintain, was addreffed to a woman ; and that woman, Elizabeth :

" A *woman's* face, with nature's own hand painted,
" Haft *thou*, the *mafter-miftrefs* of my paffion ;
" A *woman's gentle heart*, but not acquainted
" With fhifting change, as is *falfe women's* fafhion ;
" An *eye*, more bright than *theirs*, lefs falfe in rolling,
" Gilding the objeét, whereupon it gazeth ;
" " A *man* in *hue*, all heus in his [the *hues*] controuling,
" Which [hue] *fteals mens eyes*, and womens fouls
    amazeth.
" And, for a *woman* wert thou *firft created*,
" Till *nature*, as fhe wrought thee, fell *a-doting*,
" And, by addition, me of thee defeated,
" By adding one thing, to my purpofe, nothing :

" A greater Craftsman's hand thereto doth need
" That can exprefs the life of things indeed."
Compare this Sonnet, with his *fourth* Æglogue, April, which the proem tells, was intended to praife Elizabeth :

" Tell me, have ye feen her *Ange-like face*,
    " Like Phœbe fair ?
" Her heavenly 'haviour, her princely grace,
    " Can you well compare ?"

                                    " But,

" But, fince fhe [nature] *prickt* thee out for women's
 " pleafure ;
" Mine, be thy love, and thy love's ufe their trea-
 " fure (*y*)."

(*y*) The *mafter miftrefs*, which has given fuch offence,
and raifed fuch prejudices, only means, *Chiefeft*:
Mintheu fays, *Maifter*, in one fenfe, fignifies *Chief*;
So, Johnfon fays it fignifies *Chief*, head; as Mafter-
gunner from Shakfpear, Mafter-piece, mafterful: In
the Menœchmi, 1595, it is faid, " Young Women
are fo *mafterful* [Capel's Notes, 3 v. p. 466.] *Hew*, as
I have already fhown, was the appropriate word for
mien, in that age ; A man in hue, or *mien*, is the fame
thought, as Spenfer's juft defcription of Elizabeth's *Air*,
her *lofty pride*: She was a man, in *hue*: In the *Princly
Pleafures of Kenelworth Caftle*, it is faid;
  " But tydings' of our Englifh Queene,
  " Whom heaven hath deck'd with hewes."
The Creation of woman is thus defcribed in Sil-
vefter's Dubartas :
 " Source of all joys! Sweet he-fhe-coupled-one!
 " Thy *facred* birth, I never think upon,
 " But, ravis'd, I admire how God did, then,
 " Make *two* of *one*, and *one* of *two* again."
The thought of *the doting* of Nature, Shakfpeare bor-
rowed from Sydney's Arçadia, 439 :
 " O nature! *doting old;* O blind, dead Nature!"
To *prick* is often ufed by Shakfpeare for to *mark*, as
indeed the word is ufed fometimes at prefent: The
King, every year, *pricks* the Lift of Sheriffs, with a
          golden

To Shakſpeare ought ſurely to be allowed the ſame privilege, which other writers claim,

golden bodkin. But, ſince nature marked thee out for the *pleaſure*, which belongs to woman; let mine be *thy love*, " That *love*, which *virtue* begs, and *virtue* grants;" and thy *love's uſe* the *treaſure* of other women; *now chaſtity* is the appropriate treaſure of women.---It will, after all, be aſked, what *additional* circumſtance was it, which nature, in her *doting*, ſuperadded, and which defeated the poet from poſſeſſing his *maſter-miſtreſs*. I will not ſhrink from the queſtion, whatever may be its difficulty. In the mythology of Spenſer, and Shakſpeare, Elizabeth was ſprung of *heavenly race*:

" Of fair Eliza, be your ſilver ſong
" That bleſſed wight ;
" The flower of virgins, may ſhe flouriſh long,
" In princely plight :
" For ſhe is Syrix daughter, without pot;
" Which Pan, the Shepherds God, of her begot :
" So *ſprung her Grace*
" *Of heavenly race,*
" No mortal blemiſh may her blot."

Now; the *no mortal blemiſh* of Spenſer, and the *one thing* of Shakſpeare, when properly compared with the Context, convey the ſame meaning; and lead the intelligent inquirer to infer, that it was the divine origin, or high birth, of his *maſter miſtreſs*, which was the additional circumſtance, that daſhed all his hopes: For, ſhe was only a man in *hue* ; and ſhe was more than

a woman,

claim, and all critics exercife, of clearing obfcurities by the context. He has conftantly his great rival in his head, and hand. And copying the verfes, and the words of Spenfer, in his twentieth Sonnet, Shakfpeare evinces, by it, and by his twenty-firft Sonnet, that he had Spenfer for his rival, and the fame perfonage, as Spenfer, for the great objeɛt of his elaborate commendation :

" So, it is not with me, as with *that mufe* (z),
" Stirred by a painted beauty to *his* verfe ; '

---

a woman, by *addition.* Add to the before mentioned intimations what Spenfer fays of Elizabeth in his 61ft Sonnet :

" The Glorious image of the maker's beauty,
" My *Soveraign* Saint, the idol of my thought,
" Dare not henceforth above the bounds of duty
" T'accufe of pride, or rafhly blame for ought.
" For, being as fhe is, *divinely wrought,*
" And of the *brood of Angels heavenly born*;
" And with the crew of blefſed Saints upbrought,
" Each of which did her with their gifts adorn. "

(z) Compare this with Shakfpear's 80th Sonnet, wherein he points more diftinɛtly at Spenfer, and with his 83d, 84th, 85th, 86th, Son. wherein Shakfpeare fpeaks plainly of two encomiafts, himfelf, and Spenfer :

" There lives, more life in one of your *fair eyes*
" Than *both* your poets can in praife devife."

                                                  " Who

" Who Heaven itfelf for ornament doth ufe,

" *And every fair with his fair doth reherfe :*

" O! let me, true in love, but truly write.

" And, then, believe me, *my love* is as *fair*

" As any Mother's Child, though not fo bright,

" As thofe gold candles, fixed in Heaven's air."

Shakfpeare, then, having pofitively declared his purpofe, and avowed his objeƈt, forbids Commentators, from giving him another purpofe, and from affigning him a different objeƈt. The poet declared his purpofe to be the praife of one ; yet, the Commentators affert his purpofe to have been the praife of *two*, a *male love*, and a female : The poet avowed the objeƈt of his many commendations to have been a *woman* ; yet, the commentators infift, that the fame objeƈt was a *man:* The poet fpeaks of *another poet*, who now appears to be Spenfer ; whom Shakfpeare imitates, both in fentiment, and in ftyle, and emulates in his objeƈt, and ambition : Yet, the commentators affert, that Shakfpeare addreffed the *moft of his Sonnets* to a *man*, or to a *boy*, though Spenfer demonftratively addreffed his *Amoretti* to a *Queen*, to Elizabeth.

Yet,

Yet, the anonymous Critic, before mentioned, declares the twentieth Sonnet to be
too *indecent* to be quoted: " Its very *inde-*
" *cency* would have made it utterly fhame-
" lefs to prefent it to Queen Elizabeth (*a*)."
It is for impure minds only, to be continually finding fomething obfcene in objects, that convey nothing obfcene, or offenfive, to the chafteft hearts. Difcovering
nothing indecent in that Sonnet, and feeling
no difguft, at any fair conftruction of it, I
have re-publifhed it above ; and explained
its apparent meaning.   If what the prudifh
Critics of the prefent day call obfcenity,
would have poifoned Elizabeth, fhe could
not have lived out a twelvemonth of four
and forty years (*b*). The anonymous Critic
                                        feems

(*a*) Britifh Critic, vol. ix. 517.

(*b*) The Anonymous Critic never read at leaft never
regarded, Puttenham's *Arte of Englifh Poefie*, which
the Author fays was exprefsly written for *the recreation*
of the Queen.   Spenfer, in his 64th Sonnet, tells
Elizabeth,

" Her goodly *bofom*, like a ftrawberry bed,
" Her *neck*, like to a bunch of columbines,
" Her *breaft*, like lillies, ere their leaves be fhed,
" Her *nipples* like young bloffom'd jeffamines."

                                        In

feems ambitious of emulating thofe abfurd hiftorians, who conftantly apply the ways of thinking of their own times, to the principles, and practices, of the paft.

Such are the leading truths, which I have thus eftablifhed, by a thoufand proofs, in oppofition to fuppofes, conjectures, and affumptions. Now, thofe truths forbid prejudice, and criticifm, to fubftitute fuggeftions for facts, and fictions, for realities. It feems at length apparent, that the Commentators have had little knowledge of the connection between Spenfer and Shakfpeare (*c*), and ftill lefs information, with

In his 76th Sonnet he fpeaks of her
" Fair bofom, fraught with virtue's richeft treafure,
" The *neft of love*, the lodging of delight,
" And *'twixt her paps*, like early fruit in May,
" Whofe harveft feem'd to haften now apace,
" They [his frail thoughts] loofely did their wanton wings difplay:
" And, there, to reft themfelves did boldly place."

(*c*) Mr. Malone, indeed, did imagine, as I have already intimated, that Shakfpeare may have alluded in his 80th Sonnet to Spenfer; as Sewell had faid before him; but he was, at the fame time, of opinion that Daniel's Sonnets had been the model, that Shakfpeare followed. [Suppl. vol. i. 581, 645.]

regard

regard to the ambitious motives, or the
amatory objects, either of Shakfpeare, or of
Spenfer. And, wanting the loadftone of
Elizabeth to direct their devious fteps, they
were eafily mifled by the obfcurity of the
Sentiment; and as conftantly deluded, by
the defects of the language, which they
knew to be lefs accurate than their own;
particularly, in refpect to the *relatives*, and
antecedents.

In the poetical age of Spenfer, and Shakfpeare, many words, in our fpeech, bore
very different meanings, from what they do
at prefent; our language being then much lefs
precife, though more figurative, and energetic. The familiar word, *Lover*, was, in
thofe times, deemed both mafculine, and
feminine; Minfheu, the Lexicographer,
fpeaks of a *fhe-lover*, a *fhe-friend* (*d*) : And
Ben

(*d*) So, the word *love* was often fubftituted for *lover :*
[Mal. Shak. vol. ii. 114; vol. iii. 192.]
 " In our Author's time," fay Mr. Malone, and Mr.
Steevens, " this term [lover] was applied to thofe of
" the fame fex who had an Efteem for each other.
" Ben Johnfon concludes one of his letters to Dr.

Ben Johnſon ſubſcribed himſelf the *lover* of Camden. The *relatives*, which are the ligatures of language ; and which, when properly managed, give energy to the thought, and clearneſs to the expreſſion, were in thoſe times, adopted, without choice, and applied, without diſcrimination (*e*) : *His*, and *her*, and *him*, were frequently confounded : and the perſonal pronoun, *his*, was often uſed in a neutral ſenſe ; and in the ſame manner, *him*, in thoſe days, often referred to *it* ; and *himſelf* was uſed

" Donne, by telling him, he is his true *lover* ; So, in
" Coriolanus : I tell thee, fellow, thy General is my
" *lover*. Many more inſtances might be added. See
" our Author's Sonnets paſſim." [Steev. Shak. vol. v.
486 ; vol. xii. 207.] In this ſtrain, Juniper is made by
Ben Johnſon, in his *Caſe is altered*, to tell Anthony :
" Sirrah, there's one of my *fellows* mightily *enamoured*
" of thee." And in the ſame Comedy, Aurelia is
made to exclaim : " O blind excuſe ! blinder than love
" himſelf."

(*e*) The *French*, in *his* whole language, hath not one *word*, that hath *his* accent in the laſt ſyllable, ſave only *two*, called *Antepenult*. [Sydney's Defence of Poetry ; Mulcaſter's Elementarie, 1582, 76, 7 ; Sternhold and Hopkins's Pſalms, Wolf's Edit. 1590, p. 137. and the Tranſlation of the Bible, every where.]

for

for *itſelf*; *which* was commonly ſubſtituted for *who*, by Shakſpeare (*f*) : *This, their, they*, as they were often miſuſed, by our poet (*g*), darken the brilliancy of his

(*f*) Steev. Shak. vol. v. 348 ; Mulcaſter's Elementarie 82 ; Wits Common Wealth, 1598, p. 610.

(*g*) Malone's Sup. vol. i. 643, in his note on the 77th Sonnet : and ſee the Elementarie of Mulcaſter, who had been the maſter of Merchant-Taylor's ſchool from its firſt eſtabliſhment in 1561 ; and who *entreated* chiefly of *the right writing of the Engliſh tung*, which ſhall appear, when the *thing itſelf* ſhall come furth in *hir* own naturall *hew* [p. 76.] In the ſame page, he tells " that our *Cuſtom* hath already beaten out *his* own rules." In p. 77, he ſays, that " our Engliſh tung hath " matter enough in *hir* own, which maie direct *hir* own " right " In the ſame page, he talks " of *everie word* " almoſt either wanting letters for *his* neceſſary ſound." Mulcaſter, who had taught, in that celebrated ſeminary, upwards of twenty years, and was a learned ſcholar, and able writer, declared, that in 1582, " our Engliſh tung had come to the *verie height thereof*;" although he foreſaw, " that the coming Generation would " change their language as they had a right to do, the " peple having *a prerogative* to uſe both *ſpeche*, and *pen*, " at will." This learned grammarian wrote peple *hath* [have]; libertie and prerogative is [are] the cauſe. [Page 160.] Let us, then, look, with an eye of Candour on the grammatical inaccuracies of Shakſpeare !

F 2 language,

language, and enfeeble the ftrength of his fenfe. The key, which I have thus put into every hand, will be found fufficient to open the darkeft paffages of Shakfpeare's Sonnets, if the enquirer will, conftantly, bear in mind, that he has *Cynthia* for his guide.

Let me eftablifh this pofition, by a few examples; as the fubject is curious in itfelf, and goes directly, to the heart of the principal queftion. In the very opening Sonnet, we are at once *perplexed in doubt*, by the application of the relative *his*, in a neutral fenfe, to a *rofe:*

" From faireft Creatures we defire increafe,
" That, thereby, *beauty's rofe*, might never die ,
" But, as *the riper* fhould, by time, deceafe,
" *His* tender heir might bear *his* memory :"

In the fame manner, Shakfpeare again applies *his* to a *flower*, in his 94th Sonnet :

" But, if that *flower* with bafe infection meet,
" The bafeft weed out-braves *his* dignity."

Our grammarians have not, I think, obferved, that the pronoun *his* was, in thofe days, not only ufed in a *neutral* fenfe, but in a *feminine* fenfe; as by Spenfer, in his *Æglogue* of April :

And

" And, now ye dainty Damfels may depart
" Each one *his* way (*h*)."

Shakfpeare, in his 9th Sonnet, ufes *himfelf* for *itfelf*, by applying *himfelf* to *bofom*: And fo, in his 19th Sonnet, he makes *him* refer to *fair brow*; and thereby would induce a fuperficial reader to fuppofe, that the poet's *love* had been a *Male* (*i*). In the fame manner, *he* and *his*, *him*, and *fhe*, are grievoufly intermixed by Shakfpeare, in fome others of his Sonnets (*k*). And, yet,

(*h*) Mr. Malone, indeed, has obferved, that *his*, and *her*, are frequently confounded; [Shak. vol. iv. 140]; as he has equally fhown, that *this*, *their*, *thy*, are often confounded [Suppl. vol. i. p. 643]. *His* and *he*, are confounded in Shakfpeare's 63d Son. wherein we may fee *his* often applied to *time*, and *he* to knife: I fufpect, that *his*, in the laft line but one of this Sonnet, muft be underftood in a feminine fenfe, like Spenfer's *his*, when applied to a *Damfel*.

(*i*) See the 15th, 21ft, 91ft, Son.

(*k*) See the 66th, 67th, and 68th Son. The Poet, I believe, by introducing himfelf into thofe Sonnets, has created fad confufion with *his*, and *her*; with *he*, and *fhe*; and by exhaufting time, and fpace, for *conceits*, he has caufed a darknefs more dim, than his own EREBUS.

F 3   after

after plunging through a world of confusion, and conceits, he constantly returns to *one*, *only*, *she*, whom he shews by his context, to be *Cynthia*, the single Goddefs of his worship. Thus, after talking, darkly, in several consecutive Sonnets, he described Elizabeth so plainly, as to admit of no doubt, with regard to the object of his praise :

" Thofe parts of thee, that *the world's eye doth view*,
" Want nothing, that the thought of hearts can mend ;
" *All tongues* (the voice of Souls) give *thee* that due ;
" Uttering bare truth, even fo, as foes commend.
" Thy outward, thus with outward praise is crown'd ;
" But, thofe fame tongues, that give thee fo thine own,
" In other accents, do this praise confound,
" By feeing farther, than the eye hath fhown.
" They look into *the beauty of thy mind*,
" And, that, in guefs, they meafure by *thy deeds* (*l*)."

(*l*) The 69th Son. and the three preceding ones: and, compare what is faid above with Spenfer's 3d Sonnet, wherein he fpeaks of the *univerfal* praise, which *the world* beftowed on his *Soveraign beauty* ; and his 15th Sonnet, wherein he fays of Elizabeth :
" But, that which faireft is, but few behold,
" Her *mind adorn'd* with *virtues manifold*."
It is, then, apparent, that Shakfpeare had his eye on Spenfer's 15th Sonnet, when he wrote the above ; and that both the poets had the fame great object in their contemplation.

It

It has, however, been obferved to me, that the 3d Sonnet of Shakfpeare muft have been addreffed to a man, otherwife why afk the queftions :

> " For where is fhe fo fair, whofe unear'd womb
> " Difdain the tillage of *thy hufbandry ?*
> " Or, who is he, fo fond, will be the tomb
> " Of his felf-love, to ftop pofterity ?"

The context is, certainly, the beft expofitor : Now, the firft four lines of this Sonnet, and the fix laft, are plainly addreffed to the fame woman, whom the poet had wooed to wed in his firft Sonnet, and his fecond : If the *hufbandry* of Elizabeth were *celibacy,* then every woman would difdain *her hufbandry (m)* ; becaufe fhe is urged by the

---

(*m*) *Hufbandry* is generally ufed by Shakfpeare, fays Mr. Malone, for *Œconomical prudence*; [Sup. vol. i. 591 ;] and it is fo ufed in the 15th Sonnet : But, in the 3d Sonnet, it is ufed in a more appropriate, though not a very different, fenfe : In his firft Sonnet, he calls his *fair one* " tender *churl*;" in his fourth, " beauteous " *niggard*;" and " profitlefs *ufurer*." 'And this *third* Sonnet is, particularly, quoted by the faid Anonymous Critic, for proving, that it was addreffed to *a man* : But, he forbears to comment, having his mind ftill filled with the horrors of obfcenity. In this ftrain,

he

the law of nature to wed, if she can match herself fitly : Nor, is any man so foolish as

he goes on to say that, in the same Sonnet we find the person's mother was alive :

> " Thou art thy mother's glafs, and she, in thee,
>
> " *Calls back* the lovely April of her prime :"

Now; this expreffion, *Calls back*, which proves, according to the Critic, that the person's Mother was *alive*, conveys clearly to my mind, that *she was dead*; as the term implies, and the context proves; But, he afks, what are we to fay of this line ?

> " You had a father; let your fon fay fo."

Why; I fay, hiftorically, that Elizabeth had a father; and that she was courted by all the world, from the Speaker of the Houfe of Commons to Spenfer, and Shakfpeare; in order, that she might have a Son. I fay, moreover, that it was very uncritical, and unfair, to quote a *fingle line* ; difregarding the *object*, and the *context*, of the Poet. By purfuing this mode of Criticifm, and by hanging forced meanings on detached paffages, the fame Critic might very eafily fix *blafphemy* on the *Scriptures* : So, did Counfellor Erfkine infift on behalf of Stockdale, when profecuted by order of the Houfe of Commons, for a libel; and in this fpirit did Lord Kenyon direct the Jury to read the *whole book*, for finding the writer's *object*, and to compare the *Context*, in order to difcover his real meaning. If the anonymous Critic had gone on to the fourth Sonnet, he would have feen expreffions, which cannot be properly applied to a man : " Unthrifty *lovelinefs* ; *beauteous* " niggard :" If you wed not, the Poet adds :

> " Thy unus'd *beauty* muft be tomb'd with Thee."

to

to *bury his self-love*, by *stopping his posterity*,
if he can avoid his bane ; becaufe the fame
law of nature equally influences him. Over
the *illation* of Shakfpeare, there certainly
hangs a thick cloud : Yet, I think, I can,
with *fpectacles on nofe*, fee into this *darknefs
vifible*, and difcover fome glimmerings of
fenfe. The poet, probably, meant to argue,
that as every fair one difclaims fuch unfruit-
ful hufbandry as your's, why do not you
alfo difdain what is fo contrary to the nature
both of women, and of men : If your mother
had adopted your hufbandry, you had never
been ; if you continue the fame hufbandry,
where will you be hereafter ?

" Die fingle, and thy image dies with thee."

Such is the conftruction, which the poet's
context requires : and every fair conftruction ought to be made, rather than confider
Shakfpeare as a mifcreant, who could addrefs amatory Verfes to a man, " with a ro-
" mantic *platonifm of affection* (*n*)."   But, I
have

(*n*) So fays the writer, in the *Britifh Critic*, vol. ix.
p. 517. In order to juftify this imputation of *Platonifm*,
the

have freed him, I truſt, from this ſtain, in oppoſition to his commentators, by ſhewing, diſtinctly, his real object. This object, being once known, darkneſs brightens into light, order ſprings out of confuſion, and contradiction ſettles into fenſe.

This acknowledged object is the pole-ſtar, which conducts the inquiſitive reader through mazy darkneſs into open day : It plays its coruſcations on the 1ſt, 2d, 3d, 4th, 5th, 6th, the 7th, the 8th Sonnets ; and ſtill more vividly on the 9th Sonnet :

the anonymous Critic, who is very *german* to one of the *great Commentators* on Shakſpeare, ſays, that " it was " a fault of *Youth* ; and of a time when very romantic " addreſſes to friends were not uncommon." [Id.] Shakſpeare's Sonnets were certainly written, as I have proved, in 1596, or 1597, when he was two, or three and thirty, after he had been married fourteen years, and had a daughter Suſanna, who, as ſhe was baptized, on the 26th of May 1583, was then advanced to the age of puberty. It is, therefore, untrue, that Shakſpeare was a *youth*, in 1596 ; and it is altogether improbable, conſidering his ſituation, and mode of life, that he would have written ſuch *romantic addreſſes*, without having ſome great object in view, and upon ſome extraordinary occaſion.

" Is

" Is it for fear to wet a *widow's eye*,
" That *thou* confum'ft thyfelf in fingle life ?
" Ah ! if *thou* iffuelefs fhalt hap to die,
" The world will wail *thee*, like a *makelefs* wife (*o*)."

———   ———   ———

" When every *private widow* well may keep,
" By children's eyes, her hufband's fhape in mind."
This Star, again, fhines out more bright-
ly, in the 10th Sonnet, wherein he tells the

(*o*) Mr. Malone very well explains the *makelefs* wife
to mean " as a widow bewails her hufband ;" *make*, and
mate, being formerly fynonymous. [Suppl. vol. i. 588.]
In the two concluding lines, there is fome doubt thrown
on this Sonnet, which is very diftinctly addreffed to a
Woman, by applying, according to the unprecife idiom
of that age, the pronoun *himfelf* to *bofom* : For Dr.
Johnfon, from the Authority of Shakfpeare himfelf,
fays it was in ancient Authors ufed *neutrally*, for itfelf;
as :
" ———— *She* is advanc'd
" Above the Clouds, as high as heaven *himfelf*."
I do not recollect, in the writings of Shakfpeare, the
word *Widower*, which would have been the appropriate
expreffion, if the 9th Sonnet had been addreffed to a Man :
Yet, the word had been long in ufe, in its well
known fenfe, before Shakfpeare came into public life.
In Mulcafter's Elementarie, 1582, p. 225, we may
fee, *Widoer* and *Widow* : Sir John Harrington wrote
in 1599, " that my Lord Keeper is a *Widower*." [Nugæ
Antiquæ, vol. ii. p. 27.]

object

object addressed, " *thou art beloved of many*,
" be as thy *presence* is, *gracious*, and kind."
The context shows the real object through
the thin disguise, in the 11th, 12th, 13th
Sonnets, in the last of which, we may see
the unfair quotation of the writer, in the
British Critic :

" ————— *Dear, my love*, you know,
" You had a father ; let your Son say so (*p*)."

The same light shines, with sufficient
brilliance, for the dimmest sight, to see, that
the 14th Sonnet was addressed to a woman,
and to Elizabeth ; from whose *eyes* the poet
derives his knowledge ; because they are
constant stars, which show him truth, and
beauty. The context forbids any application to a *male object*, in the 15th Sonnet,
which does not give the least intimation of
a man; or in the 16th, which is quoted as
one of the proofs of our poet's *platonism :*
After courting his object to marry, by
urging *it*, to fortify *itself* against the ra-
vages of *time*, the poet exclaims :

(*p*) If the feminine expression, *Dear my love*, be not
sufficient to explain the meaning, let the Context
decide the doubt.

" Now

" Now ftand you on the top of *happy hours* ;

" And, many *maiden gardens*, yet unfet,

" With *virtuous wifh*, would bear you living *flowers*

" Much liker, t.1an *your* painted *counterfeit (q)*."

(*q*) The Britifh Critic, vol. ix. 593. It is however, to be remembered, that the *you*, in the text of Mr. Malone is *your* in the *Original*, as he very properly remark**s** [Sup. vol. i. p. 595.] My opinion is, in oppofition to the Commentators, that the original Copy was right, in printing "*your* living flowers," which ought not to have been changed, without authority. *Your* living flowers mean your living Children, in oppofition to *your* painted *Counterfeit*, or portrait ; as *Counterfeit* then meant. The allufion is plainly to the many portraits of Elizabeth, which, having given her offence, were profcribed, by proclamation. It is not quite fo certain, that Shakfpeare's *mafculine love* had, then, been *counterfeited* by the pencil. From the dark conceit of the *maiden garden* and *living flowers* the poet goes on to urge :

" So fhould the *lines* of life, that life repair,

" Which this (Time's pencil, or my pupil pen)

" Neither in *inward worth*, nor *outward fair*

" Can make you live yourfelf, in eyes of *Men*."

Mr. Malone, feeling the *darknefs vifible* of this Sonnet, fuggefts, that *lines* of life fhould be altered to *lives* of life. [Ib. 594.] But, the context fupports the original : For *Time's pencil* could more naturally paint the *lines* [outlines, or fketches] of life, than *lives* of life. The Context, by mentioning *inward worth*, and

outward

Shakfpeare proceeds forward, by the natural progrefs of his purpofe, to fpeak in his 17th Sonnet, of perpetuating " *the* " *moft high deferts*" of his love ; to eternize " the *beauty* of [her] eyes ;" and to *number*, in *frefh numbers*, all [her] graces. Can *prejudice*, whatever may be the blindnefs of

outward fair, alfo fhows the perfon addreffed to have been a woman, fince *fair* is not applied to a man, and points at Elizabeth, who was thereby praifed for her *talents :* The Context, morever, by telling her how fhe was to live in *eyes of men*, demonftrates, that the object addreffed was not a man, who was to be exhibited as an object for the *eyes of men.* Shakfpeare then proceeds to borrow a thought from Spenfer, whofe *Amoretti* he had conftantly in *his head* and *hand :*

" To give away yourfelf, keeps yourfelf ftill,
" And you muft live, drawn by your *own fweet skill.* "

Spenfer had argued, paradoxically, in his 65th Sonnet :

" The doubt, which ye mifdeem, fair love in vain,
" That fondly fear *to lofe your liberty*,
" When lofing *one*, *two* liberties ye gain,
" And make him bound, that bondage erft did fly."

It was the *paradox*, which Shakfpeare borrowed : To *give*, and to *keep* at the fame moment : To be *free*, to be *faft*, and to faften at the fame time. To the Anonymous Critic before mentioned, I will repeat, that to hang the old clothes of forced meanings, upon the *pegs* of detached lines, is a tafk, which ought to be defpifed, for its facility ; and to defy the Context requires more boldnefs than modefty and candour allow.

his

his intellect, apply the feminine epithets, *grace* of *perfon*, and *beauty* of eye, to a man, or appropriate to any other perfonage than Elizabeth, the fuper-eminent praife of " *moft high deferts*." The poet is carried forward, by the confiftency of his context, to compare the great object of his adoration, in his 18th Sonnet, " to a Summer's day ;" and to commend her " as more lovely, and " more temperate :" and, affuming a higher tone, in his 19th Sonnet, and addreffing himfelf to "fwift-footed Time," he cries out :

> " But, I forbid thee one moft heinous crime :
> " O ! Carve not, with the hours, *my love's fair brow* ;
> " Nor, draw no lines, *there*, with thine antique pen :
> " *Him*, [fair brow] in thy courfe, untainted, do allow,
> " For *beauty's pattern*, to fucceeding Men.
> " Yet ; do thy worft, old Time : Defpite thy wrong
> " My *love* fhall, in my verfe, *ever live young* (r)".

But

(r) Among a thoufand objections, which the faid Anonymous Critic makes [Britifh Critic, vol. ix. p. 516] not only, without Authority, but what is of ftill more weight, againft *The fact*, he afks : Is it credible that Shakfpeare, knowing " Elizabeth to be much older, fhould pretend to fpeak of *forty*, as a future time, and a " diftant

But, not to dwell on fmaller circumftances, the anonymous Critic aforefaid proceeds to confider the 20th Sonnet, which, with charaĉteriftic prudery, he deems too indecent to have been prefented to Elizabeth, and too bad to be laid before the public, at prefent. Without repeating my arguments, and faĉts, which prove, that this Sonnet was not addreffed to a man, and is not obfcene, I will only add; knowing the Critic, and his purpofe :

" The graver prude finks downward to a gnome,
" In fearch of *mifchief*, ftill on earth to roam."

After fuch minute examinations of fome of the moft difficult of Shakfpeare's Sonnets,

" diftant future." For the more retired life, and perfonal habits, of Queen Elizabeth, I had quoted Lord Orford's Cat. of Royal, and Noble, Authors, art. Effex; Hume's Hift. vol. v. p. 526; Whitaker's Vind. of Mary Q. of Scots, vol. ii. throughout ; which demonftrate, that fhe *daunced* as a young girl, at fixty five ; that fhe was treated by fubjeĉts, and foreigners, as an objeĉt of defire, at an older age: Spenfer addreffed his *Amoretti* to Elizabeth, in 1595, when fhe was entering into her *grand Climaĉteric:* Why, then, is Shakfpeare to be deprived of the privilege of poetic fiĉtion, in feigning Elizabeth to be only twenty-three, when fhe was fixty three? Or that, in defpite of Time, his Love fhould, in his verfe, ever live young !!

it

it cannot be reasonably expected, that I should inspect one hundred more, with the same elaboration, that I have tried to explain those encomiastic effusions, which have been deemed the most obscure. In justification of my own preconceptions, and in answer to objections, I have ascertained such facts, shown such a concatenation of circumstances, and produced such arguments, in support of the whole, as ought to confound prejudice, and to settle judgement. If I should not, however, have assigned the proper meanings to the conceits of Shakspeare, in his most difficult Sonnets, it will not follow, from my failure, in not comprehending unintelligibility, that I am wrong in my position, as to his real object; or that those critics are right, in their opinions; who, like Warburton, have assigned to this great Poet motives, which never moved him, and thoughts, that never entered his mind. I have not undertaken the hard task of commenting on Shakspeare's Sonnets, of clearing his obscurities, or of decyphering his conceits:

G But

But, my inability to perform, what feems to be beyond human capacity, does not enfeeble the ftrength of my proofs, in fupport of the main pofition, that thofe amatory Verfes were addreffed by Shakfpeare to Elizabeth.

Of thofe Amatory Verfes, it may be truly faid, that as a whole poem, which is often tied together by a very flight ligature, they have two of the worft faults, that can degrade any writing; they are obfcure; and they are tedious. Spenfer, who furnifhed the model of them, has his obfcurities, and tedioufnefs; but he has withal, more diftinctnefs, in his topicks, and more facility, in his ftyle: Shakfpeare plainly endeavoured to go beyond the mark of his rivalry; but, in affecting the fublime, he funk, by a natural cadence, into the unintelligible. Spenfer having no rival, and only a fingle object, caught at fuch topicks of praife, as he thought would pleafe the moft, and adopted fuch a ftyle, as he could moft eafily manage. Of fuch a poet, as Shakfpeare, it may eafily be conceived, that he has may happy phrafes, and elegant lines, though they are generally

darkened

darkened by conceit, and marred by affectation; with as many happy phrafes, and
elegant lines, Spenfer has fewer conceits and
lefs affeétation; having from inheritance, as
fruitful a garden of images, which he watered
from a deeper fountain of learning. Shakfpeare, "fancy's fweeteft child," fhows fometimes a manifeft fuperiority in *imagination* over
Spenfer, when this wonderful poet is forming the fame images. By an effort of his
creative powers, Shakfpeare appears to have
carried away the palm, in this great quality of a true poet, from his illuftrious rival,
even when Spenfer put forth his whole
ftrength, in cultivating the fame field. The
following is Shakfpeare's 99th Sonnet, which
was plainly written, in emulation of Spenfer's 64th:

" The forward viölet, thus did I chide:
" Sweet thief, whence didft thou fteal, thy fweet, that
   " fmells,
" If not from my love's breath? The purple pride,
" Which, on thy foft cheek, for complexion dwells,
" In my love's veins, thou haft too grofsly dy'd.
" The lily, I condemned, for *thy* hand;
" And buds of marjoram had ftol'n *thy* hair:
" The rofes fearfully on thorns did ftand;
" One blufhing fhame, another white defpair;

G 2 " A third

" A third, nor red, nor white, had ftol'n of both,

" And, to *his* robbery had annex'd *thy* breath ;

" But, for *his* theft, in pride of all *his* growth,

" A vengeful canker eat *him* up to death

" More flowers, I noted : Yet in none could fee,

" But, fweet, or colour, it had ftol'n from thee *(s)*."

Yet, this poetical defcription of a charming woman is fpecifically declared, by the anonymous Critic aforefaid, to be one of the hundred and twenty-fix Sonnets, which Shakfpeare, with his *platonifmic* pen, addreffed to a MAN (*t*). When, " in the

(*s*) With the above, compare the 64th Sonnet of Spenfer, as follows :

" Coming to kifs her lips (fuch grace I found)

" Me feem'd I fmelt a garden of fweet flowers,

" That dainty odours from them threw around,

" For damfels fit to deck their lovers bowres.

" Her lips did fmell like unto gilliflowers,

" Her ruddy Cheeks, like unto rofes red,

" Her fnowy brows like bended bellamours,

" Her lovely eyes, like pinks but newly fpred.

" Her goodly bofom, like a ftrawberry bed,

" Her neck like to a bunch of columbines,

" Her breath like lilies, ere their leaves be fhed,

" Her nipples, like young bloffom'd jeffamines :

" Such fragrant flowres do give moft odorous fmell ;

" But, her fweet Odour did them all excell ."

(*t*) Britifh Critic, vol. ix. 515—17.

orient

" *orient*, the gracious light lifts up *his*
" burning head," the said critic afferts, that
it is only the evening Star, fetting in darknefs ; when lightening flafhes conviction on
the intellect, the critical beholder infifts,
that it is only a *Will-of-the-Wifp*, playing
its delufive corufcations ; and when the context comes in to fettle every doubt, by the
decifivenefs of its inferences, the aforefaid
Critic affumes, for argument, that affertion
is more credible, than fact, and certainty
lefs convincing, than fpeculation.

The faid Critic produces, however, fomething like proof, not, indeed, of the Sonnets being addreffed to a man, the object of
the poet's *platonifm*, but of the poet's predilection for an *infant*, by quoting the 126th
Sonnet, which begins :

" O! thou, my lovely *boy*, who, in thy power,
" Doft hold time's *fickle glafs*, *his* fickle hour "

Yet, would the fame Critic have done well,
when affecting a folicitude for truth, to have
publifhed the *whole truth*. " This Son-
" net," fays Mr. Malone, " differs from
" all the others in the prefent collection, not
" being written in alternate rhimes." Mr.

G 3   Steevens

Steevens adds, that " this Sonnet only con-
" fifts of twelve lines (*u*)." The original
edition marks more ftrongly this effential
deficiency of the two lines, which contained
the explanatory point of the Sonnet. Mr.
Malone has corrected another defect of this
Sonnet, by printing *Minutes*, in his Edition,
for *Mynuit* in the original. Thefe deficiencies prove, with full conviction, that the
printer had before him a very imperfect Manufcript, which fhews neither the laft hand,
nor the full meaning of the author. We fee,
indeed, in the *twelve lines*, fuch as we have
them, that the poet gave *lovers* to the *boy;*
and wooed *him-fhe* to wed, by telling him,
that as he grows faft, he will foon grow old;
in prophetical contempt of Mr. Malone's argument, before-mentioned; and in anticipating defiance of the aforefaid Critic's *platonifm*. As we have been thus deprived of the
poet's key, which would have opened the genuine defign of the whole Sonnet, we muft
fufpend our opinions, till we know the

(*u*) Sup. vol. i. p. 681.

writer's

writer's laſt words, and truſt to the context, in judging of his real purpoſe (*x*).

(*x*) In his 115th Sonnet, indeed, we meet with the ſame thought, and even the ſame words :
  " *Love is a babe;* then, might I not ſay ſo,
  " To give *full growth,* to *that which ſtill doth grow.*"
From the Context, then, I am led to ſuſpeᵔ, that in the 126th Sonnet, the poet meant merely to ſay : Oh ! thou, my *baby love.* This ſame *boy babe,* or *baby boy,* is ſpoken of as a God, in the 110th Sonnet : After ſpeaking of his objeᵔ, as " *my beſt of love,*" he goes on to infer, that the ſame objeᵔ is, "a *God,* in love, to " whom I am confined :"
  " Then, give me welcome, next, *my heaven,* the beſt,
  " Even to thy pure, and moſt, moſt loving, breaſt."
The poet had brought forward this thought from the preceding Sonnet :
  " As from my Soul, which, in *thy breaſt,* doth lie,
  " That is my *home* of *love.*"
Of the conceits about *Love,* in the pages of poetry, there is no end ! I have not undertaken to explain all Shakſpeare's fantaſtical notions on this fruitful topick : My only endeavour has been, to make his own Context explain his own purpoſe, and his own meaning ; to free him from inconſiſtency ; and to ſettle his ſenſe. Shakſpeare himſelf was only, throughout his Sonnets, what
  " ———— all true lovers are,
  " Unſtaid, and ſkittiſh, in all motions elſe,
  " Save, in the conſtant Image of *the Creatúre,*
  " That is belov'd. ————————————

We may fee indeed, another *infant intro-duced* by Shakſpeare, in his 124th Sonnet, only two Sonnets preceding: He, herein, cries out :—

    " If my *dear love* were *but* the *child* of *State*,
    " It might, for fortune's baſtard be unfather'd,
    " As ſubject to time's love, or to time's hate :
    " No; it was *builded* far from accident ;
    " It ſuffers not in ſmiling pomp, nor falls
    " Under the blow of thralled diſcontent,
    " Whereto the inciting time our faſhion calls,
    " It fears not *policy*, that *heretick* ;
    " But, all *alone* ſtands *hugely politick*."

Now, was not Queen Elizabeth *the child of State?* And, is ſhe not deſcribed, in the ſubſequent lines, as diſtinctly as if ſhe had been named ? The poet has plainly, in his mind, a *Child of State*, which *all alone ſtands hugely politick* : And he is carried forward, by a natural courſe of thought, to deſcribe what he had obſerved, at *Court* :

    " Have I not ſeen dwellers on *form* and *favour*
    " Looſe all, and more, by paying too much rent,
    " For compound ſweet, foregoing ſimple favour?
    " Pitiful thrivers, in their gazing ſpent ! "

From his *Child of State* in the 124th Son-net, and the *Court*, and *Courtiers*, in the 125th, Shakſpeare went forward, with

theſe

thefe thoughts in his mind, to his *lovely boy,*
the *minion* of *nature,* the *Soveraign miſtreſs,*
in the 126th to whom he aſſigns *power,* and
lovers ; and going into the Exchequer, the
poet talks of *treaſure,* of the *audit,* and of
the *quietus,* which follows the *render* of accounts.   Shakſpeare has ſtill *ſome aſſociation
of ideas* in his mind : From *Time's glaſs,* and
the fickle *hour,* in the 126th Sonnet, it was
natural for him to caſt a retroſpective glance
on *the old age,* when *black was not counted
fair ;* at leaſt, it was not applied to *beautie's
name :* And, he was led on to think, in
good earneſt, of *his miſtreſs,* " whoſe eyes
" are raven black (*y*)."

(*y*) " All the remaining Sonnets, ſays Mr. Malone,
are addreſſed to *a female* ;" [Sup. vol. i. p. 682] and, the
aforeſaid Anonymous Critic joins in this affirmation,
calculating the Eſtimate from the 126th Sonnet, which
talks of *the boy:* Yet, it ſtill remains to be proved,
rather than aſſerted, that the whole of Shakſpeare's
Sonnets, from No. 1, to 126, incluſive, were addreſſed
to a man, with a *platonic* regard.   On the contrary,
I have proved, I truſt, that the whole of Shakſpeare's
Sonnets were addreſſed by him to a woman ; to a great
woman ; to Queen Elizabeth ; and I have thereby
freed our illuſtrious poet, I hope, from the odious
imputation of *platoniſm.*

We

We are induced, by this difquifition about *the object*, to whom thefe Sonnets were, originally, addreffed, to enquire what Critic, or Commentator, firft afferted, that they were addreffed to a *Man*. Thefe Sonnets, as they were plainly written in emulation of Spenfer's *Amoretti*, which were publifhed, in 1595, were probably written, in 1596, or 1597, when Shakfpeare was two, or three, and thirty. They were handed about, in Manufcript, among his *private friends*, as we are told by Meres; and were deemed very fine, at leaft, very *fweet* (z); the object, and the allufions, being then underftood, no doubt. They were not printed, during the life of Elizabeth; becaufe, probably the poet did not obtain permiffion from that faireft prude. They were publifhed, however, by Thorpe, from an

(z) Meres, in his *Wits Treafury*, 1598, calls them Shakfpeare's *Sugred* Sonnets. I obferve, that Fabyan, the Chronicler, in giving a Character of Henry 7th, fpeaks of his *fugred eloquence*. [Raftal, 1533.] Sir Philip Sydney talks of the *fugred invention* of Heliodorus, in that picture of love, in *Theagines* and *Cariclea*. [Apologie for Poetrie. 1595.]

imperfect

imperfect Copy, which may have come into the hands of W. H. who gave it to the Bookfeller, without the apparent confent of the author. But, there was no intimation, to whom they were addreffed, except that Thorpe dedicated them to W. H. as the only *begetter* (*a*) of thefe fonnets. This poem was re-publifhed by Cotes, in 1640, without a commentary. Gildon republifhed thefe Sonnets, in 1710, which, he afferted, " to " be *all of them in praife of his miftrefs* ;" as the editor adds in his Title-page. When Doctor Sewell re-publifhed thefe Sonnets, in 1728, he improved, by a poetic fiction, on this ftatement of Gildon : " A *Young* mufe," fays the Doctor, " muft have *a miftrefs*, to " play off the beginning of fancy ; nothing " being fo apt to elevate the Soul to a pitch

(*a*) See Minfheu, 1616, in vo. *to beget*, fignifying in one fenfe, to *bring foorth*. W. H, was the bringer forth of the Sonnets. *Beget* is derived by Skinner from the A. S. *begettan*, obtinere. Johnfon adopts this derivation, and fenfe : fo that *begetter*, in the quaint language of Thorpe, the Bookfeller, Piftol, the *ancient*, and fuch affected perfons, fignified the *obtainer* ; as to *get*, and *getter*, in the prefent day, means *obtain*, and *obtainer*, or to procure, and the procurer.

" of

" of poetry, as the paffion of Love (*b*)."
Theobald talked of re-publifhing the Poems
of Shakfpeare ; but lived not to perform
what has fince been done by an abler hand (*c*).
With the twenty plays of Shakfpeare, in
quarto, Mr. Steevens publifhed, literally, in
1766, *the Sonnets*, from the original Edition
of Thorpe, but without any obfervations.
At length, in 1780, Mr. Malone formally
publifhed, in his Supplement to the Edition
of Shakfpeare, 1778, *the Sonnets* and other
poems, of the great Dramatift, with the
Editor's own remarks, and the notes of his
friends. It was now, for the firft time, faid
exprefsly by Mr. Malone, that Shakfpeare
had addreffed 120 of thefe Sonnets to a *Man ;*

(*b*) The Preface, p. vii. It muft however be conftantly kept in mind, that Shakfpeare was not a *young*
mufe in 1596; and that he had a wife, with a daughter, who was ready to elevate the foul of any other
poet, or *phyfician*, to a *pitch of poetry*: In faƈt, this
daughter married Doƈtor Hall, on the 5th of June
1607.

(*c*) In Jortin's Mifcel. Obferv. upon Authors, ancient
and modern, 1732, vol. ii. p. 242, there are what have
not been much obferved, fome remarks of Theobald
on *the poems* of Shakfpeare, but not the *Sonnets*.

Mr.

Mr. Steevens, on reading the 20th Sonnet. affirmed, that it was addreſſed to a *male object* (*d*).

Theſe two commentators, then, were the firſt, who, from the moſt egregious miſconception of the poet's object, and meaning, originally wounded the fair fame of Shakſpeare. And laſt, though not leaſt, the anonymous Critic, before mentioned, who, as I have before obſerved, is *very german* to one of thoſe Commentators, was the firſt, who aſſerted, that Shakſpeare addreſſed thoſe 126 Sonnets to a *Man* " with " a *romantic Platoniſm* of Affection, (*e*)."

It

(*d*) Sup. vol. i. p. 579, 596.

(*e*) Britiſh Critic, vol. ix. 517. I have already proved that the ſtrongeſt ſupport, which is brought for this odious ſuggeſtion, "that it was a *fault* of *Youth*," is *unfounded*, by ſhewing that the Poet was two-and-thirty, when he wrote his Sonnets; having a Wife, and Children, to care for, and many avocations to occupy him : The other ſupport, that they were written at a time " when very romantic addreſſes to friends were not " uncommon," is equally groundleſs : For, the romantic addreſſes conſiſted more in words than matter; and appear more romantic to us, owing to the alteration in the import of words: When Ben Johnſon ſubſcribed

himſelf

It was referved for me to declare, for the firft
time, in the *Apology*, with *all the wildnefs*

himfelf the true *lover* of Camden, the true Lover of
Richard Martin, he meant merely to fay your affec-
tionate friend. Take an example of two very intimate
friends, Edmond Spenfer, and Gabriel Harvey, from the
following Sonnet, which has not been re-publifhed in *The
Works* of Spenfer:

" To the Right worfhipful, my fingular good *friend*,
Mr. Gabriel Harvey, Doctor of the Laws:

" Harvey, the happy above happieft men
" I read: that fitting like a looker on
" Of this world's ftage, doeft note with critique pen
" The fharp diflikes of each condition:
" And as one carelefs of fufpition,
" Ne fawneft for the favour of the great:
" Ne feareft foolifh reprehenfion
" Of faulty men, which danger to thee threat
" But freely doeft, of what thee lift, entreat,
" Like a great Lord of peerlefs liberty:
" Lifting the good up to high honours feat,
" And the Evil damning ever more to dy.
" For life, *and* death is [are] in thy doomful writing:
" So thy renowne lives ever by endighting."

Dublin: this xviij of July, 1586;
Your devoted *friend*, during life,
Edmund Spencer.

[From Foure Letters and Certain Sonnets, efpecially
touching Robert Greene." Publifhed by Gabriel Harvey, in 1592. p. 75.]

of

of Conceit, that Shakſpeare addreſſed his Sonnets to Elizabeth.   For this declaration, I aſſigned ſuch reaſons, as ſatisfied my mind, at the time: I have reviewed the whole queſtion, which, conſidering the parties, an illuſtrious Queen, and a great Poet, is very intereſting : And I now ſubmit ſuch an argument, as, I believe, cannot be eaſily anſwered, except by aſſerting what ought to be proved, and by ſurmiſing what ought to be defended by argument.

Yet, it is ſaid, by the Critic before-mentioned ; that, " when Mr. C. undertakes to " prove, as he calls it, that the Sonnets of " Shakſpeare were addreſſed to that Princeſs, " he certainly takes up one of the *wildeſt* " *Conceits* that ever aroſe in any mind (*f*)." Now ; I join iſſue on *the Wildneſs of the Conceit:* And, I appeal to Mr. Locke, Biſhop Butler, and Lord Chief Baron Gilbert, as competent judges of the theory of Logick, and of the practice of reaſoning.   I will repeat, on this occaſion, till I have taught the Cuckatoos of London, to hoot it in the ears of Critics,

(*f*) Brit. Critic, vol. ix. 515.

what

what was finely faid by Bifhop Butler, that
PROBABILITY *is the* GUIDE *of* LIFE.

With *this guide* before us, let us enquire,
which of the parties entertain the *wildeft
conceit*. Firft, Is it moft probable, that
Shakfpeare, all circumftances confidered,
addreffed One hundred and twenty-fix Amatory Sonnets to a *man*, or to a *woman ?* The
anfwer muft be, if drawn from common life,
and from found reafon, to a woman; becaufe
men ufually make love to women ; and woo
them to wed. Secondly, But, the Critic
ftates it, as *a faƐ*, that thofe Sonnets are
addreffed to *a man :* It muft be admitted, indeed, that if this pofition were true, it would
decide the point in iffue: The pofition, however, is neither true, as *a faƐ*, nor admiffi-
ble, as a *probability :* And, taking into confideration, according to the cuftom of true
Critics, and the practice of accurate judges,
the objeƐ of the writer, his context, and
his language, which laft is perplexed from
the uncertainty of the *relatives*, and the
antecedents, it will manifeftly appear, that
the whole of thofe Sonnets were addreffed

to

to a woman. Thirdly, the Critic affigns *platonifm*, as the *motive* of Shakfpeare ; the platonifm of *youth* : But, was he a *Youth ?* The anfwer is, he was two-and-thirty, a married man, and a father. The Critic tries to fupport his affertion, by faying, that there were, in that age, very romantic addreffes to friends in the world : Yet, admitting this to be true, he fails, in not producing any proof, that Shakfpeare made fuch amatory addreffes to the deareft friends : The friends, and *fellows*, of Shakfpeare, appear in his *Teftament*. From this examination, the *platonifm*, affigned, appears to be only af-fertion, without proof, affumption, without authority, fophiftry, without fenfe, and pre-fumption, againft probability. Fourthly, Does not Mr. Malone *affert*, that one hun-dred and twenty Sonnets are addreffed, by the poet, to a *man ?* Yes : but, does not Mr. Gildon, with *probability*, for his fup-port, affert, that the Sonnets were addreffed to the poet's *miftrefs:* Does not Mr. Steevens break out into indignation, when he faw Shakfpeare court his *mafter*-miftrefs ? Yes :

H   but,

but, did not Doctor Sewell, who was also
an editor of Shakfpeare, and was not frightened by a phantom, affert, that the Sonnets
were addreffed to the poet's *miftrefs*; adding,
as a proof, what has *fome fenfe*, " the young
" mufe muft have his *miftrefs* :" Mr. Gildon, and Doctor Sewell, talked, like men
of this *earth* : Mr. Malone, and Mr. Steevens fpeak, like men of fome other *planet* :
Nor, did there appear to Mr. Gildon, and
Doctor Sewell, any thing obfcene, in the
20th Sonnet, which has, indeed, no appearance of obfcenity, if it be chaftely examined,
by a chafte mind ; taking the words, as they
were then underftood, without liftening to
the fuggeftions of *platonifm*. Such are the
arguments, which have been adduced by
Commentators, and Critics, for fhewing, in
the *probation* of *The Apologift* " the *Wildeft*
" *Conceit*, that ever arofe in any mind !"

On the other hand, the *probation* of The
Apologift may be thus arranged, by the *guide*
of *probability* : Firft, Shakfpeare, who as he
was born in 1564, was two-and-thirty, in
1596, married early, and foon had children;
he

he had moreover an old father to care for, and younger brothers to help into life: Whence, it is inferable, that he had nearer objects of affection, than any mere connection of friendfhip. Secondly, Shakfpeare was by profeffion a public writer, whofe livelihood depended, chiefly, on the product of his pen: Whence, we may infer, that he had no leifure to fing the praifes of women, much lefs to woo, by amatory verfes, the affections of men. Thirdly, Shakfpeare had a vigilance of obfervation, which did not allow life to glide unheeded by him: he noted, accordingly, the paffages of the times; he faw the rife, and fall, of Courtiers; he remarked the fuccefs, and diftinguifhed the characters of writers; though Spenfer feems to be the only poet, whom he honoured by denominative praife. Fourthly, He faw men of fewer talents, than he had, raifed by adulation; he perceived poets of lefs genius, than he poffeffed, elevated by their flatteries; he felt the " vulgar fcandal ftamped upon " his brow," while in the practice of providing, by *public means*, for *daily life:* And

he

he was, in this manner, incited by emulation, and preffed by intereft, to adopt their
means, for obtaining fimilar ends. Fifthly,
He faw Spenfer, the greateft poet of his
time, addrefs many laudatory verfes to Elizabeth, and profit from them: And Shakfpeare was thus induced to turn his view to
" the *lovely gaze*, where *every eye* doth
" dwell." Knowing a *better fpirit had ufed
her name*, he tried, by his encomiaftic emulations (*g*), " to thrive," as he had thriven.
Sixthly, During the years 1596, and 1597,
when Shakfpeare wrote his Sonnets (*h*), he
was occupied as a player, and bufied as a dramatift ; who wrote, or revifed, in every year,
feveral Comedies, Tragedies, or Hiftories ;
and he had, confequently, no leifure to
write fuch Sonnets to a common man, or an
ordinary woman : But, he was induced by
two of the moft powerful motives of mankind, emulation, and intereft, to court
Elizabeth, his (*i*) *all-the-world*, who alone

(*g*) Son. 21, 80, 81, 82, 83, 84, 85, 86, all allude to
Spenfer's *Amoretti* ; and the 106th Sonnet refers minutely
to the *Faerie Queene*.

(*h*) Son. 111, 112.   (*i*) Son. 112.

had

had power to wipe the " vulgar fcandal from.
" his brow," to provide better for his life,
than by public means; and who alone had
authority " to 'oer-green his *bad*, his *good*
" *allow*." Seventhly, Knowing that lovers,
both natural, and political, had, for thirty
years, wooed Elizabeth to wed, and having
poetic licenfe, Shakfpeare feigned love for
her, like Raleigh, and Spenfer; and courted
the " *world's frefh ornament*," by appropriate topicks, which a moft fruitful imagination alone could furnifh; and which fitly
applied to no other perfon on earth, than to
her, who was *beloved of many* (*k*); who had
moft high deferts (*l*); who was endeared with
all hearts; whofe commendation was " too
" excellent for every vulgar paper to re-
" hearfe (*m*):" But, can the previous probability, which refults from all thofe intimations, be confirmed, by collateral circumftances? Yes; Queen Elizabeth is fo plainly
defcribed in many of the Sonnets, (*n*) as to
fhew,

(*k*) Son. 10. (*l*) Son. 17, 31. (*m*) Son. 38.
(*n*) In order to fee this truth moft diftinctly, we muft
attend to the 1ft Sonnet: " Thou [the object] that art

now

ſhew, diſtinctly, the real object of the poet's praiſe to *one*, and of *one*, whoſe *wondrous excellence*

" *now* the *world's* freſh *ornament*," and the *only Herald* to the *gaudy ſpring*; whereof the *topicks*, and the *words* were copied from Spenſer. [Son. 70.] See Son. 2. Thy [the object] Youth's *proud livery*, ſo gaz'd on now. In the fictions, poetical, and political, of that age, Elizabeth was conſidered as *always young*, See Son. 3, 5, and 9, wherein, the poet ſpeaks of a public, and *private, widow*. See Son. 10, 17, 20, 21, 23, wherein he ſpeaks of *looking for recompence*. See Son. 26, 29, wherein he talks, ſpiritedly, of ſcorning " to change his ſtate with *Kings*." See Son. 31, and 36, wherein he ſpeaks of his object honouring him with *public* kindneſs. See Son. 38, and 53, wherein ſpeaking ſtill of his object, he adds; " and *you*, in " *every bleſſed ſhape, we know*." See Son. 55, 57, 58, 59, 61, wherein he hints at the well known *jealouſy* of Elizabeth. See Son. 67, and 69, a very minute deſcription of her, which was borrowed from Spenſer's Son. 3, 15. See Son. 70, and 78, wherein he ſpeaks of giving *grace* a *double majeſty*. See Son. 70, wherein emulating Spenſer's Son. 81, he ſpeaks of her *worth*, as being as *wide as the Ocean*. See Son. 82, 86 and 87, wherein he feigns to have had Elizabeth, " as a dream doth flatter, in ſleep, a " King." See Son. 93, wherein he adopts the *mythology* of Spenſer:

" But, *heaven*, in thy creation, did decree,
" That, in thy face, ſweet love ſhould ever dwell."

See

excellence his verfes conftantly commended ; nay, fuch was *her worth* :

 " That we, which behold *thefe prefent days,*
 " Have *eyes* to *wonder,* but lack tongues to praife."

Eighthly, If the *probability*, then, be confirmed, by the *fact*, the probation of the Apologift is completed *:* For, we muft ever remember the leffon of the great mafters of logick, that if there be fome evidence, on one fide of a propofition, and no evidence on the other fide, every enquirer is bound, by the conftitution of his own mind, to believe in *fome* evidence, rather than in *none*.

 " To 'cide this title is impanneled
 " A 'queft of *thoughts :*"————— ———

And, the iffue being joined, it remains only, for the jury to determine, who is moft *conceitedly wild?* They who produce no legitimate evidence at all *;* or he, who, in a quef-

See Son. 96. wherein Elizabeth is minutely defcribed; talking of a *throned queen,* and of her conquefts, if fhe would ufe *the ftrength* of *all* her *State.* See Son. 94, wherein the poet fuppofes himfelf to be *crowned with her.* And fee Son. 124, wherein he defcribes her as *the Child of State.* The before quoted Sonnets are thofe, which, Mr. Malone, and Mr. Steevens affert, with a wonderful *wildnefs of conceit,* were addreffed to a Man.

H 4

tion

tion, which does not admit of demonſtration, adduces proofs, that come as near to it as poſſible.

I owed this argument, with regard to the real object of Shakeſpeare's Sonnets, to the ſubject, which, as it relates to thoſe extra-ordinary perſons, Elizabeth, Spenſer, and Shakſpeare, is intereſting in itſelf; to all the admirers of the illuſtrious dramatiſt, except the two Commentators, whoſe " ears are " more deaf than adders to the voice of any " true deciſion;" And, I alſo owed the foregoing argument to my own diſcovery, which, as I was the firſt to announce, I ought to be the laſt, in the field, to defend, againſt the aſſaults of Criticiſm, that merely dogmatizes, when it ought to prove, and only drivels, when it ought to reaſon.

In reviewing this head of my Apology, I find little to add, and nothing to retract. Having by the prefatory advertiſement to that book acknowledged the whole of the Shakſpeare-papers, which were exhibited, to be ſpurious, and the exhibition of them to be a cheat; I had no controverſy with
Mr.

Mr. Malone about the genuinenefs of Queen Elizabeth's Letter. But, I did controvert both the matter, and the manner, of his *enquiry*: I ftill difapprove of that fort of morality, which would detect an acknowledged forgery, by any means: I will continue to explode all negative argument, which is in its nature nugatory, and, in its application, extremely fallacious. The *confiftency* of *fpelling*, which was relied upon, as exifting in the age of Elizabeth, and Shakfpeare; and as fhowing at once the forgery of the papers, and the ignorance of the Believers, was fhewn to be only confiftent in its inconfiftency (*o*). In fupport of the negative argument, it was faid, that the word *ande* with a final *e* could not be found; that *forre* could not be difcovered; that *maifter* was the only fpelling of *mafter*; that *Chambe-layne* was

(*o*) Apology p. 69, 77. Add to this what is very juftly faid by the Editor of The Nugæ Antiquæ, vol. ii. Pref. viii: " The fpelling has been preferved, for the moft part, " and altho' the *fame perfons* fpelt *very differently*, it was " thought neceffary to adhere ftrictly to it, as a proof of " *there being no ftandard*, at this point of time, for writing the Englifh language, with correct orthography."

unpre-

unprecedented; that *Londonne* had never
been feen; that *Leicefter* was always written
thus (*p*); that the verb *to compliment* did not
exift, in that age; that the epithet *pretty* had
never been applied to written compofitions;
that *ourfelf* could not be found, as an unity;
that *excellence*, and *amufe*, were not then in
good ufe, as the enquirer *more than fufpects*;
all thofe words were objected to, in thofe
forms; in order to fhow, that a word does
not exift in our language; becaufe the Critic
could not find it, in his lexicography: Yet,
were all thofe affumptions difproved, with
very unexpected fulnefs, to the great difgrace of *Index-learning*. To explode, effectually, negative arguments, is of fome importance to critical reafoning: It was of ftill
more importance, on this occafion; when
negative arguments were continually brought
into action, for the obvious purpofe of obloquy. Cenforioufnefs may be at length
fhamed into filence, by finding, that they,

(*p*) In Fabyan's Chron. by Raftal, 1533, fol. CLXI, it is
faid: "This yere [1413] the Kyng helde his Parlyamente
"at Leyceter."

who

who attempt to wound without a caufe, generally receive in the conflict, " thofe
" wounds, [which] heal ill; men do give
" themfelves." The Believers, neverthelefs,
acting on accurate principles of probability,
and from the honeft motives of curiofity, or
amufement, may, with furer grounds than
Woolfey, who thought himfelf traduced, by
ignorant tongues, refolve, in his language:—

" ——————————— We muft not ftint
" Our neceffary Actions, in the fear,
" To cope malicious Cenfurers (*q*)."

(*q*) At the Conclufion of the foregoing fection, it was
faid [Apology, p. 123,] " that there were balloons, in the
" age of Elizabeth, and Shakfpeare," although the Enquirer
had taken it for granted, there were none, for the purpofe
of fixing the charge of *Anachronifm*, on the believers:
An additional proof of my pofition may be found in *The*
Philofophical Satyres, of Robert Anton, 1616, p. 20:
" Pack fool to French *Baloone*, and there at play,
" Confume the progrefs of thy fullen day."

§ III.

—— § III. ——

LORD SOUTHAMPTON and his CORRESPONDENCE.

I HAD no controverſy with Mr. Malone about the *Letter* of Lord Southampton; having explicitly admitted (*r*) that it was ſpurious: But, on this head of the *enquiry*, as on ſeveral other points, I thought I had reaſon to controvert his miſ-conceptions of

(*r*) On this point, the Anonymous Critic, before mentioned, writes [Britiſh Critic, vol. ix. p. 520] as follows: " we recollect but *one paſſage*, in which he expreſsly de-" clares his opinion that *any one* of the papers is ſpurious." Common candour required, however, that there ſhould have been added this exception, " that in the prefatory ad-" vertiſement to the Apology, the *whole of the miſcellaneous* " *Papers were acknowledged to be ſpurious*; and the ex-" hibition of them was declared to be a *Cheat:*" The Critic, in the ſame ſtrain, goes on to remark, that the Apologiſt " gives up the Letters of Lord Southampton " and Shakſpeare expreſsly, becauſe he prefers, *we know* " *not why*, one power of Attorney to two Letters." The Critic, then, cannot tell why the Apologiſt ſhould adopt a *genuine* power of Attorney, as a *touchſtone*, for trying the ſpuriouſneſs of a Letter, which was ſaid to be written by the Grantor of that power! I will apply to ſuch a Critic, Marſton's Dedication to *Detraction:*

" A canker'd verdict of malignant hate
" Shall ne'er provoke me, worſe myſelf to deem."

our

our Archaiology; to difpute the affumptions, that were apparently made, for the purpofe of mifreprefenting the Believers; and to rectify the palpable errors, which his inattentive view of the Subject had introduced into the Life of Lord Southampton. All thefe Confiderations were deemed objects of importance; as they related to Shakfpeare's earlieft Patron; and, what was of more importance, as the illuftration of thofe feveral points tended to difplay the truth with the " bleft effulgence" of the Sun in his meridian.

Now, the truth has been by nothing more obfcured, than by the Enquirer's mif-conceptions, with regard to the Cecils; who are by him reprefented as the enemies of Lord Southampton, while the Earl of Effex, is faid to have been his invariable friend. Sir Robert Cecil, as I have fhown, was the active friend of Lord Southampton: Effex was his envious opponent, until he was converted by Lord Southampton's courtfhip of

Elizabeth

Elizabeth Vernon, his Coufin (*s*). Almoft every ftriking incident, indeed, in the various Life of Lord Southampton, has been thrown into fhade, by the unfkilfulnefs of his biographer. This patron of Shakfpeare was appointed, by Mr. Malone, Vice-Admiral of the fleet, which failed under the General, Lord Effex againft the Azores, in 1597. The fact is, that Lord Southampton, who went out a volunteer, at the age of twenty-four, in the Garland, was foon commiffioned, by Effex, to command her. Sir William Monfon has recorded Lord Southampton's conduct ; which was more noted, for the bravery of youth, than the judgement of age (*t*). He was not well received at Court,

(*s*) In the Declaration of the Treafon of the Earl of Effex, [figna. D,] it is faid, " There were prefent, at this " Council, the Earl of Southampton, with whom, in " former times, he [Effex had been at fome *emulations*, " and *differences*, at Court: But, after, Southampton, " having married his Kinfwoman, plunged himfelf wholly " into his fortune," &c.

(*t*) Sir William Monfon, who was an Admiral on this expedition, relates in his " Account of the Wars with " Spain,"

Court, on his return; the Queen frowning on a Captain, who had funk a Spanifh Pinnace, without orders; in order to fhow her diffatisfaction with the General, who was unfit for fuch a fervice.

The Earl, ere long, gave ftronger proofs, that he was equally unfit for a greater fervice, and equally unfortunate, in the appointment of Lord Southampton, as a General of Horfe, as he had been two years before as a Captain of a frigate. Effex feems to have, early, refolved, on this meafure,

---

" Spain," p. 38 : " The Pinnace was a frigate of the " Spanifh fleet, who took the Garland for a galleon of " their's; but feeing the flag of the Garland fhe tried to " efcape; and the Earl purfued her, *with the lofs of fome* " *time*, when he fhould have followed the fleet; and there- " fore was defired to defift from that chace by Sir William " Monfon, who fent his boat after him: By a fhot from " my Lord, this frigate was funk." The want of fuccefs in this expedition, Monfon attributes to the want of experience and feamanfhip in the Earl of Effex. From the accurate account of Monfon, we may obferve, that Rowland White's News, about Lord Southampton's finking a great man of war, is not to be altogether credited. [Apology 136.]

contrary

contrary to pofitive injunctions (*u*). It was in the Irifh Campaign, of 1599, that a quarrel began, between Lord Southampton, and Lord Grey, which, for many years inflamed the fpirits, and diftracted the affairs, of both (*x*). The Campaign of Ireland, and the

(*u*) Ib. And fee in the Nugæ Antiquæ, vol. ii. p. 29. A Letter from Effex to John Harrington, 1599: " I fhall " provide you to a Command of Horfemen in Conforte and " Commande of the Earl of Southamptone. 1 will confer " fuch advantages as are in my powre ; for as moche as " hir Majeftie makethe me to commande peace, or ware, " to truce, parley, or fuch matter as feemethe befte for hir " realme : Be nowe affurede of my *love* for hir fake, who " byds it," &c.

(*x*) The caufe of that quarrel may be feen in Sir John Harrington's Journal of the Campaign: [Nugæ Antiq. vol. ii. 33.] " Aboute the fame tyme, the rebell prefented " himfelf, in the fight of the Caftle of Reban, whiche upon " the fighte of the Earl of Southampton, who hafted " towards them in mofte foldier-like order, retyred " themfelves to their bogges: There, the Lo. Greye, " being carried nearer to the rebell, by heate of valour " naturall to fuche yeeres and nobilitie then was reafonable, " and contrary to the Commaundmente of the Earle of " Sowthampton, was for his contempte, punifhed by the " Lord Leiufetennaunte withe a nyghtes imprifonment !"

We

the influence of Eſſex, involved Lord Southampton in treaſonable conſultations, open
rebellion, and adjudged treaſon, during the
unfortunate year 1601.

King James, contrary to his uſual logick,
ſeems to have thought, that the attack of
Eſſex, on the power of Elizabeth, was the
eſtabliſhment of his own authority. He had
hardly heard of his acceſſion, when he ſent
orders to releaſe Lord Southampton from the
Tower.(*y*)   In return, Lord Southampton
haſtened to meet the King, on his journey,
from Edinburgh to London :   And, on the
24th of April, 1604, Lord Southampton carried the ſword before the King, as he made
his public entry into Huntingdon.(*z*) Such

We may, herein ſee, alſo, Eſſex's Southamp*tone*, and
Harrington's *Sowt*hampton, excluſive of other diverſities of
Spelling.

(*y*) I had hopes of being able to preſent a Copy of the
letter, which King James wrote, on that occaſion, to the
Privy Council, for the delivery of Lord Southampton, and
Sir Henry Nevil, and which exiſted among the *Aſhmole* MSS.
at Oxford; but, upon aſking for a Copy, I was told, that
the volumn, containing it, was miſlaid.

(*z*) Chron. Pub. Edin. 1633, p. 163.

                    I   are

are the additional facts, which I have been able to collect, for freeing the biography of Lord Southampton from error, and mifre-prefentation. I will only add, that there is in *Purchas, his Pilgrimes*, vol. iv. p. 1788, a paper, figned, " Henry *Southampton* ;" and, in Camden's *Remains*, 1605, p. 156, the following *Anagram* of the Earl's name: Henricus Wriothfleius, *Heroicus, Lætus, vi virens* : In Sir John Beaumont's Poems, 1629, p. 176, there is an Elegy " on the " death of the moft noble lord Henry, " Earle of Southampton, 1624 ;" and in p. 180, there is " An Epitaph upon that " hopeful young Gentleman, the lord Wri- " othefley :"—

" What helpe can men againft pale death provide,
" When twice, within few days, Souampton dide."

The facts, and the dates, which I have now ftated, and formerly furnifhed, with regard to the life of the firft patron of Shak-fpeare, will probably be ufeful to the Bio-grapher; as fome writers find it very diffi-cult to prove what is felf-evidently true. Of this fingular truifm, the whole *Enquiry*
of

of Mr. Malone, is an irrefragable proof. His great object is to prove, that fictitious papers are falfe. I explicitly admitted, by one general acknowledgement, that the papers, in queftion, were fpurious. But, I difputed the legitimacy of the proofs, which were adduced by Mr. Malone, in order to prove them fo ; becaufe, they appeared to be as defective as the papers; and to be brought forward, full as much for the purpofe of obloquy, as for the inveftigation of truth.

To the correfpondence of Lord Southampton, and Shakfpeare, it was objected, by the Enquirer, that there was a tradition exifting, in dramatical hiftory, of a prefent of a thoufand pounds, which had been given by the Peer to the Poet. From this tradition, the Believers argued, that the letter, for which there exifted an Archetype, was probably true : on the other hand, the Sceptics, from the fame premifes, inferred, that the papers were unqueftionably fpurious. In confirmation of this inference, the Enquirer infifted, that the fpellings were fuch as no age could fhow : As a compleat

answer,

anfwer, the Apologift fhowed, that there never had been any uniform orthography, in any age(*a*).

The Enquirer went on to object to the re-duplication of the *ll* in *bllo∬oms*, and *bllooms*; and, when he was fhewn, that there remain to this day, in Englifh fpeech, analagous reduplications, he infifted, that Shakfpeare was too good a gardener, not to know, that fhrubs bloom before they blo∬om : But, in

(*a*) The anonymous Critic before mentioned afferts, however, that there is in the fpurious papers a *regular fyftem* of " Orthography ;" admitting in the fame breath " that " there are variations." [Britifh Critic, vol. ix. 520] Nay ; of fuch hot, and cold, fatyre-like critcifm out of the fame mouth there is no end. If there be variations, there is no fyftem ; and if there be no fyftem, then, the Criticifm is nothing to the purpofe. Mr. Malone objected 1ft to the fpelling of *forre*, as unprecedented ; for which fpelling, however, a precedent was found: he 2dly objected to the fpelling of *for*, in this correfpondence, between Southampton and Shakfpeare, which fhowed a deviation from a fuppofed fyftem : Thefe, then, are happy fpecimens of *Procruftic* Criticifm: If there be two *r's* one of them is lopped off; if there be only one *r*, another muft be added, for the unfair purpofe of raifing unfounded objections.

anfwer

anſwer to the objection, which was thus
drawn from the garden, it was ſhewn, that
Shakſpeare was too good a philologiſt not
to know, that *blooms*, and *bloſſoms* are mere
Synonyma. (*b*)　The Enquirer's objections,
both to the coarſeneſs of the beginning,
and the familiarity of the end of his correſpondence, were ſhown to be equally unfounded. (*k*)　He only expoſed his want of
reading, when he impugned the word *Dear*
as a familiar novelty : Sydney dedicated
his *Arcadia*, in the following terms : " To
" my *Dear* Lady, and Siſter, the Counteſs
" of Pembroke, moſt *dear*, and moſt wor-

(*b*) Apology 161 : and See Capel's Notes on Shak.
vol. iii. p. 18. l. 15.　In Chaucer's *Court* of *Love*, as
quoted by Mr. Malone [5. Shak. 263.] it is ſaid that
early on May Day—" furth goth al the Court both moſt
" and left, to fetche the flouris freſh, and *braunch*,
" and *blome*."　We may, herein, ſee, how Chaucer,
who was an excellent poetical gardener, put the *braunch*
before the *blome*.

(*k*) The objection to *Willam* is oppoſed by the Letter
of Richard 3d, in Lord Orford's *Hiſtoric Doubts*, p. 118,
about Miſtreſs Shore, the wife of *Willm* Shore.

　　　　　　　　　　　　　　　thy

" thy to be moſt *dear* Lady." And, take
the following from Du Bartas :—

" How fair art thou, my *Deer!* How *dear* to me!
" *Dear* Soule (awake), I faint, I ſinke, I ſownde!
" At thy *dear* ſight." (*l*)

As, if there had been any uniform ſpelling, in that unpreciſe period of our language, it was finally obje&ted to *freynd,*
that it was not the ſpelling of the age.   In
ſuperaddition to all former anſwers, let the
following be ſubjoined :—

" Fren*des* have Y fewe my foemen walketh thykke." (*m*)
Sir Robert Cecil aſſured the Vice Chancel-
lor of Cambridge, that he was his *loving frend:*
The Biſhop of London told the ſame Vice
Chancellor, that he was his loving*e* fre*i*nd. (*n*)

Amidſt all this want of uniformity, one
thing is certain, that he, who accuſes others
of ignorance, ought himſelf to be better
inſtru&ted.   To have been led into error
by *probability* is ſufficiently mortifying to
thoſe, who know the value of probability,
as a guide : But, to be ſcoffed at, by ignorance, for the want of information about

(*l*) Silveſter's Tranſlation, 579.
(*m*) Hern's *Aveſbury,* 265.
(*n*) Lewis's Tranſlation of the Bible.

thoſe

thofe things, that were of ufe for them to know, is a ftill harder lot, which requires " the better fortitude of patience," one of the firmeft fupport of a " a clear life."

—— § IV. ——

SHAKSPEARE's LETTER; AND VERSES TO ANNA HATHERREWAYE.

IN every conteft, there is a point of prudence, which a wife man will be ftudious to obferve ; and which prompts him never to take an untenable pofition ; becaufe the opponent is fure to attack what is weak, rather than what is ftrong. He, who affumed the tafk of convicting the *Shakfperianifms* of forgery, fell into this unhappinefs, throughout his enquiry : He ftarted a thoufand objections, which, as they were founded neither in fact, nor in argument, were, by the Apologift, either confuted, as fictions, or exploded as fophifms.

In this manner, was every one of his objections, on this head of the enquiry, minutely examined, and fatisfactorily refuted. When the enquirer faid, that fuch a name as

Anna did not then exift, in our language, he fhowed little of his learning, and ftill lefs of his difcretion. If it had not exifted before in our Bibles, in our Dictionaries, in our Dramas, it muft have been introduced, by the acceffion of King James, with Queen Anne:

" With thefe, to celebrate the genial feaſt
" Of *Anna*, ftil'd *Perenna*, (*a*) Mars his gueſt.

Had the enquirer looked into Ben Jonfon, he would have learned " that he had de-
" vifed the name of *Bel-Anna*, the Royal
" Queen of the Ocean ; and kept up the
" fame, in all his poems, wherein he men-
" tioned Her Majefty (*b*)." But, *Bel-Anna* is not the only device of Ben upon Her Majefty's name: In his *Triumph* of 1604, he has *Ori-ana*, which Whalley, moft learnedly, expounds to be *quafi Oriens-Anna* (*c*). In emulation, no doubt, of Shakfpeare's

---

(*a*) See Ben Jonfon's Works 1640, the King's entertainment, in paffing to his Coronation, p. 80, a profufion of curious learning on the great feaſt of *Anna-Perenna*, the 15th of March.

(*b*) Whalley's Edit. vol. v. 348.   (*c*) Ib. 205.

Anna,

Anna, Ben Jonſon tried to go beyond him in encomiaſtic fiction: Not content with *Bel-Anna*, and *Ori-ana*, he created *Orian:*

" See, fee, O fee, who, here, is come, a maying,
" The Maſter of the Ocean ;
" And his beauteous *Orian* (*d*) :"

Scepticiſm is the *ignis fatuus*. which continually leads into the mire, the Enquirer, who deals in *doubting things*. Thither, did it lead Mr. Malone, when he doubted, whether the *Cedar*-tree grew in England, at the acceſſion of King James. The true queſtion was, whether it exiſted in the pages of our poets. Even Gawen Douglas mentions

(*d*) The entertainment of the King and Queen at Sir William Cornwallis's houſe, at Highgate, on May-day, 1604. [Whalley, vol. v. 217.] And fee Heminge Chart. Ecc. Wigorn. vol. i. p. 289, for *Anna*: and Dugdale's Bar. vol. i. 348, in the Table of Berkley. See Blathwayte's Poems, 1621. p. 67, for *Anna*: And Heywood's Dramas, 1637, p. 203, a Dialogue between *Anna*, and Phillis, and in p. 265, an Acroſtic on Robert-*Anna*-Carr : In the Epiſtle to the reader may alfo be feen the Verb " *to compliment* ;" " Complement, I cannot," fays Heywood, the Contemporary of Shakſpeare. This collection of curious learning, Mr. Malone miſſed, by doubting the exiſtence of the name of *Anna*.

the

the *Cedir-tre* in his commendation of *maiſt reverend Virgil.* Sydney, and Spenſer, often ſing of the *Cedar.* Shakſpeare adopted this fine paſſage in his Henry VIth :

" Thus, yields the *Cedar* to the Axe's edge,"

from Marlow, who furniſhed Nixon with the very thoughts, and words, which Mr. Malone doubted the exiſtence of, in Shakſpeare's Epiſtle :

" The *lowly ſhrub doth ſeldome blaſte,* or *fade*

" Under the *Cedar's* loftie verdant ſhade. (*e*)."

Thus,

(*e*) See Anthony Nixon's Dedication to Archbiſhop Whitgift of his *Chriſtian Navy,* 1602. Nixon mentions the *Stately Eagle,* which ſhows, that he had his Eye on Marlow's *True Tragedie of Richard Duke of Yorke,* which was reprinted, in 1600. Shakſpeare's Drama of Henry 6th was not publiſhed till 1623. In the Dedication of *The Strange, wonderful* and *bloody battel betweene Frogs and Mice,* 1603, by Wm. Fowldes to Rob. Greenwood, we may ſee :

" No loftie Cedar, though in height *he* paſs,

" Eche ſev'ral plant, which deſerts foreſts yeeld.

Mr. Malone would do well, perhaps, to look into this wonderful *battel,* for ſome words, which, he ſuppoſed, did not exiſt, in 1603 :

" Once

Thus, may we fee a new example how " *doubting things go ill.*" This will, indeed, be always the fate of arguments, which are drawn from *negative* pofitions. This fort of probation, arifing more from the fcepticifm of confidence, than from the doubts of knowledge, greatly abound in the enquiry under this head of the difquifition. The *Believer* will, in every argument, have the advantage of the *Sceptick* ; becaufe, he has only to prove his affirmative pofition, whilft his opponent is drivelling among his *doubts*, and dogmatizing with his *negatives*. Meanwhile, the Believer will often find light in darknefs, and comfort in defpair :

" For, he embraceth much more earneftlie
" The gainful *praĉtice*, than cold *theorie :*
" Nor, *recks* he fo of a fophifticke pride
" Of *prattling knowledge*, too felf magnifi'd.

" Once happie in three Children born to me,
" As *pretty mife* as ever man did fee :
" And now my third, my laft beloved fonne,
" But beft beloved Sonne of all the three,
" With whome my joyes do end, my life is done,
" Moft *deare* to his Queene-mother and to me.

§ V.

—— § V. ——

SHAKSPEARE's PROFESSION of FAITH.

THE Believers were induced by the principles of their logic, and were carried forward by their guide, Probability, to regard
this profeſſion of a pious Poet, as genuine;
knowing it was a religious age, when ſuch
profeſſions were commonly made. Againſt
this document, indeed, the Enquirer pro-
feſſed to have " little to ſay;" (*a*) thinking,
no doubt, with the conſtable, in Henry V:—

> " A very little, little let us do;
> " And all is done."———

After ſome *minute* Criticiſms, which were
probably intended to mean little, the Enquirer, ſuppoſing *himſelfe* ſure *of the faĉt*,
laid his finger on an objeĉtion, which, he
doubtleſs deemed of deciſive moment : He
was aſtoniſhed to ſee the word *himſelfe* exhibited as *one word* (*b*). He ſeems, from
his objeĉtion, to have been unacquainted

(*a*) Apology 197.
(*b*) See the objeĉtion, and the anſwers, in The Apology, 202—3.

with

with Sylvefter, a Contemporary of Shakfpeare, who, in his age, had as much reputation, as our great Dramatift himfelf.
Sylvefter, who had a happy knack, at dif-
joining fyllables, and tying words, would
have inftructed our Enquirer, how to con-
nect, and feparate, the word *felfe*. Here are
fome examples :

" Our-owne-felfes Conqueft is the moft victorious :
" For in our felves ambufh our greateft foes."

" All men are faultie : none a-live can fay,
" I have not err'd ; even the perfecteft."

" 'Tis a moft bufie, yet a boot-les paine,
" To hide ones fault ; for doo the beft thou can
" Thou can'ft not hide it from thy *felfe* (though faine)
" For, who can hide him from *himfelfe* (O man)!"

" More of thy *Selfe*, than others be afham'd ;
" Thy *Selfe* art moft wrong'd by thine owne offence,
" And of thy *Selfe*, thy felfe firft (felfly blam'd)
" Muft give account to thy *felfes* Confcience. (*c*)"

We

(*c*) The Quadrains of Pibrac, Silveft. Tranfl. 710,
11, 12. In Wiclif's Tranflation of the New Teftament, we may fee *Youfilff*, for yourfelves, in James III ;
and *Uffilf*, for ourfelves, in Rom. viii; 1. Jon. 1; and in
Ebrew,

We may behold, then, in thefe fine fpecimens, how Sylvefter disjoined *Conjunc-
tive* fyllables, and *grappled* others, *with
hooks of Steel*; fuch as thofe interefting
words *our-owne-felfes*, and *himfelfe*.

Diffatisfied probably with his own affertion, our enquirer put the whole iffue, with
regard to this head of the queftion, on the
non-exiftence of the word *accede*, for a century after the death of Shakfpeare, in 1616:
Yet, ftrange to tell! Diligence difcovered
its exiftence, at an earlier period, although
confidence had miffed it in later times.
The truant, *accede*, was found in Florio's
New World of Words, 1611 (*d*). Never-
therlefs, cavil comes out in the guife of
criticifm, to affert, that the word *accede* did
exift, in our language, before the death of
Shakfpeare, and has exifted ever fince, in
Florio's *World of Words*; but, that it was

Ebrew, ch. 6, *hemfilff*, as one word. Such examples
of what has been at once refute this objection, and
deride the abfurd practice of *negative arguments*, from
the fuppofed nonentities of former times.

(*d*) See The Apology, 203, 16.

not

not in common ufe, nor likely to be introduced into Shakfpeare's confeffion (*e*).
Now, the iffue was joined upon the exiftence, or non-exiftence of the word *accede*,
during a century, after that epoch: The
word was found to exift, at an earlier
epoch: and, confequently, the iffue was
decided in favour of the finder. From that
period to the prefent, Florio's dictionary
has been in every hand; and the word *accede*, might have been, in every eye; And,
therefore, to fay, that it was not in *common
ufe*, is a negative argument, more negative,
if poffible, than any in the negative catalogue, of fuch arguments in *the Enquiry*;
becaufe it arifes from an affumption, which
is abfolutely againft proof. Indeed, it is a
confummation devoutly to be wifhed, that
our profeffed critics, would conftantly recollect, that—

> " To offend, and judge, are diftinct offices;
> " And, of oppofed natures."

(*e*) Britifh Critic, vol. ix. 519, 20.

§ VI.

—— § VI. ——

The MISCELLANIES.

BY coupling together things of such *oppofed natures*; and, thereby, converting Criticifm into Controverfy, contefts of every kind may be prolonged without end ; becaufe the combatants *muft fight their battles o'er again* ; *thrice to flay the flain.*

There cannot be finer examples of this remark, than the continued altercations about the name of Shakfpeare : The fact, indeed, feems to be, that he did not write his name uniformly. He, certainly figned both his baptifmal name and his firname differently, at different times : The former thus ; W^m. Willm. and William (*f*) ; and the latter

---

(*f*) In that, and the preceding, Age, there was as little uniformity in the fpelling of the baptifmal names, as of the firnames : In Lord Orford's Hiftoric Doubts, p. 118, there is a curious Letter of Richard 3d, about the marriage of the fair, but frail, wife of *Shore:* " Signifying unto you, that it is fhewed unto us that " our fervaunt and folicitor, Thomas Lynom, mer- " veilloufly blinded and abufed with the late [wife] of " *Willm* Shore." In Herbert's Typ. ant. vol. i. p. 543, may

latter thus ; Shak∫*peare*, Shak∫*pere*, but for
the laſt time, in his will, Shak∫peare, (*g*).
However,

may be ſeen *Wylm* Baldwyn; in p. 552, Williliam
Baldw*i*n, and *Willm* Baldwin; and in 592, Wyllym, and
William, Bonham.   In the will of Auguſtine Phillips,
our great Dramatiſt was called *Willm* Shak∫peare.
Theſe faÆs, as they exhibit remarkable diverſities, ſhow,
ſtrikingly, how groundleſs was Mr. Malone's objeÆion
to the ſpelling of *Willm*. [Apology, 271.]

(*g*) As the Enquirer was unfounded in his objeÆion
to *Willm*, ſo is he equally unfounded, in his remarks on
the Sirname of Shak∫peare : For, it was written variouſly
by himſelf, and by others.   This obſervation is equally
true, with regard to the principal poets of that age ; as
we may ſee in *England's Parnaſſus*, a ColleÆion of
Poetry, which was publiſhed, in 1600 ; Thus:

Sydney	—	S*i*dney	
Spen∫er	—	Spen*c*er.	
Jon∫on	—	John∫on	— Jhon∫on.
Dekker	—	Dekkar.	
Markeham	—	Markham	
Sylvi∫ter	—	Sylve∫ter	— S*i*lve∫ter.
Sackwill	—	Sackuil	
Fitz Geffrey	—	Fitzjeffry	— Fitz Jeffr*ay*
France	—	Fraunce.	
Mid*l*eton	—	Mid*d*leton.	
G*ui*lpin	—	G*i*lpin.	
Achell*y*	—	Achely	— Achilly — Achillye.

K   Drayton

However, one of the effects of contest is enquiry ; and enquiry, producing certainty, ends in the establishment of truth.

The objections, which were made, on this head of the enquiry, to the existence of Arabic Numerals, in that age ; to the re-ward for acting Plays; to the word *witty* ; to the term upset (*h*) ; to the Black*fryers*;

Drayton	—	Draiton
Daniel	—	Daniell.
Davis	—	Davies.
Marlow	—	Marlowe.
Marston	—	Murston
Fairefax	—	Fairfax.
Kid	—	Kyd.

Yet; is it remarkable, that in this Collection of diver-sities, our Dramatist's name is uniformly spelt Shake-speare : In whatever manner this celebrated name may have been pronounced in Warwickshire, it certainly was spoken in London, with the e, soft, thus ; Shake-speare : In the Registers of the Stationers' Company, it is written, Shakespere, and Shakespeare.

(*h*) In Chaloner's *Praise of Folie*, 1549, [sign. A. iii.] it is said that, " At *Folie's* becke onely, as oftymes, so " now also, both holy and unholy things be torned *topset-* " *tiruie*." In Bailey, *topsey-turvy* is said to mean tops in turfs ; *upside down*.

to

to fif*th* ; to *view* ; to *An. Dom.* as an unprecedented contraction ; were all anfwered
by the afcertainment of facts (*i*).   But, our
Enquirer could not find *recompence* in the
fame fenfe as *reward :* Had his diligence
been equal to his fecurity, he might have
found *recompence*, in Sternhold and Hopkins,
before Shakfpeare began to appear, with
his frequent mention of the fame animating
word :

> " His benefits they be fo great,
>> " To us, that be but fin :
> " That, at our hands, for *recompence*,
>> " There is no hope to win (*k*)."

Our enquirer objected, however, with a
firmer tone, " that at the beginning of the
" laft century, perfons of the firft rank
" were contented with *one Chriftian* name ;
" that Henry, and Charles, the heirs ap-

(*i*) Apology, 229—40.

(*k*) Edit. Wolfe, 1591. p. 137.   On the 26th of
March, 1604, Sir Oliver St. John moved in the Houfe
of Commons, "the wants, and miferies of the Irifh
" Servitors, in the late rebellion in Ireland: Their *re-*
" *compence* was prevented by her Majeftie's death.
[Com. Journal. vol. i. p. 153.]

K 2   " parent

" parent of the Crown, could boaſt of no
" ſuch diſtinction, as the having of two
" Chriſtian names (*l*)." Birch's Life of
Prince Henry, which contains the ceremonial
of his baptiſm, ought to teach dogmatiſm to
relinquiſh his uſual poſitiveneſs, with reſpect
to that Prince at leaſt : But, of the aſſertion,
with regard to Prince Charles, it may be
ſaid :

" Forth irreturnable flies the ſpoken word,
" Be it in ſcoffe, in earneſt, or in bourd."

The fact, however, is, though hiſtory ſeems
to be ſilent about it, that this Prince received the baptiſmal name of his father ;
being baptized, on the 27th of December,
1600, Charles-James, Duke of Rothſey,
Earl of Ormond, &c. (*m*) : and, upon the
demiſe of his father, he aſcended the throne,
by the name of Charles-James, which the

(*l*) Enquiry, 229.

(*m*) "Hoc Anno *Carolus Jacobus* 19 Novem. 1600
" natus Fermiloduni." [Simſon's MS Annales Eccleſ.
Scotorum:] The Abr. Chron. Edin. 1633, p. 154, ſays,
that he was born, at Dumfermlin, and baptized, on
the 27th of December, 1600, by the name of Charles
James.

heralds

heralds were ftudious to proclaim. I have,
moreover, fhown, that two Chriftian names
were not fo rare, at the commencement of
the laft Century, as Camden, with his
ufual circumfpection fuppofed: (*n*)

"———— Few words fhall fit the trefpafs beft,

" Where no excufe can give the fault amending (*o*)."

From Kings the tranfition is eafy to
players, who fometimes reprefent royal

(*n*) I will here add, in fupport of Camden, and the
truth, a few more examples of double names of baptifm,
in that age; Richard Maria Dunville, Efq. was born
in 1603; Huntingdon Haftings Corney, Efq. was born
about the fame time; Anne Maria Eftoutville; Eyfton
John Seymour; William Roberts Smith, A°. 1604;
Edward Allen Tedder.

(*o*) Apology, 255. It is a curious fact, that there was
buried, in the Church of Abergavenny, an. 1432, Sir
John Atte Hene, *Kt.* [Hern's Robert of Glofter, vol. ii.
p. 639.] Well; I will not leave this obfervation to
ftand for fome Welch Reviewer to accufe me of ignorance, in not knowing, that *Hên*, which is pronounced
Hene, in the Welch, fignifies *Old:* And that *Hene* was
added by a Welch Sculptor, in order to diftinguifh Old
Sir John, from Young Sir John Atte: It is, however,
a ftrong fact, that there was living, in 1659, at Wink-
field in Berks, Henry Hene, Efq. who had in his
Cuftody, the Monumental plate, of Sir John Atte Hene,
Kt. [Id.]

K 3   perfonages.

perfonages.   In contradiction to Pope, who
had faid, that the players of Shakfpeare's
age were not gentlemen of the ftage, but
mere players, who were led into the buttery by the Steward, Mr. Malone, and Mr.
Steevens, affert, " that there is no reafon to
" fuppofe that Shakfpeare, Burbage, *Lowin*,
" &c. who were licenfed by King James,
" were treated in this manner (*p*)."   In
this paffage, *Lowin* is made a player of
confequence : In the Enquiry, Mr. Malone
affures us, however, " That in 1608, Lowin
" was low, in his profeffion, and poor in
" his circumftances (*q*)."   In the reverfe of
the picture, we now behold, that *Lowin*,
being low, and poor, was only fit to be led
into the buttery.   " Is't good to footh him
" in thefe *contraries ?*"   Having neither
the voice, nor the heart, of flattery, I will
only anfwer, that I do not feel it good to
footh the two commentators, when they
ftate, " that Lowin was licenfed by the

(*p*) Steevens's Shak. 1793, vol. i. p. 122.
(*q*) Enq. 253.

" patent

" patent of King James ;" becaufe, the record afferts, that neither the licenfe, nor the will of Auguftine Phillips, fpeaks of *Lowin*, as a *fellow* of Fletcher, and Shakfpeare, Burbadge, and Phillips.

It is a *whimfical* circumftance, that the pride of accuracy fhould thus fall into error, after fo long a fearch. Of the family of the *whimficals*, Mr. Malone, with the help of Mr. Waldron, found, in the age of Shakfpeare, only *Whim-Wham*, and *Whimfy* (r). I have in my travels, met with another of this fatherlefs family, called *Whim-len*, in Ben Jonfon's Mafque of *Love Reftored:* Robin Goodfellow cries out, " Marry, before I could procure my pro- " perties, alarm came, that fome of the " Whim-*lens* had too much provifions (s)." Whether, amid fo much uncertainty of ex-

---

(r) Enquiry, 206—7 : In Johnfon's folio 1616; this is Whimf*ey:* In Whalley, vol. ii. p. 328, it is Whimfie.

(s) Whalley, vol. v. 404. In the Enquiry, p. 207, Mr. Malone afferts " that Volpone was firft acted in " 1607 :" But, the folio of 1616 fays 1605; and fo does Whalley, vol. ii. p. 263.

iftence,

iftence, and derivation, it were a *whim*, or a whimfey, in our Enquirer to affert, that " *oune*, for one, is the fpelling of no time " whatfoever (*t*)," I pretend not to know. One certainty, at leaft, is clear, that he feems never to have read that good old book, Wicliff's bible : " And thei hadden not " with 'hem but *oo* [one] loof [loaf] in the " boot [boat] (*u*)"   In the tranflation by Erafmus, this paffage, from Mark, Chap. VIII, may be read thus : " Neither had they " in the Shyp with them more then one " lofe (*x*)." Thus fruitlefs, are the fearches after uniformity of fpelling, in any age;

(*t*) Enq. 209.

(*u*) He who looks for the fpellings of recorded time, may find in the fame book : *aloone* for alone ; *oon* for one ; *anoon* for anon ; *ony* for any ; *oonlie* for only ; In Wicklift's *Wicket* may be found *O* for one ; and *ene* for one.   In Bifhop Pococke, 1450, may be feen [Effef. iv. 5.] " *Oon* is the Lord, *oon* feith, and *oon* baptifm." [Lewis's Tranfl. of the New Teftament, 68.] This mode of fpelling one [oon] continued in good ufe till Henry 7th's time. [See his Inftructions to his Ambaffadors to Spain.]

(*x*) The New Teftament printed by Redman 1538.

and

and thus futile, is the negative argument, for the eftablifhment of truth, in any enquiry!

Amidft all this doubting, it was to be expected, that my law, relating to Deeds, Wills, and Teftaments, fhould be called in queftion, as unprecife. However, my law was accurately ftated, although it was ludicroufly applied, for the purpofe of laughing at *a little learning*. What I faid on the authority of Weft, " that Codicils may be " made, without any Teftament, either precedent, or fubfequent (*y*)," I ftill affert to be law, in oppofition to the loofe ftatement of Blackftone, in his Commentaries (*z*)." Weft is a better authority, upon the point, than Blackftone. I will only add what the Lord Chancellor Ellefmere repeated, from Juftice Afcue, in the 37th of Henry VI: " Such a charter hath been allowed in the

---

(*y*) Weft's Symb. 1605, Lib. 2. §649, §633, §639.

(*z*) 2 Black. Com. 500—1. In oppofition to this, and in fupport of the ancient doctrine, See Bacon's Ab. in the excellent Edition of Mr. Gwillim, vol. vii. p. 328, 340.

                                                " time

" time of our predeceffors, which were as
" fage, and learned as we be (*a*)."

However true this obfervation of Afcue
may have been, in the time of Henry VI.
as to lawyers, it cannot be admitted as
juft, with regard to the commentators on
Shakfpeare. Mr. Pope, and Mr. Malone,
accufe their predeceffors, Heminges and
Cundal, of ignorance ; becaufe they were
not quite " as *fage*" as themfelves ; and
allege, that not only their Latin, and
French, but their very *Welch*, are falfe (*b*).
Whatever Mr. Malone, and Mr. Pope, may
have found in Shakfpeare, certain it is, that
Heminges, and Cundal found no *Welch*
in his dramas ; becaufe there was none to
find.   There was indeed, much Welch
fuppofed to be faid, and fung, at Glendower's, in Henry IV ; yet, was it all fung
and faid, afide.   But the truth is, that
though Shakfpeare, with the help of fuch

(*a*) Lord Chancellor Ellefmere's fpeech, in the
Exchequer Chamber ; touching the *poft nati.* Printed
for the Stationers, *An.* 1609.

(*b*) Enquiry, 271.

fcholars

fcholars as were at hand, could manage
his *fmall Latin*, and little French, the Welch
was a metal too unweildy for his anvil, as it
has been found, for that of greater fcholars,
in fubfequent times. Happy ! if the commentators on Shakfpeare had fomewhat of
his modefty : We fhould not then fee fo
many affertions, without proof ; and obfervations, without argument :

" To tire our patience, and miflead our fenfe."

—— § VII. ——

The LEARE and HAMBLETTE.

THREE words, it was faid, will fuffice,
on this head of the Enquiry (*a*) : Yet, was
our patience tired, and our fenfe mifled, by
our minute Enquirer, who affumed, without
proof, the very point, which he undertook
to fupport, by argument.

One of the three words, which was to
convict the *Leare* of fpurioufnefs, was an
objection to the ufe of *Liberty* in that age,
for *licenfe*. But, let us, paffing by Shakfpeare, look even to a prior time. In the

(*a*) Apology, 303.

con-

controverſy with Doctor Gabriel Harvey, the witty Naſh makes uſe of the word *li-berty*, in preference to *licenſe* : " As touch-
" ing the *libertie* of orators, and *poets*; I
" will conferre with thee ſomewhat gravely,
" although thou bee'ſt a gooſe cape, and
" ha'ſt no judgement : A *libertie*, thou
" ſayſt ; but, no *liberty*, without bounds,
" no licence, without limitation : Jeſu !
" what miſter wonders doſt thou tell us !
" Eevery thing hath an end, and a pud-
" ding hath two. That *libertie*, poets of
" late have uſed in their invectives, have
" exceeded, they have born their ſword up,
" where it is not lawful for a poynado,
" that is but the page of proweſſe, to in-
" termeddle." (*b*)

From this word, our Enquirer proceeds to a paſſage, which being nonſenſical, fixes,

(*b*) " Strange Newes of the intercepting certaine
" Letters, and a Convoy of Verſes, as they were going
" privilie to victual the Low Countries." By Thomas
Naſh, Gentleman, 1593. Such is the whimſical Title
of Naſhe's Confutation of Harvey's Foure Letters of
the preceding *Yere*. [Sign. E.]

according

according to his logick, the forgery, beyond a controverfy.   The objection, then,
is, that this death-giving paffage is nonfenfe.   And, he affumes, in oppofition to
the proofs of Warburton, that, in Shakfpeare, there are no paffages nonfenfical,
and feeble; and in contempt of Johnfon,
who fays, that Shakfpeare's fet fpeeches
are commonly cold and weak.   Can there
be any fpeech, colder, and weaker, than
this of Kent's?

> " I have a journey, Sir, fhortly to go,
> " My mafter calls, and I muft not fay no."

I certainly did think, and do maintain,
that the fuppofititious paffage of the furreptitious *Leare*, was more comprehenfive,
more energetic, and more Shakfperian
than the genuine fpeech (*c*).   On the other
hand, our enquirer appears to have conceived of Shakfpeare, as Donne expreffed
himfelf, on a different occafion :—

> " ———— His art did exprefs
> " A quinteffence even from nothingnefs,
> " From dull privations, and lean emptinefs."

(*c*) Apology, 309.

But,

But, againſt the opinion of the Apologiſt, who ſtill thinks that Shakſpeare might be amended, if it were allowable, the anonymous critic aforeſaid, ſhifting the queſtion from one paſſage to another, produces only his *feelings*, and his taſte (*d*). I will only reply in the words of a poet, who had both feeling, and taſte:

" There's ſomething previous ev'n to *taſte*; 'tis *ſenſe*.

But, what ſenſe is there in giving the coldneſs, and weakneſs, of the genuine verſes, in compariſon with the energy and warmth of the ſpurious lines ? Is emptineſs, then, the characteriſtic of Shakſpeare ? Or, ſhall we regard amplification in the matter, and elaboration in the ſtyle, as more Shakſperian ? Upon this reaſoning, the Apologiſt preferred ſomething to nothing : Upon a different principle, the anonymous critic prefers nothing to ſomething ; judging, no doubt, with Donne, that the very name of Shakſpeare can extract *real quinteſſence*, from *lean emptineſs*.

(*d*) Britiſh Critic, vol. ix. 521.

In

In criticifm, we may judge of grammar, which has its rules, and of argument, which has its principles: But, who difputes, in fpite of the old adage, about tafte, which has neither rule, nor principle? Who, except the Critic aforefaid? He, departing from the point in iffue, compares the *beft* in Shakfpeare, with the *worft* in his imitator. Whenever criticifm affumes the province of controverfy, abfurdity of difquifition, and impertinence of remark, will too often be the illogical effects:

‘ Now, Dulnefs fmiling:—“ Thus review the wits;
“ But, murder *firft*, and mince *them* all to bits: ”

———————

“ And you, my Critic, in the chequer’d fhade,
“ Admire new light, thro’ holes, yourfelf hath made.

—— § VIII. ——

SHAKSPEARE's NOTE of HAND.

ON this head of the queftion, our Enquirer feems to have been actuated, by the congenial fpirit of the anonymous Critic aforefaid: He firft *murdered* the Believers in Shakfpeare’s *Note* of *hand*, and *minced them*

into

into bits, afterwards:—No; by one great
ftroke of fceptical fophiftry, the Enquirer
dafhed the Shakfperian document into non-
exiftence. "Alas! it was a piteous deed!'
What he undertook to prove a furreptitious
bill, he declared to be "an evident forgery."
Such is the extent of his refearch, and the
vigour of his reafoning, that a decifive argument he has always at hand :—

"——— His parts are fo accomplifht,
"That, right, or wrong, he ne'er is nonplufht."

It was an adequate Apology for the Believers, that they produced fimilar documents,
in the fame age, by whatever denomination
they were known, whether by that of bill,
or note (*a*). The *fact* over ruled all reafoning

(*a*) Apology, 315. In addition to the notes of hand,
and fealed Bills, which were therein ftated, I will now
lay before the reader fome other fpecimens of fimilar
documents, which I found on the Regifters of the Stationers' Company:—" 29 June 1599, This day Mr.
" Bon. Norton hath promifed to pay the XX^ld, for not
" ferving the underwardenfhip within one yere next:
" And further, if his XX^ld lent to her Majeftie in this
" Court fhall be repaid before the end of the faid yere,
" that

ing upon the point, either about the effence
of it, or the Name.   Neither did it anfwer
any

" that then, it fhall go prefently upon the receipt thereof
" to the fatisfaction of the faid fine, of XX^{ld}."
[Paid accordingly 29 Dec. 1599] By me Bonham Norton.
   The fame day, Mr. Man hath promifed to pay the
iij^{ld}. vi^s. viij^d. fet upon him within one yere next · And
further that yf his money iij^{ld}. lent to her Majeftie in
this Court fhall be repaid within the end of the faid
yere, that then he fhall prefently pay the · faid iij^{ld}.
vi^s. viij^d.

                                    Thomas Man.

   The foregoing Specimens are conditional Notes of
hand.   There are fome other curious intimations in the
Stationer's Regifters, with regard to this fubject.   On
the 9th Aug. 1596, there was delivered in full court to
the Mafter and Wardens the Citie's *bill* under their
Seal for XL^{ld}. lent in M'che laft toward the Shippes.
Repayable 28th May 1597.   That money after X in
the C. was provided.—It alfo appears, that this Sum,
which was made up to LXXX^{ld}, was taken up at intereft and lent to the City for 4 months, according to
the precept.—This, then, is a fpecimen of a bill of
Debt, which was given by one Corporation to another.
We herein fee, that the City borrowed money at 10 per
Cent. in order to lend it to Queen Elizabeth, to fit out
the Shippes : The Queen borrowed alfo very fmall Sums
of Money of the private members of the Stationer's
               L   Company.

any use to infist, that by law such documents could not be negociated ; as it was shown, that such notes were, in fact, transferable, by assignment, though they were not indorsable. It was probably supposed, that any argument would be decisive, in a case, which was likely to be carried through the Court of Criticism, without a hearing. But, the authentic *fact* is the great decider of causes !—

" Afflicted sense, *thou* kindly dost set free,
" Opprefs'd with argumental tyranny."

Indeed, afflicted sense finds a safe retreat, in the silence of the anonymous Critic aforesaid, upon the point. The fact, the law, the archaiology of *the bill*, the antiquity of paper

Company. These facts, as they are thus eftablished by record evidence, exhibit a greater variety of such documents, than our Enquirer, from a narrow view of the Subject, would have us believe exifted. It was afferted, that paper-credit, or borrowing, and lending on Government Securities, might be clearly traced to Elizabeth's reign, if not to an earlier period. [Apology, 333.] It was faid in the Houfe of Commons, during the Seffion of 1605, that there were Privy-Seals, in the time of Henry 8th. [Com. Journ. vol. i. p. 289.]

money,

money, were fo fixed, by unexpected proofs,
that even hypercriticifm could not find a little
flaw.   But, in the Enquiry, a great flaw was
found by the Apologift ; which, as it was
overlooked by the Critic, fhall be paffed
over by me, although the Enquirer endeavours to make *flight work* in regard to this
Note of Hand, with the *Believers*, whom he
propofes to punifh, refpectively, according
to their degrees of guilt.   But, guilt ought to
be firft proved, before punifhment is propofed.
And, he, who brings flight proofs to fupport ftrong accufations, will, generally, be
caft into the ignoble clafs of thofe bufy men,
who are often found to accufe moft loudly,
when they can prove the leaft:

"——— of the truth herein,
" This prefent object made probation."

—— § IX. ——

Of the HISTORY of the STAGE.

THE annals of the Theatre, as they illuftrate the manners of the times, and gratify the curiofity, which is natural to mankind, will, in every age, incite enquiry, and

L 2   enchain

enchain attention. The hiftory of our ftage has exercifed the pens of Dr. Percy (*a*), of Mr. Thomas Warton (*b*), of Mr. Malone(*c*), and of other writers of diligence and learning. In addition to their curious refearches, I too prefumed to publifh many documents (*d*), which a hafty fearch difcovered among the ftate papers ; and which, as they afcertain new facts, and throw fome light upon the dark paffages of our drama, during the age of Shakfpeare, will enable the writer, to whom fhall be affigned the difficult tafk of writing a compleat hiftory of the ftage, to inftruct, by more ample notices, and to amufe, by more ftriking views of an attractive object.

After many revolutions in our public fports, both in reprefentation, and fentiment, from *jufts to myfteries*; from *myfteries* to *moralities*; and from *moralities* to *interludes*;

(*a*) In his Reliques of anc. Poetry.
(*b*) In his Hift. of Englifh Poetry.
(*c*) In his Suppl. to the Edit. of Shak. 1778, and in the Prolog. to his Edit. of Shak. 1790.
(*d*) Apology, з 39.

the

the Englifh ftage remained extremely rude, at the acceffion of Elizabeth, and ftill unformed, at the appearance of Shakfpeare. She inherited, indeed, the dramatic eftablifhments of her predeceffors; however imperfect they were in theory, and inconvenient in exhibition.   She had, evidently, as a neceffary officer, a keeper of the *veftures* of her *mafkes*, *revelles*, and *difguifings* :   And, the earlieft keeper of fuch *apparell*, from what I have been able to trace, was John Arnolde ; who died, probably, in 1573. In the fubfequent year, was appointed as his fucceffor, her well beloved fervant Walter Fyfhe, in confideration of good fervice, theretofore done to a grateful miftrefs (*e*).

A fpe-

(*e*) I lay before the reader a Copy of this curious Commiffion from the unpublifhed papers of Rymer in the Britifh Mufeum. [Afycough's Catalogue, No. 4625, p. 44.]

  " 29th Jan. De Conceffione ad vitam pro Waltero Fyfhe. [Pat. 16, Eliz. p. 4. M 24.]

  Elizabeth by the Grace of God &c. To all to whom &c. Greeting :

  Wee lett you wytt that of our Grace efpecyall cer-

A fpecimen of the *veftures*, which Walter Fyfhe was thus appointed to keep, I have already

teyne knowledge and mere mocion and in confideration of the good and faythful fervice heretofore donne unto us by our welbeloved Servaunte Walter Fyfhe we have given and graunted and by theis prefentes for us our heires and fucceffors doe gyve and graunte unto the faid Walter Fyfhe thoffice of Yoman or Keeper of our Veftures or apparell of all and fingular our Mafkes Ravelles and Difguyfings and alfo of the apparell and trappers of all and finguler our horfes ordeyned and appoynted and hereafter to be ordeyned and appoynted for our Juftes and Turneys and wee doe ordeyne con-ftitute and make the fame Walter Fyfhe by theis pre-fentes Yoman or keeper of our Veftures or Apparell of all and finguler our Mafkes Revelles and Difguyfinges and alfo of the Apparell and Trappers of all and finguler our horfes ordeyned and appoynted or hereafter to be ordeyned and appoynted for our Juftes and Turneys To have holde occupye and enjoye the faid office to the faid Walter Fysfhe and his fufficiente Deputie or Deputies for terme of the lyffe naturall of the faid Walter Fysfhe with the waiges and fees of fixpence fterling by the daye for the overfeing and falfe kepeing of the fame to be had and yerely perceaved of the Treafure of us our heires and fucceffors at the receipte of th' exchequer of us our heires and Succeffors at Weftminfter by thandes of the Treafurer and Cham-berlaynes

already exhibited to the curious beholder (f).

It was faid by me, that our earlieft actors were children : Children of St. Paul's, children of Weftminfter, children of the chapel (g). And it became, early, a common

berlaynes of Us our heires and Succeffors ther for the tyme being at the feaftes of th' annunciacion of Our Lady and Saynt Michaell th' archaungell by evin porcions and further we give unto the faid Walter Fysfhe yerely during his faid lyffe one liverye coate fuch as Yeoman Officers of our houfhold have of us to be yerely had and perceaved at our greate Wardrobe by the handes of the keeper or Clerke of the fame for the tyme beinge and to have and enjoye one fufficiente houfe or mancion to be affigned unto the faid Walter Fysfhe for the fure better and fafe keping of our faid Veftures Apparell and Trappers togeather with all manner commodities and advantages to the faid Office to be dewe and accuftomed or in any wife apperteyning in as large ample and benefyciall manner and forme as John Arnolde deceafed or any other or others Yeomen kepers of all and finguler the premiffes above mencyoned have had and enjoyed or of right ought to have and enjoye the fame albeit expreffe mencyon &c.—Tefte Regina, apud Weftm. XXIX. Januarij.

[Per breve de privato Sigillo.]"

(f) Apology, 354.

(g) Apology, 359.

L 4   practice

practice to purvey boys, who had mufical voices, for the Royal Chapel. Tuffer, who wrote *The five hundred points of good huf-bandry*, appears to have been thus taken, and appropriated, during the reign of Henry VIII. (*h*) :

> " Thence, for my voice, I muft (no choice)
> " Away of force, like pofting horfe,
> " For fundry men, had placards then,
> " Such Child to take."

The right, and the practice, of purveying fuch children, continued until the reign of James, although I know not on what prin-ciple it was juftified ; except by the maxim, that the King had a right to the fervices of all his fubjects. Sir Francis Bacon, fpeak-ing in the Houfe of Commons, upon the grievance of purveyance, on the 7th of

---

(*h*) His own Life, in verfe, p. 141, of his book, enti-tled *Five hundred points of Good Hufbandry.* Tuffer was carried by " friendfhip's lot" to St. Paul's, where he learned mufic under John Redford, an excellent mufician. [Id.] The celebrated Erafmus was a *Child of the Choir* in the Cathedral of Utrecht, till he was nine years of age: He was born, in 1467. and died in 1536.

March

March 1605-6, faid, " that children for
" the chapel may be taken (*i*)." It was,
probably, from this abundant fource, that
fome of the earlieft, and beft, of our players
originated, who derived a livelihood, and
rofe often to eminence, by amufing the public.

It is more than probable, that James
Burbadge, who appeared at the head of the
firft incorporated company of players in 1574,
may have been purveyed, like Tuffer, in
early life, and may have forgotten his ap-
rentage. Certain it is, that during the heraldic vifitation of London, in 1634, Cuthbert Burbadge, the eldeft fon of James, did
not know his grandfather ; for he could only
give an account of his brother Richard,
" the famous actor on the ftage," and of his
father James, who married Ellen, the daugh-

(*i*) Com. Jour. vol. i. 279. The fact is, that, as late
as the acceffion of Charles, the 1ft, drummers were
preffed for the army ; as we may clearly fee, in the
Privy Council Regifters.

ter

ter of Mr. Brayne, of London (*k*). Whatever may have been their originals, there
can

(*k*) For a pedigree of the Burbadges, I owe a kindnefs to Francis Townfend, the Windfor Herald, who
was fo good as to inform me, that the fame Arms
were allowed to Cuthbert, in 1634, as belonged to a
very numerous family of Burbadges in Hertfordfhire ;
a circumftance, from which a connection of family is
inferred. Cuthbert fometimes fpelt his name Burb*age*,
as did the *Burbages*, of Herts. Mr. Malone fpells the
name Bur*badge* : " But, the name ought rather, he adds,
" to be written Burbidge, being manifeftly a corruption
" of *Boroughbridge*." [Shak. 1790, vol. i. p. 2. p. 184.]
The Arms, however, of the Burbadges were three *Boar*s
heads ; and their Creft was a *Boar's* head : The heraldic
conceit of the Arms was plainly derived from the early
notion, that the original name was *Boar*-bage. We
thus, perceive, that whatever name of that age we
attempt to inveftigate, no uniformity of Spelling can
be found. We have always had *badge*, and *badger* in
our language, but not *bage*, I believe. It was faid, that
Helen Burbadge, widow, who was buried on the 8th of
May, 1613, was probably the relict of James Burbadge.
[Apology, 386.] We now fee, diftinctly, that he did
marry *Ellen* Brayne of London. Their daughter Alice,
who was baptized, on the 11th of March 157$\frac{6}{7}$, and
married one Walker, had a legacy from Nicholas
Tooley of ten pounds by the name of " Alice Walker,
the

can be no doubt, that the feveral Burbadges performed, refpectably, on that " Stage, " where every one muft play a part;" and where, many individuals play " a fad " one."

A fimilar doubt has alfo exifted, with re-gard to the origin of Edward Alleyn, though the biographers, indeed, affure us, " that " he was born of reputable parents, who " lived in good fafhion and credit(*l*)." Yet, are we ftill left, by biographical indolence, to enquire, who were the father, and mother, of that celebrated comedian, and beneficent man. The record of *the fact* is, however, to be found in the College of Heralds. His grandfather was Thomas Alleyn of Willen,

the fifter of my late Mafter Burbadge " deceafed." In the fame will, there is a legacy of ten pounds to Elizabeth Burbadge, alias *Maxey:* Now, it appears by the pedigree, which her father gave in to the College of Heralds, that fhe married for her firft hufband Amias Maxey, Gentleman, by whom fhe had James Burbadge Maxey, who was adopted, by her father: for her fecond hufband, fhe married George Bingley, one of the Auditors to King Charles the 1ft.

(*l*) Kippis's Biog. Brit. vol. i. p. 150.

in

in the County of Bucks, and of Mefham, in the County of Bedford : His father was Edward Alleyn, of Willen aforefaid : and his mother, Margaret, was the daughter of John Townley, of Townley, in the County of Lancafhire, of a refpectable family, which, to this day, " lives in good fafhion and " credit." Edward Alleyn was born on the 1ſt of September, 1566, and was baptized, as I found by fearching the parifh regifter of St. Botolph, without Bifhopgate, on the 2d of the fame month: Nor, can it now be any longer, reafonably, doubted, whether London be entitled to the honour of his birth. Though a younger man than Shakſpeare, Alleyn was fooner praifed by wits, and diftinguifhed by the world. In the *Pierce Pennyleſſe* of Nafh, which was firſt printed, in **1592,** may be feen " the *due commendation of Ned Allen:*" " Not Rof. " cius," fays Nafh, " or Æfop, thofe ad- " mired tragedians, that have lived ever " fince before Chriſt was born, could ever " perform more in action, than famous " Ned Allen." Nafh went on to add, in the

the fame ftrain of encomium, what arofe
from his enthufiaftic admiration: " If ever
" I write any thing in *Latin*, (as I hope
" one day I fhall,) not a man of any defert
" here among us, (the players particularly)
" but I will have up ; Tarleton, Ned Allen,
" Knell, Bently, fhall be known in France,
" Spain, and Italy ; and not a part that they
" furmounted in more than other, but I will
" there note, and fet down, with the manner
" of their habits and attire (*m*)." In the
filence of Nafh, we may perceive, that
neither Shakfpeare, nor Richard Burbadge,
had diftinguifhed themfelves, as players, in

(*m*) In the opinion of Ben Jonfon, who, with all his
prejudices, muft be allowed to have been a competent
judge, Ned Alleyn was the greateft actor, that had then
appeared ; or that would appear, according to Sir Richard Baker: Ben Jonfon, who always fuppofed that
his pen conferred immortality, addreffed his 89th
Epigram to Edward Allen :
  " And prefent worth in all doft fo contract,
  " As others *fpeake*, but only thou doft *act*,
   " Wear this renowne : 'Tis juft, that who did give
   " So many Poets life, by *one fhould live !*

                                        1592,

1592, when Shakfpeare, indeed, had but juft appeared, as a dramatic writer (*n*). It is a memorable circumftance, which ought to be ftrongly marked, by the hiftorian of our Stage, that fuch great actors fhould have exifted, to whom Shakfpeare, at length, fupplied dramas, which were fully equal to their powers of performance: And it will be found, perhaps, that the dramatift de-rived an advantage from the player, and the player a benefit from the dramatift. Among the players, as Alleyn was the firft, fo he appears to have been the moft diftinguifhed; and is even fuppofed, though not upon the moft fatisfactory evidence, to have furnifhed Shakfpeare, by his juft reprefentation of characters, with fome intimations of the ce-lebrated precepts, which were given to the

(*n*) In fact, it does appear, that Richard Burbadge had come out on the Stage, as early as 1589, but in the inconfiderable part of *a Meffenger*. [Steev. vol. i. 506—7.] There is reafon to fufpect, that Shakfpeare himfelf appeared as early, on the fame ftage, in as trivial a Character [Ib. 495.]

actors

actors by Hamlet. (*o*). When fuch doubts arife, from the difficulty of afcertaining facts of fo remote a period, with regard to the

(*o*) In the Apology, p. 391, it was faid, on the authotity of Mr. Malone, chiefly, that Edward Alleyn married Joan Woodward, the Daughter of Henflow's wife. It appears, however, from the funeral Certificate of this Lady, in the College of Arms, by John Gifford, the Senior Fellow, and preacher, of the College, and John Symon, the Schoolmafter thereof, and a Fellow, " that fhe was the Daughter, of the Worfhipful " Phillip Henflowe, Efquier, one of the Sewers of his " Majeftie's Chamber." On that occafion, the Arms of Henflow were impaled with the Arms of her hufband. When Alleyn entered his pedigree at the vifitation of the County of Surrey, in 1623, he gave exactly the fame account of his wife. In a doubtful point, whether her name were Woodward, or Henflow, the inference of the Heralds, from the impaling of the arms, ought to be decifive, that the wife of Alleyn was a Henflow, and not a Woodward: Yet, it appears by the written declaration of Henflow himfelf, that Edward Alleyn did marry Joan Woodward: [Mal. Shak. 1 vol. p. 288.] Thus difficult is it to afcertain a fact, even from fatisfactory evidence; though the Commentators, and Critics, demand *demonftration*, as the only proof, in the affairs of common life! In the pedigree of Edward Alleyn, he is called " Mafter of His Majefty's Game of " Bulls and Bears, and Maftif dogs."

principal

principal players, we ought not to be fur-
prifed, that ftill greater doubts fhould exift,
with refpect to the inferior actors of Shakfpeare's dramas, efpecially as we are without the fame means of giving light to
darknefs.

GEORGE BRYAN, who, like greater men,
will only be remembered from his connection
with Shakfpeare, appeared, as early as 1589,
in Tarleton's *Plat of the Seven Deadly Sins:*
he reprefented Lucius, in Gorboduck; he
played the Earl of Warwick, in Henry the
fixth, during 1592; he performed fome of
the characters in Shakfpeare's earlieft plays;
but he did not live long enough to reprefent
any part in Ben. Jonfon's *Every Man in
his Humour*, during 1598: George Bryan
was certainly dead, at this epoch; though I
have not been able to difcover either the
time, or place, of his burial; or any record
of his will.

SAMUEL CROSSE had the honour, certainly, to embody fome of Shakfpeare's fictions; and is celebrated, by Heywood, together

gether with Knell (*p*), Bently, Mills, Wilfon (*q*), and Lanam, as players, who " by
" the report of many judicial auditors per-
" formed many parts fo abfolute, that it
" were a fin to drowne their worths in
" Lethe (*r*)." Croffe died, probably, before the year 1596; though I have not been
able to find when, or where; nor, to difcover his will; nor any adminiftration to his
Eftate, if indeed he left any behind him.

THOMAS POPE played his part, as early
as 1589, in Tarleton's *Platt of the Seven*

(*p*) It appears by the parifh regifter of St. Mary Al-
dermanbury, that a William Knell was buried in the
Cemetery of that parifh, on the 24th of September,
1578 ; that a William Knell married Rebecca Edwards,
on the 30th January, 1585-6 ; that John Hemming married Rebecca Knell, widow, on the 10th of March,
1587-8 : From thefe entries we may conclude, that
Knell, one of the great actors of that period, is the
perfon, to whom they relate.

(*q*) Robert Wilfon was one of the Earl of Leicefter's
Servants, to whom the theatrical Licenfe was granted,
in 1574. A Robert Wilfon made his Will on the 29th
January, 1576-7, which was proved on the 1ft of February of the fame year.

(*r*) Heywood's Apology.

M   *Deadly*

Deadly Sins; he reprefented Arbactus, in *Sardanapalus;* he was, in 1597, and 1598, at the head of the Lord Chamberlayne's Servants, together with Hemings, who had the honour of being the firft who reprefented Shakfpeare's characters. Pope lived refpectably in St. Saviour's parifh, Southwark; and rofe to fuch eminence, as a fellow of Shakfpeare, as to have equally had a fhare in the Globe, and Curtain, Theatres; and to have employed under him theatrical fervants. He died in February 1603–4; leaving confiderable property to thofe, whom he moft regarded (*s*). Of Gabriel Singer, *Pope,* Phillips,

(*s*) I here fubjoin a Copy of the Will of Pope, " Ex-" tracted from the Regiftry of the Prerogative Court " of Canterbury ;" as it contains fome theatrical particulars, which the curious reader may wifh to fee; and as it exhibits Pope in a higher ftation, than he has hitherto been fuppofed to have held :—

" In the Name of God Amen the two and twenty of July in the year of our Lord God one thoufand fix hundred and three and the firft year of the Reign of our Sovereign Lord King James   I Thomas Pope of the parifh of St. Saviour's Southwark in the County of Surry Gentleman being at this prefent in good and perfect

Phillips, and Slye, it was remarked, by
Heywood, in 1612, " that though they be
" dead,

fect health laude and praife be given to the Almighty
God therefore do make ordain and declare this my
pnte Teftament and laft Will in manner and form following that is to fay Firft and principally I commend
my Soul into the hands of Almighty God my Maker
Saviour and Redeemer hoping and affuredly believing to
be faved through the merits death and paffion of my
Saviour Jefus Chrift and to enjoy eternal bleffednefs in
the Kingdom of Heaven   And my body I commit to
the earth to be buried in Xtian burial in the church
called St. Saviours where I now dwell   And I give
towards the fetting up of fome monument on me in the
faid Church and my Funeral Twenty pounds   Item I
give and bequeath to the poor of the Liberty where now
I dwell thre pounds   Item I give and bequeath unto
Suzan Gafquine whom I have brought up ever fince
fhe was born the fum of one hundred pounds of lawful
money of England and all my Houfehold Stuff my Plate
only excepted   Item I will that the faid Suzan Gafquine fhall have the ufe and occupation of all that
Houfe or Tenement wherein I now dwell in the parifh
of St. Saviours aforefaid during her natural life if the
Leafe and Term of years which I have in the fame
fhall fo long continue and endure fo as the faid Suzan
or her Affigns do pay the one half of the Rent referved
by the leafe to me thereof from time to time and at

fuch

" dead, their deferts yet live in the remem-
" brance of many."

ROBERT

fuch time as is limited in and by the fame Leafe amongft
others made by Francis Langley Drax deceafed and do
alfo perform fuch Covenants touching the faid Tenement as are to be done by force of the faid Leafe and if
the faid Suzan fhall happen to die before the expiration
of the faid Term then I will that my Brother John
Pope fhall have the ufe and occupation of the faid Tenement during the refidue which at the time of the
deceafe of the faid Suzan fhall be to come and unexpired of the faid Term he doing for the fame and pay-
ing from thenceforth as the faid Suzan fhould or ought
to have done if fhe had lived to the full end of the faid
Term   Item I will and bequeath unto my Brother
John Pope the Tenement adjoining to the eaft fide of
my faid dwelling houfe wherein John Moden now
dwelleth and during all fuch Term of years as I have
to come and unexpired of and in the fame by virtue of
the Leafe aforefaid fo as the faid John Pope and his Affigns during the continuance of the faid Term do pay
them half of the rent referved by the faid Leafe from
time to time and at fuch days and times as is limitted
by the fame Leafe and do perform fuch Covenants
touching only the faid Tenement to him my faid Brother bequeathed as are to be done by force of the faid
Leafe and alfo that my faid Brother do within one
month next after my deceafe enter into Bond of a reafonable

Robert Goughe, who had the honour
of reprefenting parts, in the Tragedyes, Comedyes,

fonable fum of money to my Executors for payment of
the faid moiety or one half of the faid Rent and performance of the Covenants touching the fame Tenement as aforefaid according to my true meaning and
intent in that behalf   Item I will and devife unto Mary
Clarke alias Wood all that Tenement adjoining to the
weft fide of my faid dwelling houfe wherein John
Holland now dwelleth for and during the continuance
of the Term of years which I have in the fame
(amongft others as aforefaid) by force or virtue of the
faid Leafe to me made by the faid Francis Langley to
be by her holden and enjoyed from time to time free
of any Rent to be paid for the fame fo long as fhe lives
and after her deceafe I give and bequeath my Intereft
and Term of years then to come and unexpired of and
in the faid Tenement unto Thomas Bromley who was
heretofore baptized in the parifh of St. Andrew's Un-
derfhaft in London   Item I give and bequeath to the
faid Marie Clark alias Wood and to the faid Thomas
Bromley as well all my part right title and intereft
which I have or ought to have of in and to all that
Playhoufe with the Appurts called the Curtein fitu-
ated and being in Hallywell in the parifh of St.
Leonard's in Shoreditch in the County of Middlefex as alfo all my part Eftate and Intereft which I

have

medyes, and Hiftories, of Shakfpeare, was, probably, bred by Thomas Pope. Goughe appeared,

have or ought to have of in and to all that Play-houfe with the Appurts called the Globe in the parifh of St. Saviours in the County of Surry Item I give and bequeath to the faid Thomas Bromley the fum of Fifty pounds and my Chayne of Gold being in value Thirty pounds and Ten fhillings to be paid and delivered unto him at fuch time as he fhall have accomplifhed his full age of one and twenty years provided in the mean time his Mother fhall receive thefe Legacies in regard the ufe thereof may bring up the Boy putting in good fecurity for delivering in the aforefaid Legacies at his full years of one and twenty and if the faid Thomas fhall happen to die and depart this mortal life before he fhall have accomplifhed his faid age of one and twenty years then I will give and bequeath the faid fum of Fifty pounds and the faid Cheyne of Gold unto the faid Marie Clarke alias Wood to her own ufe Item I give and bequeath to the faid Marie Clarke alias Wood the fum of Fifty pounds more provided always and my Will and Mind is that if the faid Marie fhall happen to die and depart this mortal life before the faid Thomas Bromley then the faid Fifty pounds fhall remain to the faid Thomas Bromley to be paid to him at fuch time as he fhall accomplifh the full age of one and twenty years Item I give and bequeath

appeared, with his mafter, in *Sardanapalus*, in the character of *Afpafia*; he had a legacy from

queath to Agnes Web my Mother the fum of Twenty pounds of lawful money of England and to my Brother John Pope the fum of Twenty pounds and to my Brother William Pope other Twenty Pounds   Item I give and bequeath to the Children of my faid Bretheren of John and William Pope the fum of Ten pounds to be paid and diftributed equal amongft the fame Children part and part alike   Item I give and bequeath to Robert Gough and John Edmans all my wearing apparel and all my arms to be equally divided between them   Item I give and bequeath to my Coufin Thomas Owen Five pounds   Item I give and bequeath to my loving Friend John Jackfon one Ring with a fquare Diamond in it   Item I give and bequeath to Marie Clarke alias Woode half my plate and to Suzan Gafquine the other half being equally divided between them   Item I give and bequeath to Dorothie Clark Sifter to Marie Clarke alias Wood one Gold Ring with five opalls in it   All the reft of my Rings I give to good Wife Willingfon who is now the keeper of my houfe   Item I give and bequeath unto my loving friend Bazell Nicholl Scrivenor the fum of Five pounds and to my neighbour and friend John Wrench the fum of Five pounds the refidue of all my Goods Rights and Chattels not before bequeathed my Debts and Funeral

from Pope, in 1603, of the teſtator's *wearing* apparel, and *arms*; he played in the *Second Mayden's Tragedy*, during the year 1611: But, he diſappeared, ſoon afterwards, ſo as not to be traced, either in the play bills, or at Doctor's Commons. The Puritans, who regarded plays, and actors, with a very evil eye, conſidered " players, as an abomina- " tion, that put on women's raiment."(*t*)

charge being firſt ſatisfied I wholie give and bequeath to my Mother my Brothers and their Children to be equally divided between them And I do ordain and ap- point my well beloved Friends Bazell Nicholl and John Wrench to be the Executors of this my laſt Will and Teſtament earneſtly praying and deſiring them to ſee the ſame performed in all things according to my true meaning therein And for becauſe much of this Money is out upon Bonds I do limit for the performance of this my Will ſix Months And thus not doubting but they will perform the truſt in this behalf by me in them re- poſed In Witneſs whereof I have ſet my hand and ſeal.   (Signed) Thomas Pope."
Sealed in the preſence of—John Wrench
                              John Edmans
(*t*) The Overthrow of Stage playes, 1599, without the name of the publiſher, or the place; Sign. C. iiii.

Whether

Whether Goughe, and his *fellows*, who, generally, reprefented women, were much affected by this reproach, it is not eafy to difcover, amid the difputes, about the lawfulnefs of the theatres. It feems to have been forgotten by the Puritans, in their zeal, that if recreation be neceffary to mankind, rational amufement may be juftified, as fit, from the neceffity.

SAMUEL GILBURNE, who alfo had the honour of reprefenting fome of the inconfiderable characters of our great dramatift, ferved his apprenticefhip with Auguftine Phillips, one of the fellows of Shakfpeare. When Phillips made his will, in 1605, he bequeathed to Gilborne, " his *late appren-* " *tice*, the fome of fortye fhillings, his " moufe coloured velvet hofe, and a white " taffety dublet, a black taffety fute, his " purple cloke, fword, and dagger, and his " bafe violl." Other notices about Gilborne, who probably lived, and died, in obfcurity, I have not been able to find, either in the play bills, or in the Prerogative Office.

WILLIAM

WILLIAM OSTLER, from the obfcurity
of his origin, may be fuppofed to have been
purveyed, like Tuffer, in early life, as a
finging boy. Certain it is, that as one of
the children of Queen Elizabeth's Chapel,
he reprefented one of Ben Jonfon's Characters in *The Poetafter*, during the year 1601.
When he ceafed to be a child, Oftler played
in Jonfon's Alchymift, in 1610; in *Catiline*,
during the year 1611; and in the *Dutchefs
of Malfy* of Webfter, in 1623. In Davis,
the Epigrammatift's *Scourge of Folly*, Oftler
is praifed as the *Rofcius* of the times: But,
fo many of the players were addreffed by our
Poets, by the name of the great player of
the Roman ftate, that we may reafonably
fuppofe, they did not very nicely difcri-
minate, when their defire to praife was
fcattering, with a lavifh pen, their *encomiums*,
which ceafe to be praife, if generally applied.

NATHANIEL FIELD was alfo one of the
children of the chapel, and one of the performers of Shakfpeare's charaéters. In Ben
Jonfon's *Comical Satyre*, called *Cynthia's
Revells*,

Revells, which was acted by the Queen's
Children of the Chapel, in 1600, Field
played a principal part.   In the fubfequent
year; he acted as one of the chief comedians,
in Jonfon's *Poetafter*.   When he left *the
Chapel*, he became, after the acceffion of
King James, one of the company called *the
Children of Her Majefty's Revells*.   In 1607,
he acted the part of *Buffy D'Ambois*, in
Chapman's Drama, and he performed, in
1609, one of the firft characters in Ben
Jonfon's *Silent Woman*.   Whether Field
were a writer, as well as an actor, of plays,
has admitted of fome doubt : Roberts, the
player, who, fmartly, animadverted on
Pope's preface, fpoke affirmatively, on the
point ; the intelligent writer of the *Biographia Dramatica* fpeaks, negatively ; giving
the difputable Dramas, to Nathaniel Field,
of New College, Oxford.   But, a begging
letter of Field, the player, which was preferved by Ned Alleyn, among Henflowe's
papers, and publifhed by Mr. Malone, has
decided the conteft, in the actor's favour :
For, the letter proves, that Field afked, and
received,

received, money from the liberality of honeft Henflowe, for *play writing* (*u*). Field,
the player, publifhed, in 1602, a comedie,
called, " *A Woman is a Weathercock;*" in
1618, another comedie, entitled, " *Amends*
" *for Ladies;* and, in 16 ̧2, " *The Fata*
" *Dowry*," which he wrote in co-operation/
with Maffinger (*x*), who, being equally
poor, and equally engaged in writing, when
confined in *durance* with Field, joined with
him, in begging the help of Henflowe. The
facts before ftated decide, in oppofition to
the Commentators, that Field, the player,
was the writer of the dramas. He died before the year 1641, though I have not been
able to difcover either his will, or the date
of his burial. It is a remark of Anthony
Wood, which applies pertinently to Field,
the poet-player; " So it is, and always has
" been, that poets live poor, and die in ob-
" fcuritie."

John Underwood appears to have held
nearly the fame courfe, through life, as

(*u*) Mal. Shak. pᵗ. 2. of vol. i. p. 324.
(*x*) Biog. Dram. 1. v. 159.

Nathaniel

Nathaniel Field.   Underwood was alfo one
of the Children of the Chapel; He performed in *Cynthia's Revels*, during the year
1600; in the *Poetafter*, during 1601; with
the King's Servants, he played in the *Alchymift*, in 1610, and in *Catiline*, in 1611: and
he reprefented *Delio*, in *The Dutchefs of
Malfy*, in 1623.   In this year, when Nicolas Tooley made his will, he kindly forgave Underwood the feveral fums of money,
which were due by him to the teftator.   Underwood had the honour to be one of the
performers of Shakfpeare's characters, and
enjoyed the benefit of being a fellow fharer
in the Globe, Blackfriars, and Curtain, Theatres.   He died, in January 1624–5; leaving five children, who had before loft their
mother; and now, had only their father's
" kind fellows, his Majefties Servants" to
protect their infant weaknefs.

William Ecclestone was alfo one
of the King's Servants, and equally reprefented with them Shakfpeare's characters at
the Globe, and at their ufual houfe, in the
Blackfriars.   He played in the *Alchymift*,
during

during 1610, and, during the fubfequent year, in *Catiline*. Nicolas Tooley, with his ufual benevolence, forgave Eccleftone, in 1623, all the debts, which were due to him. He difappeared, before the 6th of May, 1629, at which time he was no longer one of the King's players ; but, I have not been able to find his will in the regifters, either of the Bifhop of London, or of the Archbifhop of Canterbury. He, who acts an infignificant part, on the ftage of life, cannot hope to be long remembered, while fo many men of greater eminence are daily dif-appearing from the public eye.

Joseph Taylor is faid by tradition, which is not fupported by circumftances, to have played Hamlet, and Iago, when thefe characters were firft reprefented ; to have performed *True Wit*, in the *Silent Woman*, and *Face*, in the *Alchymift* ; though this af-fertion is not confirmed by Ben Jonfon him-felf. The player-editors ranked Jofeph Taylor, however, among thofe, who had the honour to reprefent Shakfpeare's charac-ters. He is faid to have been at the head of
the

the Lady Elizabeth's players, in 1614.
Whatever parts he may have acted, before
the year 1623, he was ftill poor, and low:
When the kind-hearted Nicolas Tooley, in
that year, made his will, he directed that,
" Whereas I ftand bound for Jofeph Taylor,
" as his furety, for payment of ten pounds,
" or thereabouts, my Will is, that my Ex-
" ecutors, fhall out of my eftate pay that
" debt for him, and difcharge him out of
" that bond." It is remarkable, that
Tooley does not call Taylor, a fellow.
Certain it is, however, that he was enume-
rated among the King's Players, on the 6th
of May, 1629, next to Hemmings, and
Lowin. In this year, he performed the
part of *Paris*, the tragedian, in Maffinger's
Roman Actor, at the private Playhoufe, in
the Blackfriars, with the King's Servants.
Among other wits, Taylor prefixed fome
encomiaftic verfes, " to his long known,
and loved friend, Mr. Philip Maffinger,
upon his *Roman Actor:*

" —————— But, why I write to thee,
" Is to profefs our loves Antiquitie,

                                    " Which

" Which to this Tragedie muſt give my teſt ;

" Thou haſt made many good, but this thy beſt."

In 1629, Taylor played the *Duke*, in Carlell's *Deſerving Favourite:* In 1630, he repreſented *Mathias*, a Knight of Bohemia, in Maſſinger's *Piƈture*, " a true Hungarian " Hiſtory." From this epoch, during many years, Joſeph Taylor aƈted, a conſpicuous part, as one of the chiefs of the King's Company, with Lowin, and Swanſton. In September 1639, he was appointed the Yeoman of the Revels, under Sir Henry Herbert, who found him an intelligent aſ-ſiſtant. Taylor was one of the ten players, who, in dedicating Beaumont and Fletcher's *Comedies and Tragedies* to the Earl of Pem-broke, in 1647, ſpoke with feeling recollec-tion of " the flowing compoſitions of the " then expired ſweet ſwan of Avon, *Shak-* " *ſpeare.*" Taylor died, in 1654, at a very advanced age, indeed, if he repreſented Hamlet, in 1596.

Robert Benfield appears to have come late into the King's Company, and to have repreſented, originally, but few of Shakſpeare's

fpeare's characters. He appeared, diftinctly, among the King's Players on the 6th of May, 1629. He buftled through feveral parts of no great difficulty; but he feems to have never rifen above the general level of the "Harlotry players." He lived to be one of the ten comedians, who, in 1647, dedicated to Philip, the Earl of Pembroke and Montgomery, Beaumont and Fletcher's *Comedies* and *Tragedies*; but I have not found any memorial of his laft Will, or of his final End.

RICHARD ROBINSON came early enough into life, and into action, to reprefent Shakfpeare's characters, in the fame fcenes, with Hemings, and Burbadge. In 1611, he acted with them, and the King's other players, in Ben Johnfon's *Catiline*. Even as late as 1616, he reprefented female characters, long after the Puritans had exhaufted their malignity, in thundering out anathemas againft fuch fuppofed profanations. In 1623, when Nicolas Tooley was difpofing of his property by will, he gave, " to Sara Burbadge, the " daughter of his late Mafter, Richard Bur-

N   " badge,

" badge, that fome of twenty nine pounds,
" and thirteen fhillings, which was owing
" to him by Richard Robinfon." He appeared in the fourth place among the King's
players, on the 6th of May, 1624. He
joined with the nine other players, in the
dedication of Beaumont and Fletcher's plays,
in 1647. There is a ftory told by Mr. Malone, which is repeated by Mr. Steevens,
that General Harrifon killed Robinfon, during the civil wars; the general crying out
with a fanatical tongue, when he gave the
ftroke of death; " curfed is he that doth
" the work of the Lord negligently(*y*)." But
the fact is, which is more credible than the
ftory, that Richard Robinfon died, quietly,
at London, in March, 1647, and was buried,
without an Anathema, in the cemetery of St.
Anne's, Blackfriars (*z*).

John Schanke was a comedian of an

(*y*) Steev. 1793, vol. i. p. 366.

(*z*) The Parifh Regifter, exprefsly, records, that
Richard Robinfon, a *Player*, was buried, on the 23d of
March, 1646–7 : So that there can be no doubt about
the identity of the perfon.

inferior

inferior caſt though he is ranked among
thoſe players, who had the honour of repre-
ſenting Shakſpeare's charaƈters. He aƈted
the *Curate* in Beaumont and Fletcher's
Scornful Lady, during the year 1616. Schanke
was a writer, as well as an aƈtor: And produced a comedy, called *Schanke's Ordinary*,
in March, 1623-4 (*a*). He ſtood the fifth,
in the liſt of the King's Players, in May,
1629. He was alſo one of Prince Henry's
Company. But, he died, probably, before
the year 1647; though I have not been able
to diſcover the time, or place, of his death,
or the will of this poetical player, who
like other poets, had little to leave behind
him, to his fellows, or relations.

JOHN RICE has ſtill leſs pretenſions to
fame, though he, too, performed ſome of
Shakſpeare's charaƈters. He aƈted the part
of *Peſcara*, in the Dutcheſs of Malfy,
during the year, 1623. He probably died

(*a*) The licenſe for this play, ſtands thus, in Sir Henry
Herbert's Regiſter: " For the King's Company;
" Shanke's Ordinary, written by Shankes himſelf, this
" 16th March, 1623."

N 2 before

before the year 1629; as he does not appear in the Lift of the King's Players, at that epoch; yet, have I not found the date of his deceafe, nor the record of his teftament.

JOHN LOWIN, who was probably born in 1576, feems firft to have appeared upon the Stage in Ben Jonfon's *Sejanus*, with Burbadge, and Shakfpeare, in 1603, after the acceffion of King James. In the fubfequent year, he came out with Burbadge, and Slye, in *the Induction* to Webfter and Marfton's *Malcontent*. The traditions, which have been handed down by Wright, and Roberts, about Lowin's reprefentations of Falftaff, Hamlet, and Henry VIII. cannot be true, if applied to any preceding period to the acceffion of Charles I. More experienced Actors performed Shakfpeare's characters, when they were firft prefented to the public. He certainly played in the *Fox* of Jonfon, in 1605, in the *Alchymift*, during 1610, and in *Catiline*, during 1611. He ftood the fecond in the enumeration of the King's players in the Lift of 1629, after Hemings, and before Taylor. In the far-
caftic

caſtic verſes, which were addreſſed to Ben
Johnſon, in conſequence of his inſolent
treatment of the public, it is ſaid :—

" Let Lowin ceaſe, and Taylor ſcorn to touch
" The loathed ſtage ; for *thou* haſt made it ſuch."

Theſe two players certainly became the
chiefs of the King's Company, after the ſe-
ceſſion of Condel, and Hemmings, about
the year 1627. In December, 1624, this
whole company, with Lowin, and Taylor,
at their head, were obliged to make a ſub-
miſſion to Sir Henry Herbert, for acting
the play, called *The Spaniſhe Viceroy*, without his licence, as Maſter of the Revels.
At a ſubſequent period, Lowin and Swanſton were obliged to aſk Sir Henry's pardon, " for their ill manners." In 1647,
Lowin, and Taylor, ſtood at the head of
the ten player-editors of Beaumont and
Fletcher's dramatical folio. In 1652, theſe
two concurred in publiſhing, as a trifling
reſource, during the miſeries of the grand
rebellion, *The wild gooſe chaſe* of Fletcher.
During a very advanced age, Lowin, for a
livelihood, kept an inn, at Brentford, called

N 3   The

The Three Pigeons. And, he finished his lengthened career of life, being buried in the cemetery of St. Martin's in the Fields, on the 18th of March, 1658–9, when administration to his goods was granted to Martha Lowin, who was probably either his widow, or his daughter. (*b*)

Such were the players, who, in conjunction with thofe more celebrated perfons, whom I formerly mentioned (*c*), were the actors, that reprefented Shakfpeare's characters, either when his dramas firft appeared, or when the original players had retired from the fcene. It was little forefeen, by any of them, that Shakfpeare's name would emblazon theirs; that their fame would be carried along the oblivious ftream of time, borne up by his ftrength, and eternized by the immortality of his renown.

It muft be allowed, however, that both the actors, and the dramatifts, owed great obligations to the Privy Council, and to

(*b*) Mal. Shak. vol. i. p'. 2. p. 205–8.
(*c*) Apology, 422 to 461.

Parliament,

Parliament, for their feveral regulations of the fcene; though they were not always grateful to their beft friends, who fupported their ufefulnefs, if at the fame time they corrected their abufes. The gentle Shakfpeare fometimes touched his fuperiors with a fine edged lancet: Ben Jonfon was prompted, by his natural ruggednefs, to ftrike them with a butcher's cleaver. In this manner, did he attempt to refift the Privy Council's order, in June 1600, " for " the reftraint of the immoderate ufe of " Playhoufes." In his Poetafter, which was acted, in the fubfequent year, by the Children of the Chapel, he made Tucca fay: " Thou fhalt have a *monopoly of play-* " *ing* confirmed to thee and thy *Covey*, un- " der the Emperor's broad Seal for this " Service (*d*)." Johnfon's farcafm incited the

(*d*) By not knowing, that there had been fuch a reftraint on the number of Playhoufes, the learned Whalley fuppofed, that awkward ftroke of the morofe Jonfon " to have been a flight gird at the practice of *mono-* " *polies*, now [then] growing into ufe." [Whalley's

N 4 Edit.

the playhoufe proprietors to perfevere in oppofing a falutary meafure; and their per-feverance, in obftinate error, induced the Privy Council to enforce, by feverer injunc-tions, an ufeful regulation.

It is from thofe regulations, as they ftand recorded, in the Council Regifters, and the Statute Book, that we now know fo many theatrical facts, which gave rife to the many conjectures of the hiftorians of our ftage. It was not known, or at leaft, had been little noticed, that, by a regulation of the fanatic Mary, which had been enforced by the wifer Elizabeth, plays had been looked into, and reviewed, even before Shakfpeare came out into fcenic life. This circumfpection, in refpect to the morals of youth, was carried to the two Univerfities, about the time, that Shakfpeare began to write for the ftage. From their attention to morality, the prudent councils of Eli-

Edit. 2. v. 99.] It cannot be too often repeated, that one fact is worth a thoufand pages of erudite con-jecture.

beth

zabeth extended their care to the interests of religion : As early as 1578, stage playing was forbidden in *Lent* ; and in 1587, the acting of plays, at the theatres, was prohibited on *Sundays*. For all the purposes of honest recreation, the number of playhouses was restrained to two, in 1600, the year when the bright Sun of Elizabeth began to set in Clouds.

The dawn of a new reign brought with it uncommon changes in the scenic world. The contemporaries of Shakspeare, who, at that epoch, were placed under a better regimen, almost all disappeared, with the effluxion of time, before the demise of James, in 1625. It is a curious fact, that at this epoch, the established Companies of London strolled often into the country; owing, no doubt, to the multiplicity of associated players, and the paucity of attractive plays (*e*). A still more remarkable fortune

(*e*) It appears from Sir Henry Herbert's Official Register, that on the 1st of July, 1625, he granted a Confirmation of the King's Company's Patent *to travel, for a year*. [Rym. Foed. 18 T. p. 120.]

attended

attended the Playhoufes than the actors. In 1589, there exifted in, and about, London, only two ; The *Theatre*, and the *Curtain* (*f*): Before the year 1629, there were erected, notwithftanding every oppofition, fifteen additional Stages, or Common Playhoufes, though thefe did not all exift, during the fame period. In 1613, the Globe Theatre was burnt, by the negligent difcharging of a peal of ordnance, during

(*f*) In Martin's *Month's Minde*, a fcarce pamphlet, which was printed, in 1589, without the name of the publifher, it was faid, fcoffingly : " And the other now " wearie of our State mirth, that *for a pennie* may have " far better by odds, at the *Theater*, and *Curten*, and " any blind playing houfe, every day."—This whimfical writer, is fuppofed to have been Thom Nafh :— " And this hath made the young youths his [Martins] " fons to chafe above meafure efpecially with the play- " ers, whom faving their liveries (for indeed they are " her Majefties men, and thefe not fo much as her " good fubjects) they call *rogues*, for playing their *en-* " *terludes* ; and affes, for travelling *all day* for a *pennie*.'' —Thefe Extracts fhew better, than has yet been done, the number of the Play-houfes, and the price of admiffion to them, about the year 1589, being the æra, probably, of Shakfpeare's acquaintance with the ftage.

the

the acting of Henry VIII; but, it was rebuilt, in the subsequent year, in a more
commodious form, and with more splendid
decorations.   In 1617, the Fortune Theatre, in Golden-Lane, was also burnt, by
negligence; but, was soon rebuilt, in a
handsomer style.   Five Inns, or Common
Oftleries, were converted into Play-houfes;
also a Cockpit, and St. Paul's singing
School; a Theatre was erected in the
Blackfriars; and during the year 1629,
another was established, in the White-
friars (g).   While Playhoufes were thus
destroyed, and built; while the managers
of public amusements did not yield prompt
obedience to public Authority; Sir William Davenant was empowered, on the
26th of March, 1639, to erect a new
Theatre, near the *Three King's Ordinary,*
in Fleet Street: But, on some difagreement
with the Earl of Arundel, the Landlord,
D'Avenant was obliged to relinquish a
project, which he was ere long enabled

(g) Howe's Chron. 103-4.

to profecute, in a different place, and form (*h*).

The

(*h*) The admirers of the Stage, and the lovers of truth, may be glad to perufe the Document, by which D'Avenant obliged himfelf to relinquifh his purpofe of building a Play-houfe in Fleet Street, which was copied from the original; and which was obligingly communicated by Mr. Craven Ord:—

This Indenture made the fecond day of October in the fifteenth yeare of the Raigne of our Soveraigne Lord Charles by the grace of God of England, Scotland, France, and Ireland King Defender of the faith &c. Annoq $\overline{\text{Dm}}$ 1639. Between the faid King's moft Excellent Ma[ty] of the firft part and William D'Avenant of London Gent. of the other part. Whereas the faid King's moft excellent Ma[ty] by his highnes Letters patents under the great Seal of England bearing date the fix and twentieth day of March laft paft before the date of theis prefents Did give and graunt unto the faid William D'Avenant his Heirs Executors Ad-miniftrators and Affignes full power licenfe and authority that he they and every of them by him and themfelves and by all and every fuch perfon or perfons as he or they fhall depute or appoint, and his and their labourers fervants and workmen fhall and may lawfully quietly and peaceably frame erect new build and fett up upon a parcell of ground lying neere unto or behinde the three Kings ordinary in Fleet Streete in the $\overline{\text{pifh}}$ of St. Dunftans in the Weft London, or in St. Brides London, or in either of them, or in any other ground in or about that place, or in the whole Streete aforefaid

The internal œconomy of the Stage,
which our theatrical hiftorians have laboured

aforefaid already allotted to him for that ufe or in any other
place that is or hereafter fhall be affigned and allotted out to
the faid William D'Avenant by the Right Honor[ble] Thomas
Earle of Arundle, and Surry Earle Marfhall of England or
any other His Ma[ts] Commiffion[rs] for building for the
time being in that behalfe a Theater or Playhoufe w[th] neceffary tyring and retyring roomes and other places convenient conteyning in the whole forty yards fquare at the moft
wherein plays muficall enterteynm[ts] fcenes or other the like
prefentments may be p[r]fented by and under certaine pro-
vifors or condicons in the fame conteyned as in and by the
faid L̄res patents whereunto relacon being had more fully
and at large it doth and may appeare : Now this Indenture
witneffeth and the faid William D'Avenant doth by theis
prefents declare his Ma[ts] intent meaning at and upon the
graunting of the faid Licenfe was and is that he the faid
William D'Avenant his heires Executors Adminiftrators
nor Affignes fhould not frame build or fett up the faid
Theater or Playhoufe in anie place inconvenient and that
the faid parcell of ground lying neere unto or behinde the
Three Kings Ordinary in Fleet Streete in the faid parifh
of St. Dunftans in the Weft London, or in St. Brides
London, or in either of them or in any other ground in or
about that place or in the whole Streete aforefaid, And is
fithence found inconvenient and unfitt for that purpofe,
therefore the faid William D'Avenant doth for himfelfe his
                                                    Heires

ed to difplay, though not in abfolute clearnefs, may receive fome illuftration from the
farcafm of a fatirift, during King James's
reign, who has been little noticed, by our

Heires Executors Adminiftrators and Affignes and every of
them covenante promife and agree to and wth o^r faid Soveraigne Lord the King his Heires and Succeffers That he the
faid William Davenant his Heires Executors Adminiftrato^rs
nor Affignes fhall not nor will not by vertue of the faid
Licenfe and Authority to him granted as aforefaid frame
erect new build or fett up upon the faid parcell of ground in
Fleet Streete aforefaid or in any other part of Fleet Streete
a Theater or Playhoufe, nor will not frame, erect, new
build or fett up upon any other parcell of ground lying in
or neere the Citties or Suburbs of the Citties of London or
Weftm^r any Theater or Playhoufe unles the faid place fhall
be firft approved and allowed by warrant under His Ma^ts
figne manuell or by writing under the hand and feale of the
faid Right Honble Thomas Earle of Arundell and Surrey.
In Witnefs whereof to the one p^t of this Indenture the faid
William D'Avenant hath fett his Hand & Seal the Day and
Yeare firft above written.

William D'Avenant. L. S.

Signed Sealed and Delived
   in the prefence of
      Edw. Penruddoks
      Michael Baker.

scenic

scenic writers. *In Follies Anatomy*, by Henry Hutton, it was said, sarcastically (*i*):

> " Blackfriers, or the Paris-garden bears,
> " Are subjects fittest to content your ears.
> " An amorous discourse, a Poet's wit
> " Doth humour best your melancholy fit.
> " The Globe to morrow acts a pleasant play,
> " In hearing it consume the irksome day :
> " Go take a pipe of *To*, the crowded stage
> " Must needs be graced with you and your page :
> " Swear for a place with each controlling fool,
> " And send your hackney servant for a stool."

Whether Henry Hutton lived to write more of *Follies Anatomy*, at a later period, I am unable to tell : Another wit of an higher vein of humour found abundant materials, for his satyric muse, during subsequent scenes of religious, and political, Contention, " when civil dudgeon first ran " high." The remnant of the commons of England, in setting forth, parliamentarily, their own merits, to the general assembly of the Kirk of Scotland, boasted, " that they had suppressed all Stage Plays,

(*i*) Printed for Walbank, 1619, in 12mo.

and

" and interludes, the nurſeries of vice,
" and profanenefs (*k*)."

—— § X. ——

Of the MASTER of the REVELS.

HOWEVER curious this fubjeét be in
itſelf; becauſe it is fo much conneéted with
our amuſements; I fear I can add little to
what I have formerly ſtated, either to gratify curioſity, by new notices, or to amuſe
the fancy, by more attraétive views of an
agreeable fubjeét.

The reign of a Monarch, who reformed
ancient eſtabliſhments, with a very rough
hand, gave origin to this eſtabliſhment
of the Revels, which was plainly a department of the Lord Chamberlain's Office (*a*).

(*k*) In a Letter from the Houſe of Commons in England
to the General Aſſembly of Scotland: Printed by Huſband,
in 1648.

(*a*) In the Apology, p. 472, it was ſaid, that to the
Lord Chamberlain belonged the high fuperintendance of
Coronations, Funerals, and Cavalcades: I now find, however, that the Heralds, who are the proper Judges of ſuch
points, doubt, whether the Lord Chamberlain's authority
extend to *Coronations*.

The

The year 1546, is the epoch of this new eftablifhment, for the regulation of public Sports. Sir Thomas Cawarden, who died in 1559, had the rule of *unwelcome revellers*, during four reigns :

"Of wondrous changes of a fatal fcene,
" Still varying to the laft." (*b*)

In thofe *various* changes, Sir Thomas Cawarden partook of his full fhare, both of merriment, and misfortune. After exhibiting before the gloomy Court of Mary, in April 1556, "A *notorious mafk* of Al-" maynes, Pilgrymes, and Irifhmen," he fell into difgrace (*c*). Whether it were, that the pulling down of St. Anne's Church gave offence to the ruling powers, who were actuated by religious zeal, I know

(*b*) In Stow's London, Edit. 1603, p. 343, it is faid, " There is a parifh church of St. Anne, within the pre-" cinct of the Black*fryers*, which was pulled down with " the *friers* church, by Sir Thomas Carden : But in the " raigne of Queene Mary, he being forced to find a church " to the inhabitantes, allowed them a lodging chamber " above a ftaire, which fince that time, to witte, the " yeare 1597, fell down."

(*c*) Apology, 478.

O   not :

not: But, it is certain, that he was obliged by the Privy Council, on the 7th of July 1556, to enter into a recognizance of £4000, to make his perfonal appearance, at a given time. He was committed to the Prifon of the Fleet, on the 15th of May, 1557. And, having made no acknowledgment " of his ill mifbehaviour to the " State," he was committed on the 14th of June 1557, to clofe prifon, with only one fervant, who was alfo fhut up with him in rigorous confinement (*d*). From this hard imprifonment, he feems to have been relieved, by the general deliverance of a new reign.

Sir Thomas Cawarden was fucceeded by Sir Thomas Berenger, or Benger, the fecond Son of Robert Berenger of Marlborough, in Wiltfhire, by Agnes, the Daughter of William Vavafor of Spaldington, in Yorkfhire (*e*). After receiving the ho-

---

(*d*) All thofe facts appear In the Privy Council Regifter of thofe dates.

(*e*) Col. Her. Vinc. Bucks, No. 138, fol. 13.

nour

nour of Knighthood, in 1553 (*f*), Benger became the fucceffor of Cawarden, both in his troubles, and his office. In 1554, Sir Thomas Benger being accufed of *Witch-craft* was committed to the Prifon of the Fleet, with only his Servant, Hutton, to attend him. On the 7th of July 1555, he was bailed. On the 27th of April 1557, he was again brought before the Privy Council; was once more committed to the fame prifon: And, he was, foon after, fent to the Affizes at Oxford, where he was probably acquitted of whatever Crime he was accufed (*g*). His fufferings under Mary were probably confidered, when he was appointed Mafter of the Revels by Elizabeth, in January 1559—60. During the rule of Benger, he had the fatisfaction to fee a progrefs in the Drama, from rude beginnings, to more mature formation, be-

(*f*) Apology, 480; wherein, Strype's Memorials, vol. ii. Apx. 11, is quoted, miftakingly, for vol. iii. Apx. 7.

(*g*) Council-Regifters, in the time of Mary, 257—261—278—610—629—638.

fore

fore the genius of Shakfpeare had produced a Tragedye, Comedye, or Hiftorye, or our Poet's Witchery had enlivened the gloom of the ancient *moralities* of the Englifh Stage. Having lived to behold *wondrous changes*, in the *varying fcene*, Benger died in March 1577; without having enjoyed any influence, or having acquired any wealth.

Edmund Tilney, who is called *Magifter Ludorum*, in the Regifters of the Herald's College, fucceeded the feeble Benger, in July 1579 (*b*). Tilney, who died in Octo-ber 1610, lived however to fee, with more fatisfaction, than his predeceffor felt, *immaturity* carried nearer to perfection, and with more vigour of mind to obtain a for-mal declaration of the precedence of his office (*i*). He faw the ftage regulated, by the

(*h*) 'See a curious account of the Tylney's in Hearne's *Langtoft*, v. ii. p. 670–75. Edmond Tilney, the Mafter of the Revels, is faid to have been the fon of Edmond, not of *Philip*.

(*i*) [The following Certificate of the precedency of the Mafter of the Revels was extracted from the Records of the College

the higheſt Authority, and the Dramas
reviewed by " honeſt, diſcreet, quiet, and
" godly,

College of Arms, by the obliging activity of Francis Townſ-
end, Windſor.]

Whereas Edmond Tylney Eſquier, Maiſter of yᵉ
Queenes Maˡˢ Office of the Revells, hath in regard of
ſome controverſies lately growne betweene him and others
for the p'cedency of theire offices being verie unwilling as
he ſaieth eyther to p'judice his ſaid office and his ſuccef-
fors therein, or to challeng yᵗ unto himſelfe yᵗ juſtly
appteyneth vnto others: Required vs by vertue of our
offices to ſett downe truly yᵉ place of his ſaid office according vnto our beſt Recordes concerning the ſame: Wee
therefore Garter Clarenceux and Norrey Kings at Armes
doe ſignifie by way of certificat vnto whome it ſhall con-
cerne yᵗ yᵉ ordering and directing of all Princely Triumphes
and Revells having ever bin an office of ſpeciall Regarde
and Accompt as well in forraine contries as within this
realme: And becauſe yᵉ cheife Comanders thereof have
likewiſe bin placed in theire precedency accordingly that in
regard of the p'miſſes it was thought good by yᵉ Right
Honorable yᵉ L. Burghley Lord High Treaſorer of England and Deputy Earle Marſhall for yᵉ tyme aſſiſted wᵗ Sʳ
Chriſtoper Hatton Lord Chancelloʳ of England and Henry
L. of Hunſdon L. Chamberlen to the Queenes Maᵗⁱᵉ yᵗ then
were wᵗ others comyſſions for thoſe cauſes aſſigned by Her
Maᵗʸ in Anno 1588 yᵗ yᵉ ſaid Maiſter of yᵉ Revels ſhould be
marſhalled amongſt other Officers of like note and accompt;

O 3   and

" godly, learned, men." He had the honour of perufing Shakfpeare's plays, as
they came from his plaftic hand ; and had
the gratification to behold Shakfpeare's characters, as they were reprefented by Burbadge, Hemmings, and Condel; who, unhappily, did not leave :

" ———— a better race to bring
" Into their vacant room."

With the confent of Tilney, no doubt,
and by his recommendation, perhaps,
George Bucke, his kinfman, obtained a
reverfionary grant of the Office of the Revells, in June 1603 ; at which time, he was
knighted, and appointed one of the King's

and yet notw'ftanding according vnto y⁰ antiquity of y‍ᵗ
office as he was by theire Lᵖˢ placed in yᵗ Recorde and
ratefied vnder theire Lᵖˢ handes : Whereby y⁰ faid Edmond Tylney Efquier Maifter of the Revells is to myngle
wᵗ fhofe Knightes Officers yt have theire p'cedencies before
all other Batchelor Knightes accordingly: And wᶜʰ Record
being our cheife and laft Warrant may not be altered or
infringed but by y⁰ the like authority otherwife then by the
faid Maifter of y⁰ Revells owne curtefie and difcrecon as
wee conceive y⁰ fame : Gyven from our office this xxviᵗʰ of
December in the xliii yeere of Her Maᵗˢ Raigne.

Gentlemen

Gentlemen of the Privy Chamber (*k*). In 1605, Sir George Bucke attended the Lord Admiral Howard, on his fplendid embaffage to Spain; wherein he was accompanied among other attendants, by four Lords, and twenty-fix Knights (*l*). Soon after his return from Spain, Sir George began to act, as affiftant to Tilney (*m*). Which-foever of the Dramas of Shakfpeare,

----

(*k*) Apology, 488 : What was faid, in that page of Sir John Bucke being attainted for helping Richard to a horfe on Bofworth-field, I have now reafon to doubt, though Sir George Bucke had ftated this, as a fact, in his Hiftory of Richard the Third.

(*l*) Old Biograph. Brit. 4th vol. p. 2679.

(*m*) The firft play, which appears in the Regifters of the Stationer's Company, as licenfed by Sir George Bucke, was the *Fleire*, on the 21ft of November 1606: On the 29th of June following, Mr. Tilney licenfed *Cupid's Whirligigge*: and on the 4th of October 1608, Mr. Segar, *the Deputy* of Sir George, licenfed *A Mad World my Mafters*. Thefe dates fhow, with fufficient diftinctnefs, when Sir George Bucke began to act, as an affiftant, and when as a principal, in the office of the Revels: And thofe dates alfo correct what was faid, on this fubject in the Apology, p. 488-9, and

confute

Shakſpeare, Sir George Bucke licenſed for
repreſentation, he licenſed but few of them
for

confute what was ſtated by Mr. Malone, in his Shakſpeare, vol. i. pᵗ. ii. p. 45.

The following plays were licenſed by Sir George
Bucke, as appears by the Stationer's Regiſters:

1606	6 May	-	*The Fleire*, provided Authority he got.
	21 November		By Aſſignment, a Comedie called, *The Fleire*.
1607	10 April	-	The Tragicall Life and Death of Claudius Tiberius Nero. [Anon.]
	20 April	-	The Whore of Babylon.
	22 April	-	The Faire Mayde of the Ex-change.
	9 May	-	The Phoenix.
	15 May	-	A Comedy called Mychaelmas-Terme.
	20 May	-	*The Woman Hater*; as it hath been lately acted by the Chil-dren of Powles.
	3 June	-	The Tragedye of Buſye Dam-boiſe, made by George Chap-man.
	29 June	-	The Travilles of the Three En-gliſh Brothers: As it was played at the Curten.

laſt

for publication.   He appears to have been
" a man well learned, and well read,
                                      " who

Laſt July -	A Tragedie:—The Miſerye of Enforced Marriage.
6 Auguſt	The Comedye of *the Puritan Widow.*
————	*Northward Ho.*
	A Comedie called, *What you Will.*
7 October	Twoo plaies:—The *Revengers Tragedie.—A Trick to Catch the Old One.*
12 October	A playe called, The *Family of Love:*—as yt hath beene lately acted by the Children of *his* Majeſty's Revels.
16 October	The Tragedie of Alexander the Sixt;—as it was played before his Majeſty.
22 October	A plai—*The Merry Devill of Edmonton.*
26 November	Mr. Willm Shakeſpeare his Hiſtorye of Kinge Lear; as it was played before the King's Majeſtie at Whitehall upon St. Stephens night at Xmaſs laſt, by his Majeſty's Servants, playing uſually at the Globe on the Bankſide.

                                      1607-8

who governed his icenic dominions, during difficult times, with great ability. He relinquifhed his adminiftration to Sir John

1607–8	22 March	The *Fyve Wittie Gallants :*—as it hath been acted by the children of the Chapell.
	28 March	A moft wytty and merry conceited Comedie, called—*Who would a thought it :* or Lawtryks.
	12 April -	A B. *Humour out of Breathe.*
	21 April -	The Characters of Twoo Royal Mafkes : Invented by Ben Johnfon.
	29 April -	The 2nd p^{te}. of the convicted Courtifan, or Honeft Whore.
	20 May -	The Booke of Pericles Prynce of Tyre. Anthony and Cleopatra.
	3 June -	A Romane Tragedie, called *The Rape of Lucrece.*
	5 June -	The Confpiracy and Tragedie of Charles Duke of Byronn : Written by Geo. Chapman.
	6 October	A playe of The Dumbe Knight.
1619	10 July -	The Temple Mafke.—An. 1618.
1621	6 October	The Tragedie of Othello.

Aftley,

Aftley, about the end of the year 1621; and died, on the 22d of September 1623, as Sir Henry Herbcrt noted in his regifter; having lived to fee the great actors of his time, fucceffively go off the Stage, of reprefentation, and of Life.

It is a fact, which has hitherto been unknown to the moft diligent inquircrs; and which is recorded in Sir Henry Herbert's Regifter, that Sir George Buck's books were burnt, though it appears not, whether by accident, or defign (*n*). I fufpect, however, that the MS. hiftory of Richard, the III. which remains, to this day, in the Cotton Library, though greatly damaged by fire, may have been fcorched, on that fad occafion. It is much to be lamented, that the books, and papers, of fo ingenious a perfon, fhould have fallen a prey to fo relentlefs a deftroyer.

(*n*) On the 3d of May 1624, Sir Henry Herbert ftates, that he had licenfed, without a fee, *Jugurth,* an old play, allowed by Sir George Bucke, and *burnt, with his other books.*

I was

I was induced, chiefly, by the ftrong affertions of Mr. Malone (*o*), to doubt, whether
The Hiftory of the Reign of Richard III. were
written by Sir George Bucke, the Mafter
of the Revels, or by George Buc, his relation. Further inquiry has convinced me,
however, that there can be no controverfy,
where there is fatisfactory information. In
the Catalogue of the Cotton Library,
which was compiled before the unlucky
fire, that did fuch irreparable damage to
that collection, this MS. is called " The
" hiftory of King Richard the third com-
" prized in five books, gathered and writ-
" ten by Sir G. Buc, Knight, Mafter of the
" King's Office of the Revels, and one of
" the gentlemen of his Majefty's Privy
" Chamber; corrected and amended in
" every page." The original MS. which
ftill remains, in the Britifh Mufeum (*p*),
though it be greatly damaged by fire,

(*o*) Shakf. 1 vol. p'. ii. p. 47, which contradicts the
New Biographia, and Anthony Wood, who were both
right, upon the point.

(*p*) Cott. MS. Tiberius E. X.

clearly

clearly proves, that the Catalogue is perfectly accurate. This MS. appears to have
been the Author's rough draught; as it is
corrected, by interlineations, and erafe-
ments, in every page. A part of the Dedication to Sir Thomas Howard, the Earl
of Arundel, &c. ftill remains, together with
" an advertifement to the Reader," which
is dated " from the King's Office of the
" Revels, St. Peter's hill, the   of
1619." This evidence, then, is decifive,
in favour of Sir George Buck, as the real
Author, againft Mr. Malone. This *Hiftory*
was firft publifhed, in 1647, by George
Buck, Efquire, who fays, indeed, in his
Dedication to Philip the Earl of Pembroke
and Montgomery, " that he had *collected*
" *thefe papers out of their duft :*" Yet, was
the publifher, whether he were the Son of
Sir George, or fome other relation, fo dif-
ingenuous, as to affume the work as his
own; and fo interefted, as to publifh for
his own profit, what, certainly, was the
property of another. It feems to have
been the fafhion, in the age of Sir George
                                              Buck,

Buck, to vindicate Richard the III. but
whether from the reprefentations of Shakfpeare, only, I am unable to tell : Sir William Cornewallis, the Younger, who wrote
an Effaye in *prayfe* of the *French Pockes,*
publifhed, before the deceafe of Shakfpeare,
an Effaye, in vindication, and praife, of
King Richard the III (*q*).   Sir George
Buck,

(*q*) I quote from the *Second* Impreffion *inlarged,*
which was publifhed, for Hawkins, in 1617.—With
regard to this curious fubject, I beg leave to fubjoin a
paffage, which I found, written in a hand of the age of
James I, on the margin of Ulpian Fulwell's Flower of
Fame, 1575 ; wherein it treats " of the Battaile fought
" at Bofworth, betweene King Henry the VII, and
" Richard that then ufurped the Crowne :"—

" Some peremtory or malicious writers (being blinded
with ignorance and wanting the vnderftanding they
profeffe to have) are not (only) content like fome cob-
lers to go beyond their laftes but in their ignorant prefumption (being lead (onely) by popular examples, by
thcir clark's imputations often defame thofe that deferve prafe and comendation amongft which King
Rich. iij of famous memery (for all fuch virtues as may
make a prince praife worthy) hath too largly (and
againft his defert) tafted of their inveterate fpleene :—
but a juft confutation of all their unjuft and falfe imputations

Buck, who will be long remembered, for his learned labours, and from his Connection with the ftage, refigned his adminiftration of *The Revels* to Sir John Aftley, in 1621.

Sir John, to whatever caufe it were owing, relinquifhed the management of the Revels to Sir Henry Herbert, even before the deceafe of Sir George Buck (r). Sir Henry, no doubt, owed this early appointment to the management of the Revels, chiefly, to his relation, Philip, the Earl of Pembroke, the Lord Chamberlain; and partly to his Brother George Herbert, whofe power of pleafing captivated King James (l).

During

putations are clerely and with truth wiped of from that inocent prince by the thrice noble and famous fcoller Sᵣ. G. Buc: in v bookes which hee hath (with fpecial knowledge) written in King Richard's defence againft all his malicious foes.   DEUS JUVIT."

(r) Apology, 495.

(s) The fucceffor of George Herbert, in the parifh of Bemerton, the Revᵈ. William Coxe, the well known
Tourift,

During the adminiftration of Sir Henry
Herbert, the Mafter of the Revels, as appears from his Official Regifter, exercifed
not only a peculiar jurifdiction over the
ftage, the plays, and the players, but alfo an
unlimited authority over every other *fhow* ;
whether natural, or artificial; whether of
trick, or ingenuity (*t*) ; with the yet greater
power

Tourift, has informed me, from the Regifter of that
parifh, " That Mr. George Herbert, Efquire, Parfon
" of Fugglefton, and Bemerton, was buried the 3d of
" March 1632-3:" He lies under the Altar, covered
with a grave-ftone, without any Infcription.

(*t*) Sir Henry Herbert granted, on the 20th Auguft
1623, a licenfe *gratis*, to John Williams, and four
others, to make *fhowe* of *an Elephant*, for a year ; on the
5th of September to make fhowe of a *live Beaver* ; On
the 9th of June 1638, to make fhowe of an outlandifh
creature, called a *Poffum* ; a licenfe to a Dutchman to
fhow two *Dromedaries*, for a year, for which, the licenfer received one pound ; a warrant to Grimes, for
fhowing *the Camell* :—On the 14th of Auguft 1624, a
licenfe was granted to Edward James to fett forth a
Showing Glafs, called the *World's Wonder* : On the 27th
of Auguft 1623, a licenfe was granted to Barth. Cloys
with three Affiftants to make fhow of a *Mufical Organ*,
with divers motions in it ; to make fhow of an *Italian
Motion* ;

power to allow, or difallow, the printing
of books: For licenfes on all thofe accounts,

Motion; to fhow *a Looking Glafs*; to fhow the *Philofopher's Lanthorn*; to fhow *a Virginal*:—A licenfe was
granted to Henry Momford, and others, " for tum-
" bling, and vaulting, with *other tricks of flight of hand* ;"
for *a prize* at the Bull by Mr. Allen, and Mr. Lewk-
ner ; to William Sands and others to fhow " the *Chaos*
" *of the World* ;" to fhow a motion called *the Creation
of the World*; to fhow certain *freaks* of *charging* and
difcharging a gun; a licenfe to Mr. Lowins, on the 18th
of February 1630, for allowing of *a Dutch vaulter*, at their
Houfes, [the Globe, and Blackfriars.] A warrant was
given to Francis Nicolini, an Italian, and his Company,
" to dance on the ropes, to ufe *Interludes*, and *mafques*,
" and to *fell his powders, and balfams* :"—to John Punc-
teus, a Frenchman, profeffing *Phyfick*, with ten in his
Company, to exercife *the quality of playing*, for a year,
and to *fell his drugs* : On the 6th of March, a licenfe
was given *gratis* to Alexander Kukelfon to teach the
art of *mufick* and *dancing*, for one year ; A licenfe to
Thomas Gibfon, to make fhew of *pictures in Wax* :
And, the mafter of the Revels appears alfo to have
licenfed books, during the reigns of King James, and
Charles the 1ft ; he received a fee, for allowing Ovid's
Epiftles, tranflated into Englifh ; he received a fee,
for a book of verfes of my Lord Brook's, called *Cælia*;
he received of Sayle, the Bookbinder, *ten* fhillings, for

P   allowing

counts, the Mafter of the Revels required a fee; and a Chriftmas box of forty fhillings, from each of the eftablifhed theatres. (*u*)

Sir Henry Herbert exercifed thofe extenfive trufts, during a long life, through difficult times, with great difcrimination of judgment, and firmnefs of decifion. He, no doubt, received fome ufeful affiftance from George Wilfon, who was fworn his Majefty's Servant, and a Groom of his Majefty's Revels, in ordinary, on the 4th of February, 1624–5 (*x*). Whether this office of Groom of the Revels were diftinct from

---

allowing to be printed two other fmall pieces of verfes, done by *a boy* of *thirteen,* called *Cowley.* I have now given fufficient fpecimens, out of a great variety, which appear on Sir Henry Herbert's Regifter; in order to evince the univerfality of the jurifdiction, which was, in thofe times, exercifed by the Mafter of the Revels.

(*u*) The fame Regifter alfo proves, that his ufual fee for licenfing a play, contrary to what was faid in the Apology, p. 520, was twenty fhillings, except when he had extraordinary trouble in making Corrections; and then he had forty fhillings.

(*x*) Sir Henry Herbert's Official Regifter.

the

the Yeoman of the Revels, I am unable to explain : Certain it is, that William Hunt, and after him, Joſeph Taylor, were Yeomen of the Revels, while George Wilſon was the Groom. With all thoſe helps, Sir Henry Herbert's duty ſometimes ſlept; owing to the multifarious nature of his office. When the ſceptre of the ſtage was delivered into his hands, there appears from the record of his office, to have been four eſtabliſhed companies of players; excluſive of ſtrangers, who ſometimes invaded their territories. The players, whether licenſed, or unlicenſed, ſeem to have been unruly ſubjeƈts, who required vigilant ſuperintendence, and powerful coercion. Refraƈtorineſs, in the governed, generally, produces tyranny in the rulers. During the turbulent period, which extended from 1623, to 1643, Sir Henry exerted the unbounded power over the dramatic world, which his royal maſters were unable to exerciſe over the ſtate. On the 12th of May, 1636, warrants were ſent to the *four* companies to ſtop the plays, on account of the peſt. Owing to the ſame

caufe,

caufe, Sir Henry, upon conference with the Earl of Effex, the Lord Chamberlain, concerning the plague, which had increafed to a hundred deaths a week, fent warrants, by Mr. Louens, on the 5th of Auguft, to the feveral playhoufes, for the purpofe of preventing their reprefentations: The plague, having decreafed to eighty fix deaths a week, induced the Lord Chamberlain to open the theatres, for the profit of the players, and the amufement of the people.

But, they were only opened to be fhut, ere long, by a power, which was full as deftructive as peftilence. The Ruler of the Revels could exert little authority, when his fubjects were difperfed, and his realms an-nihilated. Anarchy is fure to enfeeble, if it do not deftroy authority. The re-efta-blifhment of his ancient jurifdiction, did not re-eftablifh his power, even after the re-ftoration had recalled the fovereign, and given energy to the laws. The Mafter of the Revels, while his power was oppofed, felt himfelf unfupported: And, he was thus induced to retire to the quiet of the coun-

try,

try, and the enjoyment of his domain, from a fcene, which he could neither rule, nor influence. Advanced to a mellow age, Sir Henry Herbert died, in 1673; having governed, almoft half a century, with found difcretion, a

" ——— Calm region once,
" And full of peace, now toft and turbulent. '(*y*)

While

(*y*) The fubjoined Extracts, from Sir Henry Herbert's Official Regifter, are fubmitted, as a proper fupplement to what has been faid, with regard to the long Adminiftration of that able Officer; and becaufe they contain fome new, and fome curious facts :—

1622 10 May   -   A new Play, called, *The Blacke Ladye*, was allowed to be acted by the Lady Elizabeth's Servants.

    10 May   -   A new Play, called, *The Welfh Traveller*, was allowed to be acted by the players of the Revels.

    3 June   -   A new Play, called, *The Valiant Scholler*, allowed to be acted by the Lady Elizabeth's Servants.

    10 June -   A new Play, called, The Duche Painter, and the French *Branke*, was allowed to be acted by the Princes Servants at the Curtayne.

P 3 1623

While the waves were yet heaving, from
the late ftorm, Sir Henry Herbert was fucceeded

1623 27 July - For the Palfgrave's Players, a Tragedy of Richard the Third, or
the Englifh Profit, with the Reformation, written by Samuel
Rowley.

30 July - For the Prince's Players, A French
Tragedy of *the Bellman of Paris*,
written by Thomas Dekkirs and
John Day, for the Company of
the Red Bull.

Auguft For the Company at the Curtain;
A Tragedy of *the Plantation of
Virginia*; *the profanenefs to be left
out*, otherwife not tolerated.

19 Auguft For the Prince's Servants of the
Red Bull; an Oulde Playe,
called, *The Peaceable King*; or
the *Lord Mendall*, which was
formerly allowed by Sir George
Bucke, and likewife by me.

21 Auguft For the Lady Elizabeth's Servants
of the Cockpit; An Old Play,
called, *Match me in London*;
which had been formerly allowed by Sir George Bucke.

29 Auguft For the King's Players; a new
Comedy,

ceeded by Thomas Killigrew, a poet, and a wit; but an officer of lefs difcretion, with more

	Comedy, called, *The Maid of the Mill*; written by Fletcher, and Rowley.
12 September	For the Lady Elizabeth's Players; a new Comedy, called, The Cra.... Marchant, or *Come to my Country houfe*: Written by William Bonen. It was acted at the Red Bull, and licenfed without my hand to itt; be-caufe they were none of the *four* Companys.
18 September	For a Company of Strangers; a new Comedy, called, *Come fee a Wonder*: Written by John Deye.
2 October	For the Prince's Companye; a new Comedy, called, *A Fault in Friendfhip*: Written by *Young* Johnfon, and Broome. [Thefe were the *Son*, and Servant, of Ben Jonfon.]
17 October	For the King's Company, An Old Play, called, *More Diffemblers befides Women*: allowed by Sir George Bucke; and being free

more facilities. Having feen, during his youth, many revolutions in the ftate, and in

		from alterations was allowed by me, for a new play, called, *The Devil of Dowgate*, or *Ufury put to ufe :* Written by Fletcher.
1623	29 October	For the Palfgrave's Players; a new Comedy, called, *Hardfhifte for Hufbands*, or *Bilboes the beft blade*, Written by Samuel Rowley.
	19 November	For the Palfgrave's Players; a new Tragedy, called, *Two Kings in a Cottage :* Written by Bonen.
	28 November	For a Strange Company at the Red Bull; *The Faiyre fowle one*, or The *bayting of the Jealous Knight ·* Written by Smith.
	3 December	For the Queen of Bohemia's Company; *The Noble Bondman :* Written by Philip Meffenger, gent.—This was allowed to be printed on the 12th March 1624.
	4 December	For the Palfgrave's Players; *The Hungarian Lion :* Written by Gunnel.
	6 December	For the King's Company: *The Wandring Lovers :* Written by Mr. Fletcher.

1624

in his maturer age, various alterations, in the fcenic world, he died, in March, 1683; the ftage being then doom'd to feel:—

"———— A different Mafter, and a change of time."

By

1624	2 January	For the Palfgrave's Company; *The Hiftory of the Dutchefs of Suffolk*; which being full of dangerous matter was much reformed by me; I had two pounds for my pains: Written by Mr. Drew.
	6 January	For the Prince's Company; *The Four Sons of Amon*; being an Old Playe, and *not of a legible hand.*
	26 January	For the Palfgrave's Company; A Tragedy, called, *The whore in grain.*
	3 March	For the Cockpit Company; *The Sun's Darling*; in the nature of a mafque by Deker, and Forde.
	6 April -	For the Fortune; a new Comedy, called, *A Match or no Match :* Written by Mr. Rowleye.
	17 April -	For the Fortune; *The Way to content all Women,* or *how a Man may pleafe his Wife* : Written by Mr. Gunnel.

17 April

By this change, Charles Killigrew, became Mafter of the Revels, a perfon of
more

	17 April	-	For the Cockpit; *The Renegado, or the Gentleman of Venice:* Writ-ten by Meffinger.
1624	3 May	-	For the Prince's Company; A New Play, called, *The Madcap:* Written by *Barnes.*
	3 May	-	An Old Play, called, *Jugurth,* King of Numidia, formerly al-lowed by Sir George Bucke.
	15 May	-	The Tragedy of *Nero* was allowed to be printed.
	21 May	-	For the Palfgrave's Company; a Playe, called, *Honour in the End.*
	27 May	-	For the King's Company; A Co-medy, called, *A Wife for a Month:* Written by Fletcher.
	27 May	-	For the Prince's Company; A Play, called, *The Parracide.*
	11 June	-	A new Play, called, *The Fairy Knight:* Written by Forde, and Decker.
	3 September		For the Cockpit Company; A new Play, called, *The Captive,* or *The Loft recovered:* Written by Hayward.
	September		A new Tragedy, called, *A Late Murther*

more difcretion than his predeceffor, and of
equal

> *Murther of the Sonn upon the Mother :* Written by Forde, and Webfter.

15 September For the Palfgrave's Company ; A Tragedy, called, *The Faire Star of Antwerp.*

14 October For the Cockpit Company ; A new Play, called, *The City Night Cup :* Written by Davenport.

15 October For the Palfgrave's Company ; A new Play, called, *The Angell King.*

22 October For the Palfgrave's Company ; A new Play, called, *The Briftowe Merchant :* Written by Forde, and Decker.

3 November For the Cockpit Company ; A new Play, called, *The Parliament of Love :* Written by Maffinger.

For the Palfgrave's Company ; A new Play, called, *The Mafque.* The mafque book was allowed of for the prefs ; and was brought me by Mr. Jon[fon] the 29th December 1624.

1625 25 January For the Prince's Company ; A new Play, called, *The Widow's Prize ;*

equal knowledge of the theatre (z). *Under different masters*, during five reigns, he endeavoured, by prudent management, to correct the *profaneness*, which was still found in plays, and to regulate the amusements

Prize; which containing much abusive matter, was allowed of by me, on condition, that my reformations were observed.

8 February For the King's Company; An Old Play, called, *The honest Man's Fortune*; the original being lost, was reallowed by me, at Mr. Taylor's intreat, and on condition to give me a book.

11 February For the Cockpit Company; A new Play, called, Love-Tricks with Compliments.

(z) Amidst the penury of anecdotes, with regard to Charles Killigrew, I will beg leave to add, that Dryden, speaking of Varronian Satires, says that, " Among " the Moderns we may reckon the *Encomium Moriæ* of " *Erasmus*, Barclay's *Euphormio*, and a volume of Ger- " man Authors, which my *ingenious friend* Mr. Charles " Killigrew once lent me." [Dedication of Juvenal's Satires, 1702. p. xlvii.]

of

of the fcene. At length, dying in January, 1725,

> " —————————————— Amazed, he
> " Beheld th' amufive arch before him fly,
> " Then vanifh quite away."

By the deceafe of Charles Killigrew, the
difputed fceptre was delivered, in June,
1725, to Charles Henry Lee, a perfon of lefs
power, and of more obfcure exiftence. It
was, during the unfuccefsful management
of his enfeebled authority, that the frequent
rampancy of the *revelrout*, demanded the
act, *for licenfing the Stage* (*a*). He died,
in 1744, after feeing various fhifts of the
fcene; and beholding a new power impofe on it additional reftraints (*b*).

Solomon

(*a*) Apology, 537.

(*b*) I have been affured by the Reverend William Coxe,
who is known by his extenfive travels, and is refpected for
his literary labours, " That Charles Henry Lee, the Mafter
" of the Revels, could not be the fame Charles Henry Lee,
" who is faid to have died, in 1744, leaving a minor widow,
" the adminiftration of whofe effects was granted [on the
" 24th of January, 1744, Apology 537] to Elizabeth
" D'Aranda, the mother, and curatrix affigned to Martha
" Lee, the widow of the deceaft; becaufe the faid Charles
" Henry

Solomon Dayrolle fucceeded, as Mafter of the Revels, to Charles Henry Lee, in April, 1744, though it is not eafy to tell, wherein his office confifted; except that he had a lodging of no convenient extent, and a fee of no great value. His ancient jurifdiction had been transferred, in 1737, by legal authority, to a *Licenfer of the ftage*, and to the deputy licenfer, who thenceforth performed between them, all the functions

" Henry Lee was not more than twenty three years of age,
" when he died : He was page to the Princefs Amelia, at the
" time of his death, which happened in November, 1743. The
" faid Martha Lee married to a fecond hufband Dr. William
" Coxe, Phyfician to the King, and was the mother of the
" faid Reverend William Coxe, Rector of Bemerton.
" There was another Charles Henry Lee, his relation;
" they were both probably of the Litchfield family."
Such are the corrections of Mr. Coxe, from the traditions of his family. There was, no doubt, another William Henry Lee, who was the Mafter of the Revels : and who died, in the beginning of the year 1744; as Solomon Dayrolle was appointed his fucceffor, in April, 1744. But, how to diftinguifh *Antipholis* of Ephefus, from *Antipholis* of Syracufe, is beyond my powers of difcrimination. Here is a remarkable example of the foolifhnefs of demanding demonftration in the affairs of daily life!

of

of the ancient office of the Master of the Revels ; and who are, to this day, empow_ered, by legal means, to execute the invidi_ous trusts, which experience dictated, and policy conferred.

I have now supplied a few deficiences, and corrected some errors of my own, and of others. The little, which my subsequent re-searches have been able to add to the full account, given in *the Apology,* of *the Master of the Revels*, I now offer to the admirers of the Drama, as useful supplements to scenic history.

—— § XI. ——

Of the STUDIES of SHAKSPEARE.

Of such a writer, as this celebrated dra_matist, who amuses the young, and instructs the old ; who is admired the more, that he is the better understood; the universal wish must be, to know every authentic particular of *his private life*, and *literary history*, which are both involved in *palpable obscurity*, partly by the unskilfulness of his first biographers,

and

and partly by the prejudices of his fubfequent Commentators.

Twenty years have elapfed, fince Mr. Steevens wrote the life of Shakfpeare, in three lines; " All that is known" fays he, " with any degree of *certainty*, concerning " Shakfpeare, is, *that he was born at Strat-* ' *ford upon Avon ;* married, and had chil- " dren, there; went to London, where he " commenced actor, and wrote poems, *and* " *plays ; returned to Stratford, made his will,* " *died, and was buried* (*a*)." Short, as this biographical fketch is, it might have been fhortened, by excluding the uncertain, and curtailing the verbofe. The biographer, however, " confeffes his readinefs to combat " every *unfounded fuppofition* refpecting the " particular occurences of his life." Every rational man muft concur in reprobating this hoftile preparation :

" Each mind is preft ; and open every ear,
" To hear new tidings, though they no way joy us."

Yet, if the meaning of this hoftility be, to

(*a*) Mal. Sup. 1780. vol. i. p. 654.

combat

combat every propofition, about the private life, and literary hiftory, of Shakfpeare, which is not fupported by *demonftration;* every well informed perfon, who knows, that fuch enquiries do not admit of *demon-ftration*, muft revolt againft a mode of rea-foning, which would deftroy all the proba-bilities of life, and darken all the profpects of futurity. In fact, Mr. Steevens has done very little towards illuftrating the life, and literary hiftory of Shakfpeare; while Mr. Malone has laboured, with inceffant folici-tude, to illuftrate the obfcure, and to afcer-tain the doubtful, with regard to both, during twenty years, although with no great fuccefs.

About the place, and time, of the birth of Shakfpeare there has never been any difpute. Nor, is there much doubt, whether he learned his *fmall Latin* and *no Greek*, at the Free-fchool of Stratford upon Avon. It is full as certain that the grammatical inftitute, which inftructed the energetic mind of Shak-fpeare, in the elements of latinity, was the grammar of Henry VIII: For, by Queen

Q   Elizabeth's

Elizabeth's Injunctions of 1559, it was directed, " that every Schoolmaster " shall " teach the grammar set forth by King " Henrie the Eight of noble memorie, and " continued, in the time of Edward the Sixth, " and *none other* (*b*)." From those authorities, we may easily infer, what grammatical garden supplied Shakspeare with The *Floures* for *Latine Spekying*.

His English style, which is doomed to endure for ever; his poetic diction, which improved the language of his age; and his nervous manner, which rivets the attention of posterity, he derived from the vigor of his genius, and the spirit of the times: The prose of that period was poetic; as the dramas of the present day are prosaic.

The biographers, without adequate proofs, have bound Shakspeare an apprentice to some country attorney; as Mr. Malone has sent

(*b*) Injunction N° 39: The Booke of certain Cannons, 1571. p. 25, injoins, " that no other grammar shall be " taught, but only that which the Queen's Majestie hath " commanded to be read in all Schooles, through the whole " realm."

him

him, without fufficient warrant, to the defk
of fome Senefchal of a county court: But thefe
are obfcurities, that require other lights, than
conjecture, and affertion, which, by proving
nothing, only eftablifh difbelief (*c*). It can,
however, admit of neither controverfy, nor
doubt, that Shakfpeare, in very early life, fettled in a *family way*, where he was bred; as
he was born, in April 1564, was married
in Summer 1582, and had a daughter, who
was baptized, in May 1583. Where he thus
fettled, he probably refolved, that his wife,
and family fhould remain through life; although he himfelf made frequent excurfions
to London, the fcene of his profit, and the
theatre of his fame (*d*). It is ftill uncertain

　　　　　　　　　　　　　　　　　　　　at

(*c*) Apology, 553.

(*d*) The Regifter, which records the fucceffive baptifms,
marriages, and deaths, of his children, incidentally, records
the refidence of Shakfpeare's family, in Stratford upon
Avon; in 1583—1585—1596—1607—1615—1616.—
This evidence is fo fatisfactory, that it has compelled even
Scepticifm to admit my pofition to be very *probable*. It is
moreover, remarkable, that both Ben Jonfon, in his com-
mendatory verfes, and the Player-editors of Beaumont and

　　　　　　　　　　　　　　　Fletcher's

at what epoch he made his firſt excurſion to London. He had attracted ſome notice, as early as 1592; he was praiſed, in 1594; and he was celebrated, in 1598, at the age of thirty-four, as one of the greateſt poets of the reign of Elizabeth.

Whatever may have been the firſt production of his pen, certain it is, that his *Venus* and *Adonis* was written, in 1592; or at leaſt, before 1593, when Field, the Bookſeller, recorded it as his property, after having received the Archbiſhop's licenſe. It is more than probable, that he had read Wilſon's *Art of Rhetorique* (*e*), Aſcham's Scholemaſter, the Arts of Poeſy of Webbe, and of Puttenham; and perhaps Sydney's *Defence of Poetry:* Yet, is Shakſpeare ſaid, by Warton, " to have been only a reader by accident (*f*). He, certainly, was not the fel-

Fletcher's Works, in their Dedication to the ſame Philip Earl of Pembroke, to whom Shakſpeare's Dramas had been dedicated, in 1623, call Shakſpeare " the ſweet Swan " of *Avon*," *the place* of *his reſidence.*

(*e*) Apology, 559—560—562.

(*f*) Hiſtory of Poetry, v. iii. p. 393.

low

low of a College, if this honour be neceffary
to conftitute a reader by fyftem.   Shakfpeare,
however, not only read much in the volume
of life; but our poet was an attentive peru-
fer of the books, which related to *his faculty:*
And, noting down in a *Common-place-book*,
what he had read, or obferved, he prepared,
diligently, to write for immortality (*g*).

Whoever perufes with any attention, the
volumes of Shakfpeare, will readily recognize
the extent of his reading, and the carefulnefs
of his notation. In *the Apob gy*, I quoted a curious paffage from Marfton, a contemporary
fatirift, as a proof of my pofition : But, the
application of this paffage to Shakfpeare has
been difputed by the anonymous critic before
mentioned (*h*).   The chief objection is, that
the fatirift, merely, meant to draw characters in
the *general*, without any *particular* allufion.
But, is this remark warranted by *the fact ?*
The anfwer muft be, that it is not.   His firft
character, fays the critic, " is that of *a man*

(*g*) Apology. 568-9.   (*h*) Brit. Crit. v. ix. p. 518.

Q 3   " whofe

" whofe rage is dancing." No: not of *a man ;* but of a *particular* man, the writer of a *poem* on *dancing* ; " Praife but *Orchefra*," fays Marfton, " and the *fkipping art.*" Now ; who wrote *Orchefra ?* The anfwer muft be, Sir John Davis, the celebrated author of *Nofce Teipfum*, wrote the poem on dancing, entitled *Orchefra*. And, the fatirift, immediately, adds,

" ——— They'll revel with neatt jumps
" A *worthy poet* hath put on their pumps."

We have here Sir John Davis, particularly, defcribed, as a worthy poet, who wrote *Orchefra*. But, had the fatirift, Shakfpeare in his mind? Yes, in the preceding verfe the fatirift cries out :

" ——— *A hall ! A hall !*
" Roome for the Spheres, the orbes celeftial
" Will dance Kemp's jigge."

We have here more *particularity ;* the pofitive mention of *Kemp*, a living player ; and an allufion to Shakefpeare, a living dramatift ; as, indeed, he had, in a preceding fatire of the fame collection, 1599, exclaimed " A " Man ! a Man ! a Kingdom for a Man !" And, muft I, in a controverfy with a commentator

mentator on Shakfpeare, *demonſtrate*, that Marſton meant, herein, to parody Richard the third's well known exclamation on Boſworth Field (*i*)? After all thoſe *particularities*, and *alluſions*, the ſatiriſt, immediately, ſubjoins the character, not of a dramatiſt, but of a ſpecial play-writer; the writer of *Romeo and Juliet*, which play is mentioned, at the outſet of the character, as the preface to it.

Yet, cries the Critic, " Is this a picture " of our beloved Shakſpeare ?" I anſwer, yes, expreſſly : I have already proved, that the ſatiriſt was not writing of fictitious characters, but of *living Characters:* He mentions the *Orcheſtra* of Davis, the *Jigge* of Kemp, the *Romeo* and *Juliet* of Shakſpeare. The commentators, Mr. Steevens, and Mr.

(*i*) It is a fact, which cannot be diſputed, that Marſton was, in 1599, very intimately connected with Ben Jonſon, who was then at variance with Shakſpeare: Marſton, and Jonſon, afterwards quarrelled; as ſuch poets could not long be friends: Marſton again parodied Shakſpeare, in his *What you will*, 1607, wherein he ſays; " Looke ye, I " ſpeak play ſcrapes."

Malone,

Malone, have fhewn, by an enumeration of particulars, that Shakfpeare has fcarcely written a play, that he did not borrow from fome preceding drama, from fome Chronicle, or novel; taking from them, as fuited his dramatical purpofe, fentiments, fcenes, expreffions, and paffages : The commentators, then, muft be, equally, bound by what they admit, as they muft be convinced by what they prove. I have already fhewn, that " Our beloved Shakfpeare," undoubtedly, borrowed from the wealthy Spenfer.

I will repeat, what I have already faid, and prove, what is plainly demonftrable, viz. that Shakfpeare was a diligent reader, and *copious collector*. The contemporary of Shakfpeare, Webfter (*k*), who knew him perfectly, fays, in the preface to the *White Devil* (*l*), what the commentators, and critics, would do well to profit by : " *Detrac-* " *tion is the fworn friend to ignorance :* For

(*k*) For Webfter, fee the Biographia Dramatica, in vol. i. p. 465.

(*l*) Webfter's *White Devil* was publifhed, in 1612, 4°; and in 1631, 4°.

" mine

" mine own part, I have ever truly cherifhed
" my good opinion of other mens worthy
" labours, efpecially, of that free and
" heightened ftyle of Mafter Chapman:
" The laboured and underftanding works of
" Mafter Jonfon : The no lefs worthy com-
" pofures of the both worthily excellent
" Mafter Beaumont, and Mafter Fletcher:
" And, laftly, (without wrong laft to be
" named) the right happie and *copious in-*
" *duftrie* of M. Shake-fpeare, M. Decker,
" and M. Heywood ; wifhing what I write
" may be read by their light." Impoffible,
cries the Critic! Would Webfter, who was
himfelf a dramatift, rank Shakfpeare after
Chapman, Ben Jonfon, Beaumont, and
Fletcher ; and only place our illuftrious dramatift, at the laft, with fuch fcriblers as
Decker, and Heywood ; and merely fpeak
of Shakfpeare's *copious induftry ?* The *pofitive*
fact is a decifive anfwer to the queftion. The
critic-commentators, and commentator-cri-
tics, feem unable to carry their minds back
to the age of Shakefpeare ; and to judge of

men

men, and of things, according to the fentiments, and practices, of the fame age.

" Oh fie! fie !" cries the Critic ; " from
" fuch difcoveries may we be ever free!
" This, Shakfpeare ; a fellow, that never
" fpeaks but when plays, and players, are
" the fubject ; or fpeaks only common
" place fcraps, which he had written in a
" book (*m*)." Yes ; fuch is the Critic's
parody on the fatirift's character. The fact
is, Shakfpeare did delight to fpeak about
his profeffion ; Garrick delighted to fpeak
about his profeffion ; and other men of genius delight, in the prefent day, to fpeak of
their profeffions ; becaufe it is human nature
to do fo.

I have now proved, I truft, in oppofition
to the Critic, that Marfton meant to draw
particular, and not *general*, characters ; fe-
condly, that he fpoke, efpecially, of Shakfpeare ; thirdly, that our dramatift was deemed, in his day, by thofe who knew him, to
be a writer of *copious induftry* ; and, fourthly,

(*m*) Brit. Crit. 9 vol. 518.

that

that Shakfpeare did delight to talk of his profeffion (*n*): Nor, is there any thing to be deducted from the perfonal character, or the fair fame of Shakfpeare, if thofe pofitions be admitted, in their full extent:

" Bring, then, his merits to a ftrict account ;
" Make fair deductions ; See to what they mount."

I will produce another Satirift to make deductions from the character of Shakfpeare, without fearing, that it will be leffened in the amount. Ben Jonfon's fifty-fixth Epigram, " *On Poet-ape*," was intended, I believe, as a lampoon on Shakfpeare. Thus:—

" Poor *Poet-ape*, that *would be thought our chief*,
    " Whofe works are e'en the frippery of wit,
" From brokage is become fo bold a thief,
    " As we, the robb'd, leave rage, and pity it.

(*n*) The Critic goes out of the character, which the Satirift drew, and which I applied, and do apply, to Shakfpeare, when he reprobates the Character, becaufe it is faid, that our great Poet " had an inability " to talk of any thing but plays and players." [Brit. Crit. 9 v. 518.] This is a quite different propofition, which fhows, that the Critic has yet a leffon of candour to learn.

" At

" At firſt, he made low ſhifts, would pick, and glean ;
 " By *the reverſion of old plays*, now grown
" To a *little wealth*, and credit in the ſcene,
 " He takes up all, makes each man's wit his own :
" And, told of this, he ſlights it. Tut ! ſuch crimes
 " The ſluggiſh gaping Auditor devours ;
" He marks not whoſe 'twas firſt ; and after times
 " May judge it to be his, as well as ours.
" Fool, as if half-eyes will not know a fleece
 " From locks of wool, or ſhreds from the whole piece."

Fie ! Fie ! Fie ! cries the Commentator-Critic: We will not believe, that Ben Jonſon would write ſuch a lampoon on Shakſpeare ! Why will you not believe it ? becauſe, ſay ye, you do not *demonſtrate* the truth of the imputation. Nay ; my poſition does not admit of *demonſtration:* I only propoſe to ſupport my belief by *probability.* I will, however, ſay with *Gonzales:*

 " Whether this be,
 " Or be not, I'll not ſwear :

And apply to the Commentator-Critic, with *Proſpero:*

 " You do taſte
 " Some ſubtilties o' th' iſle, that will not let you
 " Believe things Certain."

In order to enable us to decide what we ought to believe, in theſe matters, as *things certain*

certain, we muſt look back upon the early
management of our theatres.   The papers
of Henſlowe, the well known manager of ſo
many theatrical companies, which Mr. Malone procured, for a valuable conſideration,
from Alleyn's College, at Dulwich, throw
many flaſhes of light on this obſcure ſub_
ject.   It is apparent, from theſe manuſcripts,
that the poets of the days of Elizabeth, and
of James, ſupplied the ſtage, with dramas,
more for profit than for reputation.   If we
except Ben Jonſon, perhaps, there were none
of the dramatiſts, including Shakſpeare, ſpe-
cifically, who cared for literary reputation.
The managers of the theatres, who paid their
money for plays, conſidered theſe plays, as
ſo much their own, that they could either
curtail them, or make *addycyons* to them: In
fact, they often paid one ſet of poets, to alter
the dramas of another ſet; without conſidering the literary reputation of the original author. (*o*)

(*o*) See Steev. Shak. vol. ii. p. 444 to 489.

It

It is to thofe caufes, that we muft trace up the circumftance of fo many defpicable dramas being attributed to Shakfpeare, which he never wrote, but which may have been altered, either by additions, or curtailments: Hence, *Pericles*, *Locrine*, *Sir John Old Caftle*, *Lord Cromwell*, *The London Prodigal*, *The Puritan*, *The Yorkfhire Tragedy* (*p*); were all attributed to Shakfpeare, during his life time, by interefted bookfellers, without caring for confequences, either immediate, or remote. Of the company, which ufually acted at The Globe Theatre, Shakfpeare was, no doubt, the revifer of the plays, which were offered for reprefentation; and the perfon, certainly, who made additions, and curtailments : From this view of the fubject, it is eafy to perceive how compleatly Shakfpeare had, within his power, the whole of the Dramas, which were acted at *The Globe*.

It is a curious fact, which has been little noticed, that Shakfpeare, as reader of his company, altered Ben Jonfon's *Sejanus*, be-

(*p*) Mr Malone's Suppl'. 1780. v. 2.

fore

fore it was acted, in 1603: Ben, however, was too proud, or self-sufficient, to allow Shakspeare's alterations to stand, when he afterwards printed this tragedy; as an appeal from the audience, who had damned it, to the public, who might save it. On this occasion, Jonson informed " the readers, that " this book, in all numbers, is not the same " with that, which was acted on the public " stage; wherein, a *second pen* had good " share; in place of which, I have rather " chosen to put weaker, and, no doubt, " less pleasing of mine own, than defraud " *so happy a genius* of his right, by my " *lothed Usurpation.*" Whalley asserts, that the *happy genius*, before alluded to, was undoubtedly Shakspeare (*q*). To this truth, add another circumstance, which is, that Shakspeare never appears to have acted in any of Ben Jonson's dramas, after the representation of Sejanus, in 1603.

There was certainly a quarrel between the two great dramatists of that accomplished

(*q*) Whalley's Ed. Jonson's Works, vol. ii. p. 130.

period.

period. In the Cambridge Comedy, called *The Return from Parnaſſus*, Kempe, the witty player, is made to ſay, in 1602: " Oh! that " Ben Jonſon is a peſtilent fellow: He " brought up Horace, giving the poets a " pill; but, our fellow Shakſpeare hath " given him a purge, that made him bewray " his credit." In what *this purge* conſiſted, it is not eaſy to tell: Shakſpeare may have *purged Sejanus* from its crudities, when it was referred to him, for reviſal, and amendment: And, Ben Johnſon was plainly offended by Shakſpeare's amendments. Add to all theſe particulars, that Marſton was, at that period, in the frequent practice of courting Jonſon, but of ſcoffing Shakſpeare.

From this excurſion, into the purlieus of the theatres, let us return to Jonſon's Epigram on *Poet-ape*. Who, then, in the contemplation of Ben Jonſon, was the *Poet-ape?* The anſwer is, " he, that would *be thought* " *our Chief* (r);" the *Chief* of the dramatic poets

(r) As early as, 1592, Shakſpeare was ſatirized by Robert Green, " As an *upſtart Crow*, beautified with *our* " *feathers*

poets; whofe works, in the envious judgment of Ben, " are e'en the fripperie of wit."
This Poet-ape would buy *the reverfion of old
plays* as a *broker:* But, by *brocage,* the *Poet-
ape* had *grown* to a *little wealth* and *credit in
the fcene.* Now, what dramatic poet, in that
age, except Shakfpeare, grew to a *little
wealth,* and credit in the fcene? *The
Poet-ape makes each man's wit his own.* The
two commentators, who have juft been
quoted, Mr. Malone, and Mr. Steevens,
have fhewn, clearly, how many of the dramas of Shakfpeare were taken from preceding
plays: Shakfpeare, then, *made each man's wit
his own;* yet, his commendation is, that he

" *our feathers*" [the Poet's feathers.]   This *upftart Crow*
" fuppofes he is as well able to bombafte out a blank
" verfe as the beft of you; and is, in *his own conceit*
" the only *Shake-fcene* in a Country." [Steev. vol. i.
486; Mal. vol i. p. 273.] The imputations caft on
Shakfpeare by the two fatirifts, Green, and Jonfon,
are fo much alike, that it is inferable, Jonfon muft have
had his eye on the farcafms of Greene. Mr. Malone,
and Mr. Steevens, after him, both agree, that the *Shake-
fcene* of Green was the Shakfpeare; the chief of the
Dramatic Poets.

R   was

was the induftrious *bee*, " which ftole the
" *honey-bag* from the *humble bees*." Tut!
this *honey-bag*, " the fluggifh, gaping, au-
" ditor devours;"—nor, " marks whofe
" 'twas firft; and oftentimes may judge it
" to be his, as well as ours." Such was
the malignity of Ben! The eye, which con-
templates thofe various circumftances, muft
be blind, indeed, if it do not fee, that Shakfpeare was *The Poet-ape* of Ben Jonfon.
Nor, was Jonfon at all overawed by Shakfpeare's fuperiority; a fuperiority, which his
felf-fufficiency leffened, and his m lice are-
viled. Jonfon had even the *Audacity*, according to Mr. Malone's expreffion, which
Mr. Steevens has adopted, " to write a play,
" after our author, on the fubject of King
" Richard III. (*s*)" And, this act of audacity furnifhes an additional probability, that
the fame audacioufnefs would lampoon the
man, whom Jonfon hated, and deride the
poet, whom a rival did not fear.

When Shakfpeare had paid to Heaven the

(*s*) Steev. vol. ii. 484.

debt

debt he owed, Jonfon came forward with a copy of verfes, which were prefixed to our poet's dramas; although the poor panegyrift has been fufficiently penurious of his praife. But, Shakfpeare was not any longer the mark of his refentment, nor a rival's fuccefs the object of envy. And Jonfon's aukward panegyrick on the poet, when dead, whom he had derided, while living, can only be confidered, as the effufions of infincerity, without the merit of commendation. It is to be remembered, alfo, that, fubfequent to the deceafe of Shakfpeare, Jonfon fpoke of him, contemptuoufly, to Drummond of Hawthornden; faying, " that Shakfpeare wanted " art and fometimes fenfe; for he had fhip- " wrecked fome mariners, in Bohemia, " where is no fea, fo near as a hundred " miles." (*t*)

Whatever Jonfon might fay, I ftrongly

(*t*) Drummond's Works, Ed. 1711. p. 225: Drummond the amiable, and acute, Drummond remarked of his friend Jonfon " that he was a great lover and praifer " of himfelf: a great contemner and fcorner of others." [Ib. 226.]

fufpect

fufpect, that fometimes Shakfpeare, like Marfton, *willingly erred* (*u*). Shakfpeare, was not only a better poet, but was alfo a man of more difcernment, and intelligence, than Marfton; though perhaps not fo good a fcholar. While Shakfpeare was yet young, the field of geography was much cultivated, on the Continent, by Mercator, and Ortelius; by Hondius, and Magini. During the reign of Elizabeth, voyages, and travels, had been made over the whole globe. Thofe parts of Science, which are connected with navigation, and geography, were much ftudied, in England, during the fame period by Cunningham (*x*), by the Diggses, and Bourne (*y*), and Blundville; by Wright

(*u*) In the preface to the *Malcontent*, 1604, Marfton avowed, " that he had *willingly erred*, in *Suppofing a* " *Duke of Genoa.*" Marfton dedicated *The Malcontent* to Jonfon, as a mark of his efteem.

(*x*) The *Cofmographical Glaffe* was publifhed, in 1559, by William Cuningham, Dr. in Phyficke.

(*y*) See William Bourne his Booke, called, *The Treafure for Traveilars*, 1598 : Of the Citie of *Prage* [the capital of Bohemia] he fays, " the Long. is 38 " Degrees

Wright (*z*), Hill (*a*), and Olyver (*b*). Even before the year 1599, a controverfy arofe, between
Wright, our countryman, and Hondius, who
was brought by Wright, to confefs, that he
had publifhed, as his own, fome difcoveries
in the theory of Navigation, which had been
made by his opponent. There were publifhed, in the fame age, Chorographical defcriptions of particular countries: And, travels into every part of Europe, Afia, and
Africa, were publifhed to the Englifh world,
during the whole period from 1592, to 1615;
a period, in which Shakfpeare exerted his

" Degrees 20 Min. the Lat. 50 Degrees 6 Min. and is
" Eaft, and a lytle to the South, 700 myles from Lon-
" don."—There was publifhed at London, in 1599, *A
Brief Defcription of the Whole World*; Wherein [Sign.
A. iii.] " *Bohemia* is defcribed as a kingdome in the
" middle of Germanie, which is compaffed round with
" a mightie Wood, called, *Silva Hicimia* [Hercinia]:
" The chiefe citie whereof is called Prage."

(*z*) Certain errors in Navigation by Edward Wright,
1599.

(*a*) The *School of Skill*, by Thomas Hill, 1599.

(*b*) The new Handling of the Planifphere: by Thomas
Olyver, 1601.

R 3   vigorous

vigorous faculties to inftruct, and pleafe, by his immortal dramas (*c*): And, Shakfpeare muft have known, therefore, the fituation of *Bohemia*, in the middle of Germany; but, it fuited the purpofe of his mufe to err, willingly. Shakfpeare appears, then, to have been *the reader*, on whofe judgement, and help, *his fellows relied*, for fatisfactory opinions, with regard to the adoption of every play : But, he was never the manager of the company, as I have formerly intimated (*d*); becaufe Hemminge, and Pope, were the managers from 1596, to 1604; when Cundel fucceeded, in this department, on the death of Pope. If it be true, as I have alfo proved, that Shakfpeare never removed his family to London, but continued through

(*c*) There was publifhed by Norton, the King's Printer, at London, in 1606, " *The Theatre of the* " *Whole World:* fet forth by that excellent Geographer " *Ortelius.*" This great work was *confecrated* by Norton to King James : The maps were in Latin; but the defcriptions were in Englifh. It is more than probable, that fuch an eye as Shakfpeare's muft have looked on this *Theatre of the World.*

(*d*) Apology, 597.

life,

life, *the fweet fwan of Avon*, he could not, owing to his diftance from London, attend to the common concerns of the company, as a manager (*e*); nor was he diverted from his ftudies, by the dull duty of providing " Clownes Sewtes, and Hermetes Sewtes, " and dievers other apparel, for the tier " houfe (*f*)."

Shakfpeare's *mufe, not wholly bent on what was gainful,* purfued fometimes ftudies lefs dramatical. And fhe produced, not in her infancy, but in her prime, *The Sonnets* which Mr. Steevens fuppofes to have been one of her *earlieft* compofitions (*g*). Certain it is, however, that Shakfpeare wrote his Sonnets, fubfequent to the publication of Spenfer's *Amoretti*, in 1595, and, probably, during the year 1597; in which year they were handed about in manufcript, among the *friends of his foul* (*h*).

It

(*e*) Apology, 597-8.

(*f*) Henflowe's *Enventary*, Steev. 2. vol. 459-461.

(*g*) Mal. Supl⁺. 2 vol. p. 594.

(*h*) *The Wit's Treafury* of Meres, which was fent to the Prefs in the Summer of 1598, fpeaks of " Shakf-

" peare's

It has not yet been fettled, upon fuch decifive circumftances, when Shakfpeare began to write for the ftage. Neither has it been fixed, by fuch facts, nor afcertained by fuch deductions, as defy criticifm, and preclude inveftigation, in what fucceffion, he wrote his comedyes, tragedyes, and hiftories. I propofe to fhow, in the fequel, that, on this interefting head, our commentators have written with more elaboration, than certainty : " People forget how little " they know, when they grow confident, " upon any prefent ftate of things."

It is an inveftigation much more eafy, in the purfuit, and more pleafing in the detail, to exhibit the courfe of ftudy, which enabled Shakfpeare to produce five and thirty dramas, within a fhort period of his life. This great performance of a vigorous mind could not have been atchieved, if Shakfpeare had not been a *diligent reader*, and a *copious collector*, as I have already fhown. Langbaine was

" peare's Sugred Sonnets among his private friends."
p. 281.

the

the firft (*i*), who pointed out diftinctly, the track of Shakfpeare's reading, in Italian Novels, Englifh Chronicles, and Plutarch's Lives, as tranflated by North. A lift of the claffic authors, which had been tranflated, into Englifh, has been fince compiled, and publifhed; in order to prove, that Shakfpeare might have known ancient hiftory, without being a claffical fcholar. It was referved for the laborious Capel, to give to the world *The School of Shakfpeare ;* exhibiting " au- " thentic extracts from divers Englifh books " that were in print, in that author's time; " and, evidently, fhowing, from whence " his feveral fables were taken, with fome " parcels of his dialogue." This volume is not only a work of extraordinary labour, but is a compilation of great ufe to thofe, par- ticularly, who are not fo fortunate as to pof-

(*i*) In his *Momus* Triump*hans* : Or the *Plagiaries* of the *Englifh Stage :* Printed, in 1688, 4°. In this work, Langbaine fhows more reading, than the late Mr. Thomas Warton, and his followers, were difpofed to allow him. The Commentators have all borrowed, co- pioufly, from Langbaine, without acknowledgement.

fefs

fefs the original writers. The refearches of
Capel evince, that Shakfpeare cultivated a
very wide field of ftudy; and the poet's
dramas demonftrate, that he had read, with
attentive difcernment, and treafured up for
ufe, with appropriate diftinctnefs, what he
had read. Capel, while compiling *The
School of Shakfpeare*, thought more of himfelf, than of others : And, when he ceafed
to labour, others thought more of themfelves, than of him. Although *prefent time
doth ever boaft itfelf above a better*; Yet,
future times are the true appretiators of the
real merits of the paft.

It muft be acknowledged, however, that
Capel was a man of but narrow comprehen-
fion, a writer of confined views; as his
School of Shakfpeare evinces. The ftudies
of Shakfpeare were commenfurate with the
Englifh literature of his age: And, *the
School of Shakfpeare* ought to contain not
only the novels, the Englifh Chronicles,
the Greek, and Roman Lives, as they had
been tranflated by North; but alfo the
whole hiftory of *letters*, during the reign of
Elizabeth :

Elizabeth : The progress of philological learning, the cultivation of the more practical parts of science, such as geography, and navigation ; and the denization of foreign erudition. Without taking in all those various departments of learning, it is impossible to show, by what artifices of study, Shakspeare acquired such various knowledge, communicated so many lessons of practick morality, and conveyed his instructions, in language, at once, easy, energetic, and sublime.

He, who undertakes the difficult task of writing *the School of Shakspeare*, ought to be extremely attentive to the current of our language, during the poet's life, as it passed along before him ; in order to catch the words as they rose, or sunk, during the different periods of an improving age. The commentators on this great writer have not always been sufficiently observant, in these respects ; to the flux, and efflux, of our speech, and to the innovations of our grammar : and they have sometimes done injustice to Shakspeare, by not attending, accu-

rately

rately, to the double meaning of words, the paft, and the prefent. I formerly exemplified this remark (*k*), by a quotation from Midfummer's Night's Dream : " No night is now with hymn, or *carol* bleft." The commentators explained this, which is fufficiently obvious to thofe, who know our ancient phrafeology, by faying, that hymns, and *Carols*, were fung in the time of Shakfpeare; but without adverting, that both in the paft, and the current fenfe, to *Carol* fignified to dance. (*l*)

Neither the compiler of *the School of Shakfpeare*, nor the commentators on his works, have been fufficiently attentive to another operative part of writing, during the period of our poet. I allude, particu-

---

(*k*) Apology, 565.

(*l*) To *Karole*, in Langtoft's Chron. means to dance: See Hearne's Glof. in Vo.—without any other fignification; fo in Robert of Glocefter: But, at the Epoch of Shakfpeare's appearance in the Theatre, the fame word had acquired the double meaning, of to fing, as well as to dance. [Gram. Anglicana, 1594, in the Gloffary.]

larly

larly, to the practice of punctuation, which
I formerly noticed (*m*). It is apparent, from
the Elementary Treatifes, which Shakfpeare muft have read, before he began to
write, that punctuation had not then been
finally fettled; though its practice had been
often taught. Among other writers, Puttenham treated of this fubject, in his *Art of
Poetry*, 1589(*n*): And, in fpeaking of the
Cæfure, he notices the Comma (,); the colon (:); the period (.); but, not the femicolon (;), which was not then known,
either in the theory of compofition, or the
practice of typography: It was, therefore,
faid by Johnfon, upon juft confiderations,
that the punctuation of Shakfpeare's text is
in the power of every commentator. (*o*)

Yet, with the truth of this obfervation
before them, our late commentators have
not been very ftudious to point the text of
Shakfpeare, upon any fyftematic principles ;
neither with any juftice to their author, nor

(*m*) Apology, p. 390-5.
(*n*) P. 61.　　(*o*) Apology, 590.

with

with any affiftance to their readers. This
obfervation could be demonftrated from
any play, in any of their volumes: But, I
will exemplify my obfervations, by a few
quotations from *All's well* :—

" Yes, [;] Helen, you might be my Daughter-in-
" Law; [:]

" God fhield, [!] you meant it not! [;] daughter, and
" mother,

" So ftrive upon your pulfe: [.] What, [!] pale
" again? [;]

" My fear hath catch'd your fondnefs: (*p*)"

I have pointed this paffage, by the interpolations, within the brackets, as the fenfe
appears to require; as diftinctnefs demands,
and propriety confirms. In order to give
the Countefs's obfervations the gravity, and
weight, which comport with her years, and
her character, there muft be a femicolon [;]
after yes, and a colon [:] after law; the
point of interjection [!] ought to follow God
fhield; for there ends the prayer. There
ought to be a full point [.] at pulfe; becaufe there ends the fenfe. The Countefs
does not mean, as the commentators fup-

(*p*) Steev. 1793. vol. vi. p. 225.

pofe

pofe, to afk a queftion ; but, to utter an exclamation, when fhe cries out: " What!
" pale again;" For, Helen cannot tell,
whether fhe herfelf be pale, or no; nor,
can fhe, in her circumftances, help her pale-
nefs. But, the commentators are, continually, confounding the points of interrogation, and interjeftion; as almoft every
page evinces. As an illuftration of this
remark, take an example, from the fame
play, in the Scene, between Lafeu, and
Parolles (*q*) :

Laf. Your Lord [,] and mafter [,] did well [,] to
make his recantation.

Par. Recantation ? My Lord ? My Mafter ?

The indignant affeftation of Parolles,
clearly, requires, that there fhould be points
of interjeftion, where the commentators
have placed points of interrogation : Recantation! My Lord! My Mafter!

Laf. Ay; Is it not a language, I fpeak ?

Par. A moft harfh one ; and [,] not to be underftood [,] without bloody fucceeding. My Mafter ? [!]

The confideration of the greateft impor-

(*q*) Ib. 266.

tance, next to the giving of the text, truly, ought to be, to point it accurately: For, without juſt punctuation, the text is un- ſettled; the ſenſe is marred; the reader is confounded; and, the inexperienced play- ers are, continually, miſled in their ſtudies, and embarraſſed in their delivery.

Theſe obſervations, I thought it neceſſary to make, in juſtice to the fame of Shak- ſpeare, who is thus injured, by careleſsneſs; and to my own argument, whilſt I am il- luſtrating the poet's *ſtudies:* Theſe remarks were alſo due to the admirers of Shakſpeare, who are conſtantly told, that *his text is now ſettled*; and that the late editions are, at length, *immaculate.*

After writing his plays, "Shakſpeare *re-* " *turned* to Stratford," ſays Mr. Steevens, in his biographical breviary, "made his " will, died, and was buried." Theſe ge- neral poſitions may be readily admitted, as they were eaſily ſtated, without requiring abſolute demonſtration; though it be not quite ſo certain, as the biographer ſuppoſed, whether Shakſpeare wrote his dramas at

London,

London, or Stratford, or on his frequent
journies, from the one to the other. It is true,
however, that his will was recorded, though
it is ſtill a point of uncertainty, when, and
by whom, it was originally publiſhed. This
publication was attributed by Mr. Malone,
and by Mr. Steevens, after him, to Theobald, with reprobation of the blunders, it
contained. From the aſperſions of hyper-
criticiſm, I endeavoured (*r*) to vindicate
Theobald, who was certainly guiltleſs,
either of the blunders, or the publication :
For, ſix years before the will was publiſhed,
Theobald had left

    " ——— This earthly world, where to do harm
    " 'Tis often laudable ; to do good, ſometimes
    " Accounted dangerous folly."

In vindicating an editor, who had de-
ſerved well of the admirers of Shakſpeare,
I ſaid (*s*), that the will was certainly publiſhed, with the original errors, in the Biographia Britannica, in 1763, for the *firſt
time*, as I believed. I formed this *belief*, by
comparing the firſt, and ſecond, editions of

(*r*) Apology, 425-7.   (*s*) Apology, 426.

S   Theo-

Theobald, with the Biographia, in 1763, without feeing Theobald's third edition, of 1752, which I have fince feen, by accident. In this *third* edition of Theobald, if any fuch there really were, the will of Shak-fpeare was publifhed, by the bookfellers, fix years after the deceafe of the editor (*t*). I looked, without fuccefs, in the Preroga-tive Office, for a will of Theobald, who probably died, as poets often die, and as hath been before remarked, without much property, for an executor to manage, or an

(*t*) The will was thruft into this Edition between the Preface and the Text; it was printed in a different cha-racter from the Preface; was paged in a different feries; and makes eight pages, or one half fheet. I have a ftrong fufpicion, that this was only a pretended Edition, with a new *Title page*, and, with the addition of the Will. For, the laft paragraph of the Preface fpeaks of the former Edi*tion*, not Edi*tions:* And the Will is obvioufly printed, in a quite different letter, from the Preface, and the Text. Nor, is this Edition of Theobald, in 1752, mentioned either by Mr. Steevens, or Mr. Ma-lone, whofe reprehenfible filence, if fuch an one there were, led my *heavy ignorance* into a petty error. My notion is, that this fabricated Edition of 1752, was in-tended to oppofe Warburton's Edition of 1747.

heir

heir to enjoy. From the Biographia Dramatica, I faid, that Theobald had died in
1742 : But, Mr. Reid ftates, with greater
probability, that he died fhortly after the
6th of September, 1744; and on the 20th
of the fubfequent October, his library, comprehending two hundred and ninety-five
old Englifh plays, was fold, at auction, by
Charles Corbet (*u*). The will of Shakfpeare
was publifhed again, in the *Biographia* Britannica, in 1763, as I formerly intimated(*x*).
It was republifhed by Johnfon, in 1766,
with all the errors. Capel feems not to
have known, when he publifhed his Shakfpeare, in 1768, that the poet's will had
then been publifhed (*y*). The will was
publifhed again by Mr. Steevens, in 1778,

(*u*) Steev. Shak. 1793 vol. i. 331.

(*x*) Apology, 426.

(*y*) At the conclufion of his Introduction, p. 74, when
inftructing the Biographer how to write a Life of Shakfpeare, he recommended, as an exifting memorial,
" his laft Will and Teftament, *extant now at* Doctors-
" Commons."

S 2   alfo

alſo with the original errors (*z*). But, Mr. Malone has the unrivalled merit of having firſt publiſhed the poet's will, from a collation with the original, in the prerogative office.

I have now rectified one of the errors, which the critic aforeſaid left, in an unlucky moment, " to the care of Mr. Ma " lone. (*a*)" I ſhould have been happy to have ſeen all my " hateful errors," diſtinctly, exhibited; that I might have had the gratifying pleaſure of ſelf-rectification: But, whatever were the imperfections of *The Apology*, it has no errors in it, which affect the argument. The error, in believing the will of Shakſpeare to have been publiſhed

(*z*) See the Edit. 1778. vol. i. p 198-9. *Buſhaxton*, for Biſhopton, *reſerved* and *preſerved*, for *received* and *perceived*; my *brown beſt bed*, for my *ſecond beſt bed*: Mr. Steevens alſo ſays, miſtakingly, [Ib. 198] " It " appears from the Regiſters in Doctors-Commons, " that Richard Burbage died in 1629: Yet, the Pariſh " Regiſter proves, that he was buried on the 16th of " March 16$\frac{18}{19}$." Mr. Malone rectified many other errors of Mr. Steevens.

(*a*) Brit. Crit. vol. ix. 520.

by

by the bookfellers, in 1763, inftead of 1752, does not invalidate the argument, wherein I vindicated the deceafed Theobald, againft the late Enquirer, who charged him with publifhing what he never publifhed. The farcafms of ignorance always fharpen the weapons of ridicule ; as want of candour is fure to receive its retribution.

Whether Theobald, whom, I have thus refcued from the pofthumous attack, of the living commentators, will be defended, with equal eafe, from another attack, of a different kind, by a very different perfon, I do not pretend to forefee. I mean the attack, which was made by Pope, at the end of his edition, in 1728, and which has been little noticed by fubfequent editors. Johnfon retained the notes of Pope; " that no frag-
" ment of fo great a writer may be loft:"
Adopting the fame apology, I will fubjoin a paffage from Pope, which appears to be as characteriftic of that celebrated poet, as any fentiment in his various writings :

" Since the publication of *our* firft Edition, there
" having been fome attempts upon Shakfpeare pub-

" lifhed

" lifhed by Lewis Theobald, (which he would not
" communicate during the time wherein that Edition
" was preparing for the Prefs, when *we*, by publick
" Advertifements, did requeft the affiftance of all lovers
" of this Author) *we* have inferted, in this impreffion,
" as many of 'em as are judg'd of any the leaft advan-
" tage to the Poet; the whole amounting to about
" *twenty-five* words.

" But to the end every Reader may judge for him-
" felf, we have annexed a *compleat Lift* of the reft;
" which if he fhall think *trivial*, or *erroneous*, either in
" part, or in whole; at worft it can fpoil but a half
" fheet of paper, that chances to be left vacant here.
" And we purpofe for the future, to do the fame with
" refpect to any other perfons, who either thro' *can-*
" *dor* or *vanity*, fhall communicate or publifh, the leaft
" thing tending to the illuftration of our Author. *We*
" have here omitted nothing but *Pointings* and meer
" errors of the Prefs, which I hope the Corrector of
" it has rectify'd; if not, I cou'd wifh as accurate an
" one as Mr. Th. [if he] had been at that trouble, which I
" defired Mr. Tonfon to folicit him to undertake.(*b*)
                                        " A. P."

I will apologize for the *prefumptuous* Theobald, in *prefuming* to know any thing of
Shakfpeare, by quoting a couplet from an

(*b*) See this very curious paffage of fuch a writer at
the end of the Index to the 8th vol. of the Edit. 1728, as
a Preface to the *various Readings*.

                                        excellent

excellent poet, who was alfo a good judge,
and an amiable man :

" THEOBALD, 'tis thine, to fhew what Shakfpeare writ;
" But, POPE fhall reign fupreme, in Poetry, and Wit."(c)

The conceitednefs of Pope, naturally,
fuggefted what his petulance eafily uttered,
that there neither was before him, nor ever
would be after him, any writer, who was
fit to revife the dramas of Shakfpeare.
Whatever Pope might think, or his partizans proclaim, the charm was difpelled, by
the appearance of Theobald's edition, in
1733 (d). The admirers of Shakfpeare had
now the fatisfaction of feeing, in the more
accurate pages of Theobald, *what Shakfpeare writ.* This laborious editor, plainly,
travelled on the right road : It was yet referved for others to travel farther, in the
fame track, with greater ftrength, and hap-

(c) See DUNCOMB's Epigram, on the Conteft, between Pope, and Theobald, in Nicols's Col. of Poems,
vol vi. p. 7.

(d) Of Theobald's Edition, there were printed no
fewer than 12,860 copies; for which he received not
lefs than 652l. 10s. [Steev. 1793, vol. i. p. 449.]

pier fuccefs. Hanmer fhowed, indeed, by his edition, in 1744, that he did not always follow the fteps of Theobald: Yet, his prefumption, in pretending to know any thing of Shakfpeare, roufed the indignation of Warburton, who had lent a few notes to Theobald. The ebullition of Warburton's various paffions of contempt, and difdain; of refentment, and emulation; appeared throughout his edition, which he publifhed in 1747. Every reader of this book was diffatisfied; becaufe no one approves magifterial dictation: And, Edwards came, in a lucky time, with his *Canons of Criticifm*, to free their minds from the bondage of a tyrant. After the preparation of many years, came out, with a milder air, a greater mafter, Johnfon, in his edition of 1765. Mr. Steevens appeared, in 1766, as the coadjutor of Johnfon, whofe previous edition was rather endured, than approved. After working under ground, for years, mole like, Capel came into open day, with his edition, in 1768, which was criticized,

and

and forgotten (*e*). After the works of Capel, followed the feveral editions of Mr. Steevens, and of Mr. Malone ; the latter of whom had furnifhed his immediate predeceffor with *feveral fupplements*. To the fucceffive labours of thefe laft editors, Mr. Ritfon, made objections, in feveral publications, which have not hitherto been fatisfactorily anfwered. It is, from this fhort furvey, apparent, that each fucceeding editor of Shakfpeare has, in fome degree, fuperfeded the former. It may eafily be obferved, that the prefent editors, Mr. Steevens, and Mr. Malone, think, and talk, with Pope, that their labours preclude future editions of other editors, who cannot poffibly hope to equal their performances, and perfections. I will only fay, with the wife man, " That to every thing there is a

(*e*) There were publifhed after the deceafe of Capel three 4°. volumes, in 1779, and 1780; confifting of a Gloffary, Various readings, Notes, Indexes, and *The School of Shakfpeare:* But, the whole is fo uncouth, as to be extremely repulfive; and fo full of affectation, as to be often unintelligible.

" feafon,

" feafon, and a time to every purpofe."
Shakfpeare alone, who has had the fate to
be mifreprefented by moft of his editors,
is immortal ; fuch was the extent of his genius, and fuch the courfe of his ftudies.

—— § XII. ——

The CHRONOLOGY of SHAKSPEARE's DRAMAS.

When Mr. Malone had attempted " to
" afcertain the order, in which the plays
" of Shakfpeare were written," Mr. Stee-
" vens, warmly, declared, " that he had
" fo happily accomplifhed his undertaking,
" that he only leaves me the power to thank
" him, for an *arrangement, which I profefs*
" *my inability* either to difpute, or to im-
" prove." This panegyrick was made, in
1778 (*a*). And, though twenty years have
elapfed, fince that attempt, this *happy arrangement* has neither been difputed by him,
nor improved by others (*b*). I propofe,
however,

(*a*) Steev. Shak. Ed. 1778, vol. i. p. 268.

(*b*) Mr. Malone has, however, difputed his own preconceptions, as to this Chronology, and has improved

his

however, whatever may be my ability, or
fuccefs, both to difpute, and to improve,
this applauded Chronology, in the following
obfervations, which I offer as an *Apology*
to Mr. Steevens, for prefuming to know any
thing about Shakfpeare; in order to fhow
him, that a *novice* can perform, in twenty
days, what a *mafter* has acknowledged his
inability to atchieve, during twenty years (*c*).
                                    Confidering

his own argument, by throwing out of it Seven of the
fpurious plays, and by changing the pofitions of feveral of
the genuine Dramas. [Compare Mr. Steevens's Edit.
1778, vol. i. p. 274, with Mr. Malone's Ed. 1790,
vol. i. p. 266, and Mr. Steevens's Ed. 1793, vol. i.
p. 470-617.] And, Mr. Steevens has, laudably, followed
the example of Mr. Malone.

(*c*) Mr. Steevens might have, furely, correded an
inftance of *falfe grammar*, which has ftood, in this
Chronology, upwards of twenty years; to the fcandal
of Criticifm, and the reproach of Editorfhip: " The
" precife *manners* of the puritans *was* [were] at this
" time much ridiculed." [Mal. vol. i. 352.] Mr.
Steevens adopted this palpable error, without perceiving its diffonance to grammar rules. [Steev. 1793,
vol. i. p. 577.] Whalley, who was a Scholar, according to Johnfon, wrote, very differently: " *Thefe*
                                    " manners

Confidering the paucity of materials, which have come down to us, with regard to the private life, and literary annals, of fo interefting a poet, every attempt to afcertain fome additional fact, to adduce fome new circumftance, or to inculcate fome ufeful principle, may juftly claim attentive indulgence, from the admirers of Shakfpeare. I muft fay, with Mr. Malone, and Mr. Steevens, " that nothing very de-" cifive can be produced, on this fubject : " *Probability alone* is pretended to," fay they (*d*). When fuch critics only promife *probabilities*, it is not for me to offer *demonftrations* : Nor, is it, for them, to call for demonftration from me, after they have claimed *probability*, as an indulgence, for themfelves. But, I propofe to fhow, that their Chronology is erroneous ; and to fub-

" manners, and moft others, which the poet has " painted, are agreeable to the character, and fuitable " to his defign." [Upton's Crit. Obferv. 2. Ed. 73.] See the word *manners* in Johnfon's Dict. which is, always, in the plural, when it fignifies *Studied Civility*, &c.

(*d*) Steev. Shak. 1793, vol. i. p. 475.

mit

mit to the admirers of Shakfpeare a jufter order, by eftablifhing new facts, and adducing pregnant circumftances :

" Of old, thofe met rewards, who could excel:
" And, thofe were prais'd, who but endeavour'd well."

Shakfpeare appears to have been as prematurely forward in his perfonal conftitution, as he was preternatural in his genius : Although he was born only in 1564, he became a hufband, in 1582, and a father in 1583. He thus entered the world, at an age, when lefs forward youths have fcarcely efcaped from the difcipline of the fchool. Like other pregnant wits, he may have written amatory verfes, while he felt the powerful incentive of love : And, he produced the Poem of VENUS *and* ADONIS, " *the firft heir* of his invention," before he had fallied from Stratford, probably; but certainly before he was known to fame (e) :

" A graver fubject could not him content
" Without love's foolifh lazy languifhment."

(e) This Poem was entered in the Stationer's Regifter, on the 13th April, 1593; and was, probably, publifhed, in the fubfequent year: It was licenfed by the Archbifhop of Canterbury.

Shakfpeare

Shakſpeare, however, was unknown, as a poet, to Webb, in 1586 (*f*); and to Puttenham, in 1589(*g*): Neither was Shakſpeare known, as a dramatiſt, to Harrington, in 1591 (*h*) ; Nor to Spenſer, in any character, at the ſame epoch (*i*). It is a curious

(*f*) When he publiſhed his *Diſcourſe on Engliſh Poetry.*

(*g*) When he printed, anonymouſly, *The Art of Engliſh Poeſy.*

(*h*) Sir John Harrington, when treating of Dramatic Poetry, in his *Apology for Poetry*, did not notice Shakſpeare.

(*i*) It ſeems impoſſible, that Spenſer, who went to Ireland, in 1580, where he continued to reſide till he was finally expelled, though he made ſome excurſions to England, could know any thing of Shakſpeare, at ſo early a period, as 1590; and, conſequently, could not allude to him in the *Tears of the Muſes*, a poem, which was firſt publiſhed, in 1591; and which contains the lamentation of *Thalia* for the death of pleaſant *Willy*, who died of late. Sir Philip Sydney is obviouſly intended by Spenſer, who, probably, wrote this, ſome time before the publication: Sydney was long lamented by the contemporary poets, contrary to the conception of the two Commentators: There were publiſhed, in the *Phoenix Neſt*, 1593, ſeveral Elegies, on Sir Philip Sydney.

curious fact, that Shakſpeare was, originally, noticed, by the malignant eye of
ſatire ; and was, firſt, mentioned, by the
ſarcaſtic pen of lampoon. It was Robert
Greene, who, (like other writers in our
own times,) is better known by the vices of
his heart, than the products of his head,
thus ſcoffed at Shakſpeare, when he wrote,
in 1592, his *Groats-worth of Witte bought
with a Million of Repentance.* When dying
of want, Robert Greene addreſſed a warning to his fellow wits, againſt truſting to
plays, for a livelihood, and to players, for
rewards. " Yes; truſt them not," ſaid he,
" For, there is an upſtart crow, beautified
" with our feathers, that with his tyger's

Sydney. I ſuſpect, however, that Gabriel Harvey, the
literary Dictator of that period, did allude to Shakſpeare, in his " *Four Letters* eſpecially touching *Robert*
" *Greene* and *other parties*, by him abuſed," which were
printed by Wolfe, in 1592 : It is in the *third* letter,
which was dated from London, on the 9th of September 1592, wherein he ſays: " I ſpeak generally to
" every ſpringing wit ; but, more eſpecially to a few :
" and, at this inſtant, *ſingularly*, to *one*, whom 1 ſalute
" with a hundred bleſſings."

" heart,

" heart, wrapped in a *player's hide*, fup-
" pofes he is as well able to bombaft out a
" blank verfe, as the beft of you ; and be-
" ing an abfolute *Johannes factotum* is, in
" his own conceit, the only SHAKE-SCENE,
" in a Country." It was Mr. Tyrwhit,
who, acutely, applied this paffage to
Shakfpeare : It was Mr. Malone, who firft
publifhed this decifive proof, that Shakfpeare had written for the ftage, as early as
1591 ; and had, by his fuccefs, attracted
the notice of difappointment, and incited
the fcoffs of envy (*k*). But, this proof may
be carried a little further back ; and may be

(*k*) Mal. Shak. vol. i. 272-3. Greene, however
did not live to publifh his *Groats-worth of Wit :* After
his death, in September 1592, Henry Chettle performed that fervice, for the real author ; as Mr. Malone
has evinced, from the acknowledgement of the publifher. [Id.] But, of this fact, I have an additional
proof, which feems to have efcaped the Commentator's
notice : There was entered, in the Stationer's Regifters, for William Wrighte, on the 20th September,
1592, " uppon the *perill* of Henry Chettle, *Green's*
" *Groat's worth of Wyt, bought* with *a million of repent-*
" *ance.*"

equally

equally applied to some other important points : Shakspeare appeared to the eyes of Greene, as " an absolute *factotum*" of the stage. This expression proves, incidentally, that Shakspeare had become, as I have intimated, *the reader* of *plays for his Theatre*, at an earlier epoch : And, he may have read, and amended, *Titus Andronicus*, in 1589 ; and may have read, and amended, *Pericles*, in 1592, *Locrine*, in 1593, Sir John Oldcastle, in 1598 ; as he, certainly, did read, and amend, Ben Jonson's Sejanus, in 1603. As Shakspeare was thus scoffed at, by a lampooner, in 1592, is it not reasonable to infer, that he who, in modern times, has been acknowledged as our greatest dramatist, might have been lampooned by a satirist, in 1599, when the public voice, had not yet allowed him that pre-eminence ?

We have now obtained something more than probability, that Shakspeare, was a reader, and writer, of plays, as early as 1591. Yet, it is a question of some difficulty to ascertain, which of his *genuine* dramas, he first wrote : Nor, is it any answer

T

to this queſtion to ſay, that he read, and
improved, the plays of others ; that he
added a letter, or a word, or a line, or a
thought, to *Titus Andronicus*, in 1589, or
to the *firſt part* of Henry VI, in 1592 ; all
which ſeem now to be acknowledged, as the
works of other poets, though Shakſpeare
may have fitted them for the ſtage.

No. I.—The Comedy of Errors, 1591.

With regard to the true epoch of this
Comedy, there have been various periods
aſſigned to it, according as opinion fluctua-
ted, between conjecture, and certainty (*l*) :
This play was originally given to the year
1596; yet, afterwards, was fixed to 1593 ;
owing to a want of attention to facts, and,
a defect in the mode of argumentation, upon
the point. It was known to Meres, in 1598,
who mentions it in his *Wits Treaſury.* It
could not be written, ſaid Mr. Malone, before 1596 ; for Warner's tranſlation of

(*l*) Steev. Ed. 1778, vol. i. p. 292 ; Mal. vol. i. 288 ;
Steev. 1793, vol. i. p. 503.

Plautus's

Plautus's Menæchmi, *from which the plot was taken*, was not publifhed till 1595. Mr. Ritfon, whofe opinion, on fuch topicks, deferves great attention, declares, that Shakfpeare had not the flighteft obligation to Warner's tranflation. In this judgment, Capel concurred, when he faid, " that " this Tranflation furnifhed Shakfpeare " with nothing but his principal inci- " dent (*m*)." The two commentators are at length difpofed to admit, that Shakfpeare may have derived fome intimations, from prior writers, on the fame fubject. The *doggerel meafure*, and the *alternate* rhimes, are, alfo, allowed to be obvious proofs, that they are the production of an inexperienced writer.

The *only note of time*, that is faid to occur, in this play, is the allufion to France being armed for war againft her heir (*n*). Now; in 1591, Queen Elizabeth fent Lord Effex with four thoufand men, to affift

(*m*) Shak. vol. i. p. 51.
(*n*) Steev. 1793, vol. i. p. 503.

Henry

Henry IV, againſt his opponents. This is a remarkable faƈt, which fixes the alluſion to 1591. That able, and artful, Prince more effeƈtually promoted his own intereſt, by embracing the religion of France, in July 1593; which ſtep led to his coronation, in February, 1594: It is apparent, then, that the events of 1594, and 1593, could not have induced Shakſpeare to ſpeak of France, as then " armed ; mak-" ing war againſt the heir." The name of *Dowſabel*, which is mentioned, in the Comedy of Errors, alſo occurs in the *Shepherd's Garland* of Drayton, which was printed, in 1593 : Yet, it is not eaſy to aſcertain, whether Shakſpeare borrowed from Drayton, or Drayton from Shakſpeare : They both probably found the name, in ſome common original; as Shakſpeare found the plot of his play in ſome unknown prototype.

But, there is another note of time, in this comedy, which the two Commentators have over-looked; and which is more ſtriking, and more inſtruƈtive, than the alluſion, fion, which is mentioned by them, of the repugnancy of France to Henry IV; that they, unconfcioufly, learned from reprobated Theobald (o). The play opens with the trial of Ægeon, a merchant of Syracufe, who went to Ephefus, contrary to *an act of trade:*

" *Ægeon:* Proceed, Solinus, to procure my fall;
And, by the doom of death, end woes, and all.
   Solinus. Merchant of Syracufa, plead no more:
I am not partial to infringe our laws.
The enmity, and difcord, which of late
Sprang from the rancorous outrage of your Duke
To merchants, our well dealing Countrymen,
Who, wanting gilders to redeem their lives,
Have feal'd his rigorous ftatutes with their bloods,
Excludes all pity from our threatning looks:
For, fince the mortal and inteftine jars
'Twixt thy feditious Countrymen and us,
It hath in folemn fynods been decreed,
Both by the Syracufans, and ourfelves,
To admit *no traffick* to our *adverfe towns* ·
Nay, more:
If any, born at Ephefus, be feen
At any Syracufan marts, and fairs:
Again, if any Syracufan born,

(o) Theob. Shakf. v. iii. p. 208–9.

         Come

Come to the bay of Ephefus, he dies,
His goods confifcate to the Duke's difpofe;
Unlefs, a thoufand marks be levied,
To quit the penalty, and to ranfom him."

Thefe allufions to the rivality of trade are fo particularly marked, as to relate, plainly, to the commercial tranfactions of that eventful period. In 1589, Queen Elizabeth feized fixty fhips, belonging to the Hans Towns, which were carrying warlike ftores to Spain (*p*). In 1590, the Hollanders complained of the Englifh depredations on their trade (*q*). In 1591, there were commercial complaints between England and Denmark. In this year, the Englifh merchant-adventurers were expelled from Staaden; but were favoured by Elbing (*r*): Here, then, are the *adverfe towns*, which are fo emphatically mentioned by Shakfpeare. Add to thofe applicable facts, that the Lord Admiral was commanded, in July, 1591, to arreft all *Hamburgh* fhips, and

(*p*) Anderfon's Chron. Hift. of Com. vol. i. p. 434-5.
(*q*) Id.
(*r*) Ib. 439.

goods,

goods, for fatisfaction of four hundred and fixty pounds to George Leate. Thefe were all very ftriking events to a commercial city, which, when mentioned by the poet, muft have been felt by the inhabitants of London: And, thofe facts, when coupled with the allufion to the repugnance of France to Henry IV, fix the time, when this Comedy of Errors was written, to 1591 (*s*).

In act the 4th, Dromeo of Ephefus fays, " Miftrefs, *refpice finem*, refpect your end." This explanation induced Warburton to refer the reader to a pamphlet of Buchanan, againft Liddington, which ended with the repetition of the wife man's warning, *Refpice finem, Refpice finem*. But, this lampoon of Buchanan, which was publifhed, foon after the birth of Shakfpeare, had been forgotten when our poet wrote his *Comedy of Errors*. I fufpect, that Shakfpeare may

(*s*) Before the deceafe of Shakfpeare, it had become proverbial to give this appellation to different Dramas, of a comick kind: Anton cried out, in his Philofophical Satires, 1616, p. 51. " What *Comedies of Errors* fwell the Stage !"

T 4   have

have feen the fame expreffions in *The Eighth Liberal Science*, or *The Art of Flattery*, which was publifhed, in 1579, *Refpice finem* (*t*); " *Alls well that ends well* (*u*)."

No. II.—Love's Labours Lost.

The frequency of the rhimes, the irregularity of the verfification, the diverfity of the dialogue, and the defects of the compofition ; all confpire to evince, that this comedy is one of the earlieft dramas of the mufe of Shakfpeare. It was, certainly, written before September, 1598 ; becaufe, it is mentioned by Meres, in his *Wit's Treafury*. It was, particularly, noticed in *Alba*, or the *Month's Mind of a melancholy Lover*, which was publifhed, in 1598. It was, originally, affigned to the year 1591 (*x*) ; yet, has it been, finally, fixed, by the editors, to 1594 (*y*) ; though the reafons, for this choice, are very infufficient to juftify the alteration.

(*t*) 7. Steev. 288.   (*u*) Sign. E. iiii.
(*x*) Steev. 1778 vol. i. p. 280.
(*y*) Steev. 1793, vol. i. p. 509.

The

The *Love's Labours Loſt* was firſt printed, in 1598. It is ſaid, in the title page of this edition, that it had been acted before Queen Elizabeth, at Chriſtmas, 1597, and to be *newly correEted*, and *augmented.* This co- medy was revived, then, in 1597, and en- larged, in the outline, which had been ſketched in ſome prior year : But, there is no ſatisfactory reaſon given, by the com- mentators, for fixing the epoch of this ſketch, in 1594, or in any other year: It is merely thought probable by them, that the firſt draft of this play was written in, or *before*, 1594 (z).

The fifth act of this very early drama opens with that *finiſhed repreſentation* of *colloquial excellence*, which was ſo emphati- cally mentioned by the late Doctor Johnſon: " I praiſe God, ſays Nathaniel to Holo- " phernes, your reaſons at dinner were " ſharp and ſententious ; pleaſant, without " ſcurrility ; witty, without affectation ; " audacious, without impudency ; learned,

(z) Steev. 1793, vol. i. p. 511.

" without

" without opinion; and ftrange, without
" hurry." But, none of the commentators feem to have adverted, that the outline
of this reprefentation was borrowed from
Sydney: In the *Arcadia*, which was firft
publifhed, in 1590, fpeaking of the fair
Parthenia, of whom Sydney fays, " that
" which made her *fairnefs* much the *fairer*
" was, that it was but a *fair* ambaffador of
" a moft *fair* mind (*a*), full of wit, which
" delighted more to judge itfelf, than to
" fhew itfelf: her fpeech being as rare as
" precious; her *filence, without fullennefs*;
" *her modefty, without affectation*; her *fhame-*
" *facednefs, without ignorance* (*b*)." Here,
then, was the original, in 1590, from which
Shakfpeare copied, in 1592.

In the 5th Act of *Love's Labours Loft*,
we may perceive much of Mufcovy, and
Mufcovites; of Ruffia, and Ruffians. War-

(*a*) Shakfpeare, in the 5th Act, repeats the epithet
fair; " A holy parcel of the *faireft* dames."—There are
repetitions of *fair* Lady, and *fair* Lord. [Steev. 1793,
vol. v. p. 326.]

(*b*) Bk. i. p. 17. of the folio Edit.

burton has well remarked, without ftating, indeed, any document for his affumption, " that the fettling of commerce in Ruffia " was, at that time, a matter that much " engroffed the concern, and *converfation* " of the public (*c*)." This converfation, and that concern, engaged the attention of the court, and city, moft particularly, in 1590, and 1591 (*d*).

No. III.—Romeo and Juliet.

This captivating drama is, probably, one of the earlieft productions of Shakfpeare; and is, certainly, the firft tragedy, which proceeded from his pen. Like other plays of this great dramatift, Romeo and Juliet was merely a fketch, in its firft draught, which was afterwards filled up, and, fuc- ceffively, improved; it was at length print- ed, in 1597, though not in its moft perfect form.

There is plainly an allufion to the Faeirie

(*c*) Steev. 1793, vol. v. p. 319.
(*d*) Hackluyt, vol. i. p. 498-9, of the Ed. 1598.

Queen,

Queen, the three firſt books of which were publiſhed, in 1590; and which was, continually, preſent, in our poet's mind; Mercutio, in his airy, and ſatiric ſpeech, cries out:

> " O, then, I ſee Queen Mab hath been with you.
> " She is the *fairies* midwife; and ſhe comes,
> " In ſhape no bigger than an aggat ſtone
> " On the fore-finger of an Alderman."

Shakſpeare, when he ſat down to ſketch Romeo and Juliet, had another poet, alſo of that period, in his mind, who was even in his eye, while he wrote the fifth act: And, the ſimilarities, between their two works, are ſo many, and ſo ſtriking, as to leave no reaſonable doubt, whether Shakſpeare borrowed from Daniel, or Daniel from Shakſpeare. In every queſtion of this kind, the probability lies againſt Shakſpeare, who, like the bee, conſtantly draws ſweets from every weed:

DANIEL:

> " And nought reſpecting death, the laſt of pains,
> " Plac'd his *pale colours*, (the enſign of his might,)
> " Upon his new got ſpoil: &c.

SHAK-

SHAKSPEARE :

" ———— beauty's *enfign* yet

" Is crimfon in thy lips, and in thy cheeks,

" And Death's *pale flag :* &c.

DANIEL :

" Decayed rofes of difcoloured cheeks

" Do yet retain fome notes of former grace,

" *And ugly Death fits fair within her face.*

SHAKSPEARE :

" Death, that hath fuck'd the honey of thy breath,

" Hath had no power yet upon thy beauty.

DANIEL :

" Ah ! now, me thinks, I fee *Death dallying feeks*

" *To entertain itfelf in love's fweet place.*

SHAKSPEARE :

" ———— fhall I believe

" That unfubftantial Death is amorous."(*e*)

Daniel's Complaint of Rofamond, from which Shakfpeare plainly borrowed, was entered in the Stationers' Regifters, on the 4th of February, 1592, and was foon after praifed by Nafh (*f*), in his *Pierce Penny-leffe* his *Supplication to the Devil* (*g*). We

(*e*) Steev. 1793, vol. i. p. 519.   (*f*) Ib. 518.

(*g*) This work of Nafh was entered in the Stationer's Regifters for Richard Jones, on the 8th of Auguft, 1592 ; being licenfed by *the Archbifhop.*

may

may eafily prefume, then, that what had attracted others, had drawn the attention of Shakfpeare, early in 1592. This prefumption is carried up to probability, by what we hear of the nurfe's talk, in the firft act; who fays, characteriftically, " that *it is now " fince the earthquake eleven years.*" Shakfpeare had been reading Gabriel Hervey's *Three proper Letters*, which were printed, in 1580, and which gave an account of *the earthquake*, which happened in April of that year. This note of time was firft mentioned by Tyrwhit, to whofe opinion great regard is certainly due : But, in forming a judgement of the true date of the firft fketch of Romeo and Juliet, we muft couple both thofe remarkable circumftances together; the recollection of the earthquake ; and the imitations from Rofamond ; which, taken together, lead us to the fpring-time of the year 1592, as the epoch of the firft fketch.

Shakfpeare refumed the confideration of this Drama, in 1595, when deficiencies were fupplied, whatever redundancies may have been taken away. There is a remark of Romeo,

meo, which points, probably, to the voyages
of Drake, and of Hawkins, in the American Seas, during the years 1594, and 1595;
perhaps, to the voyage of Raleigh, in 1595:

" I am no Pilot (*h*); yet, wert thou as far,
" As that *vaſt ſhore*, waſh'd with the fartheſt ſea,
" I would adventure for ſuch *merchandize*."

There is a mention, in the *third* act, of
" *the firſt and ſecond cauſe*," that was
probably adopted from Saviolo's treatiſe, on
honour and *honourable quarrels*, which was
publiſhed, in 1595 (*i*).

Romeo and Juliet was, originally, acted by
the ſervants of Lord Hunſden, the Lord
Chamberlain, who died, in July 1590 : This
notice of the players, by whom this play
was firſt acted, appears in the title page of
the original edition, in 1597 (*k*). The inaccuracies of the Arithmetic of the garrulous
nurſe, who by one computation makes Ju-

(*h*) Camden, in Kennet, vol. ii. p. 579-85: It is to
be recollected, that the word, *Pilot*, ſignified, in that
age, *navigator*.

(*i*) Steev. 1793, vol. i. p. 518.

(*k*) Steev 1793, vol. i. p. 518.

liet

liet eleven years old, and by another fourteen, only fhow, that Shakfpeare had compofed his play at different times, when his
attention was drawn away by diffimilar objects.

No. IV.—Henry VI.
The Firft Part, 1593.

I have the honour to concur with Mr.
Malone, in thinking, that this *hiftorie* was
not written by Shakfpeare. It is ftill more
clear, both from the account books of Henflow, and the plain intimations of the original Editors of Shakfpeare's Dramas, Hemmings, and Cundal, who perfectly knew
the tranfactions of their own theatre, that
our Poet might have made fuch alterations,
and additions, in this early play, as to have
induced them, to mingle fuch mean materials with his fineft metal.

The play of Henry the VI. was firft acted
by Lord Strange's players, on the 3d of
March 1591-2 ; and it was ere long acted
thirteen times, before ten thoufand fpecta-
tors ; fo popular was this Hiftorie, however

it

it may have been defpifed, in latter times.
For this popular reception, Whetftones appears to have prepared the way, by faying
in his *Englifh Myrror* (*l*): " By far larger
" warrant, the Englifh Kings ought to be
" called Henries: For, of eight Kings
" named Henry, fithens the conqueft, chro-
" nicles condemn not one of them to be ir-
" religious, notably wicked, or tyrannous
" oppreffors of their fubjects, but as images
" and patterns of kingly magnanimitie, of
" wonderful promeffe, of peaceable govern-
" ment, and of many other divine and he-
" roical virtues, every of them have left
" a rare monument of a noble, gracious,
" and good prince, as if by heavenly pro-
" vidence, an efpecial bleffing had been
" joined unto the name of Henry." Whether all thefe affertions could be fatisfactorily
fupported, if they were rigoroufly fcanned,
I doubt : But, it can admit of no doubt,

(*l*) The Englifh Myrror; by George Whetftones,
Gent. Printed by Windet, in 1586, fix years before
the firft appearance of Henry 6th. This writer is
fometimes called Whetftone.

U   whether

whether fuch recitals would have a powerful effect, among an uninformed people,
who had not been yet accuftomed to free
difcuffion. It was faid, alfo, by Nafh (*m*),
in 1592, and it may have had a powerful
effect on Englifh audiences, " That the
" fubftance of all plays, is borrowed out of
" our Englifh Chronicles, wherein our fore-
" fathers valiant acts are reviewed; and
" they themfelves raifed from the grave of
" oblivion and brought to plead their aged
" honours in open prefence." It is even
faid, by the commentators, with fufficient
reafon, that one of the characters, in *Henrie
the VI.* is " brave *Talbot*, the terror of the
" French (*n*)." On the contrary, Ben
Jonfon, with a peculiar repugnance to every
thing, which was properly popular, tried,
with little fuccefs, to ridicule the hiftorical

(*m*) In *Pierce Pennyleffe his Supplication to the Devil*,
which was entered in the Stationers Regifters, on the
8th Auguft 1592 ; and foon after publifhed.

(*n*) Steev. 1793, vol. i. p. 490.

plays

plays of that age, in the Epilogue to his
Every Man in his Humour, 1598.

" Fight over York and Lancafter's long jars ;
" And, in the tyring houfe, bring wounds to fcars."

No. V.—Henry VI.
The Second Part, 1595.

I alfo concur with Mr. Malone, in thinking, that Shakfpeare, as he merely improved
the firft part of Henry VI. by flight alterations, and certainly adopted into the third
part the whole of a preceding play, may
have equally adopted, for his fecond part, a
preceding play, entitled, *The firft Part of
the Contention* of *the two famous Houfes of
Yorke and Lancafter.* This play was entered
in the Stationers Regifters, on the 12th of
March, 1593–4 : Yet, the earlieft copy,
which the collectors have hitherto feen, was
printed, in 1600 : Neverthelefs, I think it
probable, that this play may have been publifhed by Millington, in 8vo. or 12mo. during
the year 1595 ; becaufe it is certain, that the
fame bookfeller did publifh, *The True
Tragedy of Richard, Duke of Yorke,* in a
12mo. form, during 1595. This probability

U 2   would

would fhow, that our poet fitted for the ftage both thofe Dramas, which now form the *fecond* and *third* parts of Henry VI, fubfequent to that year. Neither Mr. Steevens, nor Mr. Malone, feem to have known, that the firft, and fecond, parts of Henry VI were ever entered in the Stationers Regifters; which, however, do exhibit their entry together, on the 19th of April, 1602.

No. VI.—Henry VI.
The Third Part.

The years 1593, and 1594, are affigned, by the commentators, as the true epochs of the writing of this Hiftorie; being copied from a previous play of Marlow, entitled *The true Tragedy of Richard Duke of Yorke*, which they fay was firft publifhed in 1600. There are paffages in this *True Tragedy* of fufficient fplendour to juftify what has been faid of Marlow's *mighty line*. But, it is not likely, that Shakfpeare would copy from a play, which he probably had not then feen. Yet, is it demonftrable, that Shakfpeare may have feen the *True Tragedy of Richard, Duke of Yorke*, in 1595, which

was

was printed, in this year, certainly (*o*). From this prior Drama, Shakſpeare, literally, copied, in many ſcenes, the third part of Henry VI; as may be diſtinctly ſeen by in-ſpection :

MARLOW began his Hiſtorie thus :

War. I wonder how the King eſcapt our hands.

Yorke. Whilſt we purſude the horſemen of the North,
He ſlielie ſtole awaie and left his men ;
Whereat the great Lord of Northumberland,
Whoſe warlike ears could never brook retreat,
Chargete our maine battels front, therewith him
Lord Stafford and Lord Clifford all abreſt
Brake in, and were by the hands of common Soldiers
ſlain.

(*o*) This very rare book, which neither Mr. Capel, nor Mr. Malone, nor Mr. Steevens, nor Mr. Herbert, nor Mr. John Egerton, appear to have ever ſeen, is in my Library. This play, which I purchaſed at the ſale of the late Rev. Dr. Pegge's books, is entitled " The " True Tragedie of Richard Duke of Yorke, and the " death of good King Henrie the Sixt, with the whole " Contention betweene the two Houſes Lancaſter and " Yorke, as it was ſundrie times acted by the Right " Honourable the Earle of Pembrooke his Servants." Printed at London by P. S. for Thomas Millington, and are to be ſold at his Shoppe under Saint Peter's church in Cornwall. [Cornhill.] 1595, 12mo.

U 3   SHAKSPEARE

SHAKSPEARE began his Hiſtorie thus :

War. I wonder, how the King eſcap'd our hands.

Yorke. While we purſu'd the horſemen of the North,
He ſlyly ſtole away, and left his men :
Whereat the great Lord of Northumberland,
Whoſe warlike ears could never brook retreat,
Cheer'd up the drooping Army; and *himſelf*,
Lord Clifford, and Lord Stafford, all abreaſt,
Charg'd our main battel's front, and breaking in,
Were by the *ſwords* of common ſoldiers ſlain.

We ſee by this compariſon, the ſimilarity of both, and the improvements of Shakſpeare, by ſlight additions. Take another example, from the firſt act :

MARLOW :

King. Looke Lordings where the ſturdy rebell ſits
Even in the Chair of State : belike he means,
Backt by the power of Warwicke, that falſe peer,
To aſpire unto the Crown, and raigne as King.
Earl of Northumberland, he ſlew thy father,
And thine, Lord Clifford: and you both have vow'd revenge
On him, his Sonnes, his favourites, and his friends.

SHAKSPEARE :

King Hen. *My Lords,* look where the ſturdy rebel ſits,
Even in the Chair of State ! belike he means
(Back'd by the power of Warwicke, that falſe peer)
To aſpire unto the Crown, and reign as King.

Earl

Earl of Northumberland, he flew thy father;
And thine, Lord Clifford; and you both vow'd revenge,
On him, his fons, his favourites, and his friends.

Marlow :

Edw.   Et tu Brute, wilt thou ſtab Cæſar too?
A parle Sirra to George of Clarence.

Shakspeare

Difmiffed the claffical talk of *tu Brute*; and only
added, a parley is founded.

Marlow :

Alarms, and then, enter Warwicke *wounded.*
Warw.   Ah, who is nie? Come to me friend, or foe,
And tell me, who is victor York or Warwick?
Why afk I that? my mangl'd bodie fhews,
That I muft yield my bodie to the earth.
And by my fall the conqueft to my foes.
Thus yields the Cedar to the axes edge,
Whofe arms gave fhelter to the princely Eagle,
Under whofe fhade the rampant lion flept,
Whofe top branch overpeer'd Jove's fpreading tree.
The wrinkles in my brows now fil'd with blood,
Were liken'd oft to kingly Sepulchres.
For who liv'd King, but I could dig his grave?
And who durft fmile, when Warwick bent his brow?
Lo now my glory fmeer'd in duft and blood
My parks, my walkes, my mannors that I had,
Even now forfake me, and of all my lands,
Is nothing left me but my bodies length.

U 4   Shakspeare,

Shakspeare:

Alarum: Enter Edward, *bring forth* Warwick *wounded.*

   King Edw. So, lie thou there: die thou, and die our
     fear:
For, Warwick was a bug, that fear'd us all.
Now, Montague fit faft; I feek for thee,
That Warwick's bones may keep thee company. [*Exit.*
   Warw. Ah, who is nigh, come to me friend, or foe,
And tell me who is victor, York, or Warwick.
Why afk I that? my mangled body fhows,
My blood, my want of ftrength, my fick heart fhows,
That I muft yield my body to the earth:
And by my fall the conqueft to my foe.
Thus yields the Cedar to the axe's edge,
Whofe arms gave fhelter to the princely eagle,
Under whofe fhade the ramping lion flept;
Whofe top branch overpeer'd Jove's fpreading tree,
And kept low fhrubs from Winter's powerful wind.
Thefe eyes, that now are dimm'd with Death's black veil,
Have been as piercing as the mid day fun,
To fearch the fecret treafons of the world:
The wrinkles in my brows, now filled with blood,
Were liken'd oft to kingly Sepulchres;
For, who liv'd King, but I could dig his grave?
Lo! now my glory fmear'd in duft and blood;
My parks, my walks, my manors that I had,
Even now forfake me; and of all my lands,
Is nothing left me, but my body's length!
Why, what is pomp, rule, reign, but earth and duft?
And, live we how we can, yet die we muft.

It

It is not often, that fuch an opportunity has occurred of comparing the original play, with Shakfpeare's copy; the firft fketch, with Shakfpeare's improvements; the defects of the author, with the fupplements of the copyift.

Mr. Capel has quoted two lines from Shakfpeare's Henry VI:

" What will the afpiring blood of Lancafter

" Sink in the ground? I thought it would have mounted;"

in order to fhow, that he, who cannot difcern the pen, that wrote them, ought never to pretend to difcernment hereafter. The two lines above quoted, fays Mr. Malone, in refutation of Capel's dogmatifm, are found in Marlow's *True Tragedie of Richard, Duke of Yorke.* A comparifon of the two poets will evince, that Mr. Capel is totally wrong; and that Mr. Malone is not altogether right:

MARLOW.

Glof. What? will the afpiring blood of Lancafter
Sinke *into* the ground, I *had* thought it would have
   mounted.
See how my fword weeps for the poor King's death.
Now maie fuch purple teares be alwaies fhed,

For

For fuch as feek the downfall of our houfe.
If anie fpark of life remain in thee,   [*Stab him againe.*
Downe, downe to hell, and faie I fent thee thither.
I that have neither pitie, love, nor feare.
Indeed 'twas true, that Henry told me of;
For, I have often heard my mother faie,
That I came into the world with my legs forward,
And had I not reafon think you to make hafte,
And feek their ruins that ufurp our rights?
The women wept and the midwife cride,
O Jefus blefs us, he is born with teeth.

Shakspeare.

Glof.   What, will the afpiring blood of Lancafter
Sink *in* the ground? I thought, it would have mounted.
See, how my fword weeps, for the poor King's death!
O, may fuch purple tears be always fhed
From thofe who wifh the downfall of our houfe!
If any fpark of life be yet remaining,
Down, down to Hell, and fay, I fent thee thither,
                              [*Stabs him again.*
I that have neither pity, love, nor fear.
Indeed, 'tis true, that Henry told me of;
For, I have often heard my mother fay,
I came into the world with my legs forward:
Had I not reafon, think ye, to make hafte,
And feek their *ruin,* that ufurp'd our right?
The midwife wonder'd; and the women cry'd,
O, Jefus blefs us, he is born with teeth.

From thefe comparifons, we may fee the
clouds of Capel evanifh, before the effulgent
light

light of the fact. I concur with Mr. Malone, in faying, that the third part of the
Hiftorie of Henry VI. was not written by
Shakfpeare; though the outline of it received fome additional touches from our
poet's pencil: And, with Mr. Malone, I
think it more than probable, that Shakfpeare alfo adopted the fecond, and third
parts, of the *hiftorie* of the fame monarch,
from the feebler plays of inferior dramatifts;
but not with *great* additions; as that chronologift afferts, without authority.

I do not concur, however, with the commentators, in thinking, that Shakfpeare
adopted the third, and fecond parts, of
Henry VI. in 1593, or 1594 (*p*). For, there
is pofitive evidence, that he muft have adopted both, towards the end of the fubfequent
year, 1595; unlefs we could fuppofe, indeed, that the playhoufe copies had been
laid before him, for his correction: But,
the title page of Marlow's *True Tragedie*
proves, that it had been fundry times acted

(*p*) Steev. 1793, vol. i. p. 496.

by

by the fervants of the Earl of *Pembrooke*, who was not the Lord Chamberlain, in 1595, and 1594. Green, who is fuppofed to have been the author of one of thofe prior plays, died in September, 1592; and Marlow, in May, 1593. Of thefe two contemporaries of Shakfpeare, Gabriel Hervey remarked, in his *New Letter of notable Contents*, 1593, " Though *Green* were a *Julian*, " and *Marlow* a *Lucian*, they might admo- " nifh other to advife themfelves." After confidering all circumftances; what went before, as well as what followed; I am of opinion, that the epoch of the third part of Henry VI. ought to be 1595.

No. VII.—The Two Gentlemen of Verona, 1595.

This comedy bears the fame marks of an early production, as the *Love's Labours Loft*, *The Midfummer's Night Dream*, and *The Comedy of Errors*. It was originally affigned to the year, 1593 (*q*): It has been fince

(*q*) Steev. Shak. 1778, vol. i. p. 285.

given,

given, to 1595, with better reafon; though not with fatisfactory proofs. This comedy was certainly written before September, 1598; when it was mentioned by Meres, in his *Wit's Treafury*.

The principal reafon, for allowing the year, 1595, the honour of this comedy, by the commentators, is, that it alludes to the voyages of Gilbert, in 1594, and Raleigh, in 1595: Speaking of the youth of England, at that epoch, the poet fays:

" Some to the wars, to try their fortunes there;
" Some to difcover iflands far away."

The Commentators had done better to have referred to the voyage of Hawkins, in 1594, when he paffed the ftreights of Magellan; and to the expedition of Lancafter, in the fame year, who facked Fernambucca, in the Brazils (r).

There are, in act the third, fome obvious allufions to Spenfer's Sonnets of the year 1595: Of Sylvia, Proteus fays:

" You muft lay *lime*, to tangle her defires,

(r) Camden in Kennet, vol. ii. p. 579.

" By

" By *wailful Sonnets,* whofe compofed rhimes
" Should be full fraught with ferviceable vows."

The Duke replies :

" Ay ; much [is] the force of heaven-bred poefy '" (s)

Add to thefe confiderations, the warlike ftate of England, in 1595, and the hoftile tumults in Ireland, during the years 1594, and 1595. There was then a rebellion in Ireland ; there were preparations made to re-fift the Spanifh invafion, and to affift the French, in 1595 : And it was to thofe war-like events, that Shakfpeare referred, when he faid the people of England

" Put their Sons to feek preferment out ;
" Some to the wars, to try their fortunes there."

I know not, whether there be in thefe lines, fome allufion to a remarkable tranfac-tion, in 1594 : Sir Nicholas Clifford, and Sir Anthony Shirley, two *young* knights, be-haved fo bravely, under the French king, that he gave them the Order of St. Michael ; by wearing which in the city, and the court, they gave offence to Elizabeth, who fent them to prifon for their prefumption : But, as they

(s) Steev. 1793, vol. iii. p. 247.

erred

erred out of ignorance, in accepting such dif-
tinctions from a foreign prince, without her
confent, fhe releafed them from imprifonment; obliging them, neverthelefs, to refign
their honours, and to fend back their infig-
nia (*t*). Now, the obvious allufion to Spenfer's Sonnets, in 1595, feems to fettle the
epoch of *The two Gentlemen of Verona* to that
remarkable year.

No. VIII.—RICHARD III. 1595.

Shakfpeare had received fo many hints
from the perufal of Marlow's *True Tragedie*,
and fuch ftrong impreffions, from the de-
velopement, therein, of the character of Glocefter; that he was induced, immediately,
to continue the *Hiftorie* of Richard the third.
It is probable, that our great dramatift may
have been fomewhat emulous of the previous
fame of Marlow; of thofe fcenes, which
had merited the eulogy of Jonfon, when he
talked of *Marlow's mighty line*. Certain it
is, that when we open Shakfpeare's Richard

(*t*) See Camden's An. in Kennet, 2 vol. p 579.

the

the third, we feem to mount from the uniform flat, wherein we had been travelling, with uncheered fteps, to an exalted eminence, from whence we behold around us, an extenfive country, diverfified by hill and dale, refrefhed by many waters, and traverfed by roads, leading to hofpitable manfions :

Glof. Now, is the Winter of our difcontent
Made glorious Summer by this Sun of York ;
And all the Clouds, that lowr'd upon our houfe,
In the deep bofom of the ocean, bury'd.

Shakfpeare had, probably, heard that this ftory had been already " acted in St. John's, " Cambridge, fo effentially, that had the " tyrant of Phalaris beheld his bloody pro- " ceedings, it had mollified his heart : " He, certainly, knew, that an *Enterlude* entitled the *Tragedie of Richard the third*, had been exhibited, in 1593, or 1594. In fact, there was entered in the Stationers' Regifters, on the 19th of June, 1594, " An En- " terlude, intitled the Tragedie of Richard " the third, wherein is fhewn the death of " Edward the fourth, with the fmothering " of

" of the two princes in the Tower, with the
" lamentable end of Shore's wife, and the
" contention of the two houfes of Lancaf-
" ter and Yorke (*u*)." Shakfpeare's own
Tragedie of Richard the third, with the
death of the Duke of Clarence, was entered in the fame Regifters, on the 20th of
October, 1597; and it was publifhed, in the
fame year (*x*): But, it muft have been previoufly
acted, and written, before it was publifhed:
Now, thofe confiderations, when compared
with the fubfequent productions of the fame
poet, fix the true epoch of Richard the third,
in 1595, and not in 1597.

Whether it were, that the *Sun of Yorke*
began to difpel the clouds of Lancafter,
which had fo long enveloped truth, in win-

(*u*) Steev. Shak. 1793, vol. x. p. 700-1. In eftimat-
ing thofe probabilities, we ought to take into the account, that Churchyard publifhed his *Challenge*, in
1593, which comprehends " the *Tragedie of* SHORE's
" *Wife*, much augmented, with divers new additions."
This *Legend* was extremely popular, owing to its fimplicity, and moral; and by it Churchyard gained juft
celebration.

(*x*) Steev. Shak. 1793, vol. i. p. 427.

X   ter's

ter's gloom, the acceffion of King James, when *grim-vifag'd war fmoothed his wrinkled front*, appears clearly to have fet free feveral pens, that gave new luftre to hiftory. Sir George Buc, who was an antiquary, took the lead, in exhibiting jufter views of Richard's ftory, than the fcenic reprefentations of Shakfpeare had given, from the " little " underftanding" chroniclers : Yet, the life of Richard by Sir George Buc, was not publifhed till 1647; though the original draught of it had been, happily, preferved by Sir Robert Cotton. Sir William Cornewallis, the younger, publifhed, in 1616, an Effay, in *The Prayfe of King Richard the third*. The effayift feems to have lamented Richard's fate, and to have difdained the obloquy, which was daily caft up on his fame : " Neither can his blood," faid Cornewallis, " redeem him from injurious tongues, nor " the reproach offered his body be thought " cruel enough, but that we muft make him " more cruelly infamous, in *pamphlets*, and " *playes*." The late Lord Orford feems not to have known, that he had had a pre-
curfor,

curfor, in the office of apologift, in Sir Edward Cornewallis; who wrote with equal
refearch, and more learning, than himfelf.

Neither do the commentators feem to have
known, that the "much writing" Heywood
wrote a play, upon the fame fubject; as
Shakfpeare had before followed his predeceffors, over this fruitful field. Heywood
has left a *prologue*, which " was fpoken by
" a young witty lad, playing the part of
" Richard the third, at the Red Bull :"

> " If any wonder by what magick charme,
> " Richard the Third is fhrunk up, like his arme:
> " And, where in fulnefs you expected him,
> " You fee me only crawling, like a limme,
> " Or piece of that *knowne fabrick*, and no more,
> " When *he fo often hath been view'd before*." (*y*)

(*y*) See Heywood's *Pleafant Dialogues* and *Dramas*,
1637, p. 247. It is herein faid " That the Author,
" becaufe *he was* interefted *in the play*, wrote him this
" Prologue, and Epilogue." I do not fee this Richard
of Thomas Heywood noticed in any of the fcenic regifters.

No.

No. IX.—Richard II. 1596.

This *Hiftorie* was entered in the Stationers' Regifters, on the 29th of Auguft,
1597; and printed in the fame year: It was
recognized as Shakfpeare's, by Meres, in
his *Wit's Treafury*, during the year 1598.

Like other dramas of this great poet, this
Hiftorie was fuggefted to fo obfervant a
fpirit, by a former play, on the fame fubject;
though it had not Shakfpeare's adaptation to
the time, nor his proprieties of place, and
circumftance.

There is an intimation of time towards
the conclufion of the firft act, which points
directly to the true epoch of it's compofition:

Green. Now for the rebells, which ftand out in
Ireland:
Expedient manage muft be made, my liege,
Ere *further leifure* yield them *further means*,
For *their advantage*, and your *highnefs' lofs*.
K. Rich. We will ourfelf in perfon to this war.

In the Second Act, Bushy remarks:
The Wind fits fair, for news to go to Ireland;
But, none returns. For us to levy power,
Proportionable to the Enemy,
Is all impoffible.

The

The rebellion in Ireland, which was renewed, in 1594, was proclaimed, in 1595,
both in Ireland, and in England; and un-
derwent EXPEDIENT (*z*) *manage*, in 1596.
It follows, then, from thefe facts, if it were
the uniform practice of Shakfpeare to catch
at contemporary circumftances, for amufing
his audiences, that thofe ftrong remarks, on
the ftate of Ireland, in 1594, and in 1595,
when Tir Owen took the Queen's Fort, at
Blackwater, making at the fame time, many
profeffions of his *invariable loyalty* (*a*), fix
with fufficient certainty the writing of Richard II. to 1596. It ought to be remembered, to the honour of Shakfpeare, that he
laid his fatirical finger upon the weak, tem-
porizing, fhifting, policy of Elizabeth,
which gave every poffible encouragement to
the rebels; and which afforded unprincipled
traitors *further leifure;* and yielded them
further means, for *their advantage,* and *her
highnefs' lofs.* When to thofe ftriking allu-

(*z*) Camden in Ken. vol. ii. 581—587–589.
(*a*) Ib. 587.

fions,

fions, is added the concatenation of our poet's plan, in thofe hiftorical plays, it muft become apparent to every judicious eye, tha Richard II. was written in 1596; and not in 1597, as the editors have fuppofed, on weaker grounds.

After fome contrariety of opinion (*b*), and fome hefitation of judgment, the commentators feem to have finally fettled their conviction, " that there had been a former play " on this fubject, which appears to have " been called King Henry IV, in which " Richard was depofed, and killed on the " ftage (*c*)." But, none of the collectors of old plays have ever found fuch a drama; nor had Farmer, nor Tyrwhit, whofe authority for *the fact* is chiefly relied on, ever feen fuch a play : Thefe Critics, whatever weight may be due to their judgements, merely quote the acting of an old play on this fubject, by the procurement of Merrick, and other partizans of the rebel, Earl of Effex, on the

(*b*) Steev. Shak. 1778, vol. i. p. 296.
(*c*) Steev. 1790, vol. i. p. 533.

7th

7th of February, 1600–1 : On the trial of
Merrick, for high treafon, it was given in
evidence, among other treafonable facts,
" That the afternoon before the rebellion,
" Merrick, with a great company of others,
" that afterwards were all in the action, had
" procured to be played before them, *the*
" *Play of depofing Richard II;* neither was
" it cafual, but a play, befpoken by Merrick;
" and not only fo, but when it was told him
" by one of the players, *that the play was*
" *old,* and they fhould have lofs in playing
" it, becaufe few would come to it, there
" was fourty fhillings extraordinary given
" to play it; and fo thereupon played it
" was (*d*)." In oppofition to Farmer, and
Tyrwhit, I hold, though I have a great refpect for their memories, that it was illogical to argue, from a nonentity, againft an

---

(*d*) I quote from " The Declaration of the Practifes
" and Treafons attempted and committed by Robert
" late Earl of Effex and his Complices againft her Ma-
" jefty and her Kingdoms, &c." which was printed
by Barker, the Queen's Printer, in 1601 ; and which
is fuppofed to have been drawn by Sir Francis Bacon.

X 4

entity;

entity; that as no fuch play as the Henry IV, which they fpoke of, had ever appeared, while Shakfpeare's Richard II was apparent to every eye, it was in confequential reafoning, in them, to prefer the firft play to the laft: And, I am, therefore, of opinion, that *the play of depofing Richard* II, which was feditioufly, played, on the 7th of February 1600-1, was Shakfpeare's Richard II, that had been originally acted, in 1596, and firft printed, in 1597.

The acting of this play of *the depofing of Richard* II. funk deep into the heart of Queen Elizabeth. This treafonable infult, fhe never forgave, nor forgot. She fpoke, feelingly, of it to old William Lambard, when he prefented to her his *Pandecta Rotulorum*; adding, though I know not upon what information, " that this tragedy was " played forty times in open ftreets, and " houfes (*e*) "

It

(*e*) See in Nicols's curious Collection of Queen Elizabeth's Progreffes, vol. ii. " That which paffed from " the Excellent Majeftie of Queen Elizabeth, in her " Privie

It is true, indeed, that Haywarde, publifhed, in 1599. very imprudently, " The
" firft part of the life and raigne of King
" Henrie iiii; extending to the end of the
" firft yeare of his raigne," which he ftill
more imprudently dedicated, in very encomiaftic terms, to the Earl of Effex;
whether with the feditious purpofe of Merrick, I will not fuppofe. Certain it is, that
Elizabeth was highly irritated againft the
author. And fhe employed Sir Francis
Bacon to fearch the book for treafon. But,
from a charge, which involved in it the
penalty of death, he faved Haywarde, by a
joke; though not from a cenfure in the
Star Chamber, as his feditious, or his fyco-
phantic, purpofe, well deferved. Haywarde purfued the fame ftudies; publifhed
fimilar hiftories; and was knighted by King
James.

" Privie Chamber at Eaft Greenwich, 4 Augufti, 1601,
" 43 reg. fui, towards William Lambarde."—Whether
the *Pandecta Rotulorum* of Lambard were ever *printed,*
as I formerly fuppofed, I now doubt.

The

The Lord Chancellor Ellefmere, in deciding the cafe of the *Poſt nati*, pronounced a fevere cenfure on the writers of the *life*, and *reign*, of the unhappy Son of the illuftrious Prince of Wales ; " I will not re-
" member, faid that experienced Judge,
" Richard the Second's time (of which
" fome of our chroniclers do talk idly,
" and underftand little) where power and
" might of fome potent perfons oppreffed
" juſtice and faithful judges, for expound-
" ing the law foundly and truly (*f*)."
Whether Haywarde were included, in the Lord Chancellor's animadverfions, cannot now be difcovered ; but, probability leads us to fuppofe, that cenfure, will generally follow demerit, as a proper retribution.

In the 5th aɕt of Henry IV, there are intimations of what might be expeɕted of the Prince and his *loofe companions*, in the dramas, which came after it.   Boling-

(*f*) The fpeech of the Lord Chancellor of England, in the Exchequer Chamber, touching the *Poſt nati,* Printed 1609, p. 18.

broke,

broke, Percy, and other Lords being at Windfor Caftle, the father naturally afks:

Bol. Can no man tell of my unthrifty Son?
Tis full three months fince I did fee him laft:
Enquire at London 'mongft the Taverns there:
For, there, they fay, he doth frequent,
With unreftrained loofe companions;
Even fuch, they fay, as ftand in narrow lanes,
And beat our watch, and rob our paffengers.
   Percy. My Lord, fome two days fince, I faw the
      Prince;
And told him of thefe triumphs held at Oxford.
   Bol. And what faid the Gallant?
   Percy. His anfwer was, He would unto the ftews;
And from the commoneft creature pluck a glove,
And wear it as a favour; and with that
He would unhorfe the luftieft Challenger.
   Bol. As diffolute, as defperate; yet, through both,
I fee fome fparkles of a better hope,
Which older days may happily bring forth.

In thefe fketches, we may perceive the workings of the poet's mind, which had drawn an outline, that was to be filled up, and finifhed, in feveral fubfequent dramatical hiftories.

THE

No. X.—The Merry Wives of Windsor, 1596.

The epoch of the production of this fine Comedy has hitherto been fixed, in 1601, though the reasons, which have been assigned, for thus fixing it, would rather place it, at some earlier period (*g*).

It is a fact, which cannot be contradicted, that this play was merely a sketch, when it was first represented ; and was afterwards, altered, and expanded, when it was, in a subsequent reign, produced, as it at present stands. It was revised, enlarged, and amended, after the accession of King James, say the Commentators (*h*).

There are many allusions, in *The Merry Wives of Windsor*, which show, that it was originally sketched, in 1596, during the town talk about the return of Raleigh, and the publication of his lying narrative, concerning the discovery of *El Dorado*. There

(*g*) Steev. Shak. 1778, vol. i. p. 307 :—Steev. Shak, 1793, vol. i. p. 548.

(*h*) Steev. Shak. 1793, vol. i. p. 549.

are

are several metaphors, in this Comedy, which were fetched from the sea, from ships, and from sea affairs; and which seem to be unsuitable to the inhabitants of an inland town, like Windsor: But, the talk of the times turned on transmarine adventures. Of Ford's Wife, Sir John Falstaff says "She bears the purse too; " she is a region in Guiana, all gold and " bounty:" and, after sneering thus at Raleigh's *El Dorado*, Falstaff adds, with regard to Mrs. Ford, and Mrs. Page, " I " will be cheater to them both, and they " shall be exchequers to me; they shall " be my East, and West Indies; and I " will trade to them both:" Delivering his Epistles, for the *Merry Wives*, to his page, Sir John directs him—

" ———— to bear these letters tightly;

" Sail, like my pinnace, to these *golden shores*."

This *line*, which was in the first sketch of *the Merry Wives of Windsor*, shows, that it was written, say the Commentators, after Sir Walter Raleigh returned from Guiana, in 1596 (*i*).

(*i*) Steev. Ed. 1793, vol. i. p. 548.

But,

But, there is another note of time, which the Commentators have not remarked, although it is ftill more indicative of the date of this play. The *Fairy Queen* is often alluded to ; and is mentioned, in the fourth act, particularly. The whole plot, which was laid by Mrs. Page, to be executed at the hour of *fairy revel*, around Herne's Oak by *urchins*, *ouphes*, and *fairies*, green, and white, was plainly an .allufion to the *Fairy Queen* of 1596; which, for fome time, after its publication, was the univerfal talk of the time. In forming her *plot*, Mrs. Page adjufted, that,

" My Nan fhall be the *Queen* of all the *fairies*
" Finely attired, in a robe of white."

In the 5th act, *Nan*, and her *troop of Fairies*, *attend their feveral offices*, as the *moonfhine revellers*. Sir Hugh, with an encomiaftic allufion, to Elizabeth, the *Faery Queen*, *herfelf*, remarks :

" Our radient Queen hates fluts, and fluttery."

To all thofe ftriking intimations, let us add the obvious recollections of Lodge's *Devils Incarnate*, 1596, wherein he ridicules

cules the *lecherous race of Devils Incarnate,*
in our age (*k*). This *lecherous race* is expofed to ineffable ridicule, by the example
of Sir John's courtſhip of the *Merry Wives:*
When Falſtaff faw them at Herne's Oak,
he cries out, in the very language of the
Devil Luxury: "Let the Sky rain *potatoes*;
"let it thunder to the tune of Green
"Sleeves; hail kiſſing comfits; and fnow
"*eringoes:* Let there come a tempeft of
"provocation." For this profanation, Sir
John, who, according to Sir Hugh, "is
"full of *lecheries,* and iniquity," is pinched
by *the faeries,* who fing a fcornful rhime:

> "Fie on finful fantaſy!
> "Fie on luſt, and luxury!
> "Luſt is but a bloody fire
> "Kindled with unchaſte defire."

(*k*) See p. 45—46—50: Shakſpeare may have had
one eye on Lodge, as above; and the other eye on
Holingſhed, who defcribes a fimilar ſhower, as Mr.
Steevens has ſhown: [Shak. 1793, vol. iii. p. 482.]
Shakſpeare made ufe of two words, which are in Lodge,
but not in Holingſhed: Let it rain *potatoes:* and fnow
eringoes.

Such are the reasons, which convince me, that the first sketch of the Merry Wives of Windsor, was drawn, in 1596, and not in 1601.

Whether this Comedy were written by the command of Queen Elizabeth, as babbling tradition has said, and as the Commentators have as confidently repeated, as if the story had been recorded for a certainty, I think there is sufficient reason to doubt. She was certainly too feeble in 1601, to think of such toys; and she was perhaps too busy, in 1596. It is said, however, by the Commentators(*l*), that Falstaff talks, in the Merry Wives of Windsor, as if he were still in favour at Court; "*if it should come to the ear of the* " *Court how I have been transformed:*" But, this passage, I have not found: I see, indeed, in the first sketch, that Sir John, after he had been exposed at Herne's Oak, remarks,

" Well; if the *fine wits of the Court hear this,*

_____

(*l*) Steev. Shak. Ed. 1793, vol. i. p. 548.

" They'l

" They'l fo whip me with their keen jefts,
" That they'l melt me out like tallow (*m*)."

It is, moreover, faid, though I have not found the paffage, that Page difcountenances Fenton's addreffes to his daughter ; " *becaufe he kept company with the wild* " *Prince, and with Poyntz.*" Fenton does, indeed, tell Miftrefs Anne, that her father had objected, " my *riots paft*, my *wild fo-* " *cieties* :" (*n*) But, nothing is faid of the Prince, or Poyntz. After the tormenting faeries ran away, and a noife of hunting is heard, Sir John cries out: " What ; hunt- " ing at this time at night ! I'll lay my " life, the *mad Prince of Wales* is ftealing " his father's deer !" (*o*) On the whole, it is fufficiently apparent, that the firft fketch of this charming comedy was extremely imperfect, and the firft printed copy of it was ftill more defective: Nothing can be more filly than this joke of Falftaff's about

(*m*) Steev. Ed. 1766. H. 2. This paffage feems to have been left out of the improved Edition.
(*n*) Steev. 1793, vol. iii. p. 428.
(*o*) Steev. Ed. 1766, Sig. H. 2.

Y   the

the *mad Prince ſtealing his father's deer.* On ſuch an occaſion, Sir John could not have been ſuch a *blunt witted knight.* And, we ſee nothing of this impertinent interpolation, in the improved edition, which, originally, appeared in the firſt folio.

The precife time, " when the alterations, " and additions, were made, has not been " aſcertained," ſay the commentators (*p*). It was certainly altered, and amended, after the acceſſion of James I. becauſe, the king is expreſsly mentioned in the firſt ſcene. There is alſo emphatical talk about *the knights,* in alluſion, as the commentators think, to the numbers, which were made by that monarch, on his journey from Scotland. Miſtreſs Quickly tattles about the *coaches,* which came to the inſtallation; and this leads the commentators to tell, how coaches did not come into *general uſe* till the year 1605 (*q*). But, I have formerly ſhown, from the Journals of Parliament, that a bill was introduced, during

(*p*) Steev 1793, vol. i. p. 549.
(*q*) Steev. 1793, vol. i. p. 550.

the

the feffion of 1601, " to *reftrain* the *exceffive*
" ufe of *coaches* (*r*)." What is faid, by the
commentators, about the *Cotfwold games*, is
too indefinite to afcertain a date (*s*). There
is

(*r*) 1ft Jour. 602.

(*s*) In the firft act of the enlarged edition, Slender
naturally afks Page, " How does your fallow grey-
" hound, Sir? 1 hear he was outrun at *Cotfale.*" Slender alluded to the games at Cotfwold, in Glocefter-
fhire, which are faid to have been inftituted by Robert
Dover, an attorney, during the reign of James. Doctor Farmer doubts, whether Dover were not rather the
reviver than the *founder* of thefe rural fports. Mr. Steevens agrees with Doctor Farmer. Mr. Malone adopts
the opinion of Anthony Wood, that thofe manly games
were inftituted by Dover about the year 1603, with the
leave of King James, and the encouragement of Endymion Porter. [Steev. 1793. vol. i. p. 551-2.] The
fact, however, is, as we may learn from Rudder's Hiftory of Glocefterfhire, [p. 23-4.] That, in more
early times, there was at Cottfwold a cuftomary meeting, every year, at Whitfontide, called an *ale*, or
Whitfon-ale, which was attended by all the lads, and the
laffes, of the *villegery*, who, annually, chofe a Lord
and Lady of the *Yule*, who were the authorized rulers
of the *ruftic revellers.* There is in the Church of Ci-
rencefter, fays Rudder, an ancient monument, in *baffo-
relievo*, that evinces the antiquity of thofe games,

Y 2   which

is a note of time, however, that the commentators have overlooked, though it would have fhewn them the year, which they fearched for. I mean the ftatute(*t*), to reftrain the abufes of players. This act was made, " for preventing the *great abufe* of " the *holy name of God*, in ftage plays, en-" terludes, May-games, fhows, and fuch " like." This prohibitory law compelled Shakfpeare to foften down the character of Slender, who was a fwaggerer, in the firft

which were known to Shakfpeare, before the acceffion of King James. They were known, alfo, to Drayton early in that reign : For upon the map of Glocefter-fhire, which precedes the *fourteenth fong*, there is a re-prefentation of a *Whitfun-ale*, with a *maypole*, which laft is infcribed, " *Heigh for Cotfwold :*"

" Afcending, next, faire Cotfwold's plaines,
" She *revels* with the *Shepherds* fwaines;
" And fends the daintie nymphes away,
" 'Gainft Tame and Ifis wedding day."

[I quote from the *Poly-Olbion* of the year 1613. In addition to the *Annalia Dubrenfia*, 1636, there is a copy of verfes in D'Avenant's Poems, 1638, " In celebra-" tion of the yearely preferver of the games at Cotf-" wold."]

(*t*) 3 Ja. i. ch. 21.

draught;

draught; and who fwore, often, in the prefence of Anne Page (*u*): But, in the improved play, " the abufe of the holy name
" of God" is expunged. Slender no longer
talks ftoutly of *taking a bear by the muzzle.*
And he is fweated down to a *fimpleton,* who
difcovers, that Miftrefs Anne Page fpeaks
fmall like a woman; who cannot diftinguifh
a boy from a girl in the dark; and who
protefts, " if he had married the poftmaf-
" ter's boy, for all the boy was in woman's
" apparel, he would not have had him."
The ftatute, then, obliged Shakfpeare to
change the whole character of Slender,
much for the better, from *Swaggerer* to
Simpleton. Thefe fuggeftions feem to fix
the epoch of the alterations, and amendments, of this comedy, to 1606. On reading Falftaff's love letter, Mrs. Page exclaims: " Why I'll *exhibit a Bill in Parlia-*
" *ment,* for the putting down of fat men (*x*)."

(*u*) Steev. Ed. 1766. Sign. E. 4.
(*x*) This parliament began the 5th of November 1605,
and ended the 26th May 1606. 1 C. Journal of thofe
dates.

This

This obvious farcafm on the many bills, which were unadvifedly moved, in that Parliament, was not, probably, ventured till after the prorogation, on the 26th of May, 1606. On the whole, it is apparent, from thofe facts, and circumftances, that the commentators conjectured, erroneoufly, both with regard to the original fketch, when they fixed it, in 1601, and the amended drama, which they placed, in 1603.

No. XI.—Henry IV.
The Firft Part, 1596.

This drama was mentioned by Meres, in 1598. It was, in fact, entered in the Stationers' Regifters, on the 25th of February, 1597–8, and was printed, in 1598: And, from thefe facts, the commentators infer, that this play was written, in 1597.

There are other circumftances, however, which fpeak with ftronger evidence, that the firft part of Henry IV. was written, in 1596. The firft fcene opens with the King's reflections on his own health, and the ftate of the nation:

" So

" So fhaken as we are, fo wan with care,
" Find we a time for *frighted peace to pant* ;
" And breath fhort winded accents of *new broils,*
" To be *commenced in ftronds a far remote."*

This paffage, plainly, alludes to the re-
newal of hoftilities with Spain, in 1596;
and to the failing, in June, of the expedition to Cadiz, from which place, Howard,
and Effex, having facked it, departed
thence, on the 5th of July, 1596 (*y*).

Falftaff, when concerting a robbery, for
recreation fake, remarks, with a biting fneer,
that " the poor abufes of the time want
" countenance." While the military preparations were making, in 1596, fays Camden, " there were a parcel of loofe fellows,
" who went about the kingdom, under
" the counterfeit authority of *the Queen's*
" *Purfuivants,* with fham warrants, taking
" away, by force, plate, jewels, and what-
" ever they could find." (*z*). That fuch
abufes *of the time* fhould have exifted under
the wife reign of Elizabeth, and under the
difcreet adminiftration of Burleigh, would

(*y*) Camden in Kennet, vol. ii. 592-3.   (*z*) Ib. 595.

Y 4   be

be incredible, if they were not related by Camden, and confirmed by incontrovertible evidence: There ftill remains a Proclamation, dated the 3d of May, 1596, "againft " fundry abufes, practifed by divers lewd " and audacious perfons, falfley naming " themfelves Meffengers of Her Majefty's " Chamber, travelling from place to place, " with writings counterfeited, in form of " warrants; to the great flander of her " Majefty's fervice, and abufe of her loving " fubjects." It appears, moreover, by the proclamation, that though divers of thofe andacious perfons had, for fuch practices, been fet in the pillorie, had loft their ears, and had been marked in the face, for their notable *abufes*; yet, fuch were the audacious difpofitions of thofe moft vile perfons, fays the proclamation, that they more and more continued this *notorious abufe*. Such, then, were the *poor abufes* of the time, which were ridiculed, by the farcafms of Falftaff, in this play. When Prince Henry, laughing at Sir John, fays, " I fee a good " amendment of life in thee, from praying

" ing to purfe taking ;" Falftaff cries out,
" Why, Hall, 'tis my *vocation*, Hall! 'tis
" no fin for a man to labour in his *voca-*
" tion !" The fatire is here, plainly, levelled at the *Meffengers* of the *Queen's Cham-*
ber; the purfuivants; who, under pretence
of authority, levied contributions on the
people: And this fatire muft have been
highly applauded, by the auditors, who had
feverely felt the grievance. Shakfpeare
may poffibly have had in his mind, at the
fame time, Ratcliff's *Politique Difcourfes*,
of 1578, which gave the etymology and de-
finition of the word *vocation*; as Dr. Farmer remarked (*a*).

There are other allufions to the year,
1596. The carriers lamenting, in act II.
the death of Robin, the oftler, at Rochefter,
remark, that " the poor fellow never joy'd
" fince *the price of oats rofe*; it was death
" to him." The price of grain rofe to a
very uncommon height, in 1596, " by co-
" lour of the *unfeafonablenefs of this fom-*

(*a*) Steev. 1793. vol. viii. p. 380.

" *mer:*"

" *mer:*" And, on the laſt day of July, 1596, the Queen iſſued " *A Proclamation* for the " *Dearth* of *Corne*," againſt ingroſſers, and the makers of ſtarch.

The impetuous Hotſpur, grown impatient at the tedioufneſs of Glendower, exclaims : He angers me, with telling—

" ——— Such a deal of ſkimble-ſkamble-ſtuff,
" As puts me from my faith : I tell you what ;
" He held me, but laſt night, at leaſt nine hours,
" In reckoning up the feveral *devils names*,
" That were his lackeys."

Here, again, is another ſtroke at the *Devils Incarnate* of Lodge, in 1596, which have all appropriate names. There are even alluſions to the year preceding : To Daniel's *Civil Warres*, of 1595; and, to a collection entitled, *Wits*, *Fits*, and *Fancies*, of the fame year : and, moreover, an alluſion to the Letter of Amurah the Great Turk, to Chriſtendom, in 1594 (*b*).

(*b*) Steev. 1793, vol. i. p. 537.

No.

No. XII.—Henry IV.

The Second Part, 1597.

The late Dr. Johnfon has remarked,
" That thefe two plays [Henry IV. the firft
" and fecond parts] will appear to every
" reader, who fhall perufe them, without
" ambition of critical difcoveries, to be fo
" connected, that the fecond is merely a
" fequel to the firft; to be two, only, be-
" caufe they are too long to be one (*c*)."
It was entered in the Stationers' Regifters,
on the 23d of Auguft, 1600, and was
printed, in the fame year. Ben Jonfon,
certainly, alluded to the *Juftice Silence* of
this play, in his *Every Man in his humour,*
which was firft acted in 1599; but was probably written, in 1598, as the flownefs,
and circumfpection of Ben, are fufficiently
known.

No. XIII.—Henry V. 1597.

This Chronicle Hiftorie of Henry V. was
entered in the Stationers' Regifters, on the

(*c*) Mal. Shak. vol. v. 279.

14th

14th of Auguft, 1600; and was printed, though imperfectly, in the fame year. It is evident, fays Mr. Tyrwhit, that Shak-fpeare had formed the plan of Henry V. when he concluded his Henry IV; though it is, equally, apparent, that fome time elapfed, and other objects intervened, before he finally executed his preconceived purpofe: The *Epilogue* to Henry IV. told the audience, according to the theatrical practice of that age: " If you be not too " much cloyed with *fat meat*, our humble " author will continue the ftory with *Sir* " *John* in it, and make you merry with " fair Katherine of France; where [in the " play] for any thing I know, Falftaff " fhall die of a fweat, unlefs already he be " killed with your hard opinions."

There is, indeed, a note of time, in this dramatical *Hiftorie*, which is fo demonftrative of the epoch, when it was produced, as to be decifive of the fact. At the commencement of the 5th act, the *Chorus* enters, with an explanation of *the Story*, and

due

due *courfe of things :* and defires the audience
to " behold

" In the quick forge and working houfe of thought,
" How London doth pour forth her citizens !
" The Mayor, and all his brethren, in beft fort,
" Like to the Senators of antique Rome,
" With the Plebeians, fwarming at their heels,
" Go forth, and fetch their conquering Cæfar in :
" As by a lower but by loving likelihood,
" Were *now* the General of our gracious Emprefs
" (As in good time he may) from Ireland coming ;
" Bringing rebellion broached on his fword,
" How many would the peaceful city quit,
" To welcom him ?"

Effex, *the general of our gracious Emprefs,*
went to Ireland, fay the Commentators, on
the 15th of April, 1599; and returned to
London, on the 28th of September of the
fame year(*d*). " About the end of March,"
fays Camden (*e*), " the Earl of Effex fet
" forward for Ireland, and was accompa-
" nied out of London with a fine appear-
" ance of nobility, and gentry, and the moft
" chearful huzzas of the common people."

(*d*) 5 Mal. Shak. 585.—Vol. i. 320.—1 Steev. 539.
(*e*) In Kennet, vol. ii. p. 614.

In

In fact, the Queen iffued, on " the laft day
of March, 1599," her proclamation; " de-
" claring her princely refolution, in fending
" over of her army into the realm of Ire-
" land." There was, at the fame time,
ordered a public *prayer*, " for the good
" fuccefs of her Majefty's forces in Ireland."
Thefe facts prove, that the rebellion in Ireland, during the year 1599, the raifing of a
great army for its fuppreffion, and the appointment of Effex, as Lord Deputy, and
General, were brought, as ftriking objects,
before the eyes of the people of England:
The ftrong allufion of the *Chorus* muft have
been, therefore, received with popular applaufe.

Yet, it is more than probable, that this
appropriate paffage may have been interpo-
lated, in April, 1599; in order, on the reproduction of this martial *Hiftorie*, to gratify the temper of the times. It is a fact,
which the theatrical books of Henflow
prove, incontrovertibly, that the managers
of the theatres, in the age of Shakfpeare,
were in the conftant practice of employing
play-

play-wrights to *alter*, *mend*, and *add* to former plays: Rowley, Decker, Drayton,
Heywood, Ben Jonfon, and Maffinger, were
thus employed, to make frequent reparations
of decayed ftructures (f). It is, moreover,
a fact, that Shakfpeare altered, and amended,
his own dramas, and fometimes made *reparations* in the plays of contemporary dramatifts. From all thofe facts arife the pro-

---

(f) See Mal. Shak. vol. i. p^t. ii. p. 308-325. On the
17th of Auguft 1602, forty fhillings were paid by Henflow to Decker " for *new adycions* to *Owld-caftell.*" Mr.
Malone has the merit of having retrieved, and preferved,
the account-books of Henflow, from which he has favoured the public with extracts. [Ib. 288-325.] The
Editor has not, however, been always as happy in his
conjectures, as he was lucky in retrieving thofe perifhing
MSS.; which MSS. fhow, that there was acted by the
Lord *Admerall's* players, on the 11th of May, 1597,
" The Comedy of *Humers.*" This he conjectures to
have been Ben Jonfon's Every Man in his *humour.* [Ib.
299.] But, the *Humers* of Henflow was plainly Chapman's pleafant Comedy, entitled, *An Humerous Day's
Myrth*; which had been fundry times acted by the *Lord
High Admiral*, his fervants; and which was publifhed, in
1599: This fpecification precludes Mr. Malone's conjecture.

bability,

bability, that Shakſpeare amended his *Hiſ-torie* of Henry V; as new occurrences de-manded ſuitable additions.

The firſt ſketch of Henry V. was drawn, I believe, in the winter of the year 1597. The play opens with a converſation, be-tween the Archbiſhop of Canterbury, and the Biſhop of Ely, which alludes to an oc-currence of that period:

Cant. " My Lord, I'll tell you, that ſelf bill is urg'd,
" Which, in the eleventh year o'the laſt king's reign
" Was like, and had indeed againſt us paſs'd,
" But, that the ſcambling, and unquiet, time
" Did puſh it out of further queſtion.
Ely. " But, how, my Lord, ſhall we reſiſt it now?
Cant. " It muſt be thought on: If it paſs againſt us,
" We loſe the better half of our poſſeſſion:
" For all the temporal lands, which men devout,
" By Teſtament, have given to the church,
" Would they ſtrip from us."

If it be true, as the commentators have ad-mitted, and the fact demonſtrates, that Shakſpeare, like every other dramatiſt, both before, and after him, took advantage of the ſcenes of life, as they paſſed before him, to captivate the million, by alluſions to fa-miliar objects, it will follow as a ſtrong pro-bability,

bability, that Shakfpeare alluded, in the opening of the firft act, to the proceedings of the Parliament, in November, 1597. On the 14th of that month, it was remarked in the Houfe of Commons, " That although " her Majeftie had formerly been exceeding " unwilling, and oppofite, to all manner of " innovations in ecclefiaftical government; " yet, underftanding at this parliament, of " divers great abufes therein, fhe not only " gave liberty to the Houfe of Commons, " to treat thereof, but alfo encouraged them " to proceed in the reformation thereof, by " a meffage brought by Sir John Fortefcue, " the Chancellor of the Exchequer."(*g*) On the 22d of the fame November, the bill, for the relief of the poor out of *Impropriations*, and *other Church Livings*, was, after fome fpeeches, rejected, on the queftion, for the commitment, on a divifion of one hundred and feventeen, to a hundred and forty fix, votes(*h*). On the 23d of November, the bill, concerning leafes, made by

(*g*) D'Ewes's Journ. p. 557.   (*h*) Ib. 561.

Z   arch-

archbiſhops and biſhops, was, upon the ſecond reading, alſo rejected (*i*). Theſe paſſages muſt have attracted the public attention, owing to their accompanying circumſtances, and been felt by the audiences
of thoſe times.

In this drama, there is much ſaid, during
the conſultations againſt France; about the
intendment of the Scot: And King Henry,
wiſely, obſerves:

 " We muſt not only arm to invade the French ;
 " But, lay down our proportions to defend
 " Againſt the *Scot,* who will *make road upon us,*
 " With all advantages."

This applies, with more propriety, to the
occurrences of 1597, than to the tranſactions

(*i*) Ib. 562 : " Thus runs the Bill ;" ſays the Archbiſhop of Canterbury : " This would drink deep ; anſwers the Biſhop of Ely : " 'Twood drink the cup and
" all ;" replies the Archbiſhop.——" But my good
" Lord," reſumes the Biſhop, " How now for mitiga-
" tion of this Bill, urged by the Commons? Doth his
" Majeſty incline to it, or no ?"—The Archbiſhop concludes: " He ſeems indifferent, or rather, ſwaying
" more upon our part, than cheriſhing the exhibiters
" againſt us." [Steev. Shak. vol. ix. p. 270-4.]

of

of 1599: For, in 1599, King James sent Elizabeth notice, that there were twelve thousand men preparing, in Spain, to land in Ireland (*k*): The entrance of the *Ambassadors of France* accords better with 1597, than with 1599. Add to all those circumstances, the palpable allusion to them; and it appears to my eye a *confirmation strong*, that Henry V was originally sketched, in 1597. In mistress Quickly's admirable account of the death of Falstaff, a conversation arose about what Sir John said, on his death bed:

Nym. " They say, he cried out of sack.
Quick. " Ay; that 'a did.
Bard. " And of women.
Quick. " Nay; that 'a did not.
Boy. " Yes; that 'a did; and said, they were *devils incarnate.*"

The *Devils Incarnate* of Lodge, which was published, in 1596, appears never to have been out of Shakspeare's mind in 1597: An allusion to this striking publication would have, therefore, come too late, in 1599, to

(*k*) The Brit. Chronologist, vol. i. p. 174.

elevate,

elevate, and furprife, an audience, whofe minds are generally fixed on the paffing time, without thinking on that, which is paft. It was this confideration, which induced Shakfpeare to introduce the *chorus*, fpeaking of the *Emprefs's General*, when he departed for Ireland, in April 1599; becaufe the people's minds had been drawn to this fub- ject by a *royal proclamation*, and a *public prayer*. It was that confideration, alfo, which induced Shakfpeare, foon after the conference at Hampton Court, on the 14th of January, 1603–4 (*l*), to introduce a cha- racter of King James, that was out of place, if applied to Henry V: The Bifhop of Ely, having remarked, " We are bleffed in the " change of hydra-headed wilfulnefs," with an allufion to the reform of Henry V, this

---

(*l*) A pamphlet, containing the *fum* and *fubftance* of this conference, wherein King James acted as mode- rator, was publifhed by the Rev. Dr. Barlow, the Dean of Chefter, in 1604, 4to; by the direction of Arch- bifhop Whitgift, who died before the publication of it.

observation

obfervation gave the Archbifhop an occafion
to remark :

> " Hear him but reafon in Divinity,
> " And, all-admiring, with an inward wifh,
> " You would defire, the King were made a Prelate:
> " Hear him debate of Commonwealth affairs,
> " You would fay, it hath been all-in all his ftudy:
> " Lift his difcourfe of War, and you fhall hear
> " A fearful battle render'd you in mufick :
> " Turn him to any caufe of Policy,
> " The gordian knot of it he will unloofe,
> " Familiar as his garter ; that, when he fpeaks,
> " The air, a charter'd libertine, is ftill."

This is a finifhed delineation of one part
of King James's character, which clearly
diftinguifhes his powers of *difcourfe*, from
his faculties of action. Shakfpeare, indeed,
had penetrated into the whole character of
King James; as we fhall fee, in the fequel.
But, fuch were the colloquial powers of the
King, when he difcourfed on *Divinity*, on
War, or on *Policy*, that he impofed on that
difcerning minifter, Sir Francis Walfingham;
who was fent by Elizabeth, to difcover the
real character of James, while he was yet
young. I concur, then, with Warburton,
in thinking, " that this fcene was added

Z 3   " after

" after King James's acceffion to the throne."
But, I do not concur, in the inference, which
the fame critic, immediately, draws, " that
" we have no way of avoiding its being
" efteemed a compliment to *him*, but by
" fuppofing it a compliment to his *bifhops*."
Warburton's *impertinence* is not, however,
approved by Doctor Johnfon; who cannot
conceive, " why an opportunity fhould be
" fo eagerly fnatched, to treat with con-
" tempt that part of his character, which
" was leaft contemptible: If the poet had
" James in his thoughts, he was no very
" fkilful encomiaft." Yet, fuch was the
judgment of Shakfpeare, that he commends
the king for thofe colloquial accomplifhments, in which he excelled; at a time too,
[1604] when this part of his character was
beft known to his Englifh fubjects. The
king too, as he came through Berwick, had
fhewn his attendants, both by his *talk* and his
performance, that he knew, full as much as
kings generally do, of the *art* and *practick*
of gunnery. Mr. Steevens has added a note,
which, as it is equally inapplicable to the
fubject,

subject, neither confirms the remarks of Johnson, nor expofes the inaptnefs of Warburton (*m*). Notwithftanding what is thus, feebly, faid, by the three critics, I am of opinion, that Shakfpeare meant, in 1604, to offer to King James, a panegyric, which the audience felt to be juft; becaufe the accomplifhments were real: The poet may have been induced to make an offering of his panegyric; partly from motives of gratitude, and partly from feelings of emulation; Shakfpeare had received favours from King James; and he faw, at the fame time, Daniel, and Drayton, Ben Jonfon (*n*), and Dugdale (*o*), offering, feverally, their encomiaftic ftrains.

Such are the reafons, which induce me to be of opinion, that Shakfpeare made interpolations in his own play, in 1604, as well as in 1599. Nor, is it any ftrong objection,

(*m*) Steev. Shak. 1793, vol. ix. p. 371-2.

(*n*) Ben Jonfon publifhed, in 1604, a briefe panegyric of his Majefty's firft and *well aufpicated* entrance to his High Court of Parliament.

(*o*) *The Time Triumphant*, 1604.

to

to fay, that Meres did not mention Henry V, in 1598: For, Meres did not mention other undoubted dramas of our poet, which had been certainly produced, before the *Wit's Treafury* was written: Neither can a negative argument be oppofed, effectually, to affirmative circumftances.

On the whole, it appears to me, from weighing all probabilities, that the four dramas, which derive much of their intereft, from the character of Falftaff, were all written, fucceffively, in 1596, and in 1597: But, Henry V, was, undoubtedly, produced the laft In it, Falftaff does not come out upon the ftage, but dies of *a fweat*, after performing lefs than the attentive auditors were led to expect: And in it, ancient Piftol appears, as the hufband of Miftrefs Quickly; who alfo dies, during the ancient's abfence, in the wars of France.

Yet; do the commentators bring the Knight to life, and revive, and unmarry, the dame, by affigning the year 1601, as the epoch of the *Merry Wives of Windfor*. Queen Elizabeth is faid, by the critics to have commanded

manded thofe miracles to be worked, in
1601; a time, when fhe was in no proper
mood for fuch fooleries. The tradition, on
which is founded the ftory of Elizabeth's
command to exhibit the facetious knight *in
love*, I think too improbable for belief. The
maiden queen knew perfectly well, that Sir
John had, all his life, been an intriguer
among the wretched women of the town;
and fhe might thence infer, that it would
be no great feat to bring fo crafty a fharper
to intrigue with the merry women of Windfor. But, it was a harder tafk, which the
omnipotence of Elizabeth could not perform,
to bring Falftaff to real life, after being pofitively *as dead as nail in door*. Whatever a
capricious queen might have wifhed to have
feen, the audience would not have born to
fee the dead knight, on the living ftage; the
buried Quickly put on again the intriguing
chambermaid; and the married Piftol transformed into an old batchelor. Such tranfi-
tions are too violent, for fiction to create;
for credulity to believe, or fimplicity to admire !

The

The conclusion of the second part of Henry IV, was not very favourable, for Falstaff's speedy appearance among the *Merry Wives of Windsor*. Sir John had been sadly frowned on, by royal Hal, as *a vain man;* the Knight, who owed a thousand pounds to Master Shallow, was subjected to this disgrace, before the disappointed eyes of the Glocester Justice; and Falstaff was, by the Lord Chief Justice, committed to *the Fleet:* When Sir John took his bed, whence he never rose, Mistress Quickly, who knew his *conditions*, remarked, " the King has killed " his heart." Nym, soon after, adds, " the King hath run bad humours on the " Knight; that's the even of it." Pistol, immediately, subjoins,

" Nym, thou hast spoke the right;
" His *heart* is *fracted*, and corroborate."

With all his gaiety, and spirits, both natural, and assumed, Falstaff's *heart* became *fracted* when he saw himself scorned by the King; when he found himself committed by the Chief Justice; and feeling the infirmities of age, and fearing the dangers of
want,

want, he loft hope ; and " a burning quo-
" tidian tertian" fent him, from the houfe
of Miftrefs Quickly, to his " difhonourable
" grave."

It is apparent, therefore, that " the plea-
" fant and conceited comedy of Sir John
" Falftaff and the Merry Wives of Windfor"
could not, by any propriety of fiction, or
confiftency of judgement, be interpofed
between the fecond part of Henry IV, and
Henry V. If it be true, as Doctor Johnfon
affirmed, that the firft, and fecond parts of
Henry IV, are only two, becaufe they were
too long to make one ; if it be true, as the
firft act of the fecond part evinces, that Sir
John, foon after *doing good fervice at Shrewf-*
bury, was fent off, with fome charge, to
Lord John of Lancafter, at York ; He could
not, confiftently, faunter to Windfor, after
his rencounter with the Chief Juftice. When
to all thofe reafons are added the allufions,
and intimations of the Merry Wives of Windfor ; and when it is confidered, as it muft be
admitted, that the objections of the commentators are groundlefs ; it will be found,
that

found, that the true epoch of that comedy is 1596; and, that its proper place is before the firft part of Henry IV : Thus will the propriety of the poet's fiction, and the confiftency of action in his characters, be happily preferved!

No. XIV.—The Merchant of Venice, 1597.

This fine Comedy had forced itfelf on the notice of the world, before Meres wrote his *Wit's Treafury*, in 1598. It was, indeed, entered, for publication in the Stationers' Regifters, on the 22d of July, 1598. Yet, it does not follow as an inference, from the foregoing facts, that the *Merchant of Venice* was written, in 1598, as the Commentators affert (*p*).

The circumftance of *The Bond* was certainly taken, as Dr. Farmer fuggefted, from *The Orator*, which was publifhed in 1596. This intimation proves, that the Merchant of Venice may have been written, either, in

(*p*) Steev. 1793, vol. i. 538.

1597,

1597, or in 1596. From this ſtate of uncertainty, we may be relieved, by attending to
an alluſion, which did not catch the commentator's eyes: The merchant exclaims:

    "——— Nor, is my whole eſtate
    " Upon the fortune of *this* preſent year."

The queſtion then, is, what year was it,
which was a year of dread to traders? Monday, the chronicler, ſhall anſwer the queſtion: After taking notice of the loſſes of
Spain, from the capture of Hulſt, in 1596, he
adds: Then, did the " King of Spain diſ-
" penſe with himſelf for payment of his
" debts, which made many merchants in
" Spain, *Italy*, Antwerp, Amſterdam, and
" Middleburgh, to become *banquerouts(q)*."
While the balance was thus vibrating, between the years 1596, and 1598, this curious
faët fixes it for 1597.

No. XV.—Hamlet, 1597.

This captivating Tragedy, like other dramas of Shakſpeare, appears to have been
preceded by a play, on the ſame ſubjeët, and

(*q*) Monday's Briefe Chron. 1611, p. 422.

with

with a fimilar title, as early as 1589. On
this foundation, deriving fome materials
from the profe hiftory of Hamlet, this fkilful dramatift built his celebrated play of the
fame name; though it is not eafy to afcertain, exactly, the true epoch of its compofition. It was certainly printed, in 1604;
having been previoufly entered in the Stationers' Regifters, on the 26th of July, 1602.
Gabriel Harvey feems to have feen fome
copy of Shakfpeare's Hamlet, as early as
1598: while Meres appears, at the fame
time, not to have heard of what had already
attracted the notice of the dramatical world.
In Lodge's *Devils Incarnate*, 1596, there is
an allufion, indeed, to " *the Ghoft*, who cried
" fo miferably in the theatre, *Hamlet, re-*
" *venge* (*r*)." If this paffage could be,
clearly, fhown to allude to Shakfpeare's
Hamlet, the fact would prove, in oppofition to the commentators, that this play was
written, in a prior year.

There are feveral intimations, in this play,
which, plainly, refer back to the year 1596,

(*r*) P. 56.

as

as already paft. The enterprize of Fortin-
bras on the fkirts of Norway, is fuppofed
to be ;

" ———— The main motive of our preparations;
" The fource of this our watch; and the chief end
" Of *this poft-hafte* and *romage* in the land (s)."

In the midft of the commotions in Ireland, the Archduke of Auftria, fuddenly, attacked Calais; and Queen Elizabeth, hearing of this event, ordered fome forces to be
raifed, *the fame day*, being *Sunday*, during
divine fervice; in order to affift the French
King, and to fecure her own kingdom (t).
In April, 1596, a thoufand men were levied
in Kent, for the relief of Calais (u): On the
23d of May, a levy of a number of foldiers
was made, who were to repair to Dover for
the defence of Calais (x). In July, 1596,
the Queen's caftles, along the Kentifh coaft,
were furnifhed with great quantities of mu-
nition (y). In September, 1596, two thou-

(s) Steev. 1793, vol. xv. p. 14-15.
(t) Camden in Kennet, vol. ii. p. 591.
(u) Burleigh's Diary, in Murden St. pap. 808.
(x) Ib. 809.   (y) Id.

fand

fand men were fent to France, under the
conduct of Sir Thomas Bafkerville (*z*).
Speaking of the *portentous* appearance of the
ghoft, the poet adds, as a circumftance, which
forboded fome great event:

" ———— *And the moift Star*,
" Upon whofe influence Neptune's Empire ftands,
" Was fick almoft to Dooms-day with eclipfe.

Now; it is a fact, fufficiently known, by
the fad effects, that the fummer of 1596,
was a feafon remarkably *wet;* fo that the
hufbandmen could fcarcely fecure their
crops; the prices of grain rofe to an unex-
ampled height (*a*): And, in December,
1596, the ports were opened for the importation of corn (*b*): All thefe were deemed
by the poet:

" The prologue to the Omen coming on
" How heaven and earth together demonftrated
" Unto our Climatures and Countrymen.

While fo much doubt exifts, with regard
to the true epoch of this tragedy, thofe
facts, and circumftances, fix it, with fuffi-

(*z*) Burleigh's Diary, in Murden St. Pap. 809.
(*a*) Chron. prices. (*b*) Murden 811.

cient

cient certainty, to the beginning of the year, 1597.

There is another intimation, indeed, which muſt refer to a ſubſequent period: It is the announcing of the *players* by Roſencrantz to Hamlet, who aſks, " How " chances it they travel?" " I think," ſays Roſencrantz, " their inhibition comes, by " means of the late *innovation.*" The commentators have, grievouſly, miſcarried, in attempting to explain this paſſage, which was firſt quoted by Holt; becauſe, they did not know the fact, to which the dramatiſt alluded (c): The alluſion applies, pertinently, to the Order of the Privy Council, of the 22d of June, 1600, "for the *reſtraint* of the " *immoderate* uſe of *play-houſes;*" which, naturally, drove the *tragedians of the city,* into the country. There appears to be no other ſtriking event, in ſcenic ſtory, to which the *inhibition,* by *innovation,* could relate, without going back to the year 1589; in which year, regular commiſſioners were ap-

(c) Steev. 1793, vol. xv. p. 122—3.

A a   pointed,

pointed, for reviewing the productions of our
dramatifts. The ftatute of the 39th of Elizabeth (*d*), for preventing *common players*
from *wandering abroad*, which has been
quoted in explanation of that allufion, by
Mr. Malone, would have had a quite contrary effect, than the confequence of driving
the *Tragedians* of *the City* into the *Country*.
This paffage, then, as it was thus plainly
pointed to a remarkable event, in June 1600,
muft have been added, among other *addicyons*, before the republication of this tragedy, in 1604: For, the title-page of it declares this play to have been *enlarged to almoft as much again as it was, according to the
true and perfect copy* (*e*). From all thofe
facts, and allufions, it is more than probable, that Hamlet, like other dramas of
Shakfpeare, was firft fketched, early in
1597, and, ultimately, finifhed, in 1600,
with *addicyons*, which well fuited that portentous year.

(*d*) Ch. 4.
(*e*) Steev. 1793, vol. xv. p. 15.

If

If Gabriel Harvey, whofe book I have not feen, had not fpoken fo pofitively, in 1598, of the previous publication of Shakfpeare's Hamlet, I fhould have been induced, by facts, to have fixed the *original* fketch of Hamlet, in 1600. There were, in this year, long continued difputes with the Danes, in refpect to trade, and fifhery. The royal Dane confifcated the Englifh fhips; the Queen refented this arbitrary conduct; and commiffioners were appointed to fettle, by treaty, a trade, which had been begun by private intereft, and was now difcontinued by falfe policy (*f*). Such altercations muft have made fuch a play uncommonly attractive to a London audience. During this year too, there were conftant complaints of a fad fcarcity of corn; owing to *immoderate rains*, which had fallen in the autumn of 1599, and to the cold fpring time of 1600 (*g*). The notice of our obfervant dramatift was ftrongly drawn, no doubt, to thofe various events, which created public clamour.

(*f*) Camden, in Kennet, vol. ii. p. 625.
(*g*) Ib. p. 626.

No.

No. XVI.   King John, 1598.

This tragedy exhibits, to the difcerning eye, another example of Shakfpeare's cuf- tom, of borrowing, continually, from pre- ceding writers, *plots*, fentiments, fpeeches, and language (*h*).   As early as 1591, there had been a play, entitled, *The troublefome Raigne of John King of England*.   Shak- fpeare's tragedy was known to Meres, in 1598; as he names it in his *Wit's Treafury*, among our poet's other tragedies.   It was, foon after, ftill better known to Marfton, who plainly copied, as his cuftom was, when it fuited him, a line of Shakfpeare's drama into his *Infatiate Countefs*, which was pub- lifhed, in 1603.

> *Shak.*   " Why holds thine eye that lamentable rheum,
> " *Like a proud river peering o'er his bounds ?*"
> *Mars.*   " Then, how much more in me, whofe youthful veins,
> " *Like a proud river, overflow their bounds* (*i*)."

(*h*) Steev. 1793, vol. viii. p. 1.
(*i*) Mal. Shak. vol. i. p^t. 1. p. 314.

Such

Such are the proofs, which fhow pretty certainly, that Shakfpeare's King John, was written, between 1591, and 1598. In order to draw thefe extreme points clofer together, Mr. Malone fays, that Shakfpeare having loft his only fon, in 1596, was brought, by this misfortune, into a proper temper, for writing the pathetic lamentations of Conftance, on her Arthur's death. But, at what time of his life, was Shakfpeare unfit for drawing fimilar fcenes of deeper diftrefs? Johnfon has obferved, in a note, on this play, what applies more pertinently to the purpofe, " that many paffages, in " our poet's works, evidently fhow, how " *often he took advantage of the facts then,* " *recent, and the paffions, then in motion.(k)*" The fact is, that there are many allufions, in Shakfpeare's King John, to the events of 1596, and to fome, in 1597; though the commentators have not been very diligent, to collect them. The Pope publifhed a Bull, againft Elizabeth, in 1596; and the

(*k*) Mal. Shak. vol. i. p². 1. p. 312 : Steev. 1793, vol. viii. p. 81.

Pope's

Pope's Nuntio made fome offers to Henry
IV, againft Queen Elizabeth (*l*). The fcene
with *Pandulph*, the papal legate, which alludes to thofe offers, muft, as Johnfon remarks, have been at the time it was written,
during our ftruggles with popery, a very
captivating fcene (*m*). The contradictory,
fhifting, policy of England, and France, as
reprefented in King John, forms an admirable parody on the *adverfe*, friendly, conduct
of Elizabeth, and Henry the IV (*n*). Let
the fiege of Angiers, in King John, be compared with the lofs, and recapture of Amiens,
in 1597, chiefly by the valour of the Englifh
reinforcements, under the gallant Bafkerville. The altercations between the baftard,
Falconbridge, and *Auftria*, while the conduct
of the Archduke Albert was fo unpopular in
England, muft have afforded a rich repaft to
an Englifh audience: There is a ftrong allufion, particularly, in the laft act, to the
quarrel between Effex, and Raleigh, which

(*l*) Camden in Kennet, vol. ii. p. 601.
(*m*) Steev. vol. viii. p. 81.
(*n*) Camden in Kennet, vol. ii. p. 595.

began

began at Calais, in 1596, and rofe to a more remarkable height, in 1597 (*o*). Owing to the many piques among the great, occafioned by the felfifh ambition of Effex, the concluding remark of Falconbridge muft have been felt, and applauded, by the auditory :

" ———— Nought fhall make us rue,
" If England to itfelf do reft but true.

If to all thofe intimations, we add the remark of Johnfon, how much advantage Shakfpeare, conftantly, derived from facts *then recent*, and the *paffions then in motion*, there can no doubt remain, but that our poet's King John muft be fixed to the fpring time of 1598; as the true epoch of its original production.

No. XVII.—A MIDSUMMER'S NIGHT'S DREAM, 1598.

This is fuppofed to be one of Shakfpeare's moft early Dramas, from the livelinefs of its imagery, and the reiterations

(*o*) Camden in Kennet, vol. ii. p. 594, 597.

of

of its rhimes; the narrownefs of its fable, and the indiftinctnefs of its principal characters. It is certain, indeed, that this play was entered in the Stationers' Regifters, in 1600; and is even mentioned by Meres, in 1598 (*p*).

The year 1595 was, originally, affigned, as the epoch of the Midfummer's Nights Dream (*q*). This date has, however, been, fince, altered to 1592 (*r*), by one of thofe *wondrous changes of a fatal fcene*, which we frequently meet with, in this dramatical chronology. I fee no good argument, for changing the epoch from 1595, to 1592: But, for better reafons, I am of opinion, that it was written, early in 1598.

In the fine fpeech, with which Thefeus opens the 5th act (*s*), in anfwer to Hippolyta's exclamation, " 'Tis ftrange, that " thefe lovers fpeake of," he remarks:

" One fees *more devils* than *vaft hell can hold*."

(*p*) Wit's Treafury.
(*q*) Steev. 1778, vol. i. p. 285.
(*r*) Steev. 1793, vol. i. p. 497.
(*s*) 5 Steev. 1795, p. 140.

This

This is, plainly, a farcafm on Lodge's pamphlet, called " Wits Miferie, and the " Worlds Madneffe ; difcovering the *In-* " *carnate Devils* of this age," which was publifhed, in 1596. Thefeus had already remarked, in the fame fpeech :

" The lunatic, the lover, and the poet,
" Are of imagination all *compact.*"

Lodge has the fame word *compact*, as fingularly coupled : " Heinoufous thoughts " *compact* them together." It is curious to fee, in the prefent day, the characters, which Lodge, then, beftowed upon thofe contemporary poets, whom he thought the moft celebrated, in 1596 (*t*): Lilly is famous for facility in difcourfe ; Spenfer is beft read in ancient poetry ; Daniel is choice in word and invention ; Drayton is diligent and formal ; T. Nafh is the true Englifh Aretine. But, forgetting Shakfpeare, Lodge only fays, generally : " All " you unnamed profeffors, or friends of " poetry (by me inwardly honoured) knit

(*t*) Incarnate Devils, p. 57.

" your

" your induſtries in private to unite your
" fames in public : Let the ſtrong ſtay up
" the weak, and the weak march under
" the conduct of the ſtrong." Owing to
this preference given to other poets, Shakſpeare, who had certainly read Lodge's
pamphlet, becauſe he borrows thoughts,
and expreſſions, from it (*u*), now returned
marked diſdain, for contemptuous ſilence.
There is another paſſage in Lodge's Satire,
which Shakſpeare may have felt (*x*):
" They ſay likewiſe, there is a *Plaier-*
" *Devil*, or handſome ſon of Mammons ;
" but yet, I have not ſeen him, becauſe
" *he ſkulks in the country :* If I chance to

(*u*) Incarnate Devils, p. 40.

(*x*) In p. 46, Lodge, in deſcribing his *Lecherous Devil*,
the patron of Peticote-lane, ſays, " If he take up Com-
" modites, it is Cock-ſparrows, potato's and herringes
" [Eringoes] and the hotteſt wines are his ordinary
" drink, to increaſe his courage." With this, compare
what Shakſpeare ſays, in The Merry Wives of Windfor ; " Let the ſky rain *potatoes*, hail kiſſing comfits,
and ſnow *Eringoes :*" And mark what is ſaid in *Troilus
& Creſſida*, " How the *Devil luxury*, with his fat rump
" and *potatoe finger*, tickles theſe together."

" meet

" meet him againſt the next impreſſion,
" he ſhall ſhift very cunningly, but I'll
" pleaſantly conjure him ; and though he
" hath a high hat to hide his huge horns!
" I'll have a wind of wit to blow it off
" ſpeedily : If they uſe but Entrapelian
" urbanity, and pleaſure mixed with ho-
" neſty, it is to be born with all ; but,
" filthy ſpeaking, ſcurrilitie unfit for chaſte
" ears, that, I wiſh with the Apoſtle,
" ſhould not be named among Chriſtians :
" Again, in ſtage plays, to make uſe of
" hyſtorical ſcripture, I hold it, with the
" *Legiſts*, odious ; and as the Council of
" Trent did, I condemn it."

There was a poem, entitled, *Pyramus
and Thiſbe*, publiſhed by Dr. Gale, in
1597 ; but, Mr. Malone believed this to be
poſterior to *The Midſummer's Night's Dream*.
On the contrary, I believe, that Gale's *Pyramus and Thiſbe*, was prior to Shakſpeare's
moſt lamentable " Comedy of Pyramus
" and Thiſby." The Author of the Comedy of *Doɛtor Dodipol*, which was publiſhed, in 1596, or before this year, either
borrowed

borrowed a line from Shakſpeare; or Shakſpeare borrowed from him; as indeed, Mr. Steevens has acutely ſhown:

Dr. Dodipoll:

" 'Twas I that led you through the painted mead,
" Where the light faeries danc'd upon the flowers;
" *Hanging in every leaf an Orient pearl.*"

Midſummer's Night's Dream:

" And hang a *pearl* in every Cowſlip's ear."

Again:

" And that ſame dew, which ſometimes on the buds,
" Was wont to ſwell, like round and *Orient pearls,*
" Stood now within the pretty flourets eyes,
" Like tears, &c."

I am thus led, by my premiſes, to infer, that Shakſpeare, according to the laudable practice of the bee, which ſteals luſcious ſweets from rankeſt weeds, derived his extract from Dodipol; and not Dodipol from Shakſpeare.

It is to be remembered, that the ſecond volume of the *Faiery Queen* was publiſhed, in 1596; being entered in the Stationers' Regiſters, on the 20th January 1595-6. This, for ſome time, furniſhed town-talk; which never fails to ſupply our poets with
dramatical

dramatical topicks. The Faiery Queen helped Shakfpeare to many hints. In the Midfummer's Night's Dream, the fecond act opens with a fairy fcene : The *fairy* is forward to tell,

" How I ferve the *fairy queen*,
" To *dew her orbs upon the green:*
" And jealous Oberon would have the child
" *Knight* of his train, to trace the forefts wild,"

Here, then, are obvious allufions to the *Faery Queen* of 1596; as may alfo be inferred from the imitations from *Dr. Dodipol*, and from other allufions to the *incarnate Devils :* If to thefe two, we add the *Faiery Queen* of 1596, the couplement will give a demonftration, that the *Midfummer's Night's Dream* was written fubfequent to 1596.

In the firft act of *The Midfummer's Night's Dream*, Egeus comes in, *full of vexation*, with complaint againft his daughter, Hermia, who had been bewitched by Lyfander with *rhimes*, and *lovetokens*, and other *meffengers of ftrong prevailement in unharden'd youth :* And claimed, of the Duke, the

the ancient privilege of Athens; infifting either to difpofe of her to Demetrius, or to death,

> " ———— according to our Law,
> " Immediately provided, in that cafe."

Warburton, who has always at hand, his fagacity, or his learning, to find what is not to be found, has remarked, on this paffage, that, by a law of Solon, parents had the power of life and death over their children; that the poet may have fuppofed, that the Athenians had fuch a law before the age of Solon; that perhaps the Drama-tift neither thought, nor knew, any thing of the matter (*y*). But, Shakfpeare never went to a diftance, for what he faw paffing before him. Our obfervant Dramatift, pro-bably, alluded to the proceedings of Par-liament, on this fubject, during the feffion of 1597. On the 7th of November of that year, the bill was committed, for depriving offenders of clergy, who, againft the ftatute of Henry VII, fhould be found guilty of

(*y*) 5 Steev. 8.

the

the taking away of women againft their wills (z). On the 14th of November 1597, there was a report to the Houfe, touching the abufes from *licences for marriages, without bans*; and alfo touching *the ftealing away of men's children without the affent of their parents* (a): On the fame day, the Chancellor of the Exchequer, brought a meffage from the maiden Queen, about " the horrible and great inceftuous mar- " riages, which had been difcovered in " the Houfe; minding due punifhment of " the fame, in particular of the members " of the Houfe (b)." Thefe obvious allu- fions to ftriking tranfactions, of an intereft- ing nature, carry the epoch of this play beyond that feffion of Parliament, which ended on the 9th of February, 1597-8 (c).

(z) D'Ewes Journal, 552.

(a) Ib. 556: vid. 39 Eliz. ch. 9, particularly, the recital thereof: This, then, is Shakfpeare's law; "im- " mediately provided, in that cafe."

(b) Id. And fee what is faid about Adultery and Bigamy in *The Incarnate Devils*, 1596. p. 51.

(c) D'Ewes, 546.

In

In the fecond fcene of the fecond act of Midfummer's Night's Dream, there is a fine defcription, of a very unfavourable feafon :

    " Contigious fogs, which falling in the land,

    " Have every pelting river made fo proud,

    " That they have overborn their Continents :

    " The Ox hath therefore ftretch'd his yoke in vain ;

    " The Ploughman loft his fweat; and the green Corn,

    " Hath rotted, ere *his* youth attain'd a beard."

In fact, the prices of corn rofe to a great height in 1597 (*d*) ; and, during the fame year, in addition to the miferies of famine, there was a great plague in London, which carried off eighteen thoufand perfons (*e*). Thefe facts confirm the previous circum-ftances, which would fix the epoch of this fairy play, to the beginning of the year 1598.

It has been fuppofed, however, upon very flight grounds, that there is an allu-fion to the death of Spenfer, " *late* deceafed,

(*d*) Cambrone's Enquiry into the prices of grain, p. 32.

(*e*) The Brit. Chronologift, 173.

                                                 " in

" in beggary :" But, this bewitching Drama was certainly written before September 1598 : And, at that time, Spenfer was living, very quietly, in his Caftle of Kilcolman, within the county of Cork ; and was deftined, by the Queen, to be High Sheriff of that fhire (*f*): It was in October, 1598, that the Irifh rebellion, breaking out with the inftantaneous force of a flafh of lightning, involved Spenfer in ruin. Such are the facts, and arguments, which have convinced me, that the Midfummer's Night's

(*f*) The diligence of Mr. Malone has difcovered a Letter from Queen Elizabeth, dated the laft day of September 1598, to the Irifh Government; recommending Spenfer to be Sheriff of Cork: Mr. Malone had before the merit of difcovering the penfion to Spenfer. If to thefe acts of munificence of the Queen, we add the grant of his land and caftle, the total is a demonftration, that Spenfer was not neglected: And, confequently, that Slander ought no longer to caft her obloquy on Elizabeth and Burleigh, but on the Irifh rebellion. It feems unneceffary to remark, that if the Lord Treafurer Burleigh had fet himfelf againft the poet, he never would have obtained either his penfion, or his land.

B b   Dream

Dream was not written, in 1595, or in 1592, but in 1598.

No. XVIII.—The Taming of the Shrew, 1598—1606.

Among the commentators, there have been various opinions, both with regard to the writer, and the time of writing, of the Taming of *the Shrew*. The beft informed critics feem now to acknowledge, that this comedy was written by Shakfpeare, as, indeed, the play itfelf evinces; but, that a very different dramatift wrote, about the fame time, perhaps, a comedy called *the Taming of a Shrew*. After afcertaining a few facts, and adjufting fome circumftances, I am of opinion, that Shakfpeare, originally wrote *his* comedy, in 1598; and afterwards revived, and improved it, in 1606.

The commentators have remarked, that as it abounds in doggerel verfes, which indicate inexperience, and in the play of words, which he latterly condemned, it muft be of early compofition. And, Meres, who mentions twelve of Shakfpeare's dramas,

mas, in his *Wit's Treasury*, which was finished before September 1598, did not mention the Taming of *the* Shrew, among our poet's plays. Shakspeare obviously borrowed the names of two of his characters from *The Supposes* of Gascoyne, which was first acted in 1566, and published among his works, which were printed, a second time, in 1587; adopting, moreover, from Gascoyne's comedy, sentiments, and language. Add to all these proofs of an early composition, that there certainly was a similar Taming of *a* Shrew, published before 1596, perhaps, in 1594; from which Shakspeare may have borrowed both the moral, and the name.

There is in Shakspeare's Taming of *the* Shrew, a remarkable passage, that the commentators have overlooked; as they did not know the contemporary history, to which it related :—

" 'Tis death for any one in Mantua
" To come to Padua : Know you not the cause?
" Your Ships are stay'd at Venice : And the Duke,
" For private quarrel, 'twixt your Duke and him,
" Hath published, and proclaimed it openly :

'Tis

" 'Tis marvel ; but that, you 're but newly come,
" You might have heard it elfe proclaimed about."

This fignificant paffage, plainly, related to the commercial warfare between the Emperor, and Elizabeth, which ended in avowed prohibitions, by open proclamations. The Emperor Rudolph publifhed an edict, at Frankfort, on the 10th of September, 1597; banifhing the merchant adventurers of England from their refidence at Stade. In retaliation, Queen Elizabeth iffued a proclamation, on the 14th of January, 1597–8 ; commanding the merchants of the Hans Towns, to depart out of her dominions : The Mayor, and Sheriffs of London, were directed to remove the foreign merchants, who ufually refided in *the Steelyard*; and who, however, had addrefs enough to obtain the refpite of a month (*g*). It is eafy to perceive, that fuch tranfactions muft have made noife enough, in fuch a City as

(*g*) Thofe curious documents are contained in a mifcellaneous volume, which once belonged to Mr. Henry Powle, the Speaker of the Houfe of Commons, at the Revolution ; and which is now in my Library.

London,

London, to reach the quick and obfervant
ears of Shakfpeare. There is fomething
faid in the 3d and 4th acts, about irregular marriages, which may have alluded to
the proceedings of Parliament, in 1597, on
the fame fubject. Before circumftances,
pregnant as thefe are, loofe conjecture,
from vague declamation, muft give way to
accuracy of dates, and fubmit to decifivenefs of facts.

There are, moreover, fufficient grounds,
for believing, that Shakfpeare revifed, and
improved, the firft fketch of the Taming
of *the* Shrew, in 1606. The old play, on
the fame fubject, was revived, and publifhed, about the fame time; being entered
in the Stationers' Regifters, on the 22d
January, 1606–7. Shakfpeare's comedy
was entered, in the fame Regifters, on the
17th November, 1607. A very particular
occafion, which the commentators have
overlooked, gave rife to a competition at
the theatres, and among the bookfellers.
It was the arrival of the *Royal Dane*, in
London; and, the banqueting on that joy-

B b 3   ous

ous event. Lord Salifbury, the Secretary of State, wrote to the Ambaffador Winwood, on the 19th of July, 1606, " the " King of Denmark arrived yefterday at " Greenwich, being met firft by the King " and the Prince below Gravefend : It is " thought his abode here will be forty " days (*h*)." He, in fact, departed, on the 14th of Auguft, 1606. While he remained, there were nothing but caroufals ; royal, no doubt ; yet grofsly intemperate, and highly voluptuous. According to Shakfpeare, there was

" Nothing but fit and fit, and eat and eat."

Sir John Harrington has, indeed, left us a very amufing account of one of thofe banquets (*i*) ; wherein " the reprefentation of " Solomon's Temple, and the coming of " the Queen of Sheba, was made after " dinner. The lady who did play the " Queen, coming to prefent precious gifts " to the Kings, and forgetting the fteps,

(*h*) Winw. Mem. vol. ii. 247.

(*i*) This extremely interefting Letter is in the *Nugæ Antiquæ*, vol. ii. 126.

arifing

" arifing to the canopy, overfet her cafkets
" into his Danifh Majefty's lap, and fell at
" his feet : Napkins were at hand to make
" all clean : His Majefty then got up, and
" would dance with the Queen of Sheba,
" but he fell down, and humbled himfelf
" before her ; and was carried to an inner
" chamber, and laid on a bed of ftate,
" which was not a little defiled with the
" prefents, fuch as wine, cream, jelly,
" which the Queen had beftowed on his
" garments (*k*)." The *Induction* to the
Taming of the Shrew, which exhibits
drunkennefs to the eye, and the underftanding, in the moft ridiculous light ; was
properly revived, at a moment, when
" the Englifh Nobles, whom I never could
" get," fays Sir John Harrington, " to tafte
" good liquor, now wallow in beaftly de-
" lights : The ladies, abandoning their
" fobriety, are feen to roll about in intox-
" ication." There is another allufion to
that period, which feems to fhew, that the

(*k*) The whole Letter is well worthy of perufal.

original

original outline may have been now filled up, from an attention to recent events :

   " At laſt, though long, our jarring Notes agree.
   " And time it is, when raging war is done,
   " To *ſmile* at *'Scapes* and *perils over blown* (*l*)."

This may have alluded, ſpecially, to *the Gun-powder plot* of November, 1605, or it may have related, more generally, to foreign warfare : For, on the 16th of November, 1606, Winwood wrote to the Secretary of State (*m*), " that the *leaguer is* " *diſſolved.*"

No. XIX.—All's Well that ends Well, 1599.

This play is ſuppoſed, by the commentators, to have been mentioned in *The Wit's Treaſury* of Meres, in 1598, under the name of " Love's Labours *Won*." There is ſaid to be, in this comedy, an alluſion to the diſpute with the Puritans, which began in 1598, and continued, during the remainder of the reign of Queen Elizabeth. Theſe are

(*l*) Steev. vol. vi. 544. (*m*) Mem. vol. ii. 264.

the

the principal reasons, for their assigning the year 1598, as the true epoch of *All's Well that Ends Well* (*n*).

But, let us search for more satisfactory reasons, to justify the adoption of that epoch. The examination of *Parolles* will perhaps furnish a better argument. " This " is Monsieur *Parolles*," says the first Lord, " the gallant *militarist* (that was his own " phrase) that had the whole *theorick* of " war in the knot of his scarf, and the " practice in the chape of his dagger." In 1597, was published, as the commentators remark, " the *theorique and practice* of " *warre*, written by [to] Don Philip Prince " of Castil, by Don Bernardino de Mendoza. " Translated out of the Cistilian tongue in " [to] Englishe, by Sir Edward ⌈e⌉ Hoby, " Knight (*o*)."—4to. [without the name of the printer, the publisher, or the place.] I am of opinion, however, that this *translation* is not the book, which was alluded to by Shakspeare. In 1598, there was pub-

(*n*) Steev. 1793, vol. i. p. 538.
(*o*) Ib. vol. vi. p. 324.

lished,

lifhed, by Ponfonby, " The *Theorike* and
" *Practicke* of moderne warres difcourfed
" in *dialogue wife* : Written by Robert
" Barret." This author was the *gallant militarift :* For, he tells himfelf, as Shakfpeare
intimates, " that he had fpent moft part of
" his time in the profeffion of arms, and
" that, amongft foreign nations." He adds
a prayer " for *true martial valour* to the
" fervice and defence of our dread fove-
" raigne and deare countrie." In this book
of Barret's, there is much knowledge, but
ftill more affectation : He particularly
affects *foreign words :* Abanderado, Ambuf-
cado, Bando, Burgonet, Camerada, Ca-
mifada, Efcalada, Efquadra, Fila, Fronte,
Garrita, Hargulatier; and a thoufand
others, which are equally uncouth : " The
" word *Caporal,* which is a mere Italian,
" we do *corruptly* write *Corporal,*" fays this
gallant militarift. We now fee the fource of
the foreign terms, which Shakfpeare ufes,
in the examination of *Parolles : Portotar-
taroffo, Bofco chimurcho, Boblibindo chicur-
murco*

murco (*p*). The whole examination of Parolles appears to me, to be a continued farcafm on Barret's *Theorike* and *Practike* of Warre, written *dialoguewife*. Shakfpeare, whofe recollection of the paft, was equal to his obfervance of the prefent, may have had in his mind, " the examination " of one of Henry the Eighth's Captains, " which had gone over to the enemy in the " *Life of Jack Wilton*, 1594 ;" as Mr. Ritfon has obferved (*q*). For thefe reafons, it appears to me very probable, that *All's Well that Ends Well*, which was neither entered in the Stationers' Regifters, nor printed till 1623, was written, early in 1599, rather than in 1598 ; becaufe, the poet muft be allowed time to form his plan, to collect his thoughts, and to give them expreffion.

No. XX.—MUCH ADO ABOUT NOTHING, 1599.

This comedy, which is celebrated for its reciprocations of fmartnefs between Bene-

(*p*) Steev. Shak. 1793, vol. vi. p. 323.
(*q*) Steev. 1793, vol. vi. p. 323.

dick

dick, and Beatrice, was printed in 1600 ; and was, previouſly, entered in the Stationers' Regiſters, on the 23d of Auguſt, in the ſame year : But, it was not mentioned by the well informed Meres, in 1598. From the foregoing premiſes, the commentators inferred, that this comic drama was firſt written, in 1600 ; without reflecting, that it muſt have been repreſented on the ſtage, before it was entered in the Stationers' Regiſters ; and that it muſt have been written, before it was repreſented.

In the midſt of this uncertainty, about the preciſe year, it is reaſonable to enquire, for ſome note of time, which would give us more certainty about the epoch. In the opening ſcene, Leonato aſks Don Pedro's meſſenger, " How many gentlemen have " you loſt in this action?" Beatrice immediately enquires, " Is Signior Montanto, " (meaning Benedick,) returned from *the* " *wars* ?" *The wars*, which, at that time, fixed the attention of the court, the city, and the country, were Eſſex's campaign in Ireland, during the Summer of 1599. Being

told

told by the meffenger, that Benedick was returned, and as pleafant as ever; Beatrice follows up her queftion, with fome other enquiries: " I pray you how many men " hath he killed, and eaten, in *thefe wars?* " —But how many hath he killed? for " indeed, I promifed to eat all of his killing." The meffenger anfwers; " He hath done " good fervice, lady, in thefe wars." Beatrice, who was not to be foiled, readily replied: " Yes; you had *mufty victuals,* " and he hath holp to eat it." There can be but little doubt, that *the wars,* which were thus mentioned, alluded to the Irifh campaign of 1599. The fact is, as we may learn from Camden, and from Moryfon, that there were complaints of the badnefs of the provifions, which the contractors furnifhed the Englifh army in Ireland. And fuch a farcafm, from a woman of rank, and fafhion, and fmartnefs, muft have cut to the quick; and muft have been loudly applauded by the audience; who, being difappointed by the events of the campaign, would be apt enough to liften to a lampoon,

on

on the Contractor, rather than on the General ; who, by his great pretenfions, and fmall performances, had difappointed the expectations of the Queen, and the hopes of the nation. From all thofe intimations, it appears to be more than probable, that *Much Ado About Nothing* was originally written, in the autumn of 1599.

No. XXI.—As You Like It, 1600.

The genuine epoch of this Comedy has never been fettled, by fatisfactory reafons. It was certainly written, in the period, between 1596, and 1600 ; and it was entered in the Stationers' Regifters, on the 4th of Auguft, 1600. In Orlando's verfes, in praife of his miftrefs, it is faid :

" From the *Eaft* to *weftern Ind*,
" No jewel is like Rofalind:
" Her worth being mounted on the wind,
" Through *all the World* bears Rofalind.

Here are obvious allufions to the frequent voyages for diftant difcovery, which feem to have ended, for a time, in 1596. The fountain, which Stow relates to have been

    fet

set up, during the year 1596, in Cheapside, with *Diana* in *the fountain*, is plainly alluded to in *As You Like it*. In this Comedy, there is quoted a line of Marlow's *Hero* and *Leander*, which was certainly published before the year 1598 (*r*). It seems to be more than probable, that the intrigues at Court, which became apparent to every eye, after the return of Essex from Ireland, on the 28th of September, 1599, may have extorted the following sarcasm of Shakspeare :

> *Duke Sen.* Now, my Co-mates, and brothers in exile,
> " Hath not old custom made this life more sweet
> " Than that of painted pomp ? Are not these woods
> " *More free* from *peril* than the *envious Court ?*"

If there be any allusion, in these reflections, to the fall of Essex, who was sequestered from Court, soon after his arrival, the epoch *of As You Like it*, must be fixed in the winter of 1599. There can be no doubt, that it was imitated by Drayton, in

(*r*) Steev. 1793, vol. i. p. 547.

his

his *Owl,* which was firſt publiſhed, in 1604 (*s*).

No. XXII.—Troilus and Cressida, 1600.

This play, like other dramatical productions of Shakſpeare, was preceded by an earlier drama of a very different poet, on the ſame ſubject (*t*): The Troilus and Creſſida of Shakſpeare was entered in the Stationers' Regiſters, on the 7th of February 1602-3; though it was not printed 'till 1609: And, it was, therefore, probably, written, in 1602, ſay the Commentators (*u*). It was certainly acted before the acceſſion of King James: For, it is a fact, which is recorded, in the Stationers' Regiſters, that *Troilus and Creſſida* had been acted by the *Lord Chamberlain's men,* who became the King's ſervants, at his acceſſion to the throne (*x*).

Yet, none of thoſe intimations ſettle the

(*s*) Harden's Biog. Mirror, vol. i. p. 104-5.
(*t*) Steev. 1793, vol. ii. p. 482.
(*u*) Ib. p. 565.   (*x*) Id.

precife

precife epoch, when *Troilus and Creffida* was written. This drama, however, was plainly burlefqued, as the Commentators remark (z), by the comedy, entitled, *Hif-triomaftix*, which though publifhed, in 1609, was written before the demife of Elizabeth. It is that paffage in Shak-fpeare's drama, wherein, at parting, Troi-lus gives Creffida his fleeve ; and fhe, in return, gives him her glove : *Hiftriomaftix* ridicules it, in an interlude, wherein Troi-lus and Creffida held the following col-loquy :

Troil. " Come, Creffida, my Creffit light,
" Thy face doth fhine both day and night,
" Behold, Behold, *thy garter blue*
" Thy Knight his valiant Elbow wears,
" That when he fhakes his furious fpeare,
" The foe, in fhivering fearful fort
" May lay him down in death to fnort."
Creff. " O Knight, with valour in thy face,
" *Here, take my fkreene,* weare it for grace ;
" Within thy Helmet put the fame,
" Therewith to make thy enemies lame (z).

(*y*) Ib. p. 565. (*z*) Steev. 1793, vol. i. p. 567.

C c   As

As there can be no doubt, that Shakfpeare's *Troilus and Creſſida* was attacked by
ridicule, ſince the ſarcaſm is ſo palpable,
the only queſtion, among accurate reaſon-
ers, muſt be, when *Hiſtriomaſtix*, or the
Player-whipt, was originally written? *Hiſtriomaſtix* was, certainly, written, as the
Commentators acknowledge, in the time of
Elizabeth; ſince ſhe is greatly panegyrized
by the moſt obvious flattery, in the laſt
ſcene, under the name of *Aſtræa*. The
Player-whipt was probably written, in
1601, during Eſſex's conſpiracy; becauſe,
it ſpeaks of *the wars*, and talks of *a new
plot:* There is, beſides, a fine ſcene of
anarchy; the anarchiſts enter, calling out
for *liberty*; and depart, exclaiming *liberty* (*a*). *Hiſtriomaſtix* was, moſt probably,
written before Juſtice had yet inflicted pu-
niſhment on the traitors: For, Chriſoga-
nus, the ſcholar, or wiſe man, ſpeaks of
" *driving back* the *roaring torrent* on the
" *authors heads*; that all eyes may ſee,

(*a*) Sign F. 2.

" juſtice

" juſtice hath whips to ſcourge impiety."
Theſe alluſive paſſages ſeem to imply, that
the appropriate puniſhments had not yet
been inflicted on Eſſex, and his followers (*b*). If this theory be true, then, Shakſpeare's Troilus and Creſſida was written,
in 1600.

Add to all thoſe intimations ſome analo-
gous paſſages, which caſt a very vivid light
upon a dubious point. Shakſpeare appears
to have ſcoffed at Lodge's *Incarnate Devils*,
1596; and to have been himſelf ridiculed,
by the author of the *Player-whipt*; though
the ſhortſightedneſs of the Commentators
ſeem to have allowed this ſatiric current to
glide unheeded by them. In Shakſpeare's
Troilus and Creſſida, Therſites exclaims:
" How the *Devil luxury*, with his fat rump,
" and *potatoe-finger*, tickles theſe together !

(*b*) Eſſex, Rutland, Southampton, and their aſſociates,
were declared rebels, by the Queen's proclamation,
dated the 15th of February, 1600-1. On the 19th of
February, Eſſex, and Southampton, were brought to
their trials : And a few days after ; Merrick, Blount, and
Danvers, were executed.

" Fry

" Fry luxury fry !" The *Player-whipt*, for the purpofe of ridicule, introduces a merchant's wife, with her apprentice, in the market place :

Wife. " Ha' ye any *potatoes?*

Seller. " Th' abundance will not quit coft the bringing.

Wife. " What's your *Cock-fparrows* a dozen ?

Seller. " A penny, Miftrefs.

Wife. " There's for a dozen (*c*)."

This Comedy, which was thus fruitful in itfelf, and the caufe of fruitfulnefs in others, was fo much monopolized, by the Court of the maiden Queen, that it appears

(*c*) Sign B. 3. There is a moft learned difquifition by Mr. Collins, in Steev. Shak. 1793, vol. ii. p. 453, on the *fruĉtuous* qualities of the potatoe, in that age; which has been reprobated, for its *lufcioufnefs*, with all the prudery of *Oldmaidifm* by the ftill more learned writer of the profe-poetry, yclept, *The Purfuits of Literature :* It would be worthy of the deepeft refearch of this Omnifcient Scribbler, to inveftigate the caufe, why the *potatoe* fhould have preferved to this day its *fruĉtuous* powers in Ireland; yet to have loft its *invigorating* qualities in Britain, fince the aufpicious reign of the Maiden Queen; who, yet, did not die a maid, if we may believe the obftetrick Mr. Steevens. [Shak. 1793, vol. i. p. 557.].

to

to have been with-held from *the million*, during her reign : Certain, however, it is, from the before-mentioned facts, that *Troilus and Creſſida* was produced, in 1600 ; and not in 1602, as the Commentators aſſert (*d*).

No. XXII.—TIMON OF ATHENS, 1601.

The writing of this drama, which is ſaid, by Johnſon, to be *a domeſtic Tragedy*, is placed by the Commentators, in 1609 ; becauſe, they did not know where to place it (*e*). The ſtory had been forced upon the attention of Shakſpeare, by many preceding writers. Mulcaſter, the grammarian, had remarked in his *Poſitions*, 1581 ; " But, " ſome *Timon* will ſay, what ſhould women " do with learning." *Critic Timon* was, indeed, mentioned, in *Love's Labours Loſt*.

(*d*) Mal. Shak. vol. i. part 1. p. 342, and for an intimation, that this Comedy had been monopolized by the Court. [Ib. p. 343].

(*e*) Mal. Shak. vol. i. p. 372 ; Steev. 1793, vol. i. p. 599. In Steev. 1778, vol. i. p. 337 ; the epoch aſſigned to Timon was 1610.

The

The fame character was ftill more elabo-
rately difplayed in *The Incarnate Devils*,
1596: In expofing the *Fiend Tepidity*, Lodge
obferves: " This made certain difcontented
" (as Timon, and Apermantus) (*f*) waxe
" carelefs of body and foule, fretting them-
" felves at the worlds ingratitude, and get-
" ting over all diligent endeavour to ferve
" the fury of their unbridled minds : The
" ftories regiftered are full of men thus af-
" fected; and who confidereth the moft com-
" monwealths of Chriftians, fhall, I fear,
" (and let me write it with griefe) find more
" opportunity loft by coldnefs, flacknefs,
" and delay, than confideration can remedy
" with many years heart break, and ftudy."

This is a *domeftic Tragedy*; and, therefore, ftrongly faftens on the attention of
the reader, fays Johnfon : The cataftrophe
affords a very powerful warning againft
that oftentatious liberality, which fcatters
bounty, but confers no benefits ; and buys
flattery, but not friendfhip. The fcene lay

(*f*) It is to be noted, that *Apemantus* is the Churlifh
Philofopher in Shakfpeare's Timon.

in

in Athens; but, the moral was applied to London. In this drama, there are feveral intimations, which prove, that it was written, during the reign of Elizabeth; fince the *wars* are often fpoken of; and there were commotions in the city of London, which did not exift there, during the fubfequent reign : the firft thief fays:

" Let us firft fee peace in Athens."

The whole play is an accurate delineation of the ftate of men, and things, in London, during the year 1601, and the exiftence of Effex's rebellion : In perfuading the return of Timon, the firft fenator obferves:

" ———— So foon we fhall drive back
" Of Alcibiades, the approaches wild,
" Who, like a boar too favage, doth root up
" His Country's peace."

Here is as exact a picture of Effex, as, at that period, it was fit to draw. The fenators, in the laft fcene, defcribe the various meffages, which were fent by the Queen to Effex :

" ———— Noble and Young,
" When thy firft griefs were but a mere conceit,
" Ere thou hadft power, or we had caufe of fear,

" We

" We fent to thee ; to give thy rages balm,
" To wipe out our ingratitude, with loves
" Above their quantity."

We may even learn, from Timon's ex-
clamations, that execution had been done
on fome of Effex's followers :

" ———— Thatch your poor thin roofs
" With *burdens* of the *dead*; *fome that were hang'd*;
" No matter".

Nor, could the poet give plainer intimations, without departing from dramatical
propriety. Add to thofe facts, and circumftances, that there was produced, in
1600, a play on the fame fubject, which
ftill remains in MSS. ; and from which
Shakfpeare, obvioufly, borrowed, what he
has amply repaid (*g*). Such are the reafons, which, as any argument is more perfuafive than none, induce me to be of opinion, that Timon of Athens was written,
in 1601 ; but was neither entered in the
Stationers' Regifters, nor publifhed, till it
was printed, in the firft folio, in 1623.

The Commentators, however, have their

(*g*) Mal. Shak. vol. viii. p. 4.

objections

objections at hand. Yes; I am ready to cry out, with *Hotſpur*, they have

" Such a deal of ſkimble ſkamble ſtuff, as puts me from my Faith."

When Shakſpeare once began to ſtudy North's Plutarch, ſay they, it is not probable, that he would ceaſe, till he had exhauſted it of all its dramatic ſubjects. On the foundation of this ſuppoſition, another was built : Julius Cæſar, Anthony and Cleopatra, Timon, and Coriolanus, are ſuppoſed to have been written in ſucceſſion : While he was writing Cymbeline, in 1605, and Macbeth, in 1606, there is reaſon to believe, ſay they, that he began to ſtudy Plutarch, with a view to the ſtage(*h*). The Commentators ſpeak of the editions of Sir Thomas North's Tranſlation of Plutarch, in 1579, 1602, 1603; but they appear not to have known, that there was an edition, in 1595 (*i*), which is probably the

(*h*) Steev. 1793, vol. i. p. 600.

(*i*) I have in my Library the Edition of 1595; ſo that there can be no diſpute about the fact of its exiſtence.

very

very edition, which our poet ſtudied ; as
the firſt edition came too early, and the laſt
editions too late, for his inſtructive peruſal :
When he wrote Hamlet, in 1596, Shakſpeare appears to have been then perfectly
acquainted with the Roman Story ; and,
he is ſaid, by the Commentators, to have
acquired, from North's Plutarch, his acquaintance with the Roman Annals. In
Hamlet, Shakſpeare ſpeaks, familiarly, of
" the Portends, which foretold the death
" of mightieſt Julius:" Again, when he
is about to meet the Queen, Hamlet exclaims ;

" ———— Soft ; now to my mother.
" O heart ! loſe not thy nature ; let not ever
" The *Soul of Nero enter this firm boſom :*
" Let me be cruel ; not unnatural :
" I will *ſpeake* daggers to her, but, *uſe* none."

The inferences, then, from the ſuppoſed
ſtudies of Shakſpeare, in *North's Plutarch*,
during the reign of King James, are thus
overthrown by more pregnant circumſtances ; which remove all objections, and
leave upon the mind conviction.

No.

No. XXIII.—THE WINTER'S TALE, 1601.

The *Doraſtus* and *Faunia* of Green, which was publiſhed, in 1588, furniſhed Shakſpeare with the plot of this Comedy; and, it ſeems to have been preceded, like the other dramas of Shakſpeare, by a *Winter Night's Paſtime*, in 1594: The Winter's Tale was neither publiſhed, nor entered in the Stationers' Regiſters, till 1623; nor was it mentioned by Meres, in 1598.

The commentators gave it, originally, as their opinion, that *the Winter's Tale* had been written, in 1601, or 1602; but, they have ſince fixed the epoch of it, on very ſlight evidence, to the year 1604 (*k*). They appear to have been carried away from the vicinity of truth, on this occaſion, by a quotation of Blackſtone, from Shakſpeare, which furniſhed a proof to him, and to them, that the Winter's Tale was not written till after the demiſe of Elizabeth:

" ———— If I could find example
" Of thouſands, that had ſtruck *anointed* Kings

" And

" And flourifh'd after, I'd not do it ; but, fince,
" Nor brafs, nor parchment bears not one,
" Let villainy itfelf forfwear it."

Thefe lines, fay Blackftone, and the commentators, could never have been intended for the ear of her, who had deprived the Queen of Scots of life: To the fon of Mary they could not have been very agreeable (*l*). Now, mark how a plain tale fhall put down a confident affumption. Strype, who cannot be too much praifed for his labours, informs us, that " *after* the rebellion " of the Earl of Effex, were certain pray- " ers, fit for the time, fet forth, by au- " thority, to be ufed thrice a week, on the " prayer days, in the churches." This laborious hiftorian has preferved two of thofe prayers (*m*): The firft is a thankfgiving " prayer for the merciful deliverance of our " moft dread Sovereign Lady, thy vicege- " rent, in her dominions, Queen Elizabeth, " as ever heretofore, fo at this time, from " the traiterous attempts, and defperate de-

(*l*) Steev. 1793, vol. i. p. 576.
(*m*) An. Reform, vol. iv. 354—5.

" fignments

" fignments of fundry moft unkind, and
" difloyal-like perfons, who forgetting their
" duty to thee, O Lord, and towards thine
" *anointed*, have, in the *height of their pride*,
" after a popular fort, with divers falfe pre-
" tences, and many flanderous calumnia-
" tions, fought, in open rebellion, not only
" the *extinguifhment* of thy fervant, our com-
" fort, and our glory, but the tragical over-
" throw of this our native country." The
prayer then befeeches " the God of Hofts
" to defend ftill the facred perfon of our
" Sovereign Lady, from all fuch dangerous
" defignments, her kingdoms from all trea-
" cherous practices, and us, her fubjects,
" from the crafty alurements of all *popular*,
" and *ambitious diffembling* Abfoloms." The
fecond prayer fpeaks of thy handmaid, *thine
Anointed*; and of thine own *anointed Magif-
trate*. Shakfpeare, then, feems to have
merely tranflated the fentiments of thofe
public prayers, into dramatic poetry, as he
frequently did the profe narratives of Hollingfhed; and to have adopted the emphatical expreffion, *anointed Kings*, inftead of

anointed

anointed Magistrate. He was induced to do this, according to his usual custom of catching every temporary topick; in order to captivate the audience; who, while under the influence of those prayers, must have received the quoted passage with loud applause.

During that momentous period, neither Elizabeth, nor her people, entertained one thought of Mary Stuart, who fell, by the stroke of a *legal* instrument, at least; which was used, in consequence of an address of Parliament, and of a popular call: The unhappy Queen of Scots fell by a stroke of a very different kind, from that of Shakspeare at anointed *Kings*, by that *tumultuous villainy*, which was so strongly reprobated in those authorized prayers.

Blackstone's remark discovers, then, a mind, which was not very amply stored with historical knowledge, relating to that eventful age. There is, in the second scene of the first act, a passage, which was much more likely to *tent* Elizabeth to *the quick:*

> *Leontes.* " Thou mightst bespice a Cup,
> " To give mine Enemy a lasting wink;
> " Which draught to me were cordial."

Cam.

Cam. ———— " Sir, my Lord,
" I could do this, and that with no rafh potion,
" But with a lingering dram, that fhould not work
" Malicioufly, like poifon: But, &c."

It is an hiftorical fact, which is incontrovertibly certain, that Elizabeth employed
agents to take off her hated rival, by a *lingering dram* (*n*): And, upon the principle
of Blackftone, fhe might have *blench'd*, at
the recital of *Leontes' folicitation* to *befpice
a cup*.

There is a farcafm, in *the Winter's Tale*,
levelled at the *Puritans*; which is an additional proof, that this comedy was written
about the period of Effex's confpiracy:——
" There is but one *Puritan*, among them,
" and he *fings pfalms* to hornpipes." Hiftory has recorded the popular tricks of that
ambitious anarchift; how he courted the
Puritans; how he had *pfalm-finging* in Ef-
fex-houfe: And, Hume, the hiftorian,
breaks out againft thofe *religious artifioes*
with unufual warmth.

There is another note of time, in the firft

(*n*) See Tytler's Inquiry, 4 Ed. 1790, p. 320.

fcene

scene, of the fifth act, which furnishes a decisive proof against *the theory* of the commentators. Leontes laments the wrong he did himself; " which was so much, that " *heirless* it hath made my kingdom." Dion remonstrates to Paulina, who objected to Leontes' second marriage:

> " ———— If you would not so,
> " You pity not the state, nor the remembrance
> " Of his most sovereign name; confider little
> " What dangers by his highnefs' *fail of iffue*,
> " May drop upon his kingdom, and devour
> " Incertain lookers on."

The pertinence of this paffage would have struck the audience; and every one must have felt the *danger*, by *her highnefs's fail of iffue*, which *might devour* even *incertain lookers on*. The whole allusion was finely adapted to the state of the public mind; which had been haraffed by the difpute about the fucceffion. The fufpence, wherein the whim of Elizabeth kept *incertain lookers on*, to the laft, about her fucceffor, no longer exifted, after the acceffion of James, who was far from *heirlefs*. After this event, the audience would have difdained that fine paf-
sage,

fage, as idle declamation. *The crown* had now *found an heir.* And, to have longer talked about the dangers of uncertainty, when none were felt, nor forefeen, would have been rejected by the audience, as fenfelefs fiction.

For the foregoing reafons, I concur with Horatio Walpole, the late Lord Orford, in thinking, that *the Winter's Tale* is one of Shakfpeare's *hiftorical* plays which was defigned as a compliment to Elizabeth, during a moment of unhappinefs: But, I do not confider this drama *as a fecond part to Henry VIII,* which was written, at a fubfequent period, and on a different occafion. I prefume to think, that the proofs, which I have adduced, are quite fufficient to fatisfy any reafonable mind, that the *Winter's Tale* was written, in the troublous year 1601. Mr. Malone, indeed, mentions the report, which was entered in the Stationers' Regifters, in 1604, of a monftrous fifh, that appeared in the *form of a woman;* and that may have been alluded to by Shakfpeare: But, fuch a ftory is too deftitute of the cer-

D d   tainties

tainties of time, place, and circumſtance, to repel the ſtronger proofs for a prior epoch.

No. XXIV.—Measure for Measure, 1604.

For the ſtory of this drama, we are re-ferred, by Pope, to *Cinthio's Novels;* and by Farmer, with more certainty, to the *Hiſtorie of Promos and Caſſandra* of Whetſtone; though the hints, which were derived from Whet-ſtone are ſo ſlight, according to Mr. Stee-vens, that it is almoſt impoſſible to trace them (*o*): Yet, amidſt all this reſearch, for the true origin of *Meaſure for Meaſure,* it was forgotten, that it is obviouſly founded on the departure of King James, from his ancient kingdom, when he ſet out for his new dominions; and that, though the ima-ginary ſcene was laid at *Vienna,* the real ſcene was at London (*p*). This comedy muſt

(*o*) Steev. 1793, vol. iv. p. 176—7.

(*p*) Among the ornaments, which have been pro-vided, by Harding, for Shakſpeare, there is prefixed to this Comedy *a View of Vienna:* There had been much more

muft have been written, then, fubfequent
to April, 1603, and before the year 1607,
when it was plainly imitated by Barkfted(*q*),
who adopted a thought from him, that
might well lend a little, fince he had borrowed much from fo many others himfelf.

There is not one of Shakfpeare's plays
more darkened than this, by the peculiarities of its author, the unfkilfulnefs of its
editors, and the negligence of tranfcribers,
faith Johnfon: Thefe remarks are fo juft,
Mr. Steevens fubjoins, that he declined to
attempt much reformation. The opening
fpeech of *the Duke* is, indeed, fo embar-
raffed, as to have puzzled all the commentators; and they have, at laft, left it but nonfenfe:

more propriety, and ufe, in giving an accurate draught
of London, at the acceffion of King James; fince there
is fo much talk about a proclamation, which was iffued
by him, for the pulling down of new houfes in the
fuburbs.

(*q*) In Myrrha, the Mother of Adonis, or Luft's Pro-
digies, by Wm. Barkfted, a poem, 1607. [Mal. Shak.
vol. i. p. 345.]

Duke.

Duke. " Of Government, the properties to unfold,
Would feem, in me, to affect fpeech, and difcourfe;
Since *I* am put to know, that your own fcience,
Exceeds, in that, the lifts of all advice,
My ftrength can give you : Then, no more remains, [for
    me]
But that, to your fufficiency, as your worth is able,
And [I] let them [fufficiency and worth] work : The
    nature of our people.
Our City's inftitutions, and the terms
For common juftice, you are as pregnant in,
As art, and practice, hath enrich'd any,
That we remember : There is our Commiffion,
From which, we would not have you warp."

The commentators feem not to have remarked, that the character of *the Duke*, is a
very accurate delineation of that of King
James, which Shakfpeare appears to have
caught, with great felicity, and to have fketched, with much truth. The obfcurity, and
the uncouthnefs, of this fpeech, are partly
owing to the purpofed affectation of the
poet; but ftill more to the blunders of the
tranfcribers. Knowing that King James's
writings; his *Bafilikon Doron;* his *True Law
of free Monarchies;* and other treatifes; had
been, emuloufly, republifhed, in 1603, by
                                                    the

the London bookfellers, in many editions,
Shakfpeare could not fitly give a clofer parody. With fuch a key to the real purpofe
of the poet, this declamation on the *proper-*
ties of *government* muft appear, at once, appropriate, and humourous. The darknefs
of this fpeech, which the commentators have
failed to illuminate, after fhowing their
lights, begins to be impenetrable in the fifth
line: we are to recollect, that the Duke is
fpeaking, unfitly, fometimes in the plural
[we], and fometimes in the fingular [I];
and, beginning to reafon from the foregoing
premifes, he infers:

" ———— Then, no more remains, [for me,]
" But that, to your fufficiency, as your worth is able,
" [I] (*r*) let them [your fcience, fufficiency, worth,]
    work.

This fimple alteration of *I* for *and* makes

(*r*) The pronoun perfonal [I] was often confounded,
in writing, with *aye*, or yes; particularly, in Town-
fhend's *Tables*, and in D'Ewe's Journals; and Shakfpeare more than once writes *I* for *aye*, as Johnfon
obferves: Now, I conjecture, that the blunder of the
tranfcriber was begun by writing *aye* for *I*; and was
completed, by writing *and* for *aye*.

D d 3   complete

complete fenfe; though the fpeech be rendered obfcure by impropriety, and confounded by affectation.

In the fecond fcene of the third act, the
character of the Duke is fully inveftigated,
with a ftriking allufion to the real character
of King James (*s*). It may not be difpleafing to the reader to fee a fketch of the character of King James, as it was drawn by a
fpy of Queen Elizabeth's, in 1586; when
that prince was under twenty one years of
age (*t*): " Generally, he feemeth defirous
" of peace, as appeareth by his difpofition
" and exercis; viz. ift. his great delight in
" hunting; 2dly. his private delight in en-
" diting poefies; and in one, or both of
" thefe, commonly, he fpendeth the day,
" when he hath no public thing to do;
" 3dly. his defire to withdraw himfelf,
" from places of moft accefs, and company,
" to places of more folitude, and repofe,
" with very fmall retinue; 4thly. his readi-

(*s*) See Mal. Shak. vol. ii. p. 77-78-79.
(*t*) From a MS. in Mr. Aftle's Library.

" nefs

" nefs to compofe matters, that might trou-
" ble his peace, though with fome difad-
" vantage. In religion, he is foundly af-
" fected, as may be prefumed from thefe
" reafons: 1ft. His hearing the word of
" God almoft daily, viz. on Sundays, fore-
" noon, and afternoon; on Wednefdays,
" and Fridays, in the forenoon, befides a
" chapter read, and fome expofition after
" every meal. 2dly. His promptnefs in the
" fcriptures, wherein he is thought to be as
" ready, as any man within his realm.
" 3dly. His care to give good example, by
" repairing to the ordinary fermons in Edin-
" burgh Church. 4thly. His often deriding
" popery, in his common difcourfe, and
" denying mafs to the French Ambaffador.
" 5thly. His life, and converfation, which
" though it be touched fomewhat with
" the common faults of the country, viz.
" with fwearing fometimes; and whereof
" a fpecial caufe is, the want of found com-
" pany about him; yet, he keepeth it in
" good order; and as a young prince is of a
" ftayed behaviour, void of licenfioufnefs

" and

" and notorious faults; fhowing good figns
" of modefty, as blufhing fometime, when
" he fpeaketh in prefence; and the report
" is of thofe, who are neareft about him,
" very chaft, and yet defirous of marriage."
Several of thofe charaƈteriftics are alluded
to throughout *Meafure for Meafure:*

" ———— I love the people,
" But, do not like to ftage me to their eyes:
" Though it do well, I do not relifh well
" Their loud applaufe, and aves vehement:
" Nor, do I think the man of fafe difcretion,
" That does affeƈt it."

This is faid, by the commentators, to be
intended as a *courtly apology*, for the *ftately*
and *ungracious* demeanor of King James, on
his entry into England (*u*). No: The fault
of this prince was *too much familiarity*, and
not ftatelinefs; he was good natured, and
not ungracious; he did not like to *ftage* himfelf to the people's eyes; becaufe, he delighted in retirement, in the company of a
few, in ftudy, and in writing. His character appears to have been ftrangely mifrepre-

(*u*) Steev. 1793, vol. i. p. 568.

fented

fented by Mr. Malone, and by Mr. Steevens; who would delude others, as they
were themfelves deluded by Wilfon, the moft
prejudiced, and factious, of hiftorians. On
the contrary, Shakfpeare did not intend to
make any apology, but merely to give *traits*
of character, which the commentators did
not comprehend.

King James found the nation engaged in a
twenty years war with Spain, which is often
alluded to in this comedy. A peace was
concluded, at London, on the 18th of Auguft, 1604: And, the treaty was printed by
Barker, the royal typographer, from authority, in 1605: The allufions to the war are
not, then, *decifive proofs* of the writing of
this play, in 1603, as the commentators affert, with more confidence than ratiocination.

There is much allufion alfo to the pluck-
ing down of houfes in the fuburbs. The
clown afks the bawd : " You have not heard
" of *the proclamation*, have you?" " What
" proclamation, man?" anfwers the bawd,
" All houfes in the fuburbs muft be plucked
" down,"

" down," rejoins the clown, How much fuperior is Shakfpeare to his commentators ! He makes fuch characters, as the clown, and bawd, talk vaguely, and vulgarly, like fuch perfons : The commentators fearch every where for illuftrations, except in *the procla-mation* itfelf. Let us inveftigate, fully, what will carry us, directly, to the point in quef_tion.

During the whole reign of Elizabeth, it was a policy, which her councils continually enforced, to prevent the increafe of London. In the 35th of Elizabeth (*x*), a bill was paffed for reftraint of buildings in London. On the 7th of July 1580, a proclamation was iffued, commanding all perfons to defift from new buildings (*y*) : On the 22d of June, 1602, this proclamation was renewed, and enforced (*z*). After the acceffion of King James, the fame policy was purfued. A proclamation, againft inmates, and for the pulling down of *new erected* buildings, was

(*x*) 1 Lord's Journal, 521, D'Ewes, 521.
(*y*) Rym. Foed. Tom. 16. p. 449.
(*z*) Id.

iffued

iffued on the 16th of September, 1603. But it had as little effect upon intereft, and fafhion, as any former edict (*a*). On the 1ft of March, 1604–5, a fimilar proclamation was iffued ; but with as little effect. A frefh proclamation was iffued on the 12th of October, 1607, which was enforced by profecutions in the Star Chamber : Yet, the building fpirit of the town was not to be re-preffed, even by the Star Chamber. In 1614, more proclamations were, therefore, iffued : And, from this year, is faid to have begun a reformation in the buildings (*b*).

In order to enable us to decide againft which of thofe proclamations, Shakfpeare threw out his fatire, from the tongues of the clown, and bawd, we muft carry our inveftigation a ftep further. In the fecond fcene of the firft act, the bawd announces the bad news of Claudio being imprifoned " for getting Madam Julietta with child." Claudio complains of " *the neglected act*

(*a*) Howes's Stow, 828.
(*b*) Strype's Stow. Hift. of London, vol. i. p. 8.

" *being*

" *being enforced against him.*" Isabella laments her being the sister of one Claudio, condemned, on the *act of fornication*, to lose his head. Now; the act, which was thus alluded to, though not with the precision of an Old Baily Solicitor, " was the statute to " restrain all persons from marriage, until " their former wives, and former husbands " be dead," for which such persons, so of-fending, were to *suffer death*, as in cases of felony (c). It was against this act, then, which did not operate till after the end of the session, on the 7th of July, 1604, that Shakspeare's satire was levelled. All those events must have actually taken place; and must have created some bustle, and town talk, before our dramatist exhibited his cha-racters on the stage, speaking of them. From all those facts, and circumstances, *Measure for Measure* appears to have been

---

(c) 2 Ja. 1. ch. 11; 1604. Yet, the offenders were, and are entitled to the benefit of clergy; there had been a former act, on this subject, 1 Edw. vi. ch. 11, which justifies Claudio's complaint, that a *neglected Act had been enforced against him.*

written,

written, in 1604, inftead of 1603, which laft epoch cannot be fupported, againft fuch coincidences of proof.

No. XXV.—KING LEAR, 1605.

The Commentators have traced, with great diligence, the various fources, whence Shakfpeare may have derived his hints, and helps, when he fat down to write his *Lear:* The Faery Queen, the Arcadia of Sydney, the Remaines of Camden, the Chronicle of Hollingfhed, the Mirror for Magiftrates, the True Chronicle Hiftory of King Leir, and the moft famous Hiftorie of Leire, King of England, and his three daughters (*d*):

But

(*d*) While the Commentators were collecting every mention of Leire and his Daughters, they might have added " A Defence of Brutes and Brutan's Hiftory," 1593, by Edward Harvey, the Brother of the famous Gabriel Harvey. The Author gives, in p. 16, " The " Geneology or iffue of Brute:"—" Bladud begat " Leyr; Leyr begat three Daughters; the firft was " Gonorill, the fecond Ragan, and the third *Cordeil:* " Leyr gave half his goodes to his two eldeft daughters, " at their marriage; and made them mightier than
" himfelfe,

But none of thefe authorities influenced him in the choice of the particular moment to fit down, and write " The Tragedy of Lear, " which is defervedly celebrated among the " dramas of Shakfpeare."

If I might adopt the argument of the commentators, I fhould fay, that Shakfpeare read, no doubt, what every body elfe read, in 1603, the *Bafilikon Doron* of King James ; or His Majeftie's Inftructions to his deareft Sonne: Herein the poet faw what was written before the King's acceffion: " In

" himfelfe, for fpeaking to him *pointedly* ; but he gave " nothing with Cordeil to her Dowry, becaufe fhe " told him an open truth without anie forgerie." We may herein alfo fee, that from Ragan defcended *Gorbodug*, who begat *Ferrex* and *Porrex*. Edward Harvey, being a young man, undertook the hard tafk of defending Geffry Monmouth againft Mafter Buchanan, *the trumpet of Scotland:* " We may beft areede, who is " moft credible a Monmouth, or a Scot, a *Moonke*, or a " *Travailer*," concludes Edward Harvey; who wanted neither learning, nor fpirit. Like fome of the Scholars of the prefent day, on the fubject of Troy, a kindred tale, he thought it " a *dangerous pofition* to refufe the " offspring of *Brute*, both in regard of all reverend " antiquities, and in refpect of our own Countrymen."

" cafe

" cafe it pleafe God to provide you all thefe
" three kingdoms, make your eldeft fonne
" Ifaac, leaving him all your Kingdoms, and
" provide the reft with private poffeffions:
" Otherwife, by dividing your kingdoms,
" yee fhall leave the feed of divifion, and
" difcord, among your pofteritie; as befel
" this ifle, by the divifion, and affignment
" thereof, to the three fonnes of Brutus:
" Locrine, Albanact, and Chamber (*e*)."
The poet knew, alfo, that the King had
ftrongly recommended to his firft Parliament, *the union* of his two Kingdoms; which
was not received with the fame fentiment of
conciliation, nor an equal fenfe of policy,
in the Houfe of Commons (*f*); though an act
did pafs, " appointing commiffioners to treat
" for *the weal* of both Kingdoms (*g*)." On the
15th of September, 1604, a proclamation was
iffued; appointing the 20th of October, and
the Painted Chamber, for the day, and place

(*e*) Norton's Edit. 1603, p. 66. Polidore Virgil was
King James's hiftorian, for this Britifh Story.

(*f*) 1 Jour. everywhere.

(*g*) 2 Jac. 1. ch. 2.

of

of meeting of the Commiffioners, for this interefting treaty. From all thofe facts, it is eafy to infer, that this recent circumftance, which had thus drawn the public attention, alfo fixed the determination of Shakfpeare, to write, dramatically, on the ftory of Lear. Whether he adopted, for his drama, the *Britifh* ftory, by defign, or accident, I know not ; if by defign, his choice was moft ju-dicious ; if by accident, it was moft lucky : For, our Britifh anceftors were always ruined by *their divifions;* wanting nothing but peace *at home*, to make them invincible. The *moral* of Lear, then, is the moft important, which can be exhibited by fcenic action, to a people ; in order to inculcate, by ex-amples, the dangers of divifion, and the benefits of union.

Shakfpeare, certainly, borrowed the fan-taftical names of fpirits, which appear in this Tragedy, from Harfnet's *Declaration of Popifh Impoftures*, which was publifhed, in 1603. Lear is afcertained, to have been

(*h*) Rym. Foed. 16 tom.

written,

written, after the month of October, 1604 ;
fay the Commentators : For, King James
was proclaimed King *of Great Britain,* on
the 24th of October, 1604 ; and, it is evident, that Shakfpeare made a minute change
in an old rhyming faw :

" ———— Fy, fa, fum,
" I fmell the blood of an *Englifh man;*"

which Shakfpeare, with great attention to
the times, changed, in the following manner :

" His word was ftill, Fie, foh, fum,
" I fmell the blood of a *Britifh* man. '

But, the fact is, that there was iffued
from Greenwich a royal proclamation, on
the 13th of May, 1603 ; declaring that, till
a compleat union, the King held, and
efteemed, the two realms, as *prefently*
united, and as one kingdom : and, the
poets, Daniel, and Drayton, who wrote
gratulatory verfes, on his acceffion, fpoke
of the two kingdoms, as united, thereby,
into one realm, by the name of Britain ;
and of the inhabitants of England and
Scotland, as one people, by the denomina-

tion

tion of Britifh (*i*). Lear was entered in the
Stationers' Regifters, on the 26th November, 1607, and is, therein, mentioned to have
been played, during the preceding Chriftmas, before his Majefty at Whitehall : But,
though this may have been the fact ; yet the
inference does not follow, that it had never
been, formerly, acted before any audience.
After weighing the whole evidence, I concur with the Commentators, that Lear was,
probably, written, early in 1605; though

(*i*) Before King James arrived at London, Daniel
offered to him " A Panegyrike congratulatory, deli-
" vered to the King's moft excellent Majefty at Burleigh-
" Harrington in Rutlandfhire ;" which was printed,
in 1603, for Blount, with a Defence of Rhime :
  " Lo here the glory of a greater day
  " Than *England* ever heretofore could fee
  " In all her days.———— ————— —————
  " And now fhe is, and now in peace therefore
  " *Shake hands with union*, O thou mightie ftate
  " Now thou art all *great Britain*, and no more,
  " *No Scot*, no *Englifh* now, nor no debate."
This very rare publication of Daniel confutes, by the
fact, the Commentators reafoning, from the proclama-
tion : For, we fee how a poet did write, before any
proclamation iffued upon the point.

they

they are, undoubtedly, miſtaken, in ſome of their premiſes (*k*).

No. XXVI.—CYMBELINE, 1606.

The writing of this Drama, which, like Lear, is founded on the Britiſh Story, was originally aſſigned by the Commentators to the year 1604 ; as there appeared to be *no* intrinſick evidence, to direct the dubious courſe of the chronologiſt (*l*): But, the date is now fixed, miſtakingly, by them, in 1605 ; becauſe there is *little* internal evidence, by which this uncertainty might be aſcertained : Neither was the play publiſhed, nor entered in the Stationers' Regiſters, till the general publication of Shakſpeare's Dramas, in 1623. In Fletcher's Philaſter, which was firſt acted in 1611, and written, as early as 1609, or perhaps as 1608, there is ſuch an imitation of Cymbeline, as ſhows, that the riſing dramatiſt

(*k*) See Steev. 1793, vol. i. p. 577–79.
(*l*) Steev. Shak. 1778, vol. i. p. 320.

may

may have had his eye on the eftablifhed poet (*m*).

Yet, is there an intimation of time, in Cymbeline, which efcaped the fearch of the Commentators, and which will give an anfwer to the queftion, when was this play written ?   In the firft fcene of the fecond act, Cloten complains of a jackanapes, *who took him up for fwearing*.   This is a flight ftroke at the ftatute, for *reftraining the abufes of players*, by impofing penalties, on fuch dramatifts, as profanely ufed the name of God (*n*), in any play, or interlude.   Shakfpeare aimed many a ftroke at the correcting hand of the player's abufes, although he was, at the fame time, deriving benefits from it : But, he cuts, delicately, with a razor, and never, like Ben Jonfon, with a cleaver.   By putting his complaint into the mouth of fuch a Prince as Cloten, our poet fhows his ufual fkill in the knowledge of mankind, and gives an additional fpeci-

(*m*) Steev. 1793, vol. 1. p. 580.

(*n*) Com. Jour. vol. i. p. 293-4-300; 3 Jac. 1. ch. 21. 4 Blacks. Ed. Chrift. p. 60.

men

men of his difcrimination of character. This reforming ftatute commenced its operations on *the players*, from the end of the feffion, on the 27th of May, 1606 : And, confequently, Cymbeline was written, while the yoke ftill fat uneafy on their necks, in 1606.

There is a little word, in this play, which, though it bear upon the time, afforded no light to the darkling chronologift ; becaufe he did not underftand it. Belarius, moralizing on his way of life, exclaims :

" ———— O ! this life
" Is nobler, than attending for a check ;
" Richer than doing nothing for a *babe*."

The word *babe*, in this paffage, which plainly means a petty *coin*, has defied the Commentators, who have fearched in vain for its meaning (*o*). Yet, is *babe*, merely, the *babee* of the Scots coinage (*p*), which Shakfpeare introduced, in Cymbeline, as a

(*o*) Mal. Shak. vol. viii. 385.
(*p*) Cardonel's Numifmata, p. 33. The *babee*, is probably, derived from the *Ba-billion*.

fly

fly ftroke at the Scots coin, which King James had regulated by proclamation. In Moryfon's Itinerary, 1617, we are told by that accurate obferver (*q*): " Alfo the Scots " have a long time had fmall brafs *coynes*, " which, they fay, of *late are taken away*, " namely, *Babees*, efteemed by them, of " old, for fix pence, whereof two make " an Englifh penny." The editors have only to change the fpelling to Bab*ee*; and the player to pronounce it *trippingly on the tongue*; and the whole paffage will have a fenfe, and fmartnefs, which have been hitherto perverted by affectation, and obfcured by ignorance.

No. XXVII.—Macbeth, 1606.

With regard to this Drama, which has been always celebrated for its defign, its execution, and its moral, there has never been any doubt, whether it were written before the acceffion of King James. As, however, it was not entered in the Station-

(*q*) P. 283.

ers'

ers' Regifters, nor publifhed, till the epoch of the firft folio, in 1623, no helps can be derived from thofe circumftances, for fixing the year, when it was, originally, written.

It feems, now, more than probable, that Shakfpeare was, greatly, indebted, for his *Witchery*, in Macbeth, to the tragi-coomo- die of *the Witch*, which is faid, in the title page, " to have been long fince acted *by* " *his Majefties Servants*, at the Blackfri- " ers." As we now know, with fufficient certainty, that King James adopted the Lord Chamberlain's players, as the *royal fervants*, this fact would, alone, fettle the writing to be fubfequent to that great event ; though the commentators have doubted the precifion of the inference, from their ignorance of the fact (r). The au- thor of the Witch, Middleton, when he de- dicated his play to Holmes, remarked that, " witches are *(ipfo facto)* by the law con-

(r) Steev. 1793, vol. i. p. 589. Mr. Steevens has the merit of having firft difcovered how much Shakfpeare had been obliged to Middleton, for much of the *machi- nery* of Macbeth.

E e 4   " demn'd."

" demn'd." This is an obvious allufion to the 2d Jac. 1. ch. 12, in 1604, for which the Commentators have fubftituted 1603.

When King James vifited Oxford, in 1605, an interlude was acted before him, wherein the outline of Macbeth was reprefented fo forcibly, as to ftrike the *royal pedant*, fays Mr. Malone (*s*). Hearing of this favourable reception, Shakfpeare determined to write his tragedy, knowing that he could readily find materials in Hollingfhed's Chronicle, his common magazine. The writer of *the Puritan*, which was publifhed, in 1607, appears certainly to have fcoffed at Banquo's ghoft, who intruded at Macbeth's *banquet :* " We'll ha' the ghoft " i' th' white fheet fit at upper end o' th' " table (*t*)."

The author of the tragedy of *Cæfar and Pompey*, which was publifhed, in 1607, had plainly feen Macbeth :

(*s*) Mal. Shak. vol. i. p. 357.

(*t*) Steev. 1793, vol. vii. p. 476. The reference to the Puritan was firft made by Dr. Farmer.

" Why,

" Why, think you, lords, that 'tis *ambition's spur,*
" That *pricketh* Cæsar to those *high attempts?*

The thought, and the expression, in these lines, were obviously borrowed from the celebrated passage in Macbeth :

" ———— I have no *spur*
" To *prick* the sides of my intent, but only
" Vaulting *ambition,* which o'er leaps itself,
" And falls at the other."

In Macbeth, we find a strong allusion to the healing *benediction,* which King James *inherited* with the English crown ; rather than arrogated from royal self-sufficiency, as Doctor Percy has, mistakingly, said (*u*) :

" ———— Comes the King forth, I pray you?
" Ay, Sir: There are a crew of wretched souls,
" That stay his cure :
" ———— What's the disease he means?
" ———— 'Tis called *the Evil.*

Shakspeare had some intimation of this passage from Hollingshed, his usual historian, as Mr. Malone has remarked. But, the fact is, that our poet was prompted to this allusion, by what he learned from Camden's Remains, in 1605 : " As for that ad-

(*u*) Steev. 1793, vol. vii. p. 535.

mirable

" mirable *gift hereditary* to the anoynted
" princes of this realm [of England] in
" curing the King's Evil, I refer you to
" the learned *difcourfe* thereof *lately writ-*
" *ten* ;" [*Charifma* of Doctor Tooker] (*x*)."
An attention to this extract from Camden
clearly explains a paffage in Shakfpeare,
which the commentators have miftaken :

" ———— And *'tis fpoken,*
" To *the fucceeding royalty* he leaves
" The healing benediction."

Such are the reafons, which induce me
to concur with the Commentators, in thinking Macbeth was written, in 1606.

This interefting tragedy, opens with the
entrance of three witches, in a ftorm of

(*x*) Cam. Rem. p. 4. It appears from the dedication
to Sir Robert Cotton, that thefe *remains of a greater work*
were fent to the prefs, as early as the 12th June, 1603.
In Herbert's Typograph. vol. ii. p. 1232, may be feen
Charifma five Donumfanationis : Seu explicatio totius quæf-
tionis de mirabilium fanitatum gratia, &c. Auctore Guil.
Tookero, S. T. D. 1597. On the back are the Queen's
Arms, to whom the book was dedicated. See alfo
Dodfley's old plays, Ed. 1780, vol. xii. p. 428; whereby
it appears, that Dr. Borde wrote on the fame fubject,
during the reign of Henry VIII.

thunder

thunder and lightning, who hold fuch a converfation as was perfectly fuitable to their fuppofed characters :

> 1*ft Witch.* When fhall we three meet again ;
> In thunder, lightning, or in rain?
> 2*d Witch.* When the *hurly burly's* done;
> When the battle's loft and won.

The commentators have been diligent to fhow, that Shakfpeare had feveral precedents, as well as claffic authority, for his *hurly-burly,* which might, otherwife, give offence to modern ears (*y*). But, their refearches feem to have miffed an example, which would have applied clofer to the bufinefs, and *the time:* In Hake's *Gold's Kingdom, and this unhelping Age,* which was publifhed in 1604 (*z*), there is a paffage, on " the commendable government of the " City of London, in the late times of the " ficknefs, and deceafe, of the renowned " Queen Elizabeth :"

> " Fear, horror, trembling, and difmay of heart,
> " Were eachwhere feen upon reports, that went,

(*y*) Steev. 1793, vol. vii. p. 325.
(*z*) London, for Windet, 4to. p. 22.

" That

" That our late Queen lay fick :—

" In fine, when certainty of death was known,

" Of her our Queen, did *hurly burly* rife ?

" No, none at all : A bud then ftraightway blown

" On felf fame ftalk, did London well fuffice,

" To meafure all things with an upright fize :

" The keys were kept for him, who did fucceed,

" And nought was heard, that *difcrepance* might breed."

It is curious to remark, that when Heylin
firft printed his *Cofmography*, in 1621, he
publifhed the ftriking ftory of Macbeth,
without feeming to know, that Shakfpeare
had dramatized it. But Shakfpeare's drama
was firft publifhed in 1623 : " We proceed
" to the ftory of Macbeth," fays Heylin,
" than which for variety of action, and
" ftrangenefs of events, I never met with
" any more pleafing. The ftory in brief,
" is this : Duncan, King of the Scots, had
" two principal men, whom he employed in
" all matters of importance, Macbeth, and
" Banquo. Thefe two, travelling together
" through a foreft, were met by three
" fairies, witches, (*weirds*, the Scots call
" them) whereof the firft, making obey-
" fance unto Macbeth, faluted him Thane

" of

" of Glammis, the fecond, Thane of
" Cawder, and the third, King of Scotland.
" This is unequal dealing, faith Banquo, to
" give my friend all the honours, and none
" unto me; to which one of the weirds
" made anfwer: That he indeed fhould
" not be a King; but out of his loynes
" fhould come a race of Kings, that fhould
" for ever rule the Scots. And, having
" thus faid, they all fuddenly vanifhed.
" Upon their arrival at court, Macbeth
" was immediately created Thane of Glam-
" mis; and not long after, fome new fervice
" of his requiring new recompence, he
" was honoured with the title of Thane of
" Cawder. Seeing, then, how happy the
" prediction of the three weirds fell out in
" the former, he refolved not to be wanting
" to himfelf, in fulfilling the third; and
" therefore, he firft killed the King; and
" after by reafon of his command among
" the foldiers, and common people, he
" fucceeded to his throne. Being fcarce
" warm in his feat, he called to mind the
" prediction given to his companion
" Banquo,

" Banquo, whom hereupon fufpecting to
" be his fupplanter, he caufed him to be
" killed with his pofterity ; Fleance, one of
" his fons, efcaping only, with no fmall
" difficulty into Wales." Thus far Heylin,
who adds fome other particulars, which
were ftill more fictitious ; though not more
fictitious, than the fpecimens of Scottifh
hiftory, and Celtic jurifprudence, which
the Commentators have retailed, in their
notes, on this play, which is " defervedly
" celebrated for the propriety of its fictions,
" and folemnity, grandeur, and variety of
" its action."

No. XXVIII.—Julius Cæsar, 1607.

The Commentators have fteadily perfe-
vered, in their firft judgements, with regard to the epoch of .this tragedy. Like
moft of the other dramas of Shakfpeare,
Julius Cæfar appears to have had a *prototype.*
William Alexander, who rofe by his talents,
to be Earl of Stirling, and Secretary of
State for Scotland, publifhed in 1607, *The
Monarchicke Tragedies* ; Croefus, Darius,
the

the Alexandræan, and *Julius Cæsar* ; *newly
enlarged.* From this laft circumftance, we
may fairly infer, that the Julius Cæfar of
Alexander had been formerly written, for
the amufement of his mafter, Henry,
Prince of Wales. In arguing the queftion,
whether Alexander borrowed from Shakfpeare, or Shakfpeare from Alexander, the
Commentators have drawn their deduﬅions
from modern, rather than from ancient
modes of reafoning, with regard to both
the dramatifts : As Shakfpeare was in the
habit of borrowing from every one, who
had any thing to lend, it is more likely that
he would borrow from Alexander, than *Alexander* from him ; as there is no proof, that
Alexander ever borrowed of any, except
from the ancients. It is more than probable, that *the argument* of Alexander's play
fupplied Shakfpeare, with his outline ; as
the play itfelf furnifhed Shakfpeare with
thoughts, and expreffions, to fill up the
figure. It is, therefore, improbable, that
our poet produced his *Julius Cæfar* before
the year, 1607.

It

It is more difficult to fix, by incontrovertible evidence, the precife time, when Shakfpeare wrote his Julius Cæfar. There is fome reafon to believe, that this drama preceded, in point of time, the play of Anthony and Cleopatra, which was entered in the Stationers' Regifters, on the 20th of May 1608 (*a*). Attending to thofe dates, and weighing all circumftances, we may conclude, with reafonable certainty, that Shakfpeare produced his Julius Cæfar, in 1607. I have not obferved any note of time, in the play itfelf, which would make this inference more certain.

No. XXIX.—Anthony and Cleopatra, 1608.

This Tragedy, like Julius Cæfar, and other preceding dramas, had been fuggefted to the obfervant mind of Shakfpeare, by prior intimations. Daniel had publifhed a tragedy, in 1594, which was written, in-

(*a*) Mr. Steevens has the fecond of May, miftakingly, [Shak. 1793, vol. i. p. 432.]

deed,

deed, upon the ancient models, entitled *Cleopatra* ; and entered in the Stationers' Regifters, on the 19th of October, 1593. The *argument* of this poem may have furnifhed the more dramatic genius of Shakfpeare with feveral hints, which he well knew how to work into a better form. He had feen in *The Devils Incarnate*, in 1596, which he had attentively read, what Lodge had remarked, how " Anthony, dallying " in delights with Cleopatra, gave Cæfar " opportunitie of many victories." It is certain, however, that Shakfpeare's *Anthony and Cleopatra* was entered in the Stationers' Regifters, on the 20th of May 1608 (*b*). If it be true, that Shakfpeare wrote this tragedy, which Upton praifes for its elevation of language, and Johnfon cenfures, for want of difcrimination of characters, as a fequel to his Julius Cæfar, it may, perhaps, have been written, in the beginning of the year 1608. It was not printed till the

(*b*) Steev. 1793, vol. xii. p. 405 ; wherein the date is again miftakingly placed on the *fecond* of May ; as I have before remarked.

F f   pub-

publication of the firſt folio, in 1623. The
Naval Combats of this drama of Shakſpeare's, which, no doubt, had their attrac-
tions, are ſuppoſed to have been ridiculed
by Ben Jonſon, in his *Silent Woman*, 1609;
wherein *Moroſe* is made to remark; " Nay;
" I would fit out a play, that were nothing
" but *fights at ſea*, drum, trumpet, and
" target." (*c*)

XXX.—Coriolanus, 1609.

This Tragedy, which is ſaid by Johnſon,
to be one of the moſt amuſing of our author's
performances, was neither entered in the
Stationers' Regiſters, nor printed till the
publication of the firſt folio, in 1623. The
writing of Coriolanus has been aſſigned,
though with a heſitating tone, to the year
1610 (*d*). Mr. Malone ſeems to have proved,

(*c*) Ib. vol. i. p. 599.
(*d*) Mal. Shak. vol. i. p. 372. Steev. 1793, vol. i.
p. 599; yet, what was before aſſigned to the year 1610,
in the end, is given, to 1609. [Steev. 1793, vol. xii.
p. 3.]

with

with fome acutenefs, indeed, that the fpeech of Menenius, in the firft act, whereby he endeavoured to convince the feditious populace, of the unreafonablenefs of their clamours, on the account of the fcarcity, by the apologue of the feveral members of the body rebelling againft the belly, was copied from *Camden's Remains*, rather than from *North's Plutarch:* Yet, this proof goes only the length of fhowing, that as Camden's work was publifhed, in 1605, Shakfpeare muft have written his Coriolanus, fubfequent to that publication: we are ftill left to enquire, even admitting this proof in its full extent, for the particular year.

Coriolanus opens with the entry of a company of mutinous citizens, who are " all re-" folved rather to die, than to *famifh.*" Caius Marcius, being deemed by them the chief enemy of the people, is, by a general *verdict*, fentenced, tumultuoufly, to death; the firft citizen crying out: " Let us kill " him; and we'll have corn enough, at our " own price." Menenius, when he came to fpeak to the citizens, remarks:

F f 2

" ―― For

" ———— For your wants;
" Your fuffering in *this dearth*, you may as well
" Strike at the Heaven with your ftaves, as lift them
" Againft the Roman ftate :

" ———— *For the dearth,*
" The Gods, not the patricians, make it."

The dearth is afterwards acknowledged, in the fenate-houfe, *to be great:* Now, the fact is, that the years 1608, and 1609, were times of *great dearth;* though the firft was a year of greater dearth, than the laft (*e*). King James, on account of the high prices of provifions, iffued a proclamation againft monopolifts, in 1608 (*f*). It is faid, in Raleigh's *Remains*, that two millions fterling were fent out, during thofe two dear years, for the importation of corn. The tragedy turns upon the *exifting dearth:* And, therefore, the play was probably written, in 1609; while the preffure was yet felt.

Mr. Malone tries, indeed, to fupport his

(*e*) Combrune's Chron. Prices, p. 38. There was an infurrection, in Northamptonfhire, on account of inclofures, in May, 1607.
(*f*) Ib. 39.

own

own epoch of the year 1610, by faying, that mulberry trees were not much known in England before the year 1609: Mr. Steevens has fome doubt, with regard to this pofition, about the mulberries. But, the books upon horticulture, which were publifhed, during the reign of Elizabeth, had made the *mul-berry tree* fufficiently familiar to our poets, of every kind. Among feveral elegies on Sir Philip Sydney, there is a pretty poem, by Mathew Roydon, which was publifhed, in *The Phoenix Neft*, in 1593, and which fpeaks of—

" Alcides fpeckled poplar tree,
" The palme that monarchs do obtain,
" With love juice ftain'd the *Mulberie*,
" The fruit that dews the poet's braine,
" And Phillis philbert there away,
" Compar'd with myrtle and the bay."

The fact, however, is, that King James, in order to encourage the breeding of filk worms, fent circular letters all over England, in 1609 (*g*), to incite the inhabitants to plant the mulberry tree: Thefe letters, probably,

(*g*) And. Com. vol. i. p. 472.

F f 3   induced

induced Shakfpeare, while he was writing his *Coriolanus*, to draw a comparifon, from what was already known to *graffers*, and to poets :

" Now humble, as the ripeft mulberry,
" That will not hold the handling."

No. XXXI.—The Tempest, 1613.

This drama is faid to exhibit indubitable proofs of its being a late produ&ion: And, it was neither printed, nor entered in the Stationers' Regifters, till the year 1623.

The fevere tempefts, which preceded the writing of this drama, are fuppofed by Mr. Malone, *from the* authority (*h*) of Howes, rather than of Stowe, to have fuggefted its name. There happened, fay other contemporary accounts, '' a great tempeft of thun-'' der and lightening, on Chriftmas day, " 1612 (*i*)." This intimation, neceffarily, carries the writing of *The Tempeft* into the fubfequent year, fince there is little probabi-

(*h*) Mal. Shak. vol. i. p. 379, which refers to Stowe's Chron. 913. This page fhould be 1002.

(*i*) Winw. Mem. 3 vol. 422.

lity,

lity, that our poet would write this enchanting drama, in the midſt of the tempeſt, which overthrew ſo many manſions, and wrecked ſo many ſhips.

Whatever may have been the ſource, whence Shakſpeare drew the fable of *the Tempeſt*, it is certain, that he derived ſome of the principal intimations, from contemporary publications: From Raleigh's *Diſcoverie* of the beautiful *Empire of Guiana*, which was publiſhed, in 1596, and which ſeems to have made a ſtrong impreſſion on our poet's mind, he, certainly, obtained his knowledge of the *ſtill vexed Bermoothes* (*k*). From that period, the public attention was frequently drawn to this *iſle* of *devils*, which was firſt colonized by a ſhip from the Thames, in 1612. This enterprize was followed, in the ſubſequent year, by a pamphlet, entitled, *A plane Deſcription of the Bermudas, now called the Summer Iſlands* (*l*). A MS. of Vertue's, as the commentators remark, ſpeaks of the repreſentation of *the*

(*k*) Apology, p. 578.　　(*l*) Apology, 599.

Tempeſt, in the beginning of the year 1613. Ben Jonſon, with unlucky malice, attempted to ridicule this noble effort of the great dramatiſt, in his *Barthomew Fair*, in 1614 (*m*). Add to thoſe proofs, what I have formerly ſhown, by a variety of circumſtances, that the alluſion to the *dead Indian* in *the Tempeſt*, was warranted by the faƈt : For, five Indians were brought to this country from New England, in 1611; who were all carried away, in 1614, except *one;* and that one probably died, at London (*n*), in the intermediate period.

Such are the faƈts, and the circumſtances, which have induced me to aſſign the epoch of *the Tempeſt* to the year 1613, inſtead of 1612, which the commentators had adopted, from weaker argumentation.

The meaſures, which were purſued, in 1612, for extending colonization in the new-world, upon a policy of diſputable principle, were plainly ridiculed by Shakſpeare (*o*).

(*m*) Steev. 1793, vol iii. p. 2.

(*n*) Apology, p. 585-6.   (*o*) See Apology, 583-4.

He

He even ftruck at the foundation of European appropriation of American territories, by reafon of the fucceffive difcoveries of European powers; when the poet deduced the right of King Stephano, in the following manner, which is as logical, as it is legal: 1ft. Sycorax, the witch, was the prior poffeffor of the enchanted ifland, who left it to her fon, Calyban; 2dly. Profpero, after reducing him to flavery, feized his inheritance; 3dly. Calyban reclaimed his rights, which he transferred to Stephano: 4thly, And, thereupon, Stephano became King of the *ftill vex'd Bermoothes:*

" Thefe are not natural events: They ftrengthen
" From ftrange to ftranger."

XXXIII.—Twelfth Night, 1613.

This play, which, in *the graver parts* is *elegant and eafy*, and, in fome of the lighter fcenes, is exquifitely humourous, was neither entered in the Stationers' Regifters, nor printed, till the publication of the firft folio, in 1623.

It was fuppofed, by Mr. Tyrwhit, and by

by Mr. Malone, from his fuggeſtion, that *Twelfth Night* was written, in 1614; be-caufe it alludes to *Undertakers*, who were fuppofed to be reprobated, in the Houfe of Commons, during the feffion of 1614: But, Mr. Ritfon, to whofe judgement, attention is due, doubts this application of the allufion to *Undertakers*; knowing that both *Takers*, and *Undertakers*, are often mentioned in the Houfe of Commons, during other feffions, prior to that of 1614 (*p*). The fact is, that there were well known *Undertakers* for the plantation of Ulfter; and that, on the 13th of April, 1611, King James iffued a procla-mation, requiring the Britifh *Undertakers* to repair into Ireland, according to their con-tracts, for colonizing Ulfter. In June 1613, the King being informed of the many delays, and abufes, touching this intended planta-tion, fent Sir Henry Montague, to the Lord Mayor, and citizens of London, who were the greateft *Undertakers* in that fcheme, to

(*p*) See the Com. Journal, vol. i. during King James's parliaments.

put

put them in mind of their engagements:
And the mayor and citizens, on Midfummer day, refolved, to fend over proper perfons, to fulfil their own engagements, and
the King's wifhes (*q*). Thefe domeftic events
are fufficiently ftriking, to attract the fpecial
notice of a dramatift, who is noted for vigilance of obfervation.

In *Twelfth Night*, Shakfpeare tried to effect, by ridicule, what the ftate was unable
to perform by legiflation. The duels, which
were fo incorrigibly frequent, in that age,
were thrown into a ridiculous light by *the
affair* between Viola, and Sir Andrew Ague-
cheek. Sir Francis Bacon had lamented, in
the Houfe of Comons, on the 3d of March,
1609–10, the great difficulty of redreffing
the evil of duels; owing to the corruption of
man's nature (*r*). King James tried to effect
what the Parliament had defpaired of effect-
ing; and, in 1613, he iffued " An Edict and

(*q*) Howes' Chron. 1004, under the year 1613.
(*r*) Com. Journal, vol. i. p. 405. Franklyn's Annals, p. 5.

Cenfure

Cenfure againſt Private Combats (*s*)," which was conceived with great vigour, and ex-preſſed with deciſive force; but, whether with the help of Bacon, or not, I am unable to afcertain. This is another remarkable event, in 1613, which the commentators have overlooked, though it may have caught Shakſpeare's eye.

In *Twelfth Night*, the Sophy of Perſia is mentioned as a perfonage, who was, then, very familiar to an Englifh audience: Fabian ſays, he would not give his part of the fport, in laughing at Malvolio, for a penſion of thouſands to be paid from *the Sophy:* And, Viola is faid to have been fencer to the *Sophy*, in order to frighten Sir Andrew. In 1613, Sir Anthony Shirley publiſhed his travels into Perſia; with his *dangers* and *diſtreſſes*, and his *ſtrange*, and *unexpeſted deliverances*(*t*). Sir Robert Shirley, the brother of Sir Anthony, arrived, in

(*s*) It was printed, by Barker, the King's printer, the fame year.

(*t*) This narrative, was printed, in 4to. for Nat. Butter, and Jofeph Dagfet.

October,

October, 1611, as Ambaſſador from *the So-phy*; bringing with him a Perſian Princeſs, as his wife. He remained here, through the whole of the year 1612, at an expence to King James of four pounds a day: and he departed in January, 1613 (*u*). From all thoſe intimations, it ſeems, to me, that Twelfth Night was written, in 1613; while thoſe various objects were in the eye, or in the recollection, of the public.

There is, moreover, an alluſion to the picture of *Mol Cutpurſe*, who did open penance, on the 11th of February, 1611–12. From *Deutromalia*, which was publiſhed, in 1609, Shakſpeare, who is, continually, borrowing, what he is ſure to repay with intereſt, adopted the ſcrap of a ſong, *Then three merry Men be we.* There is alſo a diſtant alluſion to Dekker's *Weſtward Hoe*, which was exhibited, in 1607. Theſe laſt

(*u*) In a letter from Chamberlain to Winwood, dated from London, on the 2d of January, 1612–13, it is ſaid: " Sir Robert Shirley and his Perſian lady are " ſhipped away homeward, in a ſhip that goes to the " Eaſt Indies." [Winw. Mem. 3 vol. 428.]

alluſions

allufions only fhow the variety, and extent, of our poet's obfervations, and the copioufnefs of his common places, without giving an earlier epoch to *Twelfth Night.*

No. XXXIII.—Henry the Eighth, 1613.

There have been many diverfities of opinion, among the Commentators, about the epoch of this fplendid tragedy. Thefe diverfities have arifen, on this occafion, as it does at times, from felf-fufficiency taking the direction of judgment, and fubftituting affertion for proof, conjecture for refearch, and affumption for argument.

Shakfpeare may, indeed, have derived fome intimations, when he fat down to write Henry VIII, as he did, on fimilar occafions, from prior poems, on the fame fubject. He had often perufed, no doubt, Churchyard's *Legend* of Cardinal Woolfey, which was publifhed in *The Mirror for Magiftrates,* during the year 1587. He may have feen a poem, entitled *The Life and Death of Thomas Wolfey Cardinal,* which

was

was entered in the Stationers' Regifters, and publifhed, in 1599. He, certainly, had feen the play, called *The Life and Death of Lord Cromwell,* which was publifhed, at London, in 1602; and which was announced, in the title page, to have been written by W. S. He undoubtedly knew, that Rowley had publifhed, in 1605, a drama, entitled *King* Henry VIII : And, thefe two laft plays were both republifhed, in 1613, by the bookfellers, with the defign, no doubt, that they fhould derive a fpecial intereft, from the paffing fcenes of the bufy world. With his vigilance of obfervation, Shakfpeare, undoubtedly, knew, that fuch things were. And, from all thofe circumftances, and prefumptions, the Commentators, contrary to the moft pofitive proofs, have fixed the year 1601, for the epoch of Henry VIII.

It is a fact, which feveral witneffes fpeak of, as a certainty, which can admit of no doubt, that the Globe Playhoufe was burnt, on the 29th day of June, 1613, while the

play

play of Henry VIII was exhibiting (*x*).
" But, Mr. Malone ftrongly fufpects, that
" the only novelty attending this play, in
" the year 1613, was its title, its decora-
" tions, and perhaps the prologue, and
" epilogue." On the other hand, Sir Henry
Wooton, who lived, at the time, and knew
what he *wrote*, does fay, explicitly, that
the Globe playhoufe was burnt, during
the exhibition of a *new* play, called, *All-is-
true*, which is acknowledged on the authority of fatisfactory evidence, to have been

(*x*)   There is a letter in Winwood's Mem. vol. iii.
p. 469, from John Chamberlain to Sir Ralph Winwood,
dated from London, the 12th of July, 1613; in which
letter it is faid : " But, the burning of the *Globe a Play-*
" *houfe*, on the *Bankfide*, on *St. Peter's day*, cannot
" efcape you ; which fell out by a *peale of chambers*
" (that I know not on what occafion were to be ufed
" in the play) the *tappin*, or *ftople* of one of them light-
" ing in the *thatch*, that covered the houfe ; burned it
" down to the ground in lefs than two hours ; and it
" was a great marvaile and fair grace of God that the
" people had fo little harm, having but *two narrow doors*
" to get out."

Henry

Henry VIII(*y*). Among accurate reafon-
ers, the only queftion can be, whether we
ought to believe the pofitive evidence of Sir
Henry Wooton, who was an attentive fpec-
tator of what he relates, or Mr. Malone,
who is groping in the dark, for what
the noonday fun might have fhown him.
Such, then, is *the fact*, which fixes the
writing of Henry VIII to 1613, in oppofition to the *conjectures* of the Commentators.

There are, moreover, in the play, intimations of the time, which add *certainty* to
fact. In the laft fcene, there is a compliment to King James, for his *policy of plantation :*

" Wherever the bright fun of Heaven fhall fhine,
" His honour, and the greatnefs of his name,
" Shall be, and *make new nations.* '

This is admitted, by the Commentators, to
be an allufion to the making of new na-

(*y*) The continuator of Stowe's Chronicle, Howes,
who lived at the time, fays exprefsly, that the play,
which was then exhibited, was Shakfpeare's Henry VIII.
[Steev. 1793, vol. i. p. 560. Mal. Shak. vol. i. p' i. p. 337.]

G g   tions

tions beyond the Atlantic (*z*): And, it is said, by them, as a proof of their remark, that there was a *lottery* granted, in 1612, for promoting the Colony of Virginia, which was originally planted, in 1607, and not in 1606 (*a*), as the Commentators have afferted. There was a *third* charter granted by King James, to the Virginia Company, on the 12th of March 1611-12, which included the *ftill vex'd Bermuthes* (*b*).

Yet; fay the Commentators, in the face of fact, and probability, the allufion to

(*z*) Lord Bacon had a picture of King James, which came into the poffeffion of Lord Grimfton; whereon this *contemptible King*, fays the fpleen of Mr. Malone, is ftyled *imperij Atlantici conditor*. Mr. Steevens adopts this vulgarity of fentiment, and expreffion. [Shak. 1793, vol. xi. p. 203.]

(*a*) The firft charter was granted in 1606; but the original colony was fettled in 1607. [See Stith's Hift of Virginia, p. 44—The epoch of this fettlement is the 13th of May, 1607, p. 45.] The commentators fay [Steev. vol. ii. p. 554] that the capital of *New England* was built in 1607, and called *James Town*: But, they fhould have faid, the capital of *Virginia*.

(*b*) Stith's Hift. Appx. No. 3, one, or more, lottery, or lotteries, were granted by this charter.

King

King James's policy of plantation was a *subsequent insertion:* But, this is merely an assumption, without authority; and an assertion against proofs.

There is mention, in the last act, of a *strange Indian* come to court, which the Commentators allow " may perhaps here-" after serve to ascertain the date of this " piece, though they had not been able to " discover to what circumstance Shakspeare " here alludes (*c*)." I, formerly, investigated this circumstance; and showed, from satisfactory evidence, that two vessels, which had been sent out to the New England Coasts, by Lord Southampton, and Sir Francis Gorges, returned to England, in 1611, with *five Indians* on board; that three of those Indians were carried back to their country, in 1614, one went upon the European Continent; and the *fifth* died in London, and was exhibited, as a show (*d*). There can be no doubt, but that one of

(*c*) Steev. Shak. 1793, vol. i. p. 559.
(*d*) Apology, 585–6.

thofe

thofe Indians is the Indian, who is mentioned by the porter in Shakfpeare's Henry VIII. Is this, too, a *fubfequent infertion* ; or is it not rather a collateral circumftance, which proves the general pofition, that this play was written, in 1613 ?

In oppofition to all thofe decifive facts, collateral circumftances, and fair inferences, the Commentators run out into general reafonings, which are, fometimes, founded on fictions, and, generally, grounded on *fuppofition* : But, what kind of logick is that, which argues againft facts, which draws deductions againft probability ; and which affumes the point, that ought to be proved? Yet, thefe are the logicians, who, on other occafions, demand demonftrations in the affairs of life, and in the contefts of literature! 1ft. It is fuppofed (*e*), that Shakfpeare was more likely to have written this Tragedy, in the reign of Elizabeth, than in the time of her fucceffor. No: Shakfpeare had too much prudence, if he had had the licenfe

(*e*) Steev. 1793, vol. i. p. 554-5-6.

of

of the Mafter of the Revels, to bring the *reigning Sovereign,* as a *public fhow,* upon the open ftage ; her father's marriage, and her own baptifm : Probability rejects fuch a fuppofition.—2dly. Would the poet write a panegyrick on Elizabeth, in the time of King James, " *who hated her memory ?*" Yes : Shakfpeare wrote what he knew would pleafe *the million,* without thinking much about the court. It is a mere af-fumption againft fact, that King James *hated the memory of Queen Elizabeth (f).* 3dly.

(*f*) See Dean Barlow's account of the conference at Hampton Court, 1604, p. 3–4 : " King James fpoke " of the laft Queen of *famous memory,* fo his Highnefs " added (for it is worth the noting, that his Majefty ne- " ver remembreth her, but with fome honourable ad- " dition.") The commentators are fo abfurd as to fay, from pure prejudice, that King James, on his acceffion to the throne, ftudioufly marked his *difregard for Eliza-beth,* by the favour, which he fhowed to Lord South-ampton, and to every other perfon, who had been dif-graced by her [on account of Effex's rebellion.] It is known to every one, except the commentators, that Sir Robert Cecil, the fteady friend of Lord Southampton, kept a *fecret correfpondence* with King James, during

fome

3dly. If it had been the poet's intention to make James the chief object in the laſt act, he would probably have given a ſhort character of Elizabeth: But, we muſt take Shakſpeare's Dramas, as we find them; without writing them, as the Commentators would have them to be written: The poet ſaid what was fit to be ſaid, both as to the matter, and the manner, during the King's reign. 4thly. If the Queen had been dead, the poet would have known more about her character, and circumſtances: The truth is, that Shakſpeare knew all, and ſaid all, which he wiſhed to ſay. 5thly, The poet has " caſt the diſagreeable parts " of her father's character as much into " ſhade as poſſible:" Why; was not King

ſome years, before the demiſe of Elizabeth; and guided that Prince, by the moſt prudent advice, to the throne; Cecil merited the higheſt commendation, and the greateſt reward, for keeping the country quiet, during ſuch a period; and preventing a civil war, from a diſputed ſucceſſion. The pardon of Eſſex's friends was, moreover, the popular act of a new reign, which affected to pleaſe all parties. [The ſecret correſpondence of Cecil was publiſhed by Sir David Dalrymple, in 1766.]

James

James defcended, directly, from the fifter
of Henry VIII; and was it not through
her, that he derived his title to the crown?
Laftly, it is faid to be " unneceffary to
" quote particular paffages in fupport of
" thofe *affertions*; but the following lines,
" which are fpoken of Anne Boleyn, by
" the Lord Chamberlain, appear fo evi-
" dently calculated for the ear of Eliza-
" beth, that I cannot forbear to tranfcribe
" them :"

> " She is a gallant creature, and complete
> " In mind and feature : I perfuade me *from her*
> " *Will fall fome bleffing to this land, which fhall,*
> " *In it, be memorized.*"

Thefe lines were, no doubt, applied,
directly, by the poet to Anne Boleyn, as
the fubject required : But, the fame lines
were applied, obliquely, by the audience
to a very different lady, as Shakfpeare fore-
faw. " On the 14th of February, 1612-13,
" Frederick, Prince Palatine, of the Rhine,
" married the King's daughter, the princefs
" *Elizabeth*; and carried her over to Ger-

" many

" many on the 10th of April (g)." Here, then, is the *complete creature*, from whom *some blessing* to this *land* was expected to be *memorized*. Well; was not Sophia, Dutchefs Dowager of Hanover, the daughter of Elizabeth, Princefs Palatine: And, have not the accefsion of the Hanover family, and the reign of his prefent Majefty, particularly, been blefsings to this land; which, in it, have been *memorized*, in fulfilment of that prophecy?

We now perceive, from the fact, that there was a royal wedding, in April 1613: And, it is eafy to infer, from it, that the poet, and the players, readily, determined to have a royal *Chriftening*, as an analagous fhow.

As there is, fcarcely, an abfurdity, that fome philofophers have not maintained; fo the commentators have, on this occafion, out-done themfelves, in the abfurdity of their reafonings: They would have us believe, that Ben Jonfon, who was in perpetual hof-

(g) Brit. Chronologift, vol. i. p. 183.

tility

tility with Shakfpeare, made *adycyons* to
Henry VIII, and even wrote the prologue
for our poet (*h*). What eye does not fee the
folly of fupporting fuch fuppofitions, in oppofition to probability, and in contradiction
to common fenfe? I lament, that truth, and
impartiality, fhould oblige me to include
Johnfon, and Farmer, in this reprobation.
Far from having retired from the ftage, as
the commentators have fuppofed, Shakfpeare wrote the Tempeft, at the fame epoch;
and Othello, the greateft of his dramas, in a
fubfequent year. Tyrwhit, whofe modefty,
and knowledge, entitle him to unqualified
praife, gave his vote, for fixing the epoch
of Henry VIII, in 1613.

XXXV.—OTHELLO, 1614.

This great work, of an uncommon *maker*,
is allowed, on account of its excellence, to
have been one of his *lateft performances*. It
was neither entered in the Stationers' Regifters, till the year 1621, nor printed, till

(*h*) Steev. 1793, vol. i. p. 561.

1622.

1622. When it was firſt written, the commentators have been unable to afcertain,
either from the play itſelf, or from any contemporary production (*i*). Warburton, indeed, whoſe ingenuity was never at a lofs for
conjectures, thought, that there was an allufion, in *Othello*, to the order of baronets,
which was created by King James, in 1611:

" ――― The hearts *of old* gave hands,

" But, our *new* heraldry is hands, not hearts.

Among other prerogatives, ſays Warburton,
the baronets had an addition to their pater-
nal arms of an *hand gules*, in an efcutcheon
argent. Mr. Malone difplays his heraldic
knowledge, in confuting Warburton, who
is partly right, and partly wrong. By what
chymiſtry could this critic extract fuch a fenfe
from fuch a paffage? afks Mr. Malone. The
anfwer muſt be, the fame fort of chymiſtry,
which fo frequently enabled the obfervant dramatiſt to captivate the audience, by his ſtriking
allufions, to the paffing fcene; to fatirize,
without lampoon; and to throw out farcafms,
without fcoffing. In the firſt fcene of the

(*i*) Mal. Shak. vol. i. p. 376-8. Steev. 1778, vol. i,
p. 339-40.

fourth

fourth act, Iago, working on the jealoufy of Othello, artfully remarks: " If you are fo " fond over her iniquity, give her [a] *patent* " to offend." The audience, who knew from their feelings, how much vexation had arifen from the *patents of monopoly*, which Queen Elizabeth, and King James, had fo frequently granted, and fo often retracted, muft have been electrified by this fine ftroke of well-timed fatire. (*k*)

Mr. Malone, who allowed this *patent* fpecimen of Shakfpeare's art, to glide unheeded by him, comments, in vain, on *heraldry;* on the name, and the thing: His diligence does not find another inftance of our *new* heraldry, which Shakfpeare fatirized, fpecifically, in Othello. Warburton was right in fuppofing, that the ftroke at the

(*k*) See the 1ft vol. of the Commons Journal, for the conftant endeavours of the Houfe of Commons, without fuccefs, to abrogate the patents of monopoly, during the reigns of Queen Elizabeth, and King James. It was indeed impoffible; if the law were, as Sir Francis Bacon ftated it to that houfe; that if you make a penal ftatute, the Queen will difpenfe with it, and grant a patent with a *non obftante*

new

new heraldry was, incidentally, aimed at the creation of baronets, which was attended with uncommon circumftances. The epoch of this order was undoubtedly May, 1611: But, unluckily, for the fpeculation of Warburton, the additional armorial bearing, of the bloody hand, was not given by the patent of creation. The order had fcarcely been created, when a difpute arofe, during thofe punctilious times, about precedence, between the baronets, and the younger fons of vifcounts, and barons. On this difficult point, King James fat *perfonally*, during three feveral days, to hear the learned counfel; to take the information of Heralds; and to confider the proofs: And, in the end, he decided againft the baronets; declaring he had not had any purpofe to wrong *third parties tacitly*, whatever he might intend to confer, by his creation, on others: But, the King, wifhing to *ampliate* his favour towards the baronets, granted them, by a *fecond* patent, dated the 28th of May, 1612, among other *preheminences*, " *the* arms of Ulfter, " that is, in a field argent, a hand *geules*, or " a *bloudie*

" a *bloudie hand* (*l*)." Spenfer will inform us, in his State of Ireland, " that the *bloody* " *hand* is *O'Neel's badge*." Such, then, was the *new* heraldry, which Shakfpeare played with; in order to pleafe his audience! Yet, we fee clearly, from the fecond patent, in 1612, that the epoch, which was affigned to Othello, in 1611, cannot be fupported: And, we muft, therefore, look for the true date, in fome fubfequent year.

The fact is, that the baronets had to en-counter a feverer fhock. A great noife was made in the Houfe of Commons, on the 23d May, 1614, about the creation of Ba-ronets. This clamour againft the King's

(*l*) There was printed, in a 4to. pamphlet, by Robert Barker, in 1612,—" The decree and eftablifhment of " the King's Majeftie, upon a controverfie of prece- " dence between the younger fonnes of vifcounts and " barons, and the baronets." See Selden's Titles of Ho-nour, 1614, p. 356–8, the 2d edition, 1631, p. 821–906. King James iffued another fpecimen of his *new* heraldry, in 1613, " on the fucceffion of Prince Charles to the " Dutchy of Cornwall, though he were not born *filius* " *primogenitus*, as required by the ftatute of Edward " the IIId."

right

right to create fuch an order, was filenced in
a committee. The baronets, amidft their
apprehenfions, might have cried out, " If
" the King be not the fountain of honours,
" what is he?"(*m*) There was, a few days
before, a ftill louder outcry raifed, in the
Houfe of Commons, with much greater
caufe, againft patents of monopoly (*n*).
Owing to thofe remarkable coincidences, and
powerful reafons, I am of opinion, that
Othello was written, in 1614; and, being
written at this epoch, was the laft, as it was
one of the greateft, of his labours.

I am aware of an objection, which, if it
were founded, would difplace this tragedy
from its order : For, Othello is faid to have
been acted, at Court, early in 1613 (*o*). A manufcript of Vertue is quoted for that pofition. I would bow to any regifter of the
time ; but, I will not allow Vertue, though
a very diligent collector, to draw deductions

(*m*) Com. Journal, vol. i. p. 494.
(*n*) Ib. 490–2.
(*o*) Mal. Shak. vol. i. p. 378.

for

for me, which are to militate againſt the ſtrongeſt probabilities. (*p*)

In this tragedy, Mr. Malone has made himſelf anſwerable for an amendment in the text, which Mr. Steevens has too readily admitted. The quarto edition of 1622, and the firſt folio, had erroneouſly printed Othello's ſpeech :—

" ——— And do undertake
" *This* preſent wars againſt the Otomites."

By not adverting to the context, the editors have amended the wrong word, *this*, inſtead of the word, *wars:* For Deſdemona ſoon after pleads:

" So that, dear Lords, if I be left behind,

(*p*) On making ſome inquiries, by a friend, what manuſcript of *Vertue's* it were, which I ſaw ſo often quoted about ſcenic matters, Mr. Steevens, was ſo obliging as to ſay: " The books, from which thoſe " extracts were made, with ſeveral others loſt, belonged " to ſecretary Pepys, and afterwards to Dr. Rawlinſon, " who lent them to Mr. Vertue. There is a MS. note, " ſubjoined to the MSS. of Vertue, which, about thirty " years ago, were lent to Mr. Steevens by Mr. Gar- " rick." Much is it to be lamented, that any MS. or book, which furniſhed an illuſtration of Shakſpeare; and having once been ſeen, ſhould ever diſappear.

" A moth

" A moth of peace, and he go to the *war*,
" The rites, for which I love him, are bereft me."

We thus perceive, that fhe fpeaks only of *one war;* the Duke had already fpoken how " the Turk, with *a* moft mighty prepara*tion* " makes for Cyprus;" and, in fact, there was only *one war* (*q*): So that the editors have only bufied themfelves to make the fault, which they did not find.

The Commentators have not been more happy in their remarks, on the well known tale of Othello :

" Wherein of *anters* vaft, and *defarts idle*,
" It was my hint to fpeak : '

Among a thoufand criticifms, I do not ob- ferve, that the Commentators have remarked, that Shakfpeare, by no very uncommon quib- ble, has ufed the expreffions, of *anters vaft* and *defarts idle*, in one fenfe, when he meant alfo another. The progrefs of the word *an- ters* feems to be this : anters, aunters, aven- ters, adventures (*r*): and, hence, the word *an-*

(*q*) Nothing more was wanting, to make the text confiftent and the grammar perfect, than to ftrike the letter (s) from the word (wars.)

(*r*) Percy's Rel. of An. Poetry. vol. ii. xlv–vi.

ters

ters came to fignify, in the language of Yorkfhire, *ftrange things*, or *ftrange ftories* (*s*):
So in a difputation *bytwene a Chryftens mon
and a Jew*, which was written before the
year 1300:

> Hur fchull we longe abyde
> Auntres [adventures] to hear. (*t*)

The play on *defarts idle* confifts, in confounding *defart* for a *wildernefs*, with *defert*,
for *merit;* and *deferts idle*, or unworthy defert might be deemed defert, *fine pulvere*.

I have now finifhed my apology to Mr.
Steevens, for pretending to know any thing
about the writings of Shakfpeare, by performing, in twenty days, what he acknowledged his inability to perform, in twenty
years: And, in making this apology, I have
not only difputed Mr. Malone's chronology
of Shakfpeare's plays, but, I truft improved
it; having formed fuch a new arrangement,
as is more confiftent with probability, and

(*s*) See the Clavis to the York. Dialogue, in its pure,
natural, Dialect. 1684, p. 79.

(*t*) Warton's Hift. Englifh Poetry, vol. ii. Amendments, fign. A. 2.

better

better fupported by fact: I here fubmit,
therefore, that arrangement to the judicious
reader; having been governed, in making
it, rather by the influence of moral certainty,
than directed by any fuppofed neceffity of
fixing fome of the dramas, to each year, according to the attempt of the original chronologift, who did not reflect that, " on our
" quickeft decrees, the inaudible and noife-
" lefs foot of time fteals, 'ere we can effect
" them."

		The Old Chronology.		The New Chronology.
1.	The Comedy of Errors -	1593	—	1591
2.	Love's Labours Loft -	1594	—	1592
3.	Romeo and Juliet - -	1595	—	1592
4.	Henry VI, the Firft Part -	1589	—	1593
5.	Henry VI, the Second Part -	1591	—	1595
6.	Henry VI, the Third Part -	1591	—	1595
7.	The Two Gentlemen of Verona	1595	—	1595
8.	Richard III - - -	1597	—	1595
9.	Richard II - - -	1597	—	1596
10.	The Merry Wives of Windfor	1601	—	1596
11.	Henry IV, the Firft Part -	1597	—	1596
12.	Henry IV, the Second Part -	1598	—	1597
13.	Henry V - -	1599	—	1597
14.	The Merchant of Venice -	1798	—	1597
15.	Hamlet - - -	1596	—	1597
16.	King John - - -	1596	—	1598

17. A Mid-

		The Old Chronology.		The New Chronology.
17.	A Midfummer's Night's Dream	1592	—	1598
18.	The Taming of the Shrew -	1594	—	1598
19.	All's Well that Ends Well -	1598	—	1599
20.	Much Ado about Nothing -	1600	—	1599
21.	As You Like It - -	1600	—	1599
22.	Troilus and Creffida -	1602	—	1600
23.	Timon of Athens - -	1609	—	1601
24.	The Winter's Tale -	1604	—	1601
25.	Meafure for Meafure - -	1603	—	1604
26.	Lear - - -	1605	—	1605
27.	Cymbeline - - -	1605	—	1606
28.	Macbeth - - -	1606	—	1606
29.	Julius Cæfar - -	1607	—	1607
30.	Anthony and Cleopatra -	1608	—	1608
31.	Coriolanus - -	1610	—	1609
32.	The Tempeft - -	1612	—	1613
33.	The Twelfth Night - -	1614	—	1613
34.	Henry VIII - - -	1601	—	1613
35.	Othello - - -	1611	—	1614

In making this attempt to fettle, upon more folid ground, the chronology of Shakfpeare's dramas, than has yet been done, I muft plead, with the Commentators, that this fubject does not pretend to the *certainties* of *demonftration* (*u*): Nothing more can be

(*u*) Steev. 1793, vol. i. p. 615.

H h 2   expected

expected, from such documents, on such a
subject, than the conviction of *probability*.
I truft, however, that in making this inveſti-
gation, which was greatly facilitated, by the
labours of my precurſors, I have aſcertained
ſome new facts, and added ſome illuſtrative
circumſtances : And, I cannot help flattering
myſelf, that the new chronology will be
found, in the reſult, more conſiſtent with
probability than the old; which was compiled by Mr. Malone, with great reſearch,
and ingenuity, I confeſs; although his ſkill,
and diligence, are leſs worthy of commendation, than the modeſty, with which he tranſ-
ferred, in the end, " the ſlender portion of
" praiſe that might reſult from the novel-
" ty of the undertaking, to ſome future
" claimaint."

I will here ſubjoin, as an appropriate ſup-
plement to this apologetical ſection, ſuch
extracts from the entries of the Stationers'
Regiſters, as ſerve to illuſtrate the chronology of Shakſpeare's dramas. Theſe extracts were firſt made, by Mr. Steevens,
with great labour, and publiſhed by him
with

with fome boaft; and they are now republifhed; in order to fhow his inaccuracies,
even when he quotes a record: The text
contains *the entries;* and the margin exhibits the errors of Mr. Steevens; confifting of
the omiffions of plays, of falfe dates, of
wrong names, and of improper fpellings.

The charter of the company of the Stationers was originally granted by Philip and
Mary, on the 4th of May, 1556; and was
confirmed by Elizabeth, in 1560 (*x*). It is
at the fame time worthy of remark, that
among the Queen's *Injunctions,* in 1559,

(*x*) Steev. 1793, vol. i. p. 422. It is herein faid,
that the firft volume of the Company's Regifters had
been either loft, or deftroyed. Mr. Malone was the
firft to announce, that this volume had been found.
The fact is, as Mr. Greenhill, the Company's treafurer,
affured me, that this volume was never loft: But, it
was only not recognized, at the time; being without
the diftinguifhing mark of A, on the back ; nor, has it
any mark upon its cover, to this day. I owe an acknowledgement of favour to the Company, for the in-
fpection of their regifters; my thanks to Mr. Chapman,
the Stationer, of King's Street, for his interpofition in
my behalf; and a kindnefs to Mr. Greenhill, for his
attentions.

H h 3   there

there was an injunction " againſt the print-
" ing of pamphlets, *playes* and *ballads* (*y*)."
We may eaſily ſuppoſe, then, that though
the entries of the ſtationers begin, on the
17th of July, 1576, there would not be many
playes, and *ballads* entered, in the face of
that injunction. The ſtrictneſs of the rule
was, however, ſomewhat relaxed, in 1599,
when the prelates Whitgift, and Bancroft,
decreed, that no *plays* ſhould be printed,
without the inſpection, and permiſſion, of
the Archbiſhop of Canterbury, or the Biſhop
of London (*z*). Such, then, were the checks,
which were thus impoſed, by authority,
either to prevent the printing of plays, or to
ſecure their being printed, inoffenſively.

I now proceed to give the extracts from
the Stationers' Regiſters, as they appear in
the record:

1562.
Recevyd of Mr. Tottle for his *lycence* for
pryntinge the tragicall Hiſtory of the Ro-

(*y*) N° 51.
(*z*) Warton's Hiſt. of Poetry, vol. iii. p. 488.

meus

meus and Juliett with *Sonnetts.* (*a*)

> A. fol. 86. a.

18 February 1582.

Mr. Totell] Romeo and Juletta. B. 193.——
5 Aug. 1596: Again, as a newe ball*ad* (*b*),
for Edward White. C. 12. b.

[This, and the foregoing, are perhaps the
original work, [works,] on which Shakſpeare founded his play of Romeo and
Juliet.—Steevens.]

3d April 1592.

Edw. White] The tragedie of Arden of
feverſham & blackwill

[This play was reprinted in 1770, at Feverſham, with a preface attributing it
to Shakſpeare. The collection parallel
of paſſages, which the editor has
brought forward to juſtify his ſuppoſition, is ſuch, as will make the reader
ſmile. The following is a ſpecimen:
Arden of Feverſham, p. 74:

" Fling down Endimion, and ſnatch him up."

(*a*) Receyvd for recevyd; l*i*cen*ſe* for lycence; ſon-
net*t*es for ſonnetts.

(*b*) Bal*let* for ballad.

Merchant

Merchant of Venice, Act 5, Sc. 1:
" Peace, ho! the moon fleeps with Endymion."

Arden of Feverfham, p. 87:
" Let my death make amends for all my fins."

Much Ado about Nothing, Act 4, Sc. 2:
" Death is the faireft cover for her fhame."

Steevens.]

18 April 1593.

Rich.ᵈ Feild] Entered as his Copy, licenfed by the Archbifhop of Canterbury, and the Wardens, a book, *in*titled Venus and Adonis: Affigned over to Mr. Harrifon, fen. 25 June 1594.—297–b. It was alfo entered by Harrifon, fen. on the 25th of June; by W. Leake, the 25th of June 1596; by W. Barret the 16th of February 1616; and by John Parker on the 8th March 1619 (*c*).

19 Oct. 1593.

Symon Waterfon] a booke intitled the Tragedye of Cleopatra. (*d*)   301. b.

(*c*) Fi*e*ld for f*ei*ld; *en*titled for *in*titled; 23d June for 25th June.

(*d*) Traged*ie* for tragedy*e*.

[I fup-

[I ſuppoſe this to be Daniel's tragedy of
Cleopatra: Simon Waterſon was one of
the printers of his other works.

Steevens.]

[Daniel's *Cleopatra* was publiſhed by Wa-
terhouſe, in 1594; this Entry, therefore,
undoubtedly related to it.   Malone.]

6 Feb. 1593.

John Danter] A booke entitled a noble
Roman Hiſt*or*ye of *Ty*tus Andronicus. (*e*)

304. b.

Entered alſo unto him, by Warrant from Mr.
Woodcock, the ballad thereof.

12 March 1593.

Tho. Millington] A booke *in*tituled the
firſ*te* parte of the contention of the twoo
famous Houſes of York and Lancaſter,
with the Deathe of the good Duke Hum-
ph*rey* and the Baniſhment and Deathe of
the Duke of *Sufk* and the tragicall Ende
of the *prowd* Cardinall of Wincheſter,
with the notable rebellion of Jack Cade

(*e*) Hiſtory for hiſtor*ye*; T*i*tus for T*y*tus.

and

and the Duke of Yor*k's* firft clay*m*e unto
the Crown*e* (*f*).   305. b.

2 May 1594.

Peter Shorte] A booke intitled, a plefant
conceyted hyftorie called the Tayminge
of a fhrowe (*g*).   306. b.

[I conceive it to be the play, that furnifhed Shakfpeare with the materials,
which he afterwards worked up into
another with the fame title.   Steevens.]

9 May 1594.

Mr. Harrifon Sen.] A booke intitled the
Ravys*h*ement of Lucrece (*h*).   306. b.

14 May 1594.

Tho. *Creede*] A booke *in*titled the famous
Victories of Henry*e* the ffyft cont*e*yning*e*
the honorable Battell of Agincourt (*i*).
306. b.

(*f*) *en*tituled for *in*tituled; fir*ft* for fir*fte*; Humphr*ie*
for Humphr*e*y; *Yorke* for *Sufk*; proud*e* for prow*d*;
York*e's* for York*'s*; clai*m*e for clay*m*e; crow*n* for crown*e*.

(*g*) Pleafaunt for plefant.

(*h*) Ravyf*h*ment for ravyf*h*ement.

(*i*) *Strode* for *Creede*; 12th for 14th; *en*titled for *in*-
titled; Henry for Henr*ye*; fift for ffyft; containing for
cont*e*yning*e*.

[This

[This may have been the very difpleafing play mentioned in the Epilogue to the fecond part of Henry IV. Steevens.]
[The earlieft Edition of this play now known to be extant, was printed in 1598. Of this Edition I have a Copy. This piece furnifhed Shakfpeare with the outline of the two parts of Henry IV, as well as with that of Henry V. Malone.]

14 May 1594.

Edw. White] A booke entituled the *mofte* famous Chronicle hiftor*ye* of Leire Kin*ge* of England and his three Daughters *(k)*.
307.
[I fuppofe this to be the play on the fame fubject as that of our author, but written before it. Steevens.]

22 May 1594.

Edw. White] A booke *en*tituled a Wynters night*es* Paftime *(l)*. 307. b.
[Query, If the Winter's Tale. Steevens.]

(*k*) *Mofte* is left out; hiftor*ie* for hiftor*ye*; King for Kin*ge*.

(*l*) *In*tituled for *en*tituled; w*inter* for w*ynters*; nyght*s* for night*es*.

19 June

19 June 1594.

Tho. Creede] An enterlude *in*titled the Tragedie of Richard the Third, wherein is
fhow*en* the Death of Edward the Fourthe,
with the Smotheringe of the twoo Princes
in the Tower with *a* lamentable End of
Shore's wife and the con*iunction* of the
tw*oo* Houfes of Lancafter and York (*m*).
309. b.

[This could not have been the work of
Shakfpeare, as the death of Jane Shore
makes no part of his Drama.—Steevens.]

20 July 1594.

Tho. Creede] The lamentable Tragedie of
Locrine the eldeft Son*ne* of K. Brutus,
difcourfinge the warres of the Bri*ttans*,
&c (*n*).   310. b. vol. C.

1 Dec. 1595.

Cuthbert Burby] A boo*k* intit*u*led Edward
the Third and the *b*lack *p*rince, their

(*m*) *E*ntitled for *in*titled; fhow*n* for fhow*en*; *the* for
a; con*tention* for con*iunction*; two for tw*oo*.

(*n*) So*n* for fon*ne*; Bri*tains* for Bri*ttans*.

warres

warres with King*e* John of Fraunce (*o*).

C. 6.

[This is aſcribed to Shakſpeare by the compilers of ancient catalogues. Steevens.]

5 Aug. 1596.

Edw. White] A new*e* ballad of Romeo and Juliett (*p*). 12. b.

[Query, If Shakſpeare's play, the firſt edition of which appeared in 1597. Steevens.]

15 Aug. 1597.

Rich. Jones] Two ballads, being*e* the *ffirſte* and ſecond parts of the Widowe of Watling-ſtreet*e*; provided that no Draper's name be ſet to them (*q*). 22. b.

[Perhaps the ſongs on which the play with the ſame title was founded. It may, however, be the play itſelf. It was not uncommon to divide one dra-

---

(*o*) Book*e* for book; inti*t*l*ed* for inti*tu*led; *B* for *b*; *P* for *p*; King for King*e*; France for Fra*u*nce.

(*p*) N*ew* for new*e*.

(*q*) Being for being*e*; fir*ſt* for *ffirſte*; ſtree*t* for ſtree*te*.

matic

matic piece, though defigned for a fingle exhibition, into two parts. See
the King John before that of Shakfpeare. Steevens.]

29 Aug. 1597.

Andrew Wife] The Tragedye of Richard
the Seconde.   23.

20 Oct. 1597.

Andrew Wife] The Tragedie of King*e* Richard the Third, with the deat*h* of the
Duke of Clarence (*r*).   25.

25 Feb. 1597-8.

Andrew Wi*ffe*] A booke *in*titled the Hifto-
r*ye* of Henry the iiii[th], with his batt*aile* at
Shrewfbur*ye* againft Henry Hottfpurre of
the Nort*he* with the conceipted Mirth of
Sir John Falftaffe (*s*).   31.

22 July 1598.

James Rober*tes*] A booke of the M*a*rchaunt
of Veny*ce*, *or* otherwife called the Jewe

(*r*) King for King*e*; deat*he* for deat*h*.

(*s*) Wi*fe* for wi*ffe*; *en*titled for *in*titled; *h*iftor*ie* fot
Hiftor*ye*; batt*le* for batt*aile*; Shrewfbury for Shrewfbur*ye*; Nort*h* for Nort*he*; Falft*off* for Falft*affe*.

of

of Venyfe. Provided that *yt* bee not prynted by the faid James Robert*es* or an*ye* other whatfoever, without *lycence* firft had from the r*i*ght honourable the Lord Chamberlen (*t*).   39. b.

27 May 1600.

To Mr. Roberts] My Lord Chamberlen's mens plaies entred viz. A Morall of Clothe breches and velvet hofe : 24 May, to hym. Allarum to London.

4 Auguft.

As you like *yt*. a book. Henry⎫
the *ffi*ft. a book. *Every man*⎟
in his humor. a book. The⎬To be ftaied
Comed*ie* of Much Ado*o* about⎟
nothing*e*, a book (*u*).   ⎭

[Probably the play before that of Shak-

(*t*) Robert*s* for Robert*es*; merchaunt for m*a*rchaunt ; Veny*fe* for Veny*ce* ; *or*, after Venyce, is left out; *i*t for *yt*; b*e* for be*e*; *any* for an*ye*; *leave* for *lycence* ; r*y*ght for r*i*ght.

(*u*) Mr. Steevens has *i*t for *yt*; *f*ift for *ff*ift; he has left out altogether, one play, viz. *Every Man in his Humor, a book*; he has left out *The*; he has comed*y* for comed*ie* ; ad*o* for ad*oo*; nothin*g* for nothin*ge*.

fpeare,

fpeare, fays Mr. Steevens : But, Mr.
Malone remarks : " Surely this muft
" have been Shakfpeare's *Henry V*,
" which as well as *Much Ado about*
" *Nothing*, was printed in 1600, when
" this entry appears to have been
" made : See the Effay on the Chrono-
" logical order of Shakfpeare's plays ;
" Article, *As you Like it*."—I concur
with Mr. Malone ; becaufe the entry
adds, that all thofe books were faid to
be, *My Lord Chamberlen's men's plaies*.
It was, doubtlefs, 1600 : Thefe Entries
feem to have been, merely, omitted in
their proper places.]

11 Auguft 1600.

Tho Pav*i*er] Firft parte of the Hiftory of
the Life of Sir John Oldcaftell Lord
Cobham. Item, The Second, *and laft*
part*e* of the Hiftory of Sir John Oldcaftell Lord Cobham, with his Martyr-
dom (*x*). 63.

(*x*) In the date, 4th for 11th ; Pav*y*er for Pav*i*er ; *and*
laft are left out ; par*t* for par*te* ; Old*caftle* for Old*caftell*.

14 Aug.

14 Aug. 1600.

Thoˢ. Pavyer] The Hiftorye of Henr*ye* the
Vᵗʰ with the *b*attel of Ag*e*ncourt(*y*). 63.

23 Aug. 1600.

And. Wife Wm. Afpley] Two books, the
one called Muc*he* Ad*oe* about Nothin*ge*;
and the other The fecond Parte of the
Hiftory of King*e* Henry the iiiiᵗʰ; with
the *H*um*o*rs of Sir John Fa*ll*ftaff: wr*y*tten
by Mr. Shakefpeare(*z*). 63. b.

8 Oct. 1600.

Tho. Fyfher] A booke called a Mydfomer
nights Dreame(*a*). 65. b.

28 Oct. 1600.

Tho. H*ai*es] The booke of the Merch*a*nt
of Venyce(*b*). 66.

(*y*) Henr*y* for Henr*ye*; *fifth* for Vth; *B* for *b*; Agincourt for Ag*e*ncourt; nor, is there an &*c.* after Agen-
court, in the Regifter.

(*z*) Muc*h* for muc*he*; ad*o* for ad*oe*; nothin*g* for nothin*ge*; King for King*e*; *fourth* for iiiith; *h*um*o*urs for
*H*um*o*rs; Fa*l*ftaff for Fa*ll*ftaff; wr*i*tten for wr*y*tten.

(*a*) Fifher for Fyfher; m*i*dfomer for mydfomer; nyght*e*
for n*i*ghts.

(*b*) Hayes for Ha*i*es; *A booke called* are not in the Regifter; Merch*a*unt for Merch*a*nt.

I i   18 Jan.

18 Jan. 1601-2.

John Bufby] An excellent and plea*fant* con‑
ceited *Commedie* of Sir John Faulft*of*,
and the Merry wyves of Winde*for* (c). 78.

Arth. Johnfon] By affign'. from Jn°. Buf‑
bye a B. An excellent and pleafant con‑
ceited comedie of Sir John Faulftafe &
the mery wyves of Windfor.   ibid.

19 April 1602.

Tho. Pavier] by Affign'. from Tho. Mil‑
lington *Salvo jure* cujufcumq. The 1ft.
and 2d. pts. of Henry the VI: 11 books (*d*).

Tho. Pavier] Titus *and* Andronicus, entered
by warrant under Mr. Setons hand (*e*).
80. b.

26 July 1602.

James Roberts] A booke, The Revenge of
Hamlett prince of Denmarke, as *yt* was

(c) Pleafaunt for pleafant; comedie for commedie;
Faulftoff for Faulftof; Windfore for Windefor.

(*d*) The entry of *the 1ft and 2d parts of Henry VI* is
compleatly left out by Mr. S.

(*e*) The words, *A booke called*, are not in the Regifter,
and the copulative *and* is left out between Titus and
Andronicus.

latel*ie*

latel*ie* acted by the Lord Chamberlayn
his fervantes (*f*). 84. b.

11 Aug. 1602.

Wm. Cotton] A booke, called the Lyfe
and Deat*he* of the Lord Cromwell, as yt
was lately acted by the Lord Chamberley*n* his fervan*ts* (*g*). 85. b.

7 Feb. 1602-3.

Mr. Roberts] The booke of Troilus and
Creffeda, as *yt* is acted by my Lo. Cham-
berlens men (*h*). 91. b.

27 June 1603.

Math. Lawe] in full Courte iij Enterludes
or playes The ffirft is of Richard the 3d.
The fecond of Richard ye 2d. The third
of Henry the 4, the firft pte. all Kings (*i*).
98.

(*f*) *It* for *yt*; late*ly* for latel*ie*; Chamberl*ain* for
Chamberl*ayn*; fervan*ts* for fervant*es*.

(*g*) Deat*h* for deat*he*; Chamberley*ne* for Chamberley*n*; fervant*es* for fervant*s*.

(*h*) Cref*f*ida for Creffeda; *it* for *yt*.

(*i*) In the date, 25 for 27th.

12 Feb. 1604-5.

Nath. Butter] *Yf* he get good allowance for the Enterlude of *K.* Henry 8th. before he beg*yn* to print it; and then procure the wardens han*ds* to yt for the entrance of yt: he is to have the fame for his copy (*k*). 120.

[This was a play entitled, When you fee me you know me, or the famous Chronicle Hiftorie of K. Henrie the eight &c. by Samuel Rowley. Printed for N. Butter 1605. Malone.]

8 May, 1605.

Simon Stafford] A booke called the tragi-call Hiftorie of King*e* Leir and his three Daughters &c. as yt was lately a&ted (*l*). 123.

John Wright] By affignment from Simon Stafford and confent of Mr. Leake the tragicall Hiftory of Kinge *Leire, and his three Daughters* provided that S. S. [Si-

(*k*) *That*, miftakingly, for *yf*; the *K.* is left out before Henry; beg*in* for beg*yn*; han*d* for han*ds*:

(*l*) King for King*e*; the *&c.* after daughters is left out; *it* for *yt*; lately for latel*ie.*

mon

mon Stafford] fhall have the printing of
this book (*m*). ibid.

[This is the *King Lear* before that of
Shakfpeare. Steevens.]

3 July, 1605.

Tho. Pavyer] A ballad of lamentable mur-
*th*er done in Yorkefhire by a Gent. upon
2 of his owne Children, fore woundinge
his Wy*f*e and Nurfe (*n*). 126.

[Query, if the play—Steevens.]

22 Jan. 1606–7.

Mr. Linge] By direction of a Court and
with confent of Mr. Burby under his
hand wrytinge thefe iij copies, viz. Romeo & Juliett. Loves labour Los*te*. 3,
The taming*e* of a fhrewe (*o*). 147

(*m*) Le*a*r for Le*i*re; and he has an *&c.* for *and his
three daughters.*

(*n*) In the Regifter there is no *a*, before lamentable;
mur*d*er for mur*th*er; w*i*fe for wyfe; and there ought to
be no *&c.* at the end.

(*o*) *Nich.* for *Mr.*; Lo*ſ*t for Lo*ſte*; taming for
taming*e*.

6 Aug. 1607.

Geo. Elde] Entered for his Copie under th'ands of Sir Geo. Bucke, Knight, and the wardens, A booke called the Comedie of the Puritan wydowe(*p*).   157. b.

6 Aug. 1607.

Tho. Thorp] Entered for his Copie under 'thands of S'Geo. Bucke Kt. and wardens, A Comed*ie* called, What you Will(*q*).
ibid.

[Perhaps this is Marſton's Comedy of *What you Will.* I have a Copy of it, dated 1607. *What you Will*, however, is the ſecond title to Shakſpeare's *Twelfth Night*—Steevens.—But, Mr. Malone adds; This was certainly, Marſton's play; for it was printed in 1607 by G. Elde for T. Thorpe.]

22 Oct. 1607.

Ar. Johnſon] Entered as his Copie under 'thands of Sir Geo. Bucke, Kt. and the wardens, a plaie called, The merry Devill of Edmonton.   159. b.

(*p*) W*i*dowe for W*y*dowe.
(*q*) Comed*y* for Comed*ie.*

[*The*

[*The merry Devil of Edmonton* is mentioned in the *Black Booke* by T. M.
1604: Give him leave to fee *The merry
Divel of Edmunton, or a woman killed
with kindneffe.*—Steevens.]

19 Nov. 1607.

John Smyth*i*ck] Under t'hands of the wardens, the books following, which did
belong to Nich͞os Lynge. 6 a booke
called Hamlett. 9 The Taminge of a
Shrewe. 10 Romeo & Julett. 11 Loves
Labour Loft (*r*). 161.

26 Nov. 1607.

Na. Butter and Jo. Bufby] Entered for their
Copie under t'hands of Sir Geo. Bucke,
Kt. and the Wardens, a booke called,
Mr. W*illm* Shakefpeare, his Hiftorye of
King*e* Lear, as *yt* was played before the
King's Majeftie at Whitehall, upon St.
Stephen's night at Chriftmas laft, by his
Majeftie's Servants playing ufually at the
Globe on the Bank-fide (*s*). 161. b.

(*r*) Smyth*w*ick for Smyth*i*ck.

(*s*) Will*i*am for Willm; Hiftor*i*e for Hifto*r*ye; King
for King*e*; *it* for *yt*.

I i 4 5 April

5 April 1608.

Jofeph Hunt and Tho. Archer.] A book
called the lyfe and death*e* of the Merry
Devi*ll* of Edmonton, with the pleafant
Pranks of Smugg*e* the Sm*y*th, Sir John
and m*y*ne Hofte of the George, about
their ftealinge of Ven*f*on—By T. B. (*t*).
165. b.

[Bound up in a volume of plays attributed
to Shakfpeare, and once belonging to
King Charles II ; but now in Mr.
Garrick's collection. The initial letters
at the end of this entry, fufficiently
free Shakfpeare from being its author.
—Steevens.]

2 May 1608.

Mr. Pavyer] A booke, *The* Yorkfhire Tragedy, written by Wylliam Shakefp*e*re (*u*).
167

20*th* May, 1608.

Edw. Blunt] Entered under t'hands of Sir

(*t*) L*i*fe for lyfe; deat*h* for deat*he*; devi*l* for devi*ll*;
fmug*g* for fmug*ge*; Sm*i*th for Sm*y*th, m*i*ne for myne;
veni*f*on for venfon.

(*u*) *A* for *The*; Shakefp*e*are for Shakefp*e*re.

Geo.

Geo. Bucke, Kt. and Mr. Warden Seton, a book called : The booke of Pericles Prynce of Tyre (*x*). 167. b.

A book by the like authoritie called Anthony and Cleopatra. ibid.

   28 Jan. 1608–9.

Rich. Bonion and Hen. Whalleys] Entered for their copie under t'hands of Mr. Segar Deputy to Sir Geo. Bucke, and Mr. Warden Lownes : A booke called, the Hiſtory of Troylus and Creſſula (*y*). 178. b.

   20th May 1609.

Tho. Thorpe]A booke called, Shakeſpeare's Sonnetts (*z*). 183. b.

   16 Oct. 1609.

Mr. Welby] Edward the Third 189.

   16 Dec. 1611.

John Brown] A booke called the Lyfe and Death of the Lo. Cromwell, by W. S. 214. b.

(*x*) In the date, the 2d for the 20th; Prince for Prynce.

(*y*) Bonian for Bonion ; Whalley for Whalleys; Creſ-ſida for Creſſula.

(*z*) Sonnets for ſonnetts.

29th Nov.

29th Nov. 1614.

John Beale] A booke called the Hiftory of George Lord Faulconbridge baftard Sonne to Richard Cordelion (*a*). 256. b.

[Query. If this was Shakfpeare's *King John*, or fome old Romance, like that of *Richard Coeur de Lion*. Steevens.]

To this Mr. Malone anfwers : It was undoubtedly the famous hiftorie of George Lord Fauconbridge, a profe Romance. I have an edition of it now before me, printed for J. B. dated 1616.]

16th Feb. 1616.

Mr. Barrett] Life and Death of Lord Crom-well. 279.

2 March 1617.

Mr. Snodham] Edward the Third, the play (*b*). 288.

17 Sept. 1618.

John Wright] The comedy called Muce-dorus 293. b.

(*a*) Hiftor*ie* for Hiftory ; *George* is left out before Lord Faulconbridge ; fo*n* for fo*nne*.

(*b*) In the date, the 20th for the 2d.

[Bound

⌊Bound up in a volume of plays attributed to Shakſpeare, and once belonging to King Charles II. See Mr. Garrick's collection. Steevens.]

8 July 1619.

Lau. Hayes] A play called the Marchaunt
of Venice (*c*)   303. V. D.

6 Oct. 1621.

Tho. Walkely] Entered for his, to wit,
under the handes of Sir George Buck,
and the Wardens: The Tragedie of
Othello, the Moore of Venice   21

8 Nov. 1623.

Mr. Blounte and Iſaak Jaggard] Mr. William Shakſpeere's Comedyes, Hiſtories,
and Trage*dy*es, ſoe many of the ſaid copies, as are not formerly entered to other
men. viz.

Comedyes ⎰ The Tempeſt.
          ⎱ Two Gentlemen of Verona.
          ⎰ Meaſure for Meaſure.
          ⎱ The Comedy of Errors.

(*c*) *Nich. Okes* for *Lau. Hayes*; Merchaunt for Marchaunt.

As

Comedyes
{ As You Like it.
All's Well that Ends Well.
Twelfe Night.
The Winter's Tale.

Hiftories
{ The Third*e* Part*e* of Henry
the Sixt.
Henry the Eight.

Tragedies
{ Coriolanus.
Timon of Athens.
Julius Cæfar.
Mac*k*beth
Anthonie and Cleopatra.
Cymbeline (*d*).   69 a.

14 Dec. 1624.

Mr. Pavier] Titus Andronnicus, Widdow
of Watling Street (*e*).   93

23 Feb. 1625.

Mr. Stanfby] Edward the Third, the play,
115

(*d*) Bloun*t* for Bloun*te*; Shakefp*e*are's for Shak-
fp*e*ere's; *Hiftories* left out after comedyes; trag*e*dies for
tragedyes; third for thir*de*; par*t* for par*te*; Ma*c*beth for
Mac*k*beth.

(*e*) Pav*y*er for Pav*i*er; Andro*n*icus for Andro*nn*icus;
w*i*dow for w*i*ddow.

3 April

3 April 1626.

Mr. Parker] Life and Death of Lord Cromwell   120

4 Aug. 1626.

Edw. Brewſter] Mr. Pavier's right in Shakeſpeare's plays

Rob. Birde] or any of them.

*The Hiſtorye of Hen. the fift, and the play of
the ſame.* Sir John Oldcaſtle a play.
Tytus *and* Andronicus — Hiſtorye of
Hamblett (*f*).   127

29 Jan. 1629.

Mr. Meighen.] *The* Merry Wives of Win-
ſor (*g*).   193

8 Nov. 1630.

Ric. Cotes] Aſſigned unto him by Mr.
Bird and conſent of a full Court : Henrye
the Fift. Sir John Oldcaſtle. Tytus
and Andronicus. Yorke and Lancaſter.

(*f*) Pavyer's for Pavier's; our editor has left out,
after any of them, *The Hiſtorye of Hen. the fift, and the
play of the ſame*; Titus for Tytus; *and* is left out after
Tytus; Hiſtorie for Hiſtorye.

(*g*) *The* is left out before Merry; Windſor for Win-
ſor.

Agincourt.

Agincourt. Pericles. Hamble*t*. Yorkefhire Traged*ie* (*h*). 208

Mr. Blount affigned unto Mr. Allott] The
fixteen plays in p. 69, were affigned by
Tho. Blount to Edward Allott, June 26,
1630 (*i*). 109

[Edward Allott was one of the publifhers
of the fecond folio 1632. Steevens].

I will only beg leave to add, in Mr.
Steevens's own words, when he finifhed his
Extracts from the Stationers' Regifters,
erroneous as they were, " The public is
" now in poffeffion of as accurate an ac-
" count of the dates, &c. of Shakfpeare's
" Works, as perhaps will ever be com-
" piled :" And, I will now clofe this Apology, with remarking that, in Editorfhip,
as it often is,

" ————————— in religion;
" What damned error, but fome fober brow
" Will blefs it."

(*h*) *And* is left out after Tytus ; Hamble*tt* for Hamble*t* ; Yorkfhire traged*y* for Yorke*fh*ire traged*ie*.

(*i*) The year 1632 is put, miftakingly, for 1630.

§ XII.

―― § XIII. ――

The POSTSCRIPT, addressed to T. J. MATHIAS, F. R. S. S. A. the author of THE PURSUITS OF LITERATURE, &c. &c. &c.

IN the midſt of this controverſy, which had, for its end, the repulſion of attack, and the defence of truth, you mingled in the fray, without either the pretenſion of injury, or the proſpeɛt of good: You came out monkey-like, *to reform literature*, at whatever hazard of miſchief, or certainty of wrong: And, like a true monkey-critic, you cenſured a book, which you had never read; and of which, the peruſal might have proteɛted you, at leaſt, from the charge of ignorance, if not ſaved you, from the diſgrace of blunder. But you would, in an unlucky moment for your own fame, " make *ſatire* a *lampoon*;" and point the finger of malice :—

" See on the critic in " his pride of place,"
" Laborious Chalmers drops his leaden mace (*a*)."

In

――――――――――

(*a*) I complain not of your couplet; as I claim no exemption from the common fate of every writer, who offers

In this weapon, I fufpect, Mr. Malone has found the toughnefs of iron; and in it, you will find, I truft, the fharpnefs of fteel. This couplet was, no doubt, deemed wonderfully witty, and it will hereafter be regarded, perhaps, as vaftly wife, to roufe an offencelefs maftiff, while repofing in the fhade, after a fuccefsful conflict. You have, however, your fubterfuges always at hand:

" My *hate* was great with child; and here 'tis eas'd;
" Vex'd all the world, fo that *myfelf* be pleas'd."

---

offers to the public either amufement, or information. Any verfe-man is perfectly welcome to *hitch me into rhyme*, either in a couplet, or a triplet, if he fee any thing ridiculous, in my productions: But, I perceived in your profe note, which was not called for, an obvious purpofe of perfonal infult. " Nay, Sir," cry you, in your common cant, " have not I added to this profe " note, in a fubfequent edition, that you are a man " of *great learning*; and do you not deem this a fuffi- " cient apology from fo great a writer, as the author of " the Purfuits of Literature." No, Sir, I confider that addition, being in your ufual ftyle of attempting ridicule by the mixture of contradictory qualities, as an aggravation of the original impertinence.

" But,

" But, Sir, Sir," fay you " have I roufed
" the maftiff?" " Am I the author of the
" Purfuits of Literature?" " Have not I
" denied my being the writer of it, and
" defired bookfellers to tell the world, that
" I am not the author of a book, which
" the greateft fcholar ought to be proud to
" own?" Yes: You have made fuch denials; and you have made a fimilar denial
to your official fuperior: But you have made
all thofe denials, with fuch circumftances
of tergiverfation, as to prove the affirmative
of the queftion. You convinced fome of
the bookfellers, that you were the true
writer, by your dubious manner of fpeaking
to them, upon the point; neither pofitively directing a denial, nor yet clearly per-
mitting an avowal of the charge. When
you were advertifed, as the author, week
after week, by a perfon, who, knowing the
fact, fent his name to the publifher of the
newfpaper, did you, on that occafion, dif-
avow your being the author of that lampoon,
as publicly, as you had been pointedly
charged? No: But, you ought to have

K k   made

made fuch a difavowal, if you had confidered your fituation, in the Queen's Treafury; having lampooned the King's perfon;
having committed a breach of privilege of
both Houfes of Parliament; and having
ridiculed the two learned Societies.   Nay;
have I not, repeatedly, declared, in *my
Purfuits of Literature,* " that I never will be
" known (*b*);" confcious, you might have
added, that I have kept my own fecret,
as faithfully as *Junius,* whom time only
has at length difcovered: Time, which has
very foon difclofed your tricks.   Let me,
however, afk with Marfton, one of the firft
and beft of our fatirifts :

   " Tell me, Mathias, haft thou *Gyges'* ring,
   " That thou prefum'ft, as if thou wert unfeen?"

   I propofe, in the firft place, to fubmit to
the inquifitive reader the evidence, which

(*b*) You again declare " that neither my name, nor
" my fituation in life, will ever be revealed." And, putting yourfelf in the threatening pofture of *ancient Piftol,*
you cry out, that, " it will be *more than foolifh* to con-
" jecture about the author." [Pur. Lit. 7 Ed. p. 226-
7-8.]

                  I have

I have collected, for proving you to be the
real author of *The Purfuits of Literature* ;
2dly. to treat of the *matter* of your work ;
and, laftly, to fpeak of the manner of it ;
conftantly adducing facts, examples, and
documents, as the proofs of my pofitions ;
in order to fatisfy the moft fceptical, and
to convince the moft incredulous.   Whatever you may fay, or others may think, I fhall
confider that to be the beft logick, which
eftablifhes every proof, with fuch elaboration, as to preclude an anfwer ; and that
to be the beft writing, which enforces conviction, by the ftrength of its argument,
and fhortens controverfy, by the efficacy of
its vigour.   Neither do I feel any great apprehenfions of your repeated *threats* of " a
" *darknefs* that may be *felt*."   For, whatever may be the danger of that *darknefs*,
I am determined to

" Be ftirring as the time ; be fire with fire ;
" *Threaten* the *threatener* ; and out-face the brow
" Of *bragging horror*."

K k 2   I PROOFS

1. Proofs of *your* being the Author.

I am neither fo abfurd myfelf, as to attempt to give, nor fo foolifh, as to approve of the abfurdity of others, who demand, *demonſtration*, in the conteſts of literature, or in the affairs of life: All, then, that can be fitly offered, or fairly required, in fuch cafes, is, fuch evidence, as the nature of the fubject admits, or the conſtitution of the mind demands.

Such is the common fenfe, which has always prevailed in this land: And, hence, it is, accordingly, an eſtabliſhed principle of the common law to admit one witnefs, as quite fufficient, to prove any particular fact; if he be a credible perfon (*c*). The writing of a book, or the publication of a libel, are facts, which any one witnefs, who knows the truth, is competent to prove. And, in the daily practice of Weſtminſter-hall, nothing more is neceſſary than to bring, as a witnefs, the perfon who bought the libel;

(*c*) Such was the judicial opinion of the Lord Chief Juſtice Holt. [Bac. Ab* Ed. Guillim, vol. ii. p. 593.]

in

in order to prove the fact of publication. If this, then, be true, in common fenfe, in common law, and in common practice, nothing more is requifite, than to produce the bookfeller, who fold the firft part of *The Purfuits of Literature*, and who, as you bufied yourfelf in the fale, and celebration of the work, made no great fcruple to fay, that you were the perfon, who fent the copy, and corrected the prefs, although you fkulked behind Macrae, your printer. Thus eafy is it to prove you *the publifher* of the lampoon in queftion. Your friends, knowing what had been faid, on this head, which could be proved, and what you had yourfelf difclofed, admit, that you were *the publifher:* But, they deny, that you are *the Author;* declaring your talents to be unequal to the tafk of writing the omnifcient *Purfuits of Literature.*

It muft be acknowledged, indeed, that the publifher of a book may not be the author of it: Cleland was the putative publifher of Pope's lampoons. But, your pride has never ftoopt to be the *Cleland* of any

poet:

poet: You had publifhed fuch writings, for yourfelf, before; but not for others: And, you had already fent into the world fimilar lampoons, either to indulge the evil habits of malice, or to gratify the felfifh paffion of vanity. Yes:

" You can add guilt to vanity, and take
" A pride to hear the conquefts, which you make "

It is fair to prefume, then, that being, certainly, the publifher, you are, probably, the author. I would even undertake to carry this probability into moral certainty: If juftice called on me, for the proofs, I would produce your firft bookfeller, to prove you the publifher; your printer to prove, that you corrected the fheets from the prefs, and your laft bookfeller, to confirm the teftimony of both. I would produce a third bookfeller to prove, that he had told you fome anecdotes, which he foon faw, in your next edition. I would produce a fourth bookfeller, who lent you feveral books, which, he perceived in your next publication, quoted as authorities. If I were hard preffed for witneffes, I would produce feveral

ral ladies, to whom you confeffed, and denied, and denied, and confeffed, that you
claimed the honour of writing " the omni-
" fcious and omnifufficient" *Purfuits of Li-*
terature: Junius, MacAulay, kept *his* fecret from his wife: You let feveral women
into your fecret, with the policy of concealing, and, at the fame time, revealing, your
fecret. Yet, though many witneffes may be
produced, one witnefs is quite fufficient, to
prove the fact, either of publifhing, or of
writing, any book, in the judicial practice
of our rational tribunals. I perceive, that
this appeal to jurifprudence makes you exclaim, in the characteriftic tone of the *Pre-*
face to your *Tranflation:*

" —————— The king-becoming graces;
" As *juftice*, *verity*, temp'rance, ftablenefs,
" *I* have no relifh of them!

Let me add to thefe proofs, a fact, which
may produce conviction in the minds of all
thofe enquirers, who are either unable, or
unwilling, to take the trouble of purfuing
a train of probabilities: I have perufed fome
of your private letters, which were written,

K k 4   not

not in your elongated hand, for the purpofe of deception, but in your ufual character, for common concerns: In thefe epiftles, I have feen your *likes*, and *diſlikes*, which have enabled me to judge of your real motives, either for praife, or for blame: and, bearing in my recollection, the previous probabilities of your being the author, I was furniſhed by thefe letters, with as complete proof, as if

" —————— Spirits that know
" All mortal confequences had pronounced it."

It is an obfervation of **Dr.** Beattie (*d*), when fpeaking of the ftyle of the Scripture, " that there are no remarks thrown in, to " anticipate objections ; nothing of that cau- " tion, which never fails to diftinguiſh the " teftimony of thofe, who are confcious of " impofture." If thefe obfervations be as true, as they are judicious, and profound, a contrary conduct, in any writer, muft eftabliſh a quite different inference: Your *Pur-* fuits are full of fuch *anticipations*, which are guardedly inferted, for the obvious purpofes

(*d*) In his Evidence of the Truth of Chriftianity, vol. i. p. 79.

of

of anfwering objections, and deluding inquiry. When you are in the act of ridi-
culing the Royal Society, whereof *you are a*
fellow, you fay, " Sometimes, *as I was told*,
" the idea of the cruelty exercifed upon
" thefe animals is loft, in the *ridiculous*
" *term, My friend told me*, that he actually
" thought, &c." (e) When you are ridi-
culing the Antiquary Society, whereof you
are alfo a member, you fay, " *I am obliged*
" *for this information* to a fellow of the S. of
" Antiquaries:"(f) Yet, the fact is, that
you were prefent at the memorable election of Mr. Wyat, the tranfaction alluded
to. Panegyrizing Mr. Samuel Lyfons, for
his work, on the remains of the *Roman villa,*
at Woodchefter, you add, " which *a friend*
" *has juft fhewn me; a friend of mine* was

(e) 6 Ed. p. 341. The words, *as I was told*; and my
friend *told me*; are printed in italics; in order, that the
reader may more clearly underftand, that this information, and ridicule, did not come from a member, who is
under a folemn engagement to fupport, and *honour* the
fociety.

(f) Ib. 284.

" much

" much entertained with the three tents :"(*g*)
You threw in the *information of a friend*, in
order to conceal your intimate connection
with Mr. Samuel Lyfons, and to give a
higher varnifh to your praife. In this fpirit,
and with the fame defign of anticipation,
you mention Dr. Rennel, with ftudied praife,
in your firft edition, and with obvious neglect,
in fome fubfequent editions :

" His learn'd *Apology* has Rennel fram'd,
" And *may* hereafter be with Barrow nam'd."(*h*)

This couplet is followed by a long note,
wherein you fay, for the obvious purpofe of
concealing your well known intimacy with
the Doctor; " I am obliged *to a Dignitary*
" *of the Church* who fent me, *as a prefent*,

(*g*) Ib. p. 285.

(*h*) 4th Part, p. 84; the fame verfes and note are
continued in the pretended third edition of your fourth
part.   In the 6th Ed. p. 350, and the 7th Ed. p. 410,
Dr. Rennel is mentioned, carelefly, in the text, as having
a *learned* name ; and Dr. Barrow is quite excluded.   In
the 6th and 7th editions, the long note is fuppreffed ;
and inftead thereof, Dr. Rennel is, merely, mentioned as
[the] author of a very able, learned, and eloquent,
Apology for the Church of England.

" the

" the fermon to which I allude." You did
not, then, receive *this prefent* from Dr. Rennel himfelf, who was not backward in prefenting his *Apology*. It muft, therefore, be
apparent to all, who know how much *your
hopes and fears are to each other known*, that
your fubfequent alterations, both in the text,
and note, were made in concert with your
friend, who was, probably, frightened at
your panegyric:

" For Fame, impatient of extremes, decays,
" Not more by envy, than excefs of praife."

You play off upon your readers other
modes of anticipation. You, who had mingled in the Chattertonian controverfy, on the
wrong fide, affect to know little about Chatterton, and Lord Orford's letter (*i*).

You

(*i*) Ib. 103. After treating very fully in your text,
of Rowley, and Chatterton, and Catcot, whom you offi-
cioufly praife, you add, in your note thereon; for
every couplet muft have its note; " when *I firft* pub-
" lifhed the firft part of this poem (1794) I had *cafually*
" *glanced* at the fubject of Rowley; but fince, I have
" perufed many of the learned treatifes upon it. I *nei-*
" *ther have*, nor *will have* any thing to do with the deci-
" fion

You practife another trick of anticipation, whilft you, at the fame time, recommend your own writings to the public notice. When you commend your *Runic Odes*, you again mention Mr. Mathias, as the author of the Effay on Rowley and Chatterton (*k*).

" fion of fuch a controverfy ," and you fubjoin in a *parenthefis* (" I fpeak from the *printed accounts.*") Now, the fact is, that your " *Effay* on the evidence external " and internal, relating to the Poems attributed to " Thomas Rowley, &c." was publifhed, in its fecond edition, during 1784 ; if indeed, a fecond edition there were, as the title page afferts. On this occafion, as we herein fee, you practife a *double impofition*, for the obvious purpofe of a ftill greater deception : you had, indeed, faid, " I draw my humble information of Chat-" terton from his life in the *new* Biographia Britannica. " They, *who have time,* may read Mr. Tyrrwhit, Mr. " Bryant, Dr. Milles, Mr. Thomas Warton, &c. but, " I confine myfelf to the general view of this contro-" verfy in Mr. MATHIAS's *candid and comprehenfive* " *Effay.*" Add to thefe anticipations, your doubts, and hefitations, about Lord Orford's letters, on this well known fubject. You now run out into an elaborate panegyrick of half a dozen couplets on Catcot, the firft patron of Chatterton.

(*k*) 6th Edit. p. 248-9.

You

You recommend your *Pair of Epiſtles* to the *Rev. Dr. Randolph :* " *my mention* of them, " you, immediately, add, may poſſibly " excite ſome curioſity (*l*)." Upon *public principles*, you recommend your *Political Dramatiſt* of the Houſe of Commons, a ſatire (*m*).

But, as anticipation knows no bounds, you play off another artifice of deception, by pretending to be a Parliament-man : " To hear Mr. Fox, ſay you, as I *perpe-* " *tually* do in the houſe (*n*)." Well : you do not ſay, that you are a member of Parliament ; you only pretend, for the purpoſe of deception, that you are *perpetually*, in the Houſe of Commons.

Yet, this practice of anticipation does not well accord with your pretended *retirement*. When you have panegyrized the *Baviad*, and the *Mæviad*, of Mr. [W] Gif-

(*l*) 6th Edit. p. 283.
(*m*) 6th Edit. p. 112-14.
(*n*) 6th Edit. p. 213. The word *perpetually* you wrote *in italicks*, in order to mark more ſtrongly your conſtant attendance in Parliament.

ford,

ford, you add, " I have not the honour of
" his acquaintance; and indeed from the
" *nature* of *my retirement*, I probably may
" never fee him (*o*)." You, who live in
Scotland Yard; who run about the bookfellers' fhops; who frequent the theatres;
who attend the learned focieties; who vi-
fit the literary clubs; live in fuch *retirement*, as, probably, never to fee Mr. William Gifford, who does not live altogether
in retirement !

But, with all your retirement, you fometimes wander through the Treafury Vaults;
you even penetrate into the Treafury Chambers : But, you lament that *you never can
fee either Mr. Pitt, or the Lords of the Treafury* (*p*). And, although you thus folicit
your

(*o*) Pur. of Lit. 6 Ed. p. 113.

(*p*) Ib. p. 35. " N. B. It often requires *miraculous*
" *diligence*, even in thefe days, to get at one's ar-
" rears. *See* Mr. Pitt and the Lords of the Treafury,
" *if you can get a fight of them.* I never could." [*I never could*, ftanding thus by itfelf, is ungrammatical.]
The fenfe of this paffage is marred, by the peculiarity
of

your claims, without feeing Mr. Pitt, and
the Lords of the Treafury, " you avow
" your poem to be the fruit and ftudy of
" an independant and difinterefted life,
" paffed without the incumbrance of a pro-
" feffion, or the embarraffment of bufi-
" nefs (*q*)."

What an Oedipus! You live, in the
world, and out of the world ; you are de-
pendent, and independent ; with a profeffion, and without a profeffion ; and you
are a parliament-man, and not a parliament-man. Well! Well! Mathias! Fact,
which is the great illuminator of obfcurities, will unriddle all thofe enigmatical *anticipations :* And, the fact is, that you are a
Clerk in the Queen's Treafury, under Lord
Aylefbury, as the Red-book fhows. With
fuch a lift of anticipations before him, the
reader is ready to cry out, with Marfton :

" For fhame! unmafk ; leave for to cloke intent ;
" And fhow, thou'rt vainglorious, impudent!"

of the pointing, which is perfectly confiftent with fimilar peculiarities of punctuation, that may be traced
through your whole writings.

(*q*) Pur. of Lit. 6 Ed. p. 111-12.

From

From fuch an accumulation of proofs, I will imitate Johnfon, in appealing neither " to the boors of Middlefex, nor to the cits of " London: For, of ftyle, and fentiment, " they take no cognizance :" But, I will ftrike a fpecial jury of the boys of Weft-minfter, and Eton, for the trial of the *if-fue*, whether you be guilty, or not guilty, of writing the *Purfuits of Literature.*

My Mafters : This is a mere fact, which may be decided, by an inveftigation of cir-cumftances, like other facts, of full as much importance, and of much more difficulty. The culprit has already publifhed feveral lampoons, which are conceived, in a fimi-lar fpirit; written, in the fame ftrain of profaic poetry, accompanied with fimilar notes, from his friend Stobæus ; and given to the world, with the like purpofe of vex-ing individuals, rather than of reforming vices (*r*) ; the characteriftic difference between

(*r*) For examples: The *Heroic Epiftle* to the Rev. Dr. Watfon, in 1780. There were publifhed about that time, *Characters of Perfons of eminence in Cambridge,*
who

tween fatire and lampoon, confifting in this, that *fatire* operates upon *vices*, but *lampoon* on *perfons.*

My Mafters : you will not be deluded, I truft, by the ftories, he tells you, from *Scaliger*, and *Erafmus*, of the infufficiency of the comparifon of ftyle, and fentiment, for eftablifhing the identity of the writer ; becaufe *general* fimilarity, and *particular* analogy, lead to very different conclufions.   In all the writings of Mathias, you fee the fame affectation of learned *mottos* ; yet, in all his tracts, you, alfo, fee, the fame want of acquaintance with his mother tongue ; whilft he pretends to know every other tongue, from the Greek, to the Hottentot ; yet, he every where difplays the fame ignorance of the idiom, and grammar, of the Englifh language(*s*).   In all his productions, you
may

who were defcribed by lines from Shakfpeare. Thefe lampoons were attributed to Mr. Mathias, when they appeared.   Add to thefe, his *Pair of Epiftles,* and his *Political Dramatift, &c. &c.*

(*s*) He appears, from his writings, not to know, that there is, in the Englifh grammar, whatever Lowth

may

may fee ftriking fpecimens of his ridiculous unfkilfulnefs in the operative part of com-pofition ; and of his being totally unin-formed, with regard to the art of pointing, which is fo effential, for the accuracy, and the clearnefs, of diction. I will fubmit to your confideration fome remarkable exam-ples : from

The Visible *Mathias :*   The Invisible *Mathias :*

When comparing the   In his note on the quef-different doctrines of the   tion about the exiftence of feveral difputants, in his   *Troy,* he fays: "Some per-

---

may inculcate, fuch a form as the *fubjunctive mood.* In his Effay on Rowley, p. 12, you may fee : " But *if* the " prefent queftion deferves any inveftigation." See his Purfuits, 6 Ed. p. 72—" If he effects ; p. 77, if he *is* appointed ; *if* a copy *is* : And fee p. 71, 75, 83, 107, 108, 160, 165, 224, &c. &c. &c. Mathias fhows every where, that he does not underftand the ufe of the Englifh *article.* Ib. p. 53, 134, the Rev. Mr. Nares, [the] editor ; 241, Dr. Gillies [the] author ; and 366 (note *e*) a remarkable inftance of his ufing *the* for *his, &c.* See his childifh ignorance of Englifh grammar, in his *Effay on Rowley,* p. 8 : " the fafety *and* well being " of mankind *is* [are] concerned ;—the animofity *and* " heat of any conteft *is* [are] not always. There *is* " [are] infanity of found, *and* fhallownefs of argu-" ment (.) ;" in his Shade of Pope, p. 5.

Effay

Essay on Rowley, he recites thus: " That, these poems " exhibit such a perfection, " &c. (.)   That our old " English poets are minute " &c. (.)   That, even in " the narrative, the writer " of these poems adopts " ideal terms.(.)   That his " propensity to personifica- " tion, is indulged, &c. (.) " They are of opinion, " That(.) That(.) That(.) " That(.)" [See p. 64, 65, 66 to 82, for a thousand re- petitions of the same im- proprieties, which show, clearly, that the writer is not aware of his own blun- ders.] And, in p. 112–13, he extends the impropriety of pointing, from the close of a sentence, to the begin- ning of a paragraph :---- " where he died unfortu- " nately three months af- " ter(.)"

" That he was not igno- " rant of the French, Saxon " and Latin tongues(.)" " That, &c. &c. [All

" sons have even declared " that Mr. Bryant had no " right to touch the sub- " ject(.) That nothing can " be more contrary to rea- " son than to suppose that " the existence of a city, " and a war, of which we " have read with delight " from our boyish days, " should be called in ques- " tion(.) That their plea- " sure is snatched from " them : and such a poem, " without any historical " fact for a basis, cannot " be interesting." [Purs. of Lit. 6 Ed. p. 236.] To these illustrative extracts, add from the Prefatory Epistle to his " Transla- " tion of passages from " [the] Greek, Latin, Ita- " lian, and French writers, " &c." the following pas- sage in p. lxv: " The pa- " raphrase *and* the meaning " of them in *a very extended* " *sense,* is [are] this [these] " (.) The time is now ar- " rived; &c."   This pas-

thofe

thofe, who are acquainted with Englifh grammar, muft perceive, that as there is nothing fully affirmed, or denied, in thefe independent paragraphs, they muft be defective, both in grammar, and in fenfe.]

fage, which is a fingular example of every poffrble fault, in writing, connects, with *hooks of Stéel,* the *tranflator,* with the *author,* and the *invifible,* with the *vifible,* Mathias, who was not aware, that his profound ignorance would thus furnifh decifive proofs of the famenefs of the writer; and, confequently, a clear detection of this mighty fecret.

I have now fubmitted to your judgements, a very remarkable *peculiarity* of *punctuation,* in the pages of the vifible, and the invifible, Mathias : There is no printer, who, without the direction of the Author, would thus infert fo many *full points, before* the *clofure* of *the fenfe.* And, by this improper mode of pointing, every fentiment is rendered ungrammatical, and the connection of reafoning intended is totally deftroyed : For, as the fenfe clofes with the point (.) there can be no grammatical reference to what goes before : This, then, is a ftrong proof,

proof, that *the Essay on Rowley*, and *the Pursuits of Literature*, were written by the same Author.—Now ; in weighing probabilities, for the purpose of *probation*, the chances are a hundred to one, that two different writers would not adopt the same *affected*, ungrammatical, and absurd, punctuation (*t*), which, by this disjunction of the sentences, leaves nothing, in them, predicated of any proposition.

My Masters : This, therefore, is a distinct consideration, from that, which a comparison of style affords, for the ascertaining

(*t*) See also the 6 Ed. p. 309 [Note *O*] " My allu-
" sion in the verse is this(.) [:]   After the profanation of
" the temple, &c."   In this note, we see, as we may
also see, in many other passages throughout this work,
the same peculiarity of pointing, the same false grammar, the same absurd reasoning.   Speaking of the Bishop
of Lincoln, he says, " he was Tutor and Secretary to
" the Right Hon. William Pitt, before he was raised to
" the Prelacy(.)   A man of learning and of ability(.)"
[Pur. Lit. 6 Edit. 162.]   This last sentence, standing thus substantively by itself, in consequence of the
full stop (.) after *Prelacy*, predicates nothing of any
person : And, therefore, the intended compliment to a
learned person is marred by appropriate unskilfulness.

L l 3   of

of the identity of the Author. The fame obfervation is equally applicable, when we fee this writer, taking the very expreffions from one of his own books, to infert them in another; outfacing his own objections to Dr. Warton: In *his Political Dramatift*, fpeaking of the Houfe of Commons, he fays, " the Houfe was up :" And, in *his Purfuits of Literature*, fpeaking of the fame fubject, he adopts the fame words, " the " Houfe is up (*x*)." Not only the fame expreffions are adopted from one work, and placed in another, of the fame writer, but the fame topicks are affumed, and re-affumed by him; conftantly miftaking lampoon, for fatire; and, throughout his writings he is only confiftent, in being uniformly inconfiftent; his conftant practice ftanding, perpetually, oppofed to his avowed principle.

How fay you, Mafters, is Mathias guilty, or not guilty, of writing *The Purfuits of Li-*

(*x*) " If from *State farces*, when *the Houfe is up*" [6 Ed. p. 111.] So, *confine*, for confinement, is ufed in his *Runic Odes*, p. 10, and alfo in his *Purfuits*, in the fame fenfe. [7 Ed. 300.]

terature ?

terature? Guilty. You fay, Guilty; and fo, you fay all? Yes(*y*).

With

(*y*) In addition to thofe already advanced, I fubmit to the reader the following facts, and confiderations, which were communicated to me by a friend; and which, having been collected for his own fatisfaction, with regard to the *real Author* of *the Purfuits of Litera-ture,* may perhaps fatisfy others; who may be ftruck, by a new arrangement, and convinced, by diffimilar proofs :—

1. It is remarkable, that the perfon, to whom that work was firft attributed was the fame perfon, on whom the public judgement has ultimately fettled : For, Mr. Mathias had addreffed a letter to the Marquis of Buckingham on the fubject of the *emigrant French Priefts.* [It was printed in October 1796.] The fame uncharitablenefs animated Mr. Mathias's converfation, and the fame virulence, on the fcore of religion, debafed the pages of *The Purfuits of Literature,* as had been already ferved up, in the epiftle to the noble Marquis, whofe name was ufed, becaufe he is eminent.

2. The fufpicions, which arofe from thofe coinci-dences of fpirit, and language, were ftrengthened in the mind of all thofe, who heard Mr. Mathias, in book-fellers fhops, daily clearing the obfcurities, and readily pointing the wit of his own *Purfuits*; particularly, the obfcurity, and the wit, of repeating *Barrifter* Erfkine; none of the literati, who frequent Payne's fhop, at the

L l 4   Mews

With all this weight of circumftantial evidence on the affirmative fide of this queftion,

Mews gate, underftanding the purpofe, or the wit, of repeating the profeffional name of a profeffional man.

3. Although Mr. Mathias denied, that he was the Author; yet, he feemed always happy, when the writer was praifed, as the Author of a poem, fo fatirical, and of notes, fo erudite.

4. Notwithftanding thofe prudifh denials, the original opinion of the public became fixed on Mr. Mathias, when it was clearly feen, that any literary miftake in *the Purfuits*, which was mentioned to *him*, was fure to be correêted in the next edition; when it was obferved, that the Author was ready to alter charaêters, in which Mr. Mathias was fhown to have been miftaken; that his praife was ufually fcattered on thofe, who fhared his efteem, whilft his cenfure was beftowed on thofe, who, having noted his defeêts, had fcarcely regarded his merits.

5. Mr. Mathias was heard, at the table of the Chaplains, at St. James's, to praife the Bifhop of Norwich, in appropriate terms, which were the more noted, as the praife was juft; and the fame praifes, in the fame words, were afterwards obferved in the fourth part of *The Purfuits of Literature*.

6. When Mr. Mathias was at the fame table, on a different day, complaining, there, as he complained fometimes, at other places, of being deemed the Author of

tion, there is not the leaft proof, that any
other perfon wrote this book, or were capable

of *The Purfuits of Literature*, Mr. Bryant afked him,
why he did not imitate the example of Doctor Rennel,
if he equally wifhed not to be thought the real Author:
But, he neither adopted this advice, nor, exprefsly,
afferverated, that he was not the Author.

7. When a perfon, who left his name with the
printer, advertifed Mr. Mathias, week after week, in
the news-papers, as the real Author of *The Purfuits of
Literature*, he remained filent, at leaft he made no public
denial; neither confeffing, nor denying, the imputation;
being plainly confcious of guilt, and knowing, that his
guilt could be proved.

8. When Mr. Bofcawen was tranflating Horace, he
told one of the Commiffioners, who fat at the fame Board
with himfelf, that he fome times tranflated a verfe, as he
rode to town; the fame Commiffioner mentioned this
anecdote to Mr. Mathias; who is faid to have been the
only perfon acquainted with it: And, in the next Edition of *The Purfuits*, that natural circumftance, of tranflating on horfeback, was made a topick of triumphant
ridicule.

9. Thofe feveral probabilities are carried up to moral
certainty by the *virtual* admiffion of Mr. Mathias himfelf: For, when Mr. Drummond publifhed his tranflation of *Perfius*, he fent a copy of it, not to Mr.
Mathias, but to " the Author of *the Purfuits of Literature :*"

pable of writing, a lampoon fo inconfiftent in principles, and fo malignant in defign : Now ; all the great mafters of logick agree in one judgement, that, if we find many circumftances on one fide, and none on the other, the conftitution of our minds requires, that we fhould yield affent to that fide, which has fome evidence, rather than to that, which has none : " The only " reafonable inquiry is," fays Hammond, " which is of *probables* the moft, or of *im-* " *probables,* the leaft fuch."

ture :" And, when Mr. Drummond foon after met Mr. Mathias, he thanked the tranflator, for his prefent ; as I have been affured. Add to this anecdote, another fact : A certain noble Lord received from the bookfeller a copy of *The Purfuits of Literature,* with thefe accompanying words, " From the Author :" Some time after, the noble Lord met Mr. Mathias, in the ftreet, who faid to him, " I hope your Lordfhip received the book, I " fent you :" " You mean *The Purfuits of Literature,*" faid his Lordfhip, " I thank you for it." Now ; circumftantial proof is generally confidered by judges, as the moft fatisfactory ; becaufe various circumftances, all converging to the fame point, lead more decifively to truth, than the evidence of a witnefs, who is liable to error.

In

In proportion as you were traced through all the doublings of your fubterfuges; in proportion as the public opinion, gradually, fettled upon you, as the author; you redoubled your activity to conceal your guilt, by your blandifhments; to conciliate individuals, by prefenting your pamphlets; and to form a faction, by your intrigues, who might favour your retreat from a dangerous pofition: And whilft you ftrengthened thefe motives by habit, and confirmed them by principle, you liftened, with willing ears, to the counfels of Brutus; who, like you, was an honourable man:

" ———— Seek no hiding place, *confpiracy!*
" Hide it in fmiles and affability :"

When I have feen you thus following that honourable counfel, at the public meetings of literary men, " *making practifed fmiles* ;" and fhaking the hands of thofe, whom you had, lately, lampooned, I was ready to exclaim with *my* Octavius:

" And fome that fmile, have in their hearts,
" I fear, millions of mifchief."

Such are the proofs of your being the Author of the Purfuits of Literature, which

I fubmit

I submit to all those, who understand the nature of evidence, and delight in the investigations of truth : They will easily perceive, that special circumstances can never be answered by general declamations. When we consider the testimony of the first publisher, the declarations of two other booksellers : the evidence of your private letters, and of your avowals to women ; your significant anticipations, and striking peculiarities of pointing ; your talk, and your intrigues ; those facts, and circumstances, must be deemed equivalent to *moral certainty*, by every person, who has not a favorite to protect, or a falsehood to propagate (z).

2. I may

(z) Since I finished the foregoing argument, I have been furnished with a strong proof of my conclusion, in the text, by the perusal of the Heroic Epistle, "with " elaborate notes, and very learned references," which was addressed to the Rev. Dr. Watson, the Regius Professor of Divinity, in Cambridge ; and which has been attributed to T. J. Mathias. [It was printed for Becket, 1780, in quarto, p. p. 28.] An accurate examination of this *Heroic Epistle* has convinced me, that it was written by the author of the Pursuits of Literature.

There

2. I may now affume it as a certainty, what is clearly proved, that *you* are *the Author*

There are, in both, the fame malignity of purpofe, and affectation in the mode of purfuing it; the fame luft of acquiring diftinction, by the fame unworthy means. And, in both, there are the fame fpecimens of uncouth verfification: For inftance, in the *Epiftle*, p. 21.

" While from his lips in theologic fume

" *Verbocinations Latial defpume.*"

In this opacity, there cannot be difcerned a glimmering of Senfe: Again, in p. 22.

" But why fhould you be deeply cogitating

" Our ftates *naufrageous* and *periclitating ?*

Such unmeaning nonfenfe, and fuch peculiar *barbarifm*, can only be parallelled in *the Purfuits :* In both may be feen the fame illegitimate rhymes; In the Epiftle: Chair, were; be, L. L. D; Air, Lanoafter; preft on, Rubicon. In the *Purfuits* too may be feen the fame affectation, which Johnfon cenfured in his *Life* of *Gray*, of giving to adjectives derived from fubftantives, the termination of participles: In *the Epiftle* may be feen: *purpled* youth, *lilied* Edward, *cloifter'd* Glyn, *willow'd* academe, *laggard* age. In thefe writings, we may every where trace the fame barbarous ufe of ftrange, and unauthorized words: In the *Epiftle*, p. 4, *Anchis'ean* alacrity, *courtier* world, p. 9, *grimy* circle, p. 17, *apronbellies*, p. 19, *Verbocinations Latial*, p. 21. *Naufrageous periclitating*, p. 22, *unlatin'd* Englifh-men: Of the author of *the Epiftle*, and of the *Purfuits*,

it

thor of the *Purfuits of Literature* ; a book,
which I will, in the fecond place, proceed
to

it cannot be faid, that he is either *unlatin'd*, or *ungreek'd*.
But, it may be faid, *Battus is come again :* For, he has,
in the Epiftle, p. 26, " *bold, intrepid,* ftrides :" In the
Purfuits, 7th ed. p. 327, may be feen " *tir'd,* and *jaded.*"
The fame writer repeats, in both, his peculiar phrafes :
In the *Epiftle,* p. 28, *my dear Doctor :* In the *Purfuits,*
my *dear Adam* : In the Epiftle p. 24, there is the unlucky barbarifm, *Academe* ; In the Purfuits 7 ed. p. 229,
there alfo is the fame barbarifm *Academe.* In the Epiftle,
p. 24, " cloifter'd Glynn, wrapt up in *Rowley* and his red
" Surtout," is celebrated as the *dilectus* IAPIS : In the
Purfuits, 7 ed. p. 419-21, there is the fame peculiar talk
of " her lov'd *Iapis* on the banks of Cam," with an exprefs reference, in the note, to " her *dilectus* IAPIS,
" *Robert* GLYNN :" This laft coincidence, then, brings this
inveftigation to a *moral certainty*, that the fame head, and
hand, conceived, and wrote, in this manner, of " the
" *lov'd* IAPIS on the banks of Cam :" For, in weighing
probabilities, the chances are a thoufand to one, that
two authors would not write, in this ftyle, and fentiment,
of fuch a perfon ; who, as he was *wrapt up in Rowley,*
was peculiarly dear to T. J. Mathias, the *Effayift on
Rowley.* In *the Epiftle* too, as in *the Purfuits,* may be
feen the fame feditious farcafms on *Britain's King,* the
fame congenial celebrations of *Junius, Macgregor,* and the
other fcribblers, who, twenty years ago, drew after
them

to examine, freely, but briefly: exhibiting
the whole under diſtinct views; and following up each poſition, by indubitable evidence.

Proofs of *your* Impertinence.

I produce, at once, the Advertisement
to your 7th edition; which was dated, the
30th of March, 1798. " The following,
" or ſimilar words," ſay you, " are *recorded*
" to have been once delivered in Parliament

them the *mob of gentlemen who write with eaſe, as monſters
make a ſhow.* But, the Rev. Dr. Watſon is praiſed in
the *Purſuits,* and *cenſured* in *the Epiſtle:* So are Mr.
Sheridan, and Mr. Steevens. By what *chymical proceſs*
theſe ſingular changes were performed, I pretend not to
know. Yet, I ſee, diſtinctly, what I maintain to be a
ſtrong proof of my general poſition, that the ſame tergiverſation of principle, and practice, prevails throughout
the whole ſatyrical writings of T. J. Mathias: He
praiſes, in one page, the perſons whom he diſpraiſes, in
the next: And when he has carried his lampoon into
libel, he often retracts what he had ſaid, in ſome preceding paragraph, or pamphlet, by adding ſome qualify-
ing paſſage, or by ſome other trick of tergiverſation, which
is peculiar to himſelf, and which he arrogates, forſooth,
as a merit.

" a few

" a few years before the rebellion in 1745.
[The true date is the 10th of March,
1740–1.] " The words are thefe.[:]   The
" heat which has offended them is the
" ardour of conviction, and that zeal for
" the fervice of my country, which neither
" hope nor fear fhall influence me to fup-
" prefs.   I will not fit unconcerned, when
" Public liberty is threatened or invaded,
" nor look in filence upon (intended) pub-
" lic robbery.   I will exert my endea-
" vours, at whatever hazard, to drag the
" aggreffors to juftice, whoever may pro-
" tect them, and whoever may (ulti-
" mately) partake of the national
" plunder."   " It is," you add, " re-
" markable: the fpeaker was William
" Pitt; the Reporter, Samuel John-
" son.[:]   No more:"   And, you quote,
for your authority, Dr. Johnfon's Parlia-
mentary Debates (*a*).   What falfehood !
What

(*a*) ' I do not hefitate to avow, that I was the perfon,
' who recommended to the bookfeller the publication of
' Johnfon's *Debates*, for the benefit of the liberal youth of
our

What impofition! What affectation! Such
is your veracity, that though the book,
which you quote, informed you, exprefsly,
that Mr. Pitt never delivered that fpeech,
you would, contrary to the declaration of
Dr. Johnfon, impofe on the world, a fiction,
for a fact. And you, ftudioufly, fubftitute
an indefinite time, for the real day, when
the fpeech is fuppofed to have been fpoken;
becaufe *fraud* delights to deal in *generals*.
That illuftrious ftatefman pronounced fo
many fine fpeeches, and did fo many great
actions, that he, who attributes to him
fpeeches, which he never fpoke, or actions,
which he never performed, only diſhonours
him. Yet, you do this, although the au-

‘ our ifland. I contributed *the Preface,* which “ acknow-
“ ledged, that Johnfon did not give fo much what the
“ Speakers, refpectively, faid, as what each ought to
“ have faid.” Johnfon was affiduous to declare thofe
‘ fpeeches to be fictitious; and, particularly, a ſhort
‘ time before his death, he expreſſed his regret, for his
‘ having been the Author of fictions, which paſſed for
‘ realities.’ [Bofw. Life, vol. i. p. 129]. With the
mere operative part of the publication of Johnfon’s *De-*
bates, I had no concern.

thor of the fpeech informed you, that it was certainly fictitious. By thus fubftituting fiction, for truth, you departed, equally, from the leffons of Johnfon, the moralift, and Dryden, the poet, which laft advifes, in portraying fuch a character, to—

" ———— Draw him ftrictly fo,
" That all who view the piece may know,
" He needs no trappings of fictitious fame."

You are determined, it feems, to watch over *public liberty*, which is either invaded, or threatened; to drag to juftice the aggreffors, who partake in the *public plunder*, whoever may protect them. Well: But, in what character are you to act? Are you a Member of Parliament? Are you an eminent Member of Parliament, as Mr. Pitt undoubtedly was, in 1741? No: Yet, you affure us, on another occafion, that " though " without authority, and in a very private " ftation, I will confider myfelf in fome " meafure, as fent forth in the public fer- " vice (*b*)." And, you might have added,

(*b*) The Prefat. Epift. to your Tranfl. lxvi.

in

in the fame tone of importance, the Reprefentatives of the people in Parliament, being
themfelves unequal to the tafk of protecting
liberty, and guarding property. Ourself
alone are equal to the mighty charge! And,
you are, of courfe, welcomed, on earth, by
honeft Noodle, in the excellent Life of
Tom Thumb, *the great:*

> Noodle.—" Sure he was fent exprefs
> " From Heav'n to be the pillar of our State.
> " Though fmall his body be, fo very fmall,
> " A Chairman's leg is more than twice as large,
> " Yet is his foul, like any mountain big;
> " And as a mountain once brought forth a moufe,
> " So doth this moufe contain a mighty mountain."

You oppofe your advertifement " to the
" enemies of the principles of your work,
" but not to the enemies of the work itfelf."
I avow myfelf the determined enemy, not,
indeed, of the work itfelf, which I defpife
for its nonfenfe, and deteft, for its jacobinifm; but, to *the principles* of your work,
which no honeft man can approve. I am
the enemy of *the principles* of your work;
becaufe you attempt to feparate the government from the conftitution, and the governed

from

from the governors; becaufe you endeavour
to confound all perfons, and all parties; becaufe attacking, perfonally, both the living
and the dead, you convert your fatire into
lampoon; becaufe you celebrate republicans,
and difpraife loyalifts; particularly, thofe
loyalifts, who, during the prefent times, have
ably, and fuccefsfully, defended the conftitution, and fupported the government, at
fome rifque, and at fome expence : I am the
more an enemy of this practice, and of that
principle of your work; becaufe, I fee your
object, and note your felfifhnefs : Thofe
writers, you fay, in the perfuafive language
of your *practice*, whatever may be their
power and their fuccefs, are but paultry
fcribblers;

" Hirelings of State, or Oppofition flaves;"(c)

When compared with Ourself, and Our
Pursuits. Well : I will allow you to be
a great writer, if you will only learn to write
Englifh with common propriety ; and admit
you to be an able conftitutionalift, if you

(c) Purfuits, 6 Edit. p. 190.

will

will but acquire habits of conſtitutional conſiſtency: I will, moreover, acknowledge,
with the king, in *Tom Thumb,* that,

> " Thy modeſty's a candle to thy merit:
> " It ſhines itſelf, and ſhews thy merit too."

Yet, who are thoſe invaders of liberty, I
wonder, and plunderers of the people,
whom, you pledge yourſelf to drag to juſtice? In the language of oppoſition, and in
the intrigue of jacobiniſm, the King's miniſters are the perſons, who are, conſtantly, held
up, as the foes of freedom, and the plunderers
of property: And, in your advertiſement, we
thus ſee confuſion worſe confounded. The
Queen's ſervant is to drag to juſtice the
King's miniſters, whoever may protect them!
In all your lampoons, you are, continually,
tilting at Mr. Pitt: And, in your laſt publication, when you, profeſſedly, come forth
to *ridicule* Mr. Grattan, you attempt, with
your uſual conſiſtency of principle, to *criminate* Mr. Pitt (*d*). A clerk in the Queen's
Treaſury

(*d*) " The want of œconomy *(I know what I advance)*
" is the *chief* and prominent defect of Mr. Pitt's ad-
" miniſ-

Treafury affumes the controul of the King's Chancellor of the Exchequer! You, thus, with a jacobin fpirit, introduce the anarchy, which Shakfpeare has finely dramatifed, by fhowing, " Liberty pluck Juftice by the " nofe; the baby beat the nurfe." What a baby; to beat fuch a nurfe!

But, you are the baby, who, in the affumed character of a fatirift, beats many a nurfe. When you put on the garb of fatire, you only clothe yourfelf in an invidious habit: And, when you pervert the meaning of the word, and the purpofe of the thing, by " convert- " ing *fatire* into *lampoon*," you merely throw off the invidioufnefs of the former, to put on the malicioufnefs of the latter. Yet, you fuppofe, that there is fomething noble, in

" miniftration." [The fhade of Alexander Pope, &c: p. 38.] I quote this paffage, at prefent, for the purpofe of proving my affertion in the text: I will, hereafter, animadvert on its inconfiftency, and falfehood. Mean time, the following paffage [Purfuits, 7th Ed. p. 131] may fairly be deemed an ufeful Commentary: " Mo- " dern State œconomy feems to confift in fpending or " fquandering the greateft poffible fums in the leaft pof- " fible time."

the

the fpirit, and fomething dignified, in the
practice, of fatire.   Buoyed up by this conceit, you defy " grim-fac'd reproof."   And,
in feveral prefaces, you employ all the artifices of fophiftry, and all the inanity of fuch
arguments, to defend your writings, and to
explain their purpofe; without making one
defence of what cannot be defended, and
without explaining, what indeed by any
other pen might be eafily explained.   Such,
however, is the fpirit of your artifice, that
you think it clothes you in the *blanket of the
night*, which enables you to fay to yourfelf,
that—

   " ——Cloud, and ever-during dark
   " Surrounds me !"

   The queftion is not, what was the practice
of lampoon at Athens, or the conduct of fatire at Rome: But, what is the proper
meaning, and the accuftomed allowance, of
both, in Britain; as the words are found in
our language, and as both are tolerated by
our manners, and fanctioned by our laws:
" SATIRE," faith Johnfon (*e*), " is a poem,

   (*e*) Dictionary.

" in

" in which wickednefs, or folly, is cenfured.
" Proper Satire is diftinguifhed, by the *ge-*
" *nerality* of the reflection, from a lampoon,
" which is aimed againft a *particular perfon;*
" but *they are too frequently confounded.*"
And, Rofcommon inftructs the fatirift :

" You muft not think, that a fatirick ftyle
" Allows of fcandalous and brutifh words."

" Lampoon," faith Johnfon, " is a *per-*
" *fonal* fatire ; is *cenfure,* written not to re-
" form, but to vex." The whole lexicography of our language; the practice of our
earlieft, and beft, fatirifts ; the amenity of
our manners; the voice of our laws; all recognize Johnfon's principle to be right, and
his definitions to be juft. If we may judge
of the tree by its fruit, you differ, widely,
from the great moralift. on this point (f):
Your

(f) Purfuits, 7 Ed. p. [8.] " A moralift and a divine
" have not the fame office with *a fatirift* ; *perfonality* is
" foreign to them." [Ib. p. 10.] We hereby fee, that
your precept correfponds with your practice: On the
contrary, I maintain, that *perfonality* is *foreign* to the duty
of a *fatirift:* The lampooner only deals in *perfonality.*
Yet, you infift that, " Satire never can have effect,
" without

Your practice is, to *lampoon* in your text,
by specifications of Names; and to enlarge
upon your text, in your notes, by " *cenfure*
" plainly written, not to reform, but to
" vex." No one objects to the legitimate
practice of proper satire, which is distin-
guished by the *generality* of its censures.
And, when you repeatedly answer objections, which were never made, you only place
yourself in the ridiculous position of the
jack pudding, who fights a fleeting shadow
with his wooden lath. The true objections
to your poems are, that you, continually,
confound satire with lampoon; and are ever
writing lampoon, for satire. You are subtle
enough to see the true objection; but your
sophistry is sufficiently alert to evade the
real question. The repetition of your an-
swers, which are always impertinent, has
enrolled you in the honourable list of AN-

" without a *perfonal* application. It must come home to
" the bosoms, and often to the offences of particular
" men." [Ib. p. 9.] This doctrine, I maintain, is ille-
gal, and libellous, irreligious and immoral.

SWER

swer-jobbers, whom Swift has denounced for having no confcience.

But, it is a hard tafk to anfwer ftrong objections, which do not admit of pertinent anfwers. Dryden, who was a fatirift, although not equal, to be fure, to you, faw the difficulty; but he could only avoid it, by acting differently from you: He admitted, honeftly, what every honeft man muft admit, that *lampoon*, or *perfonal* fatire, cannot be juftified. " In a word," fays Dryden (*g*), " that former fort of fatire, which " is known in England, by the name of " lampoon, is a dangerous fort of wea- " pon, and for the moft part *unlawful*. We " have no moral right on the repu- " tation of other men. 'Tis *taking* " *from them what we cannot reftore to them.* " There are only two reafons, for which " we may be permitted to write *lampoons;* " and I will not promife, that they can al-

(*g*) I quote from Dryden's Dedication of his Tranf-lation of Juvenal's Satires to the Earl of Dorfet. Ed. 1702, p. 58-9; being " a Difcourfe concerning the " original and progrefs of Satire."

ways

" ways juſtify us. The firſt is revenge,
" when we have been affronted in the ſame
" nature, or have been any ways notoriouſly
" abuſed, and can make ourſelves no other
" reparation. The ſecond reaſon, which
" may juſtify a poet, when he writes againſt
" *a particular perſon* ; and that is, when he
" is become a public nuiſance."   Now; I
demand what *moral right* have you on the
reputation of *other men*.   Your anſwer muſt
be, with Dryden, whom you quote as an
authority, in point (*h*), that you have no moral right over any man's reputation: And
this fair anſwer ſhows the arrogance of your
conſtant practice, which is as inconſiſtent
with our manners, as contrary to our laws.
Warburton appears to have concurred with
Dryden; when *he ſet up*, as the beſt defence
for the *Dunciad*, that the various dunces had
firſt attacked Pope.   But, who, I wonder, attacked you, before you came forth with your
lampoons?   The real offence, which you

(*h*) Purſuits, 7 Ed. p. 8: As you rely on the authority of Dryden, you ought to be concluded by it.

felt,

felt, was fubfequent; and confifted, in not taking any notice either of you, or of your writings (*i*). Well: I will allow, that to

(*i*) There was one perfon, however, a poet, and a fcholar, who, I am told, provoked lampoon by a different conduct. On perufing the firft part of the *Purfuits of Literature*, Mr. Pye expreffed his approbation of it to Mr. Owen, the original bookfeller, in rather ftrong terms; that on the next day, Mr. Owen fent him, *from the Author*, the firft part of the *Purfuits*, and *the Epiftle from the Emperor of China*; that the next time he went into Mr. Owen's fhop, he gave Mr. Pye a letter, written in a *very odd hand*, but not purporting to be from the Author; ftating, that the letter writer was pleafed to hear Mr. Pye had fpoken highly of the Poem, and that *he fhould do well* to continue to do fo, as the Author was a *perfon of eminence*, both in the *literary*, and *political* world; that Mr. Pye was, thereupon, fo ftruck with the infolence of this demand, that he faid, with fome warmth, He never would fay one word more in favour of it to any body: In the *fecond part*, appeared, accordingly, *Spartan Pye*, and the foporific Lectures of Tyrtæus, at Coxheath, and Warley. I have feveral of Mr. Mathias's threatening letters to literary men, written in the fame *odd, elongated*, hand. I underftand he is in the frequent practice of writing, in the fame hand, his flatteries, in his prefentation copies.

neglect

neglect the mighty Mathias was a great offence:

" ————*Pride* hath no other glafs
" To fhew itfelf, but *pride*; for fupple knees
" Feed arrogance, and are the proud man's fees."

But, *the dead* can neither give, nor take,
offence.   Have they alfo neglected you?
Have they raifed " a warning voice" againft
the principles of your Purfuits? You can raife
" the fhade of Pope:" But, can you lay the
ghofts of Bifhop Wilkins; of Bifhop Newton; of Dr. Adam Smith; of M. Court de
Gebelin; whofe graves you have opened,
and whofe fame you have wronged?

You attack " the wild rapture and empiric
" rage" of Ceftria's mitred lord, at the
opening of your fecond dialogue (*k*).   Wilkins was an honour to England, fays Burnet,
who was not very lavifh of his praife: Wilkins was one of the fathers of the Royal
Society (*l*):   And, thefe are, no doubt, fub-

(*k*) 6th Ed. p. 67.

(*l*) " Upon my word," fay you, " *Philofophy* is a very
" pleafant thing: It makes us laugh fometimes."   The
aftronomical difcoveries of Herschell are ridiculed in
the fame note.   [Ib. p. 68.]

ftantial

ſtantial reaſons, for dragging a biſhop from his grave, merely to furniſh topicks of lampoon. You had been poaching in the *Scribleriad* of Owen Cambridge, where you ſaw the *wild rapture* of Biſhop Wilkins, repeatedly, mentioned (*m*). In the *Scribleriad*, I had ſeen this ſubject treated, without any emotion of difguſt: But, Cambridge has playfulneſs, without malignity: Mathias has malignity, without playfulneſs.

But, why drag Biſhop Newton from his quiet grave (*n*)? He was not the Biſhop of

---

(*m*) Scrib. 1751, p. 26-7. You have killed many a partridge in the Scribleriad. You have appropriated, as your own, without the conſent of the Lord of the Manor, ſentiments, and expreſſions. Your character of *Moroſoph-os* is only the *Moroſoph* of Cambridge. [Ib. 30, bk. 5, p. 5.

O! for that *warning voice* which Cadmus heard
[Scrib. 29.]
Some *warning voice* invites to yonder ground.
[Shade of Pope, p. 1.]

(*n*) Purſuits, 7 Ed. p. 332 ; 333, Note (*g*) ; 334, Note (*qq*): In theſe *learned*, and *witty*, notes, there are ſeveral blunders: *Aculeated* for *aculeate*: *Neither* is followed by *or*, inſtead of *nor*.

St.

St. Pol. He would have emigrated, I doubt
not, rather than have relinquifhed his faith:
and he would have followed the example of
the *feven bifhops*, rather than have facrificed
his principle: But, his blamelefs life, and
his writings in fupport of Chriftianity, could
not fhield him, from the lampoon of your
charity:

" Peace, Peace, for fhame, if not for Charity !"

" Urge neither *fhame*, nor *charity* to me,"
fay you: " For refolved I am, to fatirize
" Doctor Adam Smith, who taught finance
" to a moft fpendthrift minifter (*o*):

" Prove that no dogs, as through the ftreets they range,
" Give bone for bone in regular exchange.

" My dear Adam," you add, in your
note, " this philofophy of yours is nearly of
" the fame date as your anceftors in Eden,
" and I can only fay, in reply, *Who ever ex-*

(*o*) " Adam Smith, the great writer on Wealth and
" Finance; from whom Mr. Pitt learned his art."
[Pur. Lit. 6 Ed. p. 87.]   No: Dr. Smith did not write
on Wealth and Finance; but, on *the* Wealth of *Nations.*

" *pected*

" *pected to fee a dog do fo?*"(*p*)   In return,
let me afk a queftion, which is full as pertinent, did *dear Adam* expect to fee fuch a
fight?   But, I will defend a dead philofopher from lampoon, by the authority of an
immortal poet :

> " Will any dog that hath his teeth and ftones,
> " Refign'dly leave his bitches and his bones,
> " To turn a wheel, and bark to be employ'd,
> " While Venus is by other dogs enjoy'd?(*q*)"

But, this remarkable concidence between
the queftions of the philofopher, and the
poet, does not mollify your fpirit of lampoon :   Nay; my dear Dryden, you repeat,
who ever, but the œconomical doctor, *expected to fee a dog do fo?*

This queftion, however, admits of an eafy
folution, when compared with the inquiry,
" What muft we fay to M. Court de Ge-
" belin, who has actually endeavoured to
" *reafon us into a belief* that the founders
" of the Roman ftate, Romulus, and Re-
" mus, were only allegorical perfonages."

(*p*) Purfuits, 4th Part, p. 70-3.
(*q*) Dryden's Effay on Satire.

Mr.

Mr. Court de Gebelin (*r*), with all the ingenuity, and learning, which he has difplayed in nine quarto volumes, on the *Monde
Primatif*, will never be forgiven, for drawing, by anticipation, your character : " Cri-
" tiques fuperbes & exclufifs prefque tou-
" jours ignorans :" And fo, Monf. *Critique fuperbe, & exclufif*, I leave you (if I
may fcribble in your ftyle) to trace the tale
of Romulus, and Remus, in the fictions of
hiftory, or to find them, as real perfons, in
the allegories of fable.

With thefe recent inftances before us, of
the univerfality of the fatire, in your writings, which comprehends both the living, and the dead, we may fay, with *Pi-
fanio :*

"——— Kings,

(*r*) He was a *Proteftant*, which circumftance does not
conciliate your charity; and he *died*, in 1785, which
event does not exempt him from your hypercriticifm !
When you wifh to be witty, you would do well to avoid
the appearance of blunder: " Remus, it feems, fay you,
fignified THE SUN in the Winter, and Romulus, in *the
Summer*. [7 Ed. Pur. p. 283.] You meant to fay : And
Romulus *fignified the Sun*, in the Summer.

N n

" ——Kings,(*s*) Queens,(*t*) and States,(*u*)
" Maids, (*x*) Matrons;(*y*) nay, *the secrets of the grave*;(*z*)
" This viperous flander enters.

This

(*s*) Confidering your own official fituation, and the circumftances *of the times*, you ufe too many freedoms, with *great Augustus*; particularly, in your *Chinese Epiftle*; in what you fay of Poet Mafon; and in recommending JUNIUS, an adjudged libel, as *a claffical book.*

(*t*) You fatirize Sir J. B. Burgefs's Poem, on the Princefs Elizabeth's Drawings; which poem appears to be dedicated to the Queen, by her royal permiffion : Confidering your ftation, what is this but the fcullion in the kitchen, who lampoons the dignified Miftrefs of a vaft domain.

(*u*) Both Houfes of Parliament are libelled throughout the *Purfuits of Literature.*

(*x*) A *Duke's chafte Daughter* is lampooned. [6 Ed. p. 105.]

(*y*) Mrs. Montague is lampooned for her able and elegant Vindication of Shakfpeare againft the impertinences of Voltaire.—The Marchionefs of Buckingham is lampooned as " the great PATRONESS OF THE CATHOLIC CAUSE in England." [Pair of Epiftles, p. 28.]

(*z*) I have juft fhown two Prelates of the Church of England dragged from their graves; and thofe two very able writers, in their feveral departments of literature, Dr. Adam Smith, and Mr. Court de Gebelin, ridiculed

in

This *univerfality* of your fatire, you carry
even into the profeffions of men : In your
Pair of Epiftles, you lampoon feveral eminent phyficians, lawyers, and divines: You
lampoon the profeffors, and fellows, of
colleges ; you libel the learned focieties,
their prefidents, and their fecretaries ; you
lampoon all parties, and perfons, in the
ftate ; you lampoon refpectable characters,
for their mere manner ; their habits of
fpeaking, or modes of walking ; although
every one has a right, furely, to his own
amufements, and his character.   You alfo
lampoon *perfonal defects :*

" From the *fpare* Rumford to the *pallid* Knight."

What is this, but to introduce into the literary world, and into our domeftic retire -
ments, the fame fort of monfter, who, fome
years ago, ran about the town, wounding,

in death. The amiable, and learned Tyrwhit is lampooned: The late Doctor Stukely, to whom the Archai-
ological world owe fo much, is facrificed at the fhrine
of Mr. Samuel Lyfons : [Shade of Pope, p. 68.]
    " The Dennes, and owlifh *Stukeleys* of the day,
    " Retire abafh'd at Lyfon's rifing day."

N n 2   favagely,

favagely, unprotected women. The neceffity of felf-defence demands, that the learned
focieties, the literary meetings, profeffional
men, official men, matrons, maids ;—all,
fhould be warned againft this monfter of a
lampooner : Have a care, then, good people ; fee Mathias comes !

" Frontlefs, and Satire proof, he fcours the ftreets ;
" And runs a *Malayan Muck* at all he meets."

Even Pope, who carried his fatire to the
very verge of fcurrility, declares that, " To
" a true *fatirift*, nothing is fo odious as a
" *libeller*, for the fame reafon, as to a man
" truly *virtuous*, nothing is fo hateful as a
" hypocrite (*a*)." What ! are we a libeller ? " Is there I *afk*, with *confidence*, in
" our Pursuits, any fentence or any fen-
" timent, by which the mind may be de-
" praved, degraded *and* [or] corrupt-
" ed (*b*)?" Yes : I am one of thofe *ignorant men*, who maintain, that your *Purfuits*
of *Literature* are a continued libel, which
has a neceffary tendency to deprave, de-

(*a*) Warton's Edition of Pope, vol. iv. p. 59.
(*b*) Pur. 7 Ed. p. 10.

grade,

grade, and corrupt ; and, which by its perfonal fcandal, "pand*a*rs [panders] to the vi-
" tiated tafte of the prefent times :" Your fatirical verfe, with its libellous profe, is a con-
tinual lampoon, a fpecies of writing, which is
neither legal, nor moral.   Your confidence,
however, is not to be confounded, though
it may be chaftifed.   " They," you add,
" who would confider my reprehenfions of
" authors and of the tendency of their writ-
" ings, as libels or as libellous matter, are
" as ignorant of common law, as they are
" forgetful of common fenfe, or common
" integrity and candour (*c*)."   And, you
might have added, in the fame tone of arrogance, " I AM *Sir* ORACLE ; and, when
" I ope my lips, let no dog bark."

You join iffue, then, with the *ignorant
men,* your opponents, on the libelloufnefs
of your *Púrfuits* of Literature.   You call
upon them to produce their authorities ; to
contradict Blackftone, the great fage of the
law, if they dare ; and you challenge them

(*c*) Ib. p. 11.

N n 3   to

to fhow, " that any part of your book is
" blafphemous, immoral, treafonable, fchif-
" matical, feditious, or fcandalous (*d*)."
And, confidering your context, you might
have fafely added,

> " I am to pray you not to ftrain my fpeech
> " To groffer iffues, nor to larger reach,
> " Than to fufpicion."

I will not ftrain your fpeech to larger
reach. I will fay, however, that Dryden
had warned you of the *unlawfulnefs* of *lam-poon*; of your having no moral right over
any man's reputation; I will add, that
Johnfon had taught you the difference between lampoon and fatire; the one being
general againft vices, the other, particular
againft perfons : And, you might have eafily inferred from thofe authorities, if your
own conceit had not led you aftray, that you
might fatirize wickednefs, without charging John Styles with being wicked; that
you might fatirize vice, without accufing
Thomas Nokes with being vicious; and
that you might fatirize fwindling, without

(*d*) Purfuits, 7 Ed. p. 11.

charging

charging *Foulis*, with being a swindler:
Yet, you, deliberately, differ with Dryden,
and Johnson, in your judgement of the li-
gitimate province of satire; saying, expressly, " that satire never can have effect,
" without *a personal application:* It must
" come to *the bosoms*, and often to *the of-*
" *fences*, of *particular men* (*e*)." You, thus,
set up your title to lampoon, and, expressly,
defend all the enormities of libel, a practice, which our manners reprobate, and our
laws condemn.

You appeal, for your justification, to
Blackstone (*f*), who is not the best authority, in respect to libels, without the expo-
sition of *a* Commentator, on *the* Commentator. Well: Blackstone does state the law,
in the passage quoted by you; but not the
whole law. The learned Commentator is
here speaking of *civil actions for libels*, and
he adds: " But, in a *criminal prosecution*,

(*e*) Pursuits, 7 Ed. p. 9.

(*f*) Ib. p. 11: And, with your *usual fairness*, you
quote chapter xi. of book iv. rather than the page,
wherein is contained your own refutation.

N n 4   the

" the *tendency*, which all libels have to *cre-*
" *ate animofities*, and to *difturb* the *public*
" peace, is *the whole* that the law confi-
" ders." He is teaching, that, on *criminal*
profecutions, the *truth* of the libel is not any
defence of it: For, the tendency of *all li-*
bels, whether *true*, or *falfe*, to *create ani-*
mofities, and to difturb the *public peace*, is the
whole that the law confiders, in a criminal
profecution. Now; have not your writings created animofities; have not they a
tendency to a breach of the public peace?
The fact is, that *you* have been *eagerly pur-*
fued (fuch were the expreffions reported to
me) at the Chaplain's table, at St. James's,
on account of your Pursuits: What, then,
muft be the animofity created, which could
induce grave men to carry their irritation,
to the very hazard of blows, within the
King's palace? This being true, in fact,
" the offence againft the public is com-
" plete," according to the authority, which
you have produced (*g*). I will not infift

(*g*) Blackft. 12 Ed. vol. iv. p. 150.

upon

upon the literary controverſy, which has
been raiſed about your lampoons ; nor upon
the heart-burnings ; the coldneſs among
friends ; which have all been excited by
them : But, I will add, that there are other
points of great concernment, which bring
your writings within the penalty of law.
Your frequent attacks on *Great Auguſtus,*
during ſuch times ; and your endeavours in
the ſpirit, and language, of *Junius,* to make
the King perſonally anſwerable, for what
his miniſters are alone reſponſible ; are
groſsly libellous.   Your as frequent attacks
on both Houſes of Parliament, eſpecially,
on the freedom of their debates, are high
offences : and Biſhop Horſely, whom you
conſtantly *purſue,* for his ſpeeches in the
Houſe of Lords, might either complain of
a breach of privilege in that houſe, or move
the Court of King's Bench, againſt you, for
an information (*h*).   Upon the ſame principles,

(*h*) " Sooner the people's right ſhall Horsely teach."
" I allude," ſay you, " in your note, on this line, to
" Biſhop Horſely's *intemperate,* and *unadviſed Speeches*
" in

ciples, might the members of the Houfe of Commons, whofe fpeeches are attacked, either move the Houfe, for a breach of pri vilege, or the King's Bench, for an information. But, the moft aggravated libel, among the thoufand libels, in your writings, is the attack on the Houfe of Commons (*i*), for granting money towards the relief of the emigrant French clergy, and laity : To publifh the proceedings of the Houfe, without the confent of the Speaker, is a breach of privilege; to publifh them, untruly, is an aggravation; and to publifh fuch proceedings, falfely, as you have done, in this cafe, with the defign of rendering the reprefentatives of the people, fitting in parliament, odious in the eyes of their conftituents, is a libel of the moft enormous malignity. I may now, I truft, repeat, with regard to your Pursuits; to your *Epiftle to*

" in *Parliament*. Bifhop Horfely, and Mr. Wynd-
" ham, fhould be more attentive in this particular."
[Purfuits, 6 Ed. p. 256.]

(*i*) Purfuits, 4th Part, 3 Ed. pref. xix.

the

the Marquis of Buckingham ; *to your Shade of Pope :*

" Sweet fcrawls! to fly about the ftreets of Rome:
" What's this, but *libelling* againft *the Senate ?*"

Thus much, then, in refpect to public libels ! With regard to libels, on perfons in fituations of particular truft, and on *private men*, you have quite overlooked them, in your favourite authority : You entirely forget, that for every libel on an individual, the fame individual has an action againft you, for damages ; and, what is of more importance, for reparation of his character : On this head, the law feems to be now clearly fettled, " that whatever renders a " man ridiculous, or lowers him, in the " efteem, and opinion of the world, " amounts to a libel ; though the fame ex- " preffions, if fpoken, would not have " been defamation (*k*)." This is laid down as law, in reference to private perfons : But, when it fpeaks of libel againft officers in high employments or trufts, or againft ma-

(*k*) 3 Blackft. Com. Ed. 12. p. 125, in the Note (6).

giftrates,

giftrates, it affumes a higher tone. In all your *Purfuits* you purfue the King's mi-nifter, with the unrelenting fpirit of lam-poon : In your laft publication, *The Shade of Pope*, (*l*), you fay, " the want of œcono-" my *(I know what I advance)* is the *chief* " and prominent defect of Mr. Pitt's ad-" miniftration." This, indeed, is a note on the following lines.

> " Supplies are prompt for Pitt's directing hand ;
> " Pactolus rolls through all the wealthy land:
> " Hence, Palaces for Bankrupt-Bankers rife,
> " And Monarchs wonder with inquiring eyes."(*m*)

On queftions of libel, our Judges have faid, " We will fee what every eye fees ; we will " underftand what is obvious to every intel-" lect." You accufe Mr. Pitt, as the Chan-cellor of the Exchequer, of want of œcono-my : and you fupport your unfounded affer-tion, by ftating, that he applies the *fupplies*, which are *promptly* granted by Parliament, to build private palaces, for unworthy in-dividuals (*n*). Without noticing the fcur-

(*l*) Shade of Pope, p. 38.
(*m*) Ib. p. 38-9.   (*n*) Id.

rility

rility of thofe paſſages, which is below contempt, I will ſay, that they amount to an
actionable libel, which is as malignant in
its principle, as it is odious in its application.   From that exalted character, I will
now turn to one of lower degree, indeed,
but equally entitled to the protection of
law :

" Then let the learned page once quit your fight,
" Some *Scotch* Greek *ſwindling* printer ſteals your right."

In your note, upon this text, you apply
your charge, expreſsly, to " the *Scotch*
" *Printer* Fowlis (*o*)," to whofe Printing-
houſe at Glaſgow, our ſcholars owe much,
for the accuracy, and neatneſs, of the Greek
Claſſicks.   This, then, is exactly the ſort
of libel, which the Judge, who is mentioned
by a very judicious law-writer (*p*), reprobated from the bench :   " If the party had
" been a *common ſwindler* (as alledged), the
" defendant ought to have indicted him ;
" but he had no right to libel him in that
" way :"   To publiſh of a tradeſman, that he

(*o*) Purſuits, 6 Ed. p. 114-15.
(*p*) Wooddeſon, vol. iii. p. 182.

is

is a *fwindler*, is, therefore, actionable : And
the injured Fowlis is entitled to reparation,
for an injury, which has been done him,
by your imputation on his character, founded on the groffeft mifreprefentation.

Such is your libel on a tradefman, who
is connected with literature ! Your lampoons
on men of fcience, and men of learning,
are without number. If it be true, in law,
" that whatever renders fuch perfons ridi-
" culous, and lowers them in the efteem of
" the world," is a libel, what muft be the
whole of your *Purfuits?* Your attack on
Doctor Warton, who is far your fuperior,
as a poet, as a fcholar, as a critic, and,
perhaps, I do not fay too much, if I add, as
a man, is an actionable libel. What you
repeatedly fay of the King's hiftoriographer
for Scotland, is an actionable libel.

" Or I could fcribble for hiftorick fame,
" Like Gillies, feeble, formal, dull, and tame."(q)

(q) " The epithets in the verfe, you add, in your
" Note upon the Couplet above, are defigned to *cha-*
" *racterize the Writings* of Dr. Gillies." [Purfuits, 6
Ed. p. 76-8.]

Yet ;

Yet ; with all thofe libels, both⋅ public, and private, in your *Purfuits*, you felicitate yourfelf, " that in *your work*, there is no- " thing blafphemous, immoral, treafona- " ble, fchifmatical, feditious, or fcanda- " lous (*r*)." As you, no doubt, know the meaning of your own terms, you call on the *ignorant men* to produce, publickly, fomething like proofs of thofe imputations. I will briefly ftate mine. In one of your notes, you compare your own affected feel- ings to our Saviour's agony in the garden, which feveral divines have noticed as *blaf- phemous* (*s*). There is fuch a perpetual contradiction, between your principle and practice in your *Purfuits*, as to render the whole, immorally, difhoneft : Your warm recommendation of JUNIUS, whofe Letter was adjudged a treafonable libel, for attack- ing the King's *impeccability*, is, itfelf, trea-

(*r*) Purfuits, 7th Ed. [11]

(*s*) Purfuits, 6 Ed. p. 174, Note [*r*], which ends with the blafphemous comparifon. You alfo parody the Scriptures, moft irreligioufly, [Ib. p. 70:] And again, [Ib. 13.]

fonable :

fonable . Your attempt to divide Chriftians, by reviving, and embittering, the Roman Catholick controverfy, at a time when all Chriftians ought to unite againft Atheifts, is fchifmatical : Your whole book, as far as it relates to public men, and public meafures, is highly *feditious* ; there being a conftant endeavour throughout, to feparate the governed from the governors, and the government from the conftitution : And, the very effence of the luminous pages of *your Purfuits* is avowed *fcandal.* Yet ; you poffefs not the magnanimity of Dryden, who honeftly acknowledged, " I am fen" fible of the fcandal, I have given by my " loofe writings, and make what repara" tion I am able."

But, you maintain that, " under thefe " *reftrictions,*" you have an undoubted right, to lay your fentiments before the world, on public fubjects, public men, and public books, in *any manner you think proper* (*t*). Under this claim, when fpeaking of the parliament, you commit feveral

(*t*) Pur. 7 Ed. p. 11.

breaches

breaches of privilege; faying of the Commons, affembled in Parliament, what is
pofitively falfe : In animadverting on the
King's minifters, you write concerning the
Chancellor of the Exchequer what is equally falfe : In fpeaking of books, you ftate
every thing that is unfair, and what is libellous againft the authors : and you go on,
in a tone of arrogant reclamation, to infift,
" If I am [be] denied this *right*, [of doing
" *wrong*,] there is an end of the freedom
" of the prefs (*u*)."   Yet, Blackftone, your
own authority, would have inftructed you,
had you looked into his context, that there
has never been a time, fince the revival of
learning, and the epoch of printing, when
the right, or the practice, of publication
exifted, without refponfibilities; a refponfibility to the public profecutor, for what
regards the public; and a refponfibility to
the individual, for any offence, which
might be offered to him : It is apparent,
then, as your own Mentor would have

(*u*) Purfuits, 7 Ed. p. 5.

O o   taught

taught you, that though you might publifh, without any previous reftraint, yet the fubfequent refponfibility ought to have operated as a prior defeafance of the right. It is, therefore, abfurd, and jacobinical, to fay, that you may do what you think fit, if you be anfwerable for your mifdeeds. If you will not be inftructed by your own *fage*, it may be remarked of you, as of other " *wil-* " *ful men*, the injuries, which they them- " felves procure, muft be their *fchoolmaf-* " *ters*."

Neverthelefs, what is there in this *freedom of the prefs*, more than in any other right? Are there any *abfolute rights*? Or are all rights only *relative*, as between the public, and individuals? *Wilfulnefs*, indeed, may claim *a right* to do *wrong*; but, juftice will never admit the pretenfion: So, the *tongue* has no title to the freedom of *fpeaking evil of dignities*, nor the hand any privilege to fcribble profaical poetry, or ungrammatical profe, which is a lampoon upon fcholars, and a degradation of learning.

You

You would do well, to recollect how often
" *headstrong liberty* is lashed with woe."

Of all rights, indeed, the right of
writing and publishing, what one thinks,
which constitutes *the liberty of the press*, is
the least *absolute :* It is only a *concurrent*
right, which every man, every woman, and
every child, enjoys, as fully as you enjoy
the same right: It is the same *concurrent*
right, as the right of driving on the high-
way ; whereon, if, with malicious, or ignorant, self sufficiency, you drive against, and
damage, any woman's coach, or any man's
cart, the law will compel you to make that
reparation, which, for the wrong, justice
shall prescribe.   When you are enthroned
in your dictatorial chair, clothed in your
robe of conceit, with your Gyges' ring on
your demonstrative finger, what better right
have you, than I have, to think, write,
and publish ? Yes : I am a SATIRIST, say
you, authorized by *ourself* to reform learning, and to preserve *the State :* " The pa-
" ramount necessity of securing to this
" Kingdom her political and religious ex-
O o 2   istence,

" iftence, and the rights of fociety, have
" urged me to this endeavour to preferve
" them (*x*)." Well: the French offer
liberty to every people ; telling them, " that
" when you are Free, you fhall *do* as we
" please." *You* come forward, on this
libertine principle ; to fecure the ftate, by
attacking the government; and to reform
literature, by obliging every fcholar to write,
as *you dictate*.   In the French tone, you fay,
be free : and all is fafe, from " the war-
" hoop of Jacobins, from the fhrieks of
" Witlings, from the feeblenefs of poetaf-
" ters (*y*):" The ftate is fecure, while
ourfelf threaten the national plunderers(*z*) :
It is enough :

" ————— Ourself ftill, ftill, remain,
" Cerberian forehead, and Cerberian brain !"

With all this feverity, you have your
fofter moments. In drawing characters, you
fcreen yourfelf under the mantles of Theo-
pompus, and La Brueyere.   Lord Coke's

(*x*) Purfuits, 7 Ed. p. 5.   (*y*) Ib. p. 11.
(*z*) Ib. the Advert. p. iii.

ring ;

ring; Lex eft tutiſſima caſſis; had been a better fafeguard, than either the furtout of The-
opompus, or the blanket of La Bruyere:
" But, many paffages, in your Purfuits, are
" beft defended, fay you, by the Apology of
" Horace (*a*). I fhall offer no other apo-
" logy. As to my fuppofed arrogance, a
" poet will be fometimes warmed, with the
" dignity, and importance of his fubject."(*b*)
In anfwer to *your Apology*, I will only fubjoin what Lady Mary Wortley faid to Pope:

" Horace can laugh, is delicate, is clear ;
" You, only, coarfely rail, or darkly fneer."

I will here clofe my proofs of your IM-
PERTINENCE ; of which we have had more
than enough: And, I will now proceed to
fubmit

PROOFS *of your* MALIGNITY:

I have already given fo many proofs of
your malignant practices, that a few examples will be amply fufficient, to eftablifh my
pofition.

(*a*) Purfuits, p. 12.   (*b*) Purfuits.

O o 3   " But,

" But, on the *mitred Oath* that Tucker fwore
" Parr wifely ponder'd, and his Oath forbore."

You explain your text by your note: " Jo-
" fiah Tucker, D. D: [the] Dean of Glo-
" cefter once took an oath in a pamphlet
" that he would refufe a bifhoprick." (*b*)
Yet, the fact is, that Dean Tucker never
took fuch an oath, either *in* a pamphlet, or
out of a pamphlet. If malignancy had any
memory, you would have recollected, that
the worthy Dean, who merits well of his
country, for freeing it from prejudices, was
juftly intitled to repofe at the age of *four
fcore*. The fame fpirit led to a fimilar attack on Mr. Bryant. In defence of your
Caninity, you refer to a paffage in his *Mythology*, which does not exift in it. You
mis-ftate that learned writer; in order to obtain, by means of mifreprefentation, the im-
puted farcafm of Mr. Bryant on *the* HIER-
ARCHY (*c*). This, indeed, is your ufual

(*b*) Purfuits, 7 Ed. p. 217-18. Your *mitred Oath*
is nonfenfe; becaufe an Oath cannot be *mitred*.

(*c*) Purfuits, 7 Ed. p. 92; wherein Bryant's Mythol.
vol. i. p. 329, is quoted, for what is not in the book.

practice :

practice: But, neither time, nor fpace, allows me to quote many examples of your
mifreprefentations, for the purpofe of lampoon. A moft remarkable inftance is your
attack on *Foulis*, the printer, of Glafgow,
whom, with malignant pen, you call a *fwindler*. A bookfeller, who is noted at once for
his diftinctnefs, and his probity, and knew
the tranfaction informed me, that it was,
grofsly mifreprefented in *your Purfuits* (*d*).
Indeed,

(*d*) Purfuits, 6 Ed. p. 114-15: Mr. Peter Elmfly,
who is never to be mentioned but with praife, told me,
" That fome London Bookfellers, he, and Foulis, the
" Printer, undertook to publifh an Octavo Edition of the
" *Greek Tragedians*, from a German Edition, and at the
" fame time to get Mr. Profeffor PORSON to correct the
" text, and to add fome *Scholia*. The learned Profeffor
" agreed; *the Copy*, confifting of the corrected text, and
" the promifed Scholia, was fent to Foulis, who printed
" part of the projected edition: But, Mr. Elmfley lofing
" his health, and being unable to fuperintend the work,
" the whole project failed. Whereupon Foulis, who
" had thus an intereft in *the Copy*, undertook to print
" *eighty* Copies of the Æfchylus, in a folio form, with-
" out any *Scholia*; in doing which he made ufe of Mr.
" Profeffor Porfon's printed text, as far as it went,

" without

Indeed, all thofe, who did not know your habits of malignity, were eafily led by your context, to fuppofe, that Mr. Profeffor Porfon had communicated his corrected Æfchylus to fome Lord Monboddo, or other Greek fcholar, in Scotland, who, regardlefs of the truft repofed in him, had delivered " to fome " Scotch, Greek, fwindling, printer," the facred tranfcript. By a little extenfion of your malice, you in the fame manner mifreprefent all other Scotchmen, as equally unfit for truft (*e*). Of the maligner, and the maligned, it may be remarked, that,—

" His will is moft malignant ; and it ftretches
" Beyond you to your friends."

As I have already fhewn *who*, and *what* you are, I will now fubmit

PROOFS

" without afking his confent. For this inattention to " the Profeffor, the printer was advifed to make an " apology : But, he never did ;" faying, that his affairs had been materially injured, by the failure of the projected Edition in Octavo. *The Copy* was brought back from Scotland, in 1797, and returned to Mr. Profeffor Porfon. Such is the fact ! and fuch is the offence !

(*e*) " No *Scotchman* near, no Gillies by my fide."

[Purfuits, 6 Ed. p. 339.

Proofs *of your* Jacobinism.

Barruel, and Robifon, have written hiftories of Jacobinifm; tracing it through all
its windings; exhibiting it in all its varieties;
illuftrating its principles, and fhewing its
effects: Yet, Jacobinifm, like wit, may be
more eafily defcribed, than accurately de-
fined, and more grievoufly felt, than readily
found. The Parliaments of the fifter Kingdoms have inftituted inquiries upon the
point; have purfued it in all its affociated
forms; have penetrated into all its difguifes,
expofed it in all its fubtleties; and deplored
all its grievous effects on individuals, and on
ftates: Like the tree, it is every where beft
known by its genuine fruits, anarchy, plunder, and bloodfhed.

Nay, Sir; am I a Jacobin? Have not I
made a laborious endeavour, confidering the
wayward nature of the times, and the para-
mount neceffity of fecuring to this kingdom
her political and religious exiftence, to preferve the rights of fociety (*f*)? Have I not

(*f*) Purfuits, 7 Ed. pref. 5.

declared,

declared, that the conftitution of Great Britain, even with all its real, or apparent defects, is worthy of continuance (*g*). Yes: you have written a *fatirical poem*; with notes, in libellous profe: you have written epiftles in the fame ftyle : And, avowing your right to publifh *perfonal* fatire, you have lampooned all parties and perfons; you have, under this jacobinical claim, fpoken evil of dignities; and you have attacked our eftablifhments, religious, civil, and literary. During thefe *wayward times*, this inconfiftency of your general practice, with your avowed principle, is, itfelf, a ftrong proof of Jacobinifm; becaufe the workings of the heart are beft known, by the operation of the hand: For, as you remark, *it is written, I hope we all know where*, " out of the abun- " dance of the heart the mouth fpeaketh."

The King, as the Sun of our fyftem, does infinite good, but *can do no wrong*. If you were not a Jacobin, that royal immunity would have faved his facred character from

(*g*) Ib. p. 7.

your

your jacobin animadverfions.   In your *Chinefe Epiftle* there are too many " fcoffs, and
" fcorns, and contumelious taunts," at the
King, and his minifters, if your purfuits
were fair, or your purpofe honeft.   And, in
the fame jacobin fpirit, fpeaking of the melancholy Gray, you fay:

> " Dark was his morn of life, and bleak the Spring,
> " Without one foft'ring ray from *Britain's King*."

You add, in your note, " *I wifh*, that the
" royal favour had been *offered* to the firft
" poet and the firft fcholar of the age." (*h*)
Who was to tell, that an Eton boy would be
the firft poet, and firft fcholar of his age?
When Gray at length did fhow, that he was
a poet, " he was offered *the laurel*, after the
" death of Cibber," as Johnfon diftinctly told
you (*i*) :   And, you therefore, malign *Britain's King*, with jacobin tongue.   In this
jacobin fpirit, you immediately afk:

> " Saw you not Mafon ftand with down caft-eye,
> " While *great Auguftus* pafs'd unconfcious by?"

You add, however, in anfwer to your own

(*h*) Purfuits, 7 Ed. p. 53.   (*i*) Life of Gray.

queftion,

queſtion, Mr. Maſon " muſt have been over-
" looked for a *particular reaſon*;" acknow-
ledging at the ſame time, if you were ſeri-
ous, the King's diſcernment in poetical merit. While you are warm with your jacobinical purpoſe to degrade greatneſs, you forget,
that Maſon was, all his life-time, a growl-
ing republican; that Gray, after receiving
the unſolicited appointment of profeſſor of
modern hiſtory, never diſcharged the duties
of the office.

Yet; what are theſe inſtances of your jacobiniſm, to your propagation of JUNIUS; as
if the reproduction of a libel were not itſelf
a libel: You put that adjudged libel, which
attacked the king's perſon, into the hands of
our liberal youth; in order to inſtruct them
in conſtitutional knowledge. Yet, all this
while, JUNIUS was only Hugh M'Aulay,
who was born in the county of Antrim,
during 1747; and in 1769, at the age of
two and twenty, came over to England, to
teach juriſprudence to the venerable Manſ-
field, and the Engliſh language to Engliſh-
men—

" —— From

" ————from the rattling tongue
" Of faucy and ambitious eloquence(*k*)."

JUNIUS,

(*k*) As you had, in 1780, celebrated JUNIUS, in your
Heroic Epiſtle to the Rev. Dr. Watſon; ſo in your
Pur. 7 Ed. p. 4, you call JUNIUS " a *great* and *conſum-*
" *mate writer.*" You again ſpeak of the Conſtitutional
knowledge of JUNIUS [Ib. 6th Ed. p. 273.] You renew
your panegyric, in the 7th Ed. p. 119: " I quote
" JUNIUS, in Engliſh, as I would *Tacitus,* or *Livy,* in
" Latin. I conſider him, as *a legitimate Engliſh Claſſic.*"
If you had not given ſo many ſpecimens of your own
Engliſh ſtyle, the recommendations of Junius, as an
Engliſh Claſſic, would alone demonſtrate your profound
knowledge of the Engliſh language. We may eaſily
ſuppoſe that, as Junius was not naturally overburthened
with embarraſſment, his opprobrious Letter to *Britain's
King* was elaborated with all his ſkill. I will ſay nothing
of the matter of a compoſition, which the law ſtill reprobates, as a treaſonable libel. For the benefit of our
liberal youth, however, I will briefly examine the language of this *Engliſh Claſſic*: He begins: " It is the
" misfortune of your life, and originally [was] the
" cauſe of every, &c." Who, but a boy from *Antrim,*
would write originally *is ?*" " And [is] originally the
" cauſe of every reproach *and* diſtreſs, which has"
[have.] Who but a youth, who had been taught
Engliſh by an Iriſh Woman, at Antrim, would make
the ſingular verb *has* agree with the plural nominatives

reproach

JUNIUS, then, was an *United Irishman*
by birth, by habit, and by practice; with

reproach and diftrefs? Again: " *If* England *was* [were]
" fold to France: If refentment ftill prevails." Moreover: " The rays of royal indignation, collected upon
" him, ferved only to illuminate, and could not con-
" fume" [him.] This paffage, which was, no doubt,
thought vaftly fine, is egregioufly defective, by wanting
the object, that I have fupplied. Here is another blunder
of the fame kind: " He will foon fall back into his
" natural ftation,—A filent Senator, and hardly fup-
" porting the weekly eloquence of a news-paper:"
This laft claufe ought to ftand thus: " A filent Sena-
" tor, and the feeble fupporter of a weekly news-paper."
Such are the blunders, in one letter, of a writer, whom
you recommend as, an *English Claffic*: And fuch are the
blunders, which difgrace the Edition of JUNIUS, publifhed by the writer himfelf: He did not, then, know
how to write Englifh, any more than you know what
is Englifh, when you read it in your mother tongue.
The Letters of JUNIUS, which I have lately run over,
with a view to his language, are full of fuch egregious
blunders. In the five and twenty years, which elapfed,
between the writing of *Junius* and the publication of
The Indian Obferver, Mac Aulay, who had extraordinary
capabilities from nature, greatly improved his ftyle, by
habit, and reflection: This laft work of his able hand
is written much better than the firft; although the Critics are ftill blinded, by the falfe *glare* of *Junius*.

all

all the talents, fubtlety, and fedition, of his fraternity: And, confequently, when you recommend to the public a book, which has been ftigmatized by law, you thereby act upon the fame principles, avow the fame opinions, and practife the fame jacobin-ifm (*l*).

With

(*l*) I obferve, that you more than once attribute the writing of *Junius's* letters to the late William Gerard Hamilton, who was, furely, incapable of writing papers, fo puerile, fo malignant, fo feditious : You did not re-collect, when you made thofe affertions, from the *higheft authority*, that the books, and manufcripts, of W. G. Hamilton have come to the hammer, without difclofing a fecret, which was not to be difclofed. [Chinefe Epif-tle, p. 5.] Confidering it of fome importance to afcer-tain, who was the real Author of thofe letters, I have collected documents, which completely fatisfy me, that Hugh Mac Aulay, who affumed the name of Boyd, was the real Author: He had all the genius, all the fecrecy, all the malignancy, all the feditioufnefs, which were neceffary for fuch a tafk : And it fhould be recollected by thofe Critics, who dictate on this fubject, that there is no *erudition* in Junius, nor *official* detail : There is no fort of knowledge, in Junius, but what could be eafily picked up at Court, or in Coffee-houfes, by fuch boys, as Mac Aulay, or Chatterton : I fay at Court; becaufe it is a fact, that Mac Aulay, conftantly, went to St. James's,

as

With the fame fpirit, you attack the Parliament, during *thefe wayward times:*

" If from *State farces*, when the Houfe is up,
" Some feek the green room and with Kemble fup(*m*)."

One of thefe *ftate farces* is minutely dramatized: and, in order that the dulleft reader
may comprehend the fatire, you fubjoin, as
ufual, your note, to inftruct him in the point
of your lampoon: " Alluding, you add, to
" the long debates on the Dog and Bitch
" Bill, which is a little allegorical, fome-
" times unintelligible, and often ludi-
" crous (*n*)." You muft be ignorant, indeed, if you did not know, that this attack
on the proceedings of Parliament is a breach
of privilege: But your delight in lampoon-

---

as to a Coffee-houfe, for the purpofe of collecting information: And, it was there, that he collected, with
his ready ears, the half-information, which he retailed in
his papers.

(*m*) Purfuits, 6th Ed. p. 111.

(*n*) Ib. p. 164-5. There is alfo an attack on " the
" *incomprehenfible Cavalry Act*, under George the Third
" of Great Britain." [Ib. p. 323.]

ing

ing the legiflature (*o*), induces you to take the imputation of ignorance, in that point, rather than not gratify itfelf.

Through *all your Purfuits*, the *Lords*, affembled in Parliament, are equally fubjected to the lafh of your lampoon (*p*). In your *Chinefe Epiftle*, you abound in *fcoff* at the moft dignified Peers: The Archbifhop is fcoffed at (*q*): The Chancellor is attack-

---

(*o*) Political Dramatift, 1795, p. 1.
> *The houfe was up*; the long debate was o'er:
> And Addington prefided now no more:

After the rifing of the Houfe, you introduce the Minifter:
> " His friends from idle terrors to releafe,
> " Pitt caft faint gleams of vifionary peace."

The abfurdity of this is loft in its Jacobinifm: Whether your avowed purpofe be to ridicule Mr. Sheridan, or Mr. Grattan, your fecret principle furely directs you to animadvert on Mr. Pitt: Yet the contradictorinefs of your practice to your principle ever detects your double dealing: You apologize, indeed, by faying:
> " I never deviate into honeft fenfe."

(*p*) Purf. 6th Ed. p. 256.

(*q*) Chinefe Epiftle, p. 16: Your imputation on the Archbifhop is unfounded in the fact:
> " Why flumbers the Arch-Pontiff? on the fhore,
> " Who from embodied dulnefs roufes Moore?"

You attack the Archbifhop's power of conferring degrees, in your *Pair of Epiftles*, p. 13.

P p   ed (*r*):

ed(*r*): The Bishops are satirized (*s*): And you try, by every effort of jacobinical malignity, to reduce the highest characters to a level with the lowest (*t*).

You equally bespatter both sides of the house; shewing neither respect for the ministers, nor deference to their opponents. And, you hold this *impartial pen of censure*, through all your lampoons. You peck at Mr. Pitt, and you fly at Mr. Fox: You run at Mr. Rose, and you strike at Mr. Sheridan: You lampoon Lord Loughborough, and you traduce Lord Thurlow: You bounce at Mr. Bowles, and you laugh at Lord Lauderdale: You goad Mr. J. Gifford, and you bite Mr. Barrister Erskine. Such are the facts! The motives, which produced those effects, may be traced to one of the funda-

---

(*r*) Chinese Epistle, p. 11:

"Yet still, though thron'd in Thurlow's *rightful* place,
"His words want weight which never wanted grace."

According to your jacobinical code, Lord Thurlow had *the right*, though the King had delivered *the Seal* into fitter hands.

(*s*) Ib. p. 14-16.   (*t*) Id. 11-18.

mental

mental principles of jacobinifm; viz. an endeavour to confound characters, the good
with the bad; and, thereby, to teach mankind to truſt to all-confounding anarchy:
By your indiſcriminate cenſure, you would
reduce the Britiſh dominions to the moſt piti-
able ſtate, which a nation can fall into, when
driven, by jacobinical artifice, to deſpair;
having ſhown, that there is no man, in whom
it can truſt for ſafety, nor pillow, whereon
to reſt its head. You have, however, your
anſwer at hand: You are reſolved, with your
uſual arrogance, which *the dignity of the fubject demands,*

" A while to war with dunces, fools, and knaves,
" Hirelings of State, or Oppoſition Slaves."

The ſame principle of jacobiniſm incites
you to war with *Scotland* and the *Scots:*

" —————— though Scotland's Star
" Shed brief malignant heat, and ſcorch'd afar(*u*)."

(*u*) *Chineſe Epiſtle*, p. 28 : In your *Pair of Epiſtles*,
p. 23, you ſay :

" And Gillies rules o'er all the hiſtoric Choir :
" *Scotch Mirrors*, and *Scotch Loungers*, in the rear :"
And, you libel the *Scotch* printer Fowlis.

P p 2   You

You cry out:

" No *Scotchman* near, no Gillies by my fide."

You recollected, no doubt, how *Junius* railed at Scotfmen, and, thereby, rent the nation, thirty years ago : And you were induced by the motives of that malignant writer, to divide the North from the South; at a time, when they ought to be united, in affection, and in effort. It is a fact, which was long fufpected, but is now afcertained, that it is a fundamental principle of the United Irifh-men of the prefent day, to difunite Scotland from England, and to keep Ireland feparate from both. You act upon the fame jaco-binical maxim of *divide et impera*, for a rea-fon, which is worthy of your motives, and your manners:

" How can the rogues pretend to fenfe ?
" Their pound is only twenty-pence."

The fame manners, and the fame motives, led you to raife from the grave of oblivion, where it had lain upwards of a century, and where it ought to reft in peace, the Roman catholic controverfy. If you be a chriftian,

what

what but jacobinifm could induce you, while
an attack is made, by atheifts, on chriftianity itfelf, to inflame chriftians againft each
other? But, you thought you faw the Church
in danger, becaufe her fathers flept: Sir, the
Church of England is moderate; becaufe fhe
feels, that fhe is ftrong: If fhe were weak,
fhe would, upon your principles, fet up per-
fecution: You would, from the fame motive, perfuade the people, that the French
emigrants, both laity, and clergy, were in-
vited into our ifle, by government, rather
than thrown upon our fhore, by tempeft (*x*).
You infinuate, that the King had fitted up a
palace for their pleafure, rather than given
them a barrack for their fhelter (*y*). You,
certainly, impeach the Parliament, for feed-
ing the hungry, and clothing the naked:
And, you would, thereby, tear from the national banner, one of its brighteft *quarter-*

(*x*) I quote your opprobrious *Letter to the Marquis
Buckingham,* on this fubject: And your *Purfuits* every
where.

(*y*) Id.

ings,

ings, its renown amongſt civilized mankind, for public charity (z).

You were led by ſimilar motives of jacobiniſm, to attack the King's miniſters, for employing military bodies of French emigrants : And, your jacobinical temper, ac-

(z) I will not again reprobate your attacks on Parliament, as at once unconſtitutional, and jacobinical : But, with regard to the vote of 540,000*l.* for the ſuffering Clergy and Laity of France, I will ſtate *the faƈt* againſt *your fiƈtion :* [Purſuits, 6 Ed. p. 220.] By an official ſtatement, which was laid before the Seleƈt Committee of Finance of the Sums of Money, which were taken out of the Civil Liſt revenue, for the relief of the ſuffering Clergy, and Laity of France, from the 5th January, 1793, to the 5th January, 1797, the ſame amounted to 420,600*l.* 12*s.* 0½*d.* : Now ; upon an average of four years, the total is only 105,150*l.* 3*s.* a year : Yet ; becauſe the Houſe of Commons, by a vote, made good the ſum, thus advanced, you repeatedly charge the Commons with voting, *annually,* 540 000*l.* You recur, often, to this topick of inflammation ; for the obvious purpoſe of raiſing the indignation of the Conſtituents againſt their Repreſentatives, in Parliament. Since the 5th of January, 1797, this Charity, which was before advanced out of the Civil Liſt, has been, annually, voted by Parliament.

cording

cording with that fpirit, you could not let it
pafs, but, break out:

> " Now, when the French *defend* us in difgrace,
> " French fwords, French fraud, French priefts, and
>   French grimace(*a*)."

From the *fleeping fathers* of the church,
and the Catholick controverfy, you turn
your jacobinical attention to our learned fe-
minaries. You lay your cenforious finger
on Eᴛᴏɴ-ꜱᴄʜᴏᴏʟ, as ftanding in need of
many *new*, and *ftrong*, regulations. " It
" is ᴍʏ Oꜰꜰɪᴄᴇ," you · add, " to fpeak
" openly and boldly(*b*)." It is in vain, I
believe, to fearch the Chapel of the Rolls,
for a charter, appointing you, or your fathers, the *vifitors* of Eton School. *Your*
Oꜰꜰɪᴄᴇ, then, confifts in your affuming of
the right to lampoon all perfons, and eftablifhments; for the jacobinical purpofe of
degrading them: You lampoon the Pro-

(*a*) You fay, in your Note, that this alludes to the
French Emigrant Regiments, enrolled in the Britifh
Army; " a meafure of Government unwife;—a *project*
" *of defperation.*" [Purfuits, 6 Ed. p. 303.]

(*b*) Purfuits, 6 Ed. p. 257-59.

voft,

voft, and Mafters, of Eton; in order to inculcate upon the boys more obedience to their fuperiors: Yet, the boys, you fay, are licentious. You put Junius into their hands; in order to inftil into them habits of fubmiffion; yet, you exclaim, loudly, that the fcholars form themfelves into *political parties*. Such parties there will be, while fathers and mothers, uncles and aunts, female coufins and old nurfes, fhall continue to form parties upon the point, whether *John Styles*, or *Tom Nokes*, fhall be the minifter: For this unclaffical vulgarity, of mentioning *Nokes*, and *Styles*, I beg your pardon: I meant to fay, whether *Cicero*, or *Catiline*, fhall be the King's minifter. We all know what law fays, that the fins of the fathers fhall be vifited upon the children: But, by your jacobinical code, the children's tutors are to be vifited, for the follies of their fathers, and nurfes.

From Eton School to King's College, Cambridge, the tranfition is natural. With your jacobinical cleaver, you hew down " the *infigne* of a Chancellor's authority,
" borne

" borne by a *mongrel, robustious* satellite of " a French Directory (*c*)." MY OFFICE favours much of French authority : As a judge, you condemn, without a hearing; and, as the executioner, at the same time, you mangle the condemned, with your jacobinical sabre.

From King's College, you extend the visitatorial power of MY OFFICE to the Royal Society. You find the members of it, in the exercise of their chartered rights, cultivating *natural knowledge:* And, in the like character of French judge, and executioner, you lampoon, without a hearing, the President, the Secretary, and the fellows, who only knew you as their fellow, that had solemnly engaged to support their privileges, and promote their views (*d*).

The

(*c*) Pursuits, 6 Ed. p. 61 : The *barbarous* word, *insigne*, is repeated, in the 7th Ed. p. 309; but, the opprobrious words, *mongrel,* and *robustious*, were expunged.

(*d*) Pursuits, 6 Ed. p. 31–67–321–340; Note (*q*) which is a kind of protest against the Transactions of the Royal Society: I say nothing of its want of decency, its

want

The jacobinical authority of MY OFFICE, you eafily extend, in the next place, to the Antiquary Society ; which you alfo find in the exercife of its chartered rights ; yet, in your accuftomed manner, you punifh the Society by mangling, with your fatirical fabre, its head, body, and limbs (*e*). Your engagement to fupport the Society, and your honour to fulfil that engagement, are quite blotted by you out of your jacobinical

want of fenfe, its want of grammar, and its want of truth. " I would thunder in the ears of the Prefident, " and of the whole Royal Society, as a body," fay you, " Nolumus leges NATURÆ mutari." The malignity of your imputation is blunted by your ignorance : For, you extend the famous fpeech of the Barons, which was fpoken under Henry III. to King John's age. [Purfuits, 4th Part, p. 76.] Such a perverfion of the Barons fpeech was to be expected from you, who talk of " *Natural* Science." You feem to think with *Dog-berry* that, " To be a well-favoured man is the gift " of fortune ; but, to write and read comes by *nature.*"

(*e*) Purfuits, 6 Ed. p. 59, 244 : When a Satirift ftarts up, to cenfure a Society, whofe object is the cultivation of polite literature, he ought at leaft to write common fenfe, in common grammar : " I believe, fay you, (but fee the Society's Archæologia for *the record*) that IT " took place before, &c." [Id.] *What* took place?

code.

code. So we have, in thofe examples, a true picture of jacobinifm, which difregards all engagements; and allows no object, however facred, to ftand in its way, when in purfuit of its end. The Secret Committees of the Parliaments of the fifter kingdoms have fhewn, by incontrovertible documents, that the great object of the men, who are *united*, upon the true jacobinical principle, is, to deftroy all *conftituted authorities*, for the fell purpofe of fetting up *univerfal anarchy:* And, therefore, your repeated attacks, on all conftituted authorities, afford an indubitable proof of your jacobinifm.

Nay; have not I ftrongly maintained, that " Our *ruin can* be *effected* by *political reform* alone (*f*)?" Yes; you have written as libelloufly againft reforms, as on any other topicks. The Houfe of Commons being informed of fuppofed abufes in office, appointed a Committee to enquire into the

(*f*) Purfuits, 6 Ed. p. 209.

true

true ſtate of all offices. As you, however, aſſume the character of the people's *guardian* againſt *public plunderers*, you ſpeak contemptuouſly of this conſtitutional meaſure : And, you abuſe Mr. Abbot, the Chairman of this Committee. Well : you have in a ſubſequent edition made a half-apology to Mr. Abbot, for this abuſe ; but, you have not made any apology to the Houſe of Commons, for the breach of privilege, in attacking its Committee. The Houſe of Commons being given to underſtand, that juſtice is impeded, and that wrong may be done, by the uncertainty of the expiration of ſtatutes, appointed a Committee to ſtate *the fact*. As Chairman of this Committee, Mr. Abbot again employs his abilities, his activity, to the good purpoſe, of doing conſtitutional ſervice : And, you, therefore, fall upon him, and object to ſuch conſtitutional reform (*g*). You act, as if you thought, that no conſtitutional good can be done without your advice, and no

(*g*) Purſuits, 4th Part, 3 Ed. p. 29.

public

public fervice performed, without your affiftance.   Thus, you fay (*h*):

 " But if in love with *fiction* ftill, at Court
 " Prefent in verfe fome new *Finance Report,*
 " How taxes, funds and debts fhall difappear,
 " Or in the fiftieth, or five hundredth year."

 " The violence, fedition, and daring
" wickednefs of the times (*i*)" induced his
Majefty to recommend to the confideration
of Parliament that violence, that fedition,
and that wickednefs.   The Parliament, in
purfuance of the royal recommendation,
paffed the Sedition Acts.   And, you thereupon, attack the Parliament, in the following terms(*k*):

 " But in the *wane* of Empires (mark the hour)
 " *Vice* and the *Sword* confolidate all power ;
 " *Laws pafs their bounds* ; *few Statefmen* ftand erect ;
 " *All* in their Country's name, themfelves protect ;
 " The *Conftitution founds* in *every fpeech,*
 " The words are *infult,* and *each act a breach* ;
 " The public hopes with public credit fink :
 " At *fuch* an hour when men to madnefs think,
 " What is a poet, what is fiction's ftrain ?
 " JUNIUS might probe a nation's wounds in vain."

 (*h*) Purf. 7 Ed. p. 325. (*i*) Ib. 6 Ed. p. 273.
 (*k*) Purfuits, 6 Ed. p. 273 : Each *act* a breach," of
what ? The context points to *the Conftitution.*

        Well:

Well : you have fubjoined a note ; in order
to explain, that *my* FRIEND OCTAVIUS, by
this jacobinical attack, on the King, on the
Parliament, on *the laws*, on " the ftatefmen
" all," *means nothing* (*l*), during "fuch vi-
" olent, feditious, and wicked times." You
thus come forward, like a Maidftone witnefs, to teftify for *your friend Octavius*, that
his principles are the fame as your own,
that he conducts himfelf as you do, that he
is a well affected, well meaning, fubject,
and that when he fpeaks, and acts, feditious jacobinifm, he means nothing. As
for me ; I have no other mode of knowing
what perfons are, or mean, but by comparing their avowed principles, and their
conftant practice, together. I did not want
the Maidftone witneffes to tell me any thing
about O'Connor : I had feen his fpeeches,
and his writings, and obferved his conduct,
in Ireland ; I knew, that he had fled from
the juftice of his country ; I faw him *taken
with the mainour*, in the company of men of

(*l*) Purfuits, 6 Ed. p. 273.

bad

bad fame, going to France: And, I inferred, from all thofe circumftances, that he was, what he has fince acknowledged himfelf to be, a traitor. I did not want your *Shade of Pope* to inform me, who, or what, Mr. Grattan is: I had perufed his fpeeches too, read his pamphlets, and feen his conduct, during twenty years: And, from thofe unerring data, I inferred, what the Committees of the Irifh Parliament have proved, that his principles and his conduct have been confiftent. The fame rule of logick, I apply to you. When I fee you criminate Mr. Pitt, in the fame breath, that you ridicule Mr. Grattan: When I obferve you animadvert, on Godwin, Thelwall, and other feditious characters, in one page, and in the next, attack the Parliament, for fuppreffing feditious focieties, you aftonifh me, by the glaring inconfiftency of your invariable practices with your profeffed principles. And, with thefe obfervations, I clofe MY PROOFS OF YOUR JACOBINISM.

PROOFS

Proofs *of your* Ignorance.

I have the honour to concur with Til-
lotson, in thinking that, " He who doth
" not know thofe things, which are of ufe
" for him to know, is but an ignorant man,
" whatever he may know befides." If you
had the gift of tongues, I would treat you
as an ignorant man, while you prefume to
teach others what you do not know yourfelf; and pretend to dictate, on every fubject, to every perfon: And, I am free to
think now, as you formerly thought, " that
" it is poffible for an author not to write the
" worfe, for having fome previous know-
" ledge on the fubject, about which he is to
" treat (*a*)."

As my firft proof; I will quote your laft
publication, *The Shade of Pope.* You affume it, as a point agreed, that the loyal
fpirit of Pope rofe indignant at the refidence
of the feditious Grattan at *Twit'nam*. You

(*a*) *Mathias's* Effay on the Evidence, relating to
Rowley's Poems, p. 84.

would

would not have written the worfe on this
topick, for having had fome previous knowledge of your fubject.   Had you looked into
Pope's Satires, you would have feen, that
the *poet* was to the full as feditious, as the
politician.   Pope was, continually, lampooning *Kings :* and, when the Prince of Wales
afked him, *how he could love a Prince, while
he difliked Kings*, the poet had an anfwer to
feek.   In the Houfe of Commons, Fox re-
proached Lyttelton, the friend of Pope, with
entertaining friendfhip for a lampooner, who
fcattered his ink without fear, or decency.
About this time too, Paul Whitehead was
fummoned before the Lords for his poem
called, *Manners :* But, the whole proceeding was intended, fays Johnfon, rather to in-
timidate Pope, than to punifh Whitehead.
And, Pope defifted from further attempts,
at reformation, by lampooning : " He was
" not likely ever to have been of opinion,
" that the dread of his fatire could counter-
" vail the love of power, or of money ; he
" pleafed himfelf with *being important* and
" *formidable ;* and gratified fometimes *his*

Q q   " *pride*,

" *pride*, and fometimes *his refentment*; till
" at laft, he began to think, he fhould be
" more fafe, if he were lefs bufy (*b*)."
What Pope thought, perhaps, you may live
to think: But, my bufinefs is only with
your ignorance of Pope's real character.
Pope was as ignorant of the flourifhing ftate
of the nation, in 1738, as you were of its
flourifhing ftate, in 1798.

You are led, by your ignorance, to mention William Wood, and *his affociates*, who
were confounded by the eloquence, and
energy, of Dean Swift (*c*). Yes; the *Draper*
was very eloquent, like yourfelf, in writing
of what he did not underftand; and very
energetic, like you, alfo, in oppofing, not
an evil, but a good. After a while, the li-
tigated queftion, about Wood's *halfpence*,
was referred to Sir Ifaac Newton, as Mafter-
worker of the Mint, who reported two facts :
1ft. That the contract, which had been
made with Wood, for fupplying Ireland

(*b*) Johnfon's admirable Life of Pope, throughout.
(*c*) Shade of Pope, p. 6.

with

with copper coins, was the moſt advantage-
ous, that had ever been made, for that country : 2dly. That Wood had compleatly executed his contract. The Engliſh government would not force a good upon Ireland,
at the riſk of a rebellion : The Iriſh government rejected the copper coins, which
all parties in Ireland reprobated ; but Wood
had a penſion, which no party oppoſed. I
have now drawn ſome information even out
of your ignorance ; and have ſubſtituted an
uſeful moral, for your ſeditious application
of it.

You, at length, raiſe the Ghoſt of Pope,
to frighten Grattan :

" What accents, murmur'd o'er this hallow'd tomb,
" Break my repoſe, deep founding through the gloom ?"

In the firſt line of your firſt couplet, we ſee a
wonderful ſpecimen of your ignorance of the
art of writing : You interpoſe a comma between the nominative, [accents,] and the
verb, [murmur'd]. And, from that blunder the tranſition was eaſy to the impropriety
of unfitly changing the tenſe of your verb,
from the *paſt* to the *preſent :* You might in-

deed

deed have chofen either the paft, or the prefent form of your verb : But, as you meant
to fay, and fing, what accents murmur'd,
and what accents broke my repofe, you were
bound by grammatical propriety, and your
own election, to adhere to that form, which
poetical vivacity required ; although poetical vivacity required rather the prefent form.
Poor Pope ! whofe chief boaft is accuracy, to
be thus raifed from the " hallow'd tomb ;"
and made to talk, fo inaccurately, in a fingle
couplet !

From Pope, the tranfition is not difficult
to Shakfpeare:

" Muft I for Shakfpeare no compaffion feel,
" Almoft eat up by COMMENTATING zeal."

In revenge, you have hunted the Commentators, through twenty pages " o'er bog and
" quagmire," in the text, and notes (*d*):

" Hot was the chafe ; I left it out of breath ;
" I wifh'd not *to be in* at Shakfpeare's death."

This chafe, which is written in the true
ftyle, and meafure, of Fowldes's " Strange
" wonderful battell between Frogs and

(*d*) Purfuits, 6 Ed. p. 39-60.

" Mife

" Mife (*e*)" brings to my recollection a
paffage in the *Summer's Laft-Will* of Nash:
" Faith, this fcene is a right *prandium cani-*
" *num*, a dog's dinner, which, as it is with-
" out wine, fo here is a coyle about dogges,
" without wit."

In every fyftem of mythologifts, nothing
can be more juft than, that he who has hunted
others, fhould himfelf be hunted. You truly
tell, indeed, what is not news to the readers of Shakfpeare, that our great poet was
born, in 1564, and died on his birth day,
in 1616; that his plays were firft collected,
and publifhed together in folio, in 1623, by
his principal friends, Hemming and Condel:
But, when you add, that, " they likewife
" *corrected* a fecond edition in 1632," you

(*e*) This wonderful battel was printed, in 1603:
Herein may be feen, in the Frogs and Mice, the pro-
totypes of your Dogs: Thus: Croaking Hyfiboas; Cla-
morous Polyphon; Blown-cheek Phyfignathus; Lick-
meale Lichomile; Eatcheefe Trygroglyphus; Eatcrum
Pfiaharpax: Thefe are more poetical epithets than
yours: The following is fuch a defcription of a warrior,
as you give of your hounds: *Embafichytros* is a moufe
that flily creepeth into every pot.

Q q 3

tell

tell news, indeed(*f*): For, Condel died, in 1627, and Hemming, in 1630; as you might have feen in a book, which you de_ride(*g*). As you poffefs the magical power of raifing men from the dead, fo you can, by your *hydra-headed wilfulnefs*, annihilate exiftence: " For, life and death is in thy " doomful writing." You immediately add: " It may feem ftrange to us, but it is true, " that *no other* edition of his works was at- " tempted till eighty two years after that " time, when in the year 1714, a *third* edi- " tion was publifhed by Mr. Rowe(*h*)." You thus annihilate, by your *doomful writ-ing*, the folio editions of 1664, and of 1685, and the 8vo edition of 1709. And, you, therefore, demonftrate, by *your own fhowing*, what it is to be a *Shakfpearean Commentator* of the Warburtonian fchool.

From your vaft knowledge of Shakfpearean hiftory, you give a lift of *Old Plays*, in which you include *Banks Bay horfe in a trance*,

(*f*) Purfuits, 7 Ed. p. 91. (*g*) Apology, p. 436-39.
(*h*) Purfuits, 7 Ed. p. 91.

and

and *Peirce Pennyless' Supplication to the Devil;* but these were never dramatized until
you issued your Shakspearean *fiat*.

You have, in addition to all other great
qualities, the knack of being *right pleasant*,
when you blunder most; and of being vastly
witty, by egregious interpolation, only.
" The first chapter of Markhams Booke of
" Armorie is intitled, The difference *between*
" *Charles* and Gentle*man*," say you (*i*).
The passage, as quoted by the late Dr. Farmer, is, " the difference 'twixt *Churles* and
" Gentle*men* (*k*)." If you had looked into
Bailey, for the meaning of *Churl*, your ignorance would have been saved such a blunder. But, why interpolate several &cs. for
the purpose of sarcasm ? And, why immediately add, " Reader, Mr. Steevens, and
" Dr. Farmer will tell you *all this is so*, and
" *quoted* too, though you may begin with
" a staring doubt." Steevens, and Farmer
will tell you all this, and *quoted* too !! What

(*i*) Pursuits, 7 Ed. p. 81.
(*k*) Steev. Shaksf. 1793, vol. ix. p. 441, which is
quoted by you upon the point.

blunder!

blunder! What interpolation! What non-fenfe! Let falfe grammar be added to thefe(*l*); and we fhall have compleat fpecimens of your performances, as *a* Shakfpearean Com-mentator.

Your fagacity cannot divine, it feems, by what refined abfurdity *the wills* of the actors could be *raked up*, to illuftrate Shakfpeare (*m*), Why; Sir, wills are not to be *raked up* at Doctors Commons: It requires fome refearch to difcover wills there; and fome expence to obtain copies of them, for any purpofe. The players' wills were not publifhed by Mr. Malone, nor by me, for the purpofe of illuftrating Shakfpeare's Dramas; but for the important objects, of illuftrating his life, and clearing the dark hiftory of the ftage, during his interefting age. It is, however,

(*l*) Whether their own drowfinefs, *and* that of their brother Commentators, *was* [were] in confequence? [Purfuits, 7 Ed. p. 83] If I *am* [be] rightly inform-ed:—If he *does* [do]. *Mr.* Steevens and Co. [Meffrs. Steevens and Co.]—What can be more defpicable, than *the drowfinefs of fuch a fcholar*, with his ungrammatical improprieties, and his learned follies.

(*m*) Purfuits, 7 Ed. p. 97.

apparent

apparent, that the publishing of the wills
of Hemming, and Condel, did not prevent
you from making these players the editors of
the Dramas of Shakfpeare, *after they* had
been fome years dead. To true merit ought
to be affigned the palm : And, therefore, the
blunderbufs, who can make *dead* players *living* editors of Shakfpeare, is juftly entitled
to the honours of the *fools-cap*, and *bawble*.

What! Sir, do you call me a blunderbufs,
who am now, what Gray lately was, the firft
fcholar, and the firft poet in England? Yes:
I will call any writer a *blunderbufs*, who
fcribbles, blunderingly; and yet pretends to
dictate to thofe, who know more than he,
upon the point difcuffed. "Confuls," fay
you, " do not now meet confuls in Tufcu-
" lum; and if I am [be] rightly informed,
" the *Sympofiacks* [Sympofiarchs] at Wim-
" bledon, and Holwood, have not too much
" feverity of method or equality in the
" [their] glaffes (*n*)." In this paragraph,
you, no doubt, intended, to be profoundly

(*n*) Purfuits, 7 Ed. p. 13.

learned,

learned, and vaftly witty: But, how came you, as the firft fcholar, to ufe the adjective, *Sympofiacks*, in place of the fubftantive, *Sympofiarchs* (*o*); as your context fhows, that you meant to fpeak of the *landlords*, and not of their *feafts?* In your *feverity of method*, and *equality in the glaffes*, you add nonfenfe to blunder. Wit, and blunder, cannot co-alefce. When a writer, who ftands upon the ftilts of learning, introduces into a fhort paffage bad fenfe, bad grammar, affectation, blunder, he only fhows himfelf in the cha-racter of a blunderbufs! But, you have your anfwer at hand: " If I culminate at all, it " is from the equator (*p*)." A navigator may fail, from the Equator to the Pole, be-fore he fhall difcover the meaning of this *culmination* of ignorance, which rifes to the very *vertex* of nonfenfe.

Yet; you have rifen above your own *cul-mination*, in the perfpicuous paffage follow-ing: " The time for difcrimination feems

(*o*) For the feveral meanings of Sympofiacks, and Sympofiarchs ; compare Johnfon, Bailey, and Afh.

(*p*) Purfuits, 7 Ed. p. 272.

" to

" to be come. Toleration is fully granted
" to all opinions, subject to the controul of
" *the legiſlature*, after their publication, in
" the open courts of law, by the verdict of a
" jury, in which true liberty conſiſts (*q*)."
It is certainly high time for *diſcrimination* to
interpoſe: For, chaos ſeems come again.
Toleration is allowed, *fully*, when it is exer-
ciſed under the controul of the *legiſlature;*
not, indeed, acting in its place, and character,
of the legiſlature; but, in the courts of law,
as ſuperintendant of judicial proceedings;
and, in this ſuperintendance of the legiſlature over the judicial power, *true liberty* conſiſts, according to your theory; although,
according to Monteſquieu's ſyſtem, ſuch a
ſuperintendance is real tyranny.

But, the culminations of ignorance are
confined to neither time, nor ſpace :

" Though Abram Jones and *Jaſper Wilſon* preach,
" With names uncouth, but *not unpoliſh'd ſpeech*(*r*)."

(*q*) Purſuits, 7 Ed. p. 62.

(*r*) Purſuits, 6 Ed. p. 166 : *Names uncouth*, " inſtead
" of *Cato*, Brutus, &c."   You are a true ſon of Miſtreſs
Dangle, for your admiration of " *Roman Signatures*."

In

In your accuftomed appendage of note, you add, " I more than fufpect the celebrated " Mr. Rofcoe of Liverpool in Jafper Wil- " fon (*s*)." As a logician, you place your *more than fufpect*, in oppofition to my *pofitive information*, which, decidedly, gave the work of Jafper Wilfon, to Dr. Currie. As an hiftorian, you come forth with that *more than fufpect*, after Doctor Currie, like a man, has avowed the publication, and like a fpirited man, has made an expofition of his principles. As a friend to the conftitution, you would refix in the fide of Government a thorn, which had been extracted, by my little efforts. As a judge of the Olympick games, you affign the prize, accompanied with Pindaric praifes, not to the victor, but to the vanquifhed. Ignorance cannot culminate higher in the fmoke of blunder, nor grovel lower in the mire of affectation !

(*s*) You often repeat the praifes of Mr. Rofcoe : But, from your partiality to republican principles, you fhut your eyes upon his republicanifm, which is perpetually breaking out, in his writings; nor do you open them upon a well-known club of Jacobins at Liverpool.

What !

What! Sir, do you attribute ignorance to me, who fit in the dictatorial chair, with Gyges' ring on my critical finger? Have not I inftructed every fcholar, that Juvenal was born at Acquinum, Perfius at Voltetra, and Lucilius at Aiunca? Yes: But, had not Harwood already taught our children the fame petty points, when he put into their hands " The Lives and Characters of the " Greek and Roman Clafficks "? Nay; have not I quoted, not from thofe Claffics only, but from books, in every fcience, and in every language? Yes:

" In ancient fenfe, if any needs will deal,
" Be fure, I give them fragments, not a meal;
" What Gellius, or Stobæus hafh'd before,
" Or chew'd by blind old Scholiafts o'er and o'er."

Gellius was a minute critic: Stobæus gave his common place book to the public, wherein we happen to find fuch mincemeat of old books. [Mat.] You may, indeed, acknowledge, in the words of Balandino, the Pageant Poet to the City of Milan, in Ben Jonfon's *Cafe is Altered:* " Why; I'll tell " you, Mafter Onion, I do ufe as much " *ftale ftuff*, though I fay it myfelf, as any " man

" man does, in *that kind*, I am fure. Did
" you fee the laft Pageant, I fet forth ?"
yclept, *The Shade of Pope*.

Nay; have not I fhown my extenfive *no-
ignorance* by tranflating, in the character of
a friend, " the paffages from [the] Greek,
" Latin, Italian, and French writers quoted
" in the Purfuits of Literature ?" Yes: and
you have ftumbled at the threfhold, by
committing a blunder, in the title-page ;
as I have fhewn above ; and in the laft page ;
as it thus appears : " End [*the* End] of the
" fourth and laft dialogue, &c." You,
who defy a commentary (*t*), cannot tranflate your own quotations. You have falfe
grammar, in the very firft article of your
tranflation (*u*). In your fecond trial, you
have impropriety of pointing, befides falfe
grammar ; But, I will not dwell upon the
egregious pleonafm of your " mere *babble of*

(*t*) Pref. p. xlvii.

(*u*) Pref. p. lxxix: " The merit, however, of the
" caufe itfelf, and of the warfare in which fhe is engaged,
" joined to the predilection of Stilicho, enfure*s* [enfure]
" the affection and favour of the nation." I do not
mean to object to your *paraphraftic verbofity*.

" *words* ;"

" *words* ;" the expreffion, *babble*, alone,
conveying the whole idea of idle talk, or of
puerile tranflation. In your fourth trial, you
fail, in giving either the elegance, or the
plain meaning of Cicero : " *Ne incognita pro*
" *cognitis habeamus :* Not to miftake what
" is unknown, for what is known," fay
you : In every tranflation, two rules are in-
difpenfable ; it muft be grammatical ; it
muft be idiomatical : And from both thofe
rules, you have, in the above inftance, departed egregioufly. Let us take another example from Cicero, whom you attempt to
tranflate : " De Republica *graviter* querens,
" de homine nihil dixit : He complained
" *deeply* for the fake of the ftate ; of the
" man himfelf he faid nothing." Cicero's
graviter may be tranflated *heavily, gravely,
wifely, grievoufly, forely, feverely, hardly* ;
but, to complain *deeply* is not idiomatical :
Refpect for fuch a philologift, and orator,
as Cicero was, would induce me to attempt
a tranflation of your quotation from him, in
the following manner : Complaining, grievoufly, for the Republic, he faid nothing of
the

the man.   In tranflating the motto to your
title page, from Juftin Martyr, you have
again introduced bad Englifh : " Ye, who
" from your natural difpofition [difpofi-
" tions] as well as from your education are
" in all things, &c (*x*)."   In the following *germannick queftion*, " Whether a chi-
" mæra buzzing in a vacuum, has [have]
" the power, &c. (*y*)."   And there ought
to be no (,) after vacuum, unlefs there be
one after chimæra.   But, I have done : I
have no intention " to chafe a fchoolboy to
" his common places :" Nor, have I any
defign to darn Sir John Cutler's ftockings,
which you wear, worthily, by inheritance,
from the œconomical Knight : my purpofe,
merely, is to fupport my own pofition, by
examples, that you cannot tranflate *into*
Englifh, your quotations from foreign lan-
guages.   As you cannot write Englifh ; fo
you cannot poffibly tranflate ; even if your
affectation did not mar your fenfe (*z*) : But,
amidft

(*x*) Tranf. p. 1.   (*y*) Ib. p. 12.
(*z*) Purfuits, p. 27 : " *Magnum eft vectigal parfimonia:*
" Oeconomy is a great *poffeffion*."   Here is another example

amidſt a thouſand other defects, your great
defect, both as a tranſlator, and as a writer,
is *verboſity*. With theſe obſervations, I will
cloſe *my proofs* of *your* IGNORANCE. And,
adopting the mythological principle, before
mentioned, I will only add :

" So Proteus hunted in a nobler ſhape,
" Became, when ſeized, a puppy, or an ape."

PROOFS *of your* NONSENSE.

Ignorance, and nonſenſe, may certainly
be regarded as couſins in the firſt degree ;
being deſcended from folly, and affectation,
the common parents of both. Conſidering
this deſcent, we need not be ſurprized, that
ſatyrical nonſenſe ſhould ſo often appear in
the world of letters, ſometimes, indeed, in
the garb of plauſibility, but oftener, with
the air of arrogance :

" Proſe ſwell'd to verſe, verſe loit'ring into proſe."

Such is the importance of this ſubject, to

ample, which ſhows, that you cannot tranſlate Cicero :
Vectigal ſignifies a tax, or income, which the context required ; but, not *poſſeſſion*, which conveys the idea of
ſomething more ſtable.

R r   the

the purity of our compofitions, that philofophical rhetoricians have formally inquired,
" What is the caufe that Nonsense fo often
" efcapes being detected, both by the
" writer, and by the reader (*a*) ?" This
difquifition accounts, by anticipation, why
the Critics, who have propagated *your*
Pursuits, have not detected the nonfenfe
in them ; and why the readers, who have
perufed your *profe fwelled to verfe*, your
poetry loitering into profe, did not perceive,
that they were reading Nonsense :

 " How fluent nonfenfe trickles from his tongue,
 " How fweet the periods, neither faid, nor fung !"

Thefe *phenomena* may be eafily accounted
for, indeed, by the fact, that your writings
form fuch a vaft wildernefs of *nonfenfe*, the
darknefs vifible whereof obfcures the fight,
both of the eye, and the underftanding.
But, fuch are the limited capacities of men,
that vaft objects cannot be eafily compre-

(*a*) Campbell's Philofophy of Rhetorick, vol. ii. p. 92 ;
wherein you may fee much ufeful learning, and may find
many beacons for your future courfe, although the
Author was a *Scotchman.*

        hended

hended by them, without the whole be divided into its feveral parts : Examination
may then begin ; and judgment may be at
laft pronounced.

You feem, indeed, to have excelled the
perfpicuous writer ;

> " Him, who now to fenfe, now nonfenfe leaning;
> " Tries but to *wheedle round* about a meaning."

This fort of writing may be illuftrated
by the following examples : " The reform-
" ers ftrove to buy *golden opinions,* of their
" fellow citizens, and to *wear them* in the
" neweft glofs.   The external decoration
" deceived the eye. The painted fepulchre
" was prepared and whited *without,* the
" vault and receptacle of all our ancient
" liberties, and rights, and fecurities, and
" properties, and common comforts.   Still
" we beheld all this, but went our way,
" and forgot what manner of men, thefe
" reformers were."   Thefe paffages were
intended, no doubt, to be vaftly inftruc-
tive ; but where is the fenfe of them ? You
inftruct your readers : " at this very hour,
" when the public mind was darkened that

R r 2   " it

" it could not difcern, when in every quar-
" ter of Heaven appeared vapour, and mift,
" and cloud, and exhalation." In order to
difpel thefe accumulated vapours, you quote
an Italian paffage, from the *Inferno* of *Dante*,
which makes darknefs vifible. " It was the
" morning horizon began fuddenly to red-
" den. It was the dawn. Then indeed,
" *firft in his eaft the glorious lamp was feen*,
" regent of day! This luminary was ED-
" MUND BURKE ! ! !"

Now, has the reader daylight, indeed.
" The rays of *the orb* were direct, col-
" lected, and concentrated : They had
" power to illuminate, and to confume(*b*)."
What fublime nonfenfe! Yet, thefe paffages (*c*) may be confidered, as proper fpecimens of the texture of the Prefatory Dif-

(*b*) JUNIUS had faid, as I have already remarked :
" The rays of royal indignation, collected upon him,
" ferved only to illuminate, and could not confume."
You borrowed this paffage of JUNIUS, without perceiving, that it is ungrammatical nonfenfe : This comes of
ignorant admiration!

(*c*) Purfuits, 6 Ed. p. 124-5.

courfe

courſe to your third Dialogue, which is a tiſſue of falſe compoſition, thus embroidered with nonſenſe.

But, abſolute nonſenſe, and falſe compoſition, may be found every where, throughout *your* PURSUITS: " If Biſhop Horſeley " goes [go] on in this ſtyle, whatever his " politics may be, he certainly never will " incur the danger of *The Second Philip-* " *pic*." (*d*) " Not forgetting," you add, in a ſubſequent page, " his lordſhip's *Greek* " *proſody* for Lord Thurlow and *the la-* " *dies*." (*e*) What ſpecimens of gallant " nonſenſe ! I am ready to cry out, with Marſton, the ancient ſatiriſt :

" My ſhins are broke, with groping for ſome ſenſe ;
" To know to what his words have reference."

(*d*) Ib. p. 139.

(*e*) Purſuits, 6 Ed. p. 145; and the Note (*r*) in p. 140, for ſimilar nonſenſe about the ſame Lords, and Ladies :

' Nay Thurlow once ('tis ſaid) could ſing or ſwear,
' Like *Polypheme*, " I cannot, cannot bear."
[Ib. p. 108 :] We ſee in this couplet more *plagiariſm* from the Dunciad. [8vo. Ed. p. 156.]
" Teach thou the *warbling* POLYPHEME to roar,
" And ſcream thyſelf as none e'er ſcream'd before."

R r 3   Let

Let us take an example of incomprehenfibility, from your poetical text:

" Bleft be the voice of mercy, and the hand
" Stretch'd o'er affliction's wounds with *healing bland,*
" In holieft fympathy ! Our beft of man
" Gave us to tears, ere mifery well began(*f*)."

If perfpicuity be the chief quality of writing, what purpofe can it anfwer to write what cannot be underftood ? Happy! if you would ftretch out your hand, *with healing bland,* to open our eyes, *ere mifery begin,* in order to fee in your arithmetical fyntax, that two adjectives make one fubftantive. You have, however, your anfwer at hand to every objection: This is what is called in modern jargon, *The fublime inftinct of fentiment* (*g*).

" Till *wheedling round* with metaphyfick *art,*
" You fteal religion from th' unguarded heart."

But, this may be done by what you call a *ftrange fatality,* and in *the blunder of papal*

(*f*) Ib. p. 151. Pope, indeed, has *healing balm.* [Ib. p. 88] But, with an eye of plagiarifm on Pope, you went, far beyond his pretenfions, into the regions of nonfenfe, by your *healing bland.*

(*g*) Purfuits, 6 Ed. p. 21.

meta-

metaphor (*h*); or it may be ftill better performed by the trick of fome " young law-
" yers, and boy-members of Parliament,
" of forgetting their Greek, *if ever they*
" *knew any* (*i*)." Your lawyers muft be,
indeed, ftrange jurifts, to forget the law,
which they never learned, and your boy-
parliament-men muft be ftill more extraordinary fcholars, to neglect the Greek, which
they never knew. But you deal in novel-
ties, as well as in *bulls :*

 " Armies have *fkeletons*, and fermons too (*k*);
 " So teach our Doctors warlike or [and] divine."

Your ufual note points out not only the
meaning, and the fatire, of your text, but
its nonfenfe too : " The language of the
" Houfe of Commons. It fhould have
" been in other terms. Sorrow is facred,
" and fhould have the language of confo-
" lation even from the lips of a ftatefman."
What, I wonder, fhould have been in other
terms ? You refer, for an anfwer, to the fke-

(*h*) Ib. p. 154. (*i*) Ib. p. 141.

(*k*) Ib. p. 343 : In order to make out the lame fenfe,
it fhould have been faid, and fermons too *have fkeletons*.

R r 4

letons

letons of fermons by Mr. Simeon. "This, "you add, is as ludicrous and abfurd in a "divine, as the term is offenfive and *un-* "*feeling* in *Parliament* during the miferies "of war (*l*)." But, you mitigate, in fome degree, thefe animadverfions, by remarking that, though every ftatefman knows the *rattles of office*; Mr. Burke, who was the God of your idolatry, could alone fave England "from the grand *crufhing* CABAL, "grounded and rooted in France, and "branching out and overfhadowing all "Europe (*m*). I fpeak, as I think; in fin-"cerity." But, there is no end of the fpecimens of nonfenfe, which may be taken from your *Purfuits!* They grow luxuriantly, like other weeds, from a foil, which appears to be naturally fuited to them. You were favoured by nature; but art feems not to have fupplied the neceffary cultivation of the feeds of your genius; nor, to have produced, by your education, its proper fruits:

"True

(*l*) Purfuits, p. 343.   (*m*) Ib. p. 356-7.

" True Child of fortune ; and true foe to fame,
" You lifp'd in nonfenfe ; for the nonfenfe came(*n*)."*

3. I have

(*n*) There is, as I have faid, no end to *the nonfenfe* in
your Purfuits: I will only give a very few inftances
more: In 6 Ed. p. 71, you talk of " reading a *Minifter
in Books.*" You fpeak of the *mitred* Oath that Tucker
fwore: Can an Oath be mitred? Yes; by the fame
pen, which could make the worthy Dean *fwear a mitred
Oath, in a political pamphlet.* We may fuppofe, that the
mitred Oath is to be found " in fome *pofthumous MSS.*
" of William Warburton, [the] Bifhop of Gloucefter."
[Ib. p. 159.] But, it required, in addition to the learned
Bifhop's genius, which could thus write after *inhumation,*
" an *infurrection* of talents." [Ib. p. 173.] Befides,
you have an office, " to inftruct the rifing abilities, and
" hope of England." [Ib. p. 198.] You can, indeed,
eafily erect offices, and form plans: " A diftinguifhing
" feature in all his plans for the relief of the poor, the
" idle, the abandoned, and the wretched. *The mode of
" conferring mercy* and apparent kindnefs *is not always
" mild* and merciful. I have too much refpect for my
" readers to enlarge on this virtue." [Ib. p. 181.] But,
why not enlarge your fentiment into fenfe, and your
ftyle into grammar? You, indeed, affign a fatisfactory
reafon: " Our *unfexed* female writers now inftruct, or
" confufe us and themfelves in the labyrinth of politics,
" or turn us wild with Gallick frenzy." [Ib. p. 194.]
" Are we to add corruption to corruption," you afk,

till

3.   I have now finiſhed what I had chiefly to ſay, with regard to *the matter* of the work, which you, originally, called The Pursuits of Literature ; or *What you Will.* Its general ſubject, ſay you, is *Literature* ; although, when you afterwards diverge to *What you Will,* you relinquiſh the moſt ſignificant part of your well choſen Title-page.   It is a *ſatirical poem,* with

" till there neither is, *nor can be,* a return to virtuous
" action?" [Ib. p. 198.]   " Are we to ſpare," you
exclaim, " the ſharpeſt inſtruments of authority and of
" cenſure, when public eſtabliſhments are gangrened in
" the *life organs ?*" [Ib. p. 199.]   It is not ſurprizing,
then, though you think it unfortunate, " that ſcarce a
" ſubject in literature can be intereſting without the
" *ſcience* and *matter* of politics." [Ib. p. 205.]   As you
have your *ſcience of politics* ; ſo have you your *ſtate
botany* ; and your *public victuals* : For according to your
ſcience of politics " the State has no *decent* awe." [Ib.
p. 293]   How could it? conſidering that " Dr. Moro-
" ſophos," whom you brought from the *Scribbleriad,*
" knew but little of the ſyſtem of the Lydian mode in
" the diatonick genus." [Ib. p. 290.]   How could he,
even with the help of Biſhop Horſley, whom you ridicule, in the next ſentence, becauſe he put down a
jacobinical pretender to Greek learning, know any
thing of your *ſyſtem of a mode* in a *genus ?*

Notes,

Notes, fay you : And. you have fince affumed the more arrogant denomination of
a NATIONAL *poem*(*o*).   An attack, indeed,
on all parties, and all perfons, excepting
the chofen few, is fitly called a *national
poem*; artfully compofed, with " *half ma-*
" *lice*, and half whim :" And, fuch a poem
is very properly accompanied with *a well
noted margin* ; as nothing can be more con-
confiftent, amidft fo much inconfiftency,
than notes of elucidation, to clear up the
darknefs of the text ; to explain the incom-

(*o*) A writer in the *True Briton* of the 27th of October, 1797, under the fignature of " *A Friend to the Con-*
" *ftitution, &c.*" emphatically, calls *the Purfuits of Literature*, " *the* NATIONAL *Poem.*"   In this *Puff-oblique*,
the hand of the celebrated Mr. PUFF himfelf, manifeftly, appears.   In the feries of *letters*, which are, at
prefent, publifhing in the *Morning Herald*, under the
fignature of HORATIO, *the Purfuits of Literature* are,
again, called *the* NATIONAL *Poem:*   And, again the
encomiaftic hand of the great PUFF himfelf appears, in
every paragraph of *Horatio's* Letters.   MATHIAS is a
mannerift :   And, when he does his beft, his ftyle, and
fentiment, his purpofe, and his *Puff*, manifeft themfelves fo plainly, that it is impoffible not to fee him, in
his proper perfon, and in his true character.

prehen-

prehenfible, and to point the dull. I mean to
fay little of your want of any previous plan,
or of *honeſt* purpofe. Of your plan, you write
about it, and about it, that although it be not
a *mock epick*, with a beginning, a middle,
and an end, it is a *dramatick* EXCURSUS:

" In thundring lines, your no-defign rehearfe ;
" And rant, and rumble, in a ſtorm of verfe."

As a proof of your *no-deſign*, let it be remembered, that, although your fubject be
literature, which you fay, truly, is interwoven into the web of our *politics*, you obferve nothing about the *faction*, confiſting
of *the* REVIEWERS, that domineers, in our
Literature. The public, feeling the evil
influence of that faction, encouraged competitors, in the fame department of letters.
After a while thefe competitors became
themfelves factious, though upon a different
principle. The Public now called for Reviewers of *the* Reviewers ; and the public,
without the benefit of your help, derived a
manifeſt advantage, from encouraging competition, and difcountenancing factioufnefs.
On this fubject, which is fo intimately connected

nected with our conftitution, in church,
and ftate, you are, ftudioufly, filent. By
attacking all our eftablifhments, ecclefiaftical, civil, and literary, you have engaged
the repeated applaufe of the *Monthly Review:* By animadverting on Thelwall, and
Godwin, on Volney, and Prieftley, you
have fecured the indifcriminate praifes of
the *Britifh Critic.* Thus much, then, with
regard to your *plan*, and your *purpofe*. I
will now proceed to fubmit the, very little,
I have to add, about *the* MANNER of your
Purfuits.

PROOFS of *your inability* to write POETRY.

I will produce, as my *firft proof*, the very
firft couplet of your boaftful poem :

" I, who *once deem'd* my race of labour *run*,
" *And* camps, and courts, and crowds, and fenates,
    fhun (*a*)."

Now ; here is a fad ftumble at the very
threfhold. You, who had chofen your own
tenfe, were obliged to follow up your *once
deem'd*, and run, in the firft line of the cou-

(*a*) Purfuits, 7 Ed. p. 45.

plet,

plet, which are thus doubly in the paft time, with the paft tenfe, in *fhun*, in the fecond line of it; and your conftruction ought to have been, I, who once deem'd, and fhunn'd; as in Dryden:

" So Chanticleer, who never faw a fox,
" Yet fhunn'd him, as a failor fhuns the rocks(*b*)."

Nay; Sir, fay you, fhunn'd would ruin the rhyme. Your anfwer is only a proof of my pofition. I cannot help you out of your hobble: But, I can affign you, the poetry profeffor at Oxford, and the public orator at Cambridge, as affiftants, in the neceffary work of mending your " cobbl'd rhymes."

From fuch rhymes, and fuch grammar, it was natural to expect, in the fubfequent

---

(*b*) Prieftly would have inftructed you, (Horrefco referens!) if you had looked into his grammar, that the verb to *fhun* is not irregularly inflected: And fee Afh's Dictionary *in voce*. *Once*, fays Addifon, fignifies *formerly*; at a *former time*: Formerly *fhun* will not do; but, formerly *fhunned* will do. See how uniformly Addifon preferves, in his *Campaign*, the confiftency of his tenfe, in the prefent time:

" The rout begins, the Gallic fquadrons run,
" Compell'd in crowds to meet the fate they fhun."

verfes,

verſes, ſuch obſcurity, as to involve your
readers in doubt, whether the *ſyſtems*, which
laugh to *ſcorn the avenging rod*, be in the ac-
cuſative caſe, or in the nominative (*c*). There
can be no doubt, however, whether you
introduce an anticlimax in your thirteenth
verſe, after making your *ſyſtems hurl defiance to the throne of God*, you ſing, " *Blood*
" *guiltineſs* is their crime." I ſay nothing
of your pleonaſm, in the ſame ſentence, of
foliage dark, and cypreſs gloom. But, how
came you, in the preceding verſe, to give
fleſh the power of thinking, by crying out ;
" No *fleſh*, no ſpirit, now muſt reſt *in*
" *hope ?*" In *your Mythology*, indeed, this
new quality of matter often occurs, as in
your thirtieth verſe, you aſſign to your *Lau-
rentian trumpet* not only a *ſound*, but a *ſoul*.
In this ſtyle of genuine nonſenſe, you talk,
in your ſixteenth verſe, of *ſculptur'd mockery*, as you ſpeak of *mitr'd oath* ; which
oath cannot be ornamented with a *mitre* any
more than *mockery* can be *ſculptured*. Such

(*c*) Purſuits, 7 Ed. p. 46.

are

are the blunders in the firſt ſixteen verſes of a poem, which defies a commentary !

To obſcurity, and nonſenſe, and pleon-aſm, you add an inſtance of falſe grammar, in your twenty-eighth verſe :

> " The loud Laurentian *trumpet,* through the land,
> " Sound [founds] &c. ——————
> " With ſtrength of Stentor, but Mezentian ſoul (*d*)."

I am aware, that your aſſiſtants are ready to plead, that you meant to write, in the *ſubjunctive mood,* of which your writings proclaim your ignorance : But, the context ſhows, that you intended to ſpeak *indicatively:* And, this is a proper example of the exception to the rule, which Lowth lays down, when treating of the *ſubjunctive mood* (*e*). Of ſuch verſes, with their falſe grammar, and falſe ſenſe, who is not ready to exclaim with a poet of a different ſpirit :

> " Yet

(*d*) Purſuits, 7 Ed. p. 49.

(*e*) Grammar, p. 150-1 : There is nothing *contingent,* or hypothetical, in the aſſertion, " though the Lauren-" tian trumpet found;" and, therefore, the *indicative mood* was requiſite ; as in the following example : " *Though* he *was* rich, yet for your ſakes he became " poor." [Ib. p. 151.]

" Yet, this one maxim from my pen receive,
" To middling bards, the world no quarter give."

If such bards receive no quarter; if
" middling poets are by all accurst;"
what can that bard expect, who is often
incomprehenfible, and generally nonfenfical? But, is the firft fcholar, and the firft
poet of the prefent day, ever incomprehenfible, ever nonfenfical? Yes:

" For, true *no-meaning* puzzles more than wit."

You may have examples, from any page of
the Purfuits, or *Shade of Pope* :

" Oh, for that Sabbath's dawn ere Britain wept,
" And France before the *Crofs* believ'd and flept!
" (Reft to the State, and flumber to the foul!)
" Ere yet the brooding ftorm was heard to roll(*f*)."

Can *Geneva's angel* explain this incomprehenfibility, except by a note, " without
" [an] end(*g*)?" Take a fpecimen of nonfenfe (*h*) ?"

" Brave all the joint affociates of *A. S.*
" The jeft infipid, and the idle guefs;
" Bind, copy, comment, *manufcript*, and print,
" Take from good natur'd friends fome ufeful hint."

(*f*) Purfuits, 7 Ed. p. 275.   (*g*) Ib. 6 Ed. p. 231-2.
(*h*) Ib. p. 104-5.

S s   If

If we inquire for the fenfe ; if we afk, who ever faw, in any other place, the verb *to manufcript ?* you will refer us to

" Many a page *in gorgeous Bulmer's blaze :*"

But, if I had the art of *manufcripting*, in the higheft perfection, I could neither *comment* upon one third of the improprieties of *your Purfuits*, nor copy half the errors in them :

" Mark next, how fable, language, fancy, *flies* [fly]
" To ghofts, and beards, and hoppergollops cries(*i*)."

Let us add another example of elegant poetry, and exact grammar, from *The Pair of Epiftles :*

" (Oh that their very names might Jourdan throttle)
" *Eifenach, Enrebrehtftein*, or *Wolfen-bottle*.
" Such tempting themes *unwilling* [unwillingly] I forego,
" Nor [not] ftrive to paint, what I can never know."

We may now afk, a pointed queftion, with Rofcommon :

" Why is he honour'd with a Poet's name,
" Who neither knows, nor would obferve a rule ?"

The anfwer is, if he cannot reafon, he

(*i*) *Shade of Pope*, 3d Ed. p. 51-2.

can

can rhyme, both to the ear, and to the eye. Take from *the Purfuits*, as the beft illuftration, a few examples, which, in *accuracy*, emulate Gifford, and in *precifenefs*, excel Pope:

Crachrode	-	God,
Fac fimiles	-	Fees,
Price - -	-	Clarifs
Malone -	-	me all one,
Shewn -	-	Malone,
A. S. - -	-	guefs,
done - -	-	Alciphron,
eye - -	-	dignity
equal - -	-	the fequel
vie - -	-	dignity
rule - -	-	fool
prieft - -	-	digeft.
tint - -	-	point
view - -	-	too
new - -	-	too

Thefe fpecimens, from a greater colle&ion, may well induce you to confefs, with Be-nedict, after he had made fome indifferent verfes : " very *ominous endings!* No; I was " not born under a rhyming planet(*k*)."

I will

(*k*) I will add, from your *Odes*, your *Epiftles*, and your *Purfuits*, fome additional proofs of the truth of Bene-

di&'s

I will now clofe my PROOFS, of your *in-ability* to write POETRY, with a few remarks on your *character* of *the favour'd* BARD,

dict's fentiment, and of the propriety of your adopt-ing it:

Eaft - - -	dreft
birth - - -	earth
ftrew'd - -	food
ftore - - -	pow'r
Sphere - -	difappear.
fraught - -	thought
caufe - - -	laws.
work - - -	Burke
Purfuits - -	Pufs in boots
own - - -	alone
Rolle - -	Soul
fearch - -	Church
retire - -	Choir
again - -	men
loth - - -	growth
turn - - -	difcern
horfe - -	courfe.

It was fuch *ominous endings*, which, induced the clown, in *As you like it*, to obferve : " I'll rhyme you fo, eight " years together, dinners and fuppers, and fleeping " hours, excepted : It is the right butter-woman's rate " to market." I fay nothing to your frequent facrifice of the grammar rule to the rhyme: As run—fhun; flies—cries; for *fhunn'd, fly,* &c.

which

which was written by you with great elaboration, and has been praifed by fome critics, as excellent, beyond all praife.

Little need be faid to your introduction, with "the dread refiftlefs pow'r, that works " *deep felt*," except, that your *deep felt* is not quite proper: Well: your favoured *Bard*, " with *loftier* foul, paints what he " feels." *Loftier*, than what, or whom ? Not furely than the foregoing " *dread re-* " *fiftlefs* power;" a comparifon, which would be abfurd, both in reafon, and in rhyme. If there be neither poet, nor perfon, with whom your *Bard* can be compared, in your verfes; then, your epithet, *loftier*, cannot be defended: There would not have been the fame objection, if you had given your bard the lof*tieft* foul. By leaving out two verfes (*l*), in your laft edition, in confequence of the objections of a

---

(*l*) " Paints what he feels in characters of light,
" *Hears in each blaft fome confecrated rhime,*
" *Trac'd by the fpirit of the troublous clime.*"
Hears fome confecrated rhyme trac'd! Through what
   clime ?

poet,

poet, you make your bard turn too quickly, after painting what he felt ; and turn *without a mover.* " He turns : and *inflanta-* " *neous,* all around, cliffs whiten, waters " murmur, voices found :" your adjective *inflantaneous* will not agree with your verbs *whiten, murmur,* and *found:* and it mult, therefore, be *inflantaneously,* or fome other *adverb,* fuch as *inflantly,* except, indeed, poetic licenfe allows ungrammatical impropriety.

You go on to fing that oft your bard, " his fteps ideal hafte to rock *and* [or] " groves, the wildernefs *or* wafte:" In verfes, which arrogate *fublimity,* I fay nothing to the *tautology* of groves, *wildernefes, wafies.* You now find a fit prototype for your *Bard,* in BRUNO, though not legitimate rhymes in *brow* and *below,* nor a proper accent in *fojourn.* " Then as down " ragged cliffs the torrent roar'd, *proflrate* " great nature's prefent God ador'd." *Proflrate adored* will not do, if an attention to grammatical rules be as neceffary in poetry, as in profe : you mult find an *adverb,* inftead

inftead of an *adjective*, for your *verb :* Why
not adopt *lowly*, which was ufed by Milton, in your fenfe? Well: " The powers
" of harmony refort" to your bard, after he
had been fadly frightened by your " fub-
" ftantial horrors, *and* [of] eternal doom."
By your unfkilfulnefs you now introduce
fuch *flafky darknefs* into the operations of
your *mufical powers*, that it is a hard tafk to
find the grammatical connection, between
the nominatives and verbs ; " while to their
" *numerous* [number'd] paufe, his choral
" paffions dread accordance keep." Yet
little is that obfcurity, when compared with
that " cloud of pride, which oft doth dark"
the character of your bard ; and oft doth
urge your fublimity beyond the verge of
fenfe : " Such is the *Poet*," fay you : " bold
" without *confine* (*m*), imagination's char-
" ter'd *libertine*." Your *confine*, if it were
properly accented by you, is obnoxious to
a charge of impropriety. Yes, your bard
is without *confine* ; for he can *ride* down a

(*m*) Purfuits, 7 Ed. p. 300.

S s 4

tem-

tempeſtuous tide, while other poets muſt *ſail* down ſuch a tide : And you might as well have cheered the readers of this incomprehenſible character, with this comfortable intimation from Dryden :

> " 'Twas ebbing darkneſs, paſt the noon of night,
> " And phoſphor on the confines of the light."

In this character of the *true Bard*, laboured into verſe, I have now ſhewn, though it be ſhort, many blunders. If one objection, which was drawn from an offence againſt poetic taſte, rather than from rules of grammar, induced you to omit two verſes, which were in the firſt delineation of this character, ſo many incontrovertible objections demand the expulſion of the whole character of the favorite Bard, from your *Purſuits*. I ſhall otherwiſe cry out, fy on the writer, and fy, fy, fy, on the critic; the one to ſcribble ; the other to praiſe ſuch " heroick fuſtian:

> " As, forc'd from wind guns lead itſelf can fly,
> " And pond'rous ſlugs cut ſwiftly thro' the ſky."

PROOFS

Proofs *that you* CANNOT WRITE *at all*.

He, who undertakes to write, in the Englifh language, ought to write according to the rules of the grammar of that language: Hence follows another canon, that he muft have a particular regard to *grammatical purity*. If, indeed, fuch an author fhould arrogate to himfelf the high character of being the *firft fcholar*, and the *firft poet*, of the age, it becomes ftill more neceffary that, in his compofitions, he fhould be, not only, attentive to grammatical purity, but that he fhould add the higher qualities of elocution, which give energy, and grace, to his difcourfe.

I fhall, in laying down my proofs, begin, as all grammarians begin, with the article. Although Lowth has very ably explained the *ufe*, and the *application*, of the article; which is a prefix to fubftantives, for defining their fignifications; you feem not to know, that fuch a part of fpeech exifts in our language. I will prove my pofition by examples: In [the] " advertifement to the 7th " edition," you fay " *the* [my] Poem on the " Purfuits

" Purfuits of Literature, I have *revifed* with
" *great care:*" and in this *revifed* edition,
p. 442, you fay [the] " End of the Poem :"
In thefe fhort, but remarkable, paffages, are
no fewer than three blunders. You talk of
Dr. Douglas, [the] author; of Dr. Rennel,
[the] author; of Dr. Gillies, [the] author;
of the Rev. Mr. Nares, [the] Editor of the
Britifh Critic: As to Dr. Parr, indeed, you
lament, when you think of fuch a fcholar,
and *the* [his] wafte of erudition (*a*). As
whipper-in, you mount Steevens in [the]
rear, and " Calvin in [the] front." In your
avowed works, there is the fame ignoranco
of the ufe of *the article* (*b*); a circumftance

(*a*) Purfuits, 6 Ed. p. 53.

(*b*) In your *Runic Odes*, may be feen, without the
article; advertifement; argument. In your *Effay on
Rowley*, may be obferved, without the article: preface;
contents; as to [the] metre, they are of opinion; as to
[the] ancient language. [Effay, p. 66-7.] In your
Purfuits, 7 Ed. p. 382, you fing of great ftatefmen, who:

    " ———— Some Mantuan ftrain rehearfe,
    " In [a] *fchoolboy* conteft for a hackney'd verfe."

In the laft verfe, the judicious critic may fee two blunders; the want of the article; and the no-adjective
fchoolboy.

this

this, which, with fcholars, will be deemed
a ftrong proof, that the fame author only
could commit the fame blunders.

From the article, which, in our language,
is fo important, for giving clearnefs to the
fenfe, and precifion to the ftyle, let us next
advert to *the fubftantive, the name* of whatever is written, or conceived. I have already
fhown how much you confound the *noun*
with the adjective, and the adjective with
the noun. You have *fympofiack* for *fympofi-
arch;* you fpeak often of a *mafter* work,
inftead of a *mafterly* work (*c*); of *mafter*
miffes (*d*); and you have more than once
fubftituted *two* adjectives for *one* fubftantive; as *cuftomary black, healing bland.* By
the abfurd practice of fubftituting a wrong
noun for a right one, you often make downright nonfenfe of a fentence (*e*):

" Soft;

(*c*) In your Odes, p. 24, you have committed the
fame fault, " With *meteor* glare devoid of force:" As
the proper adjective, Milton had ufed *meteorous.*

(*d*) Purfuits, 7 Ed. p. 61.

(*e*) " The fophifts unabafh'd yet rear their *head.*"
You thus give to Godwin, and to Volney, only *one*
" head:

" Soft ; and o'er *female failings* lightly pass ;

" And may *Aglaia* lead them to *their* glass."

You, thus, lead up *female failings*, instead of the *fair sex*, to *their glass.* You place *connubial glories* on the head of *female failings*, which *female failings* you make to tread life's domestic, *happier*, stage; [happier than what?] and, by an Ovidian metamorphosis, you transform the said *female failings* into

" The guardians, comforts, teachers of mankind(*f*)."

By thus *rumbling in a storm of verse*, without attending to that important part of grammar, the *noun*, you ramble into manifest nonsense. I have already shown, that you attend as little to the true use of the *adjective*. Who ever saw such an adjective as *Straw-*

---

head: Now ; the misfortune is, that they have two mischievous *heads*. [7 Ed. p. 368.] In a similar spirit of blunder, you speak of *one* Boaden, and *one* Waldron, who wrote *two* pamphlets. The fact is, that each of these Authors, who are full as well known, as a certain anonymous scribbler, wrote *one* pamphlet.

(*f*) I quote from the 7th Ed. of the Pursuits, p. 148, which Edition was *revised with great care :* By what poetic fiction, then, could you substitute *female failings* for the *fair sex*, through a dozen verses?

berry ?

berry? Strawberry Horace(*g*); fuch an adjective as mafter? Mafter miffes (*h*).   After
a thoufand mifapplications of the *adjective*,
you " proclaim *aloud* the proletarian reign,"
by giving a new fenfe to this *proletarian* adjective, with *proletarian* blunder (*i*).

In

(*g*) None but yourfelf can be your parallel: You have
your *zig-zag* verfe ; and *coxcomb ftrains* : In your
Chinefe Epiftle, p. 13, there is *plume-pluckt*, and in p.
19, is *Anglo-Ruffic :* Add to thefe adjectives, *cryptogamik,
tittle-tattle, battle-flain, goffamery.*

(*h*) For your *mafter miffes*, you furnifh proper companions, by giving them " pleafure miffes," in your
Chinefe Epiftle, p. 27. *Mafter miffes*, and *pleafure
miffes*, may do well in China; but, they will not do in
England!

(*i*) You quote Old Littelton for faying, " that *Pro-
" letarius* is a man who giveth nothing to the Common
" Wealth but only a fupply of Children." [Pair of
Epiftles, p. 30.] *Old* Spelman knew neither that *word*,
nor this fignification of it. You quote, however, with
your ufual felicity, *Ennius*, and *Aulus Gellius*, on the
point. The firft fcholar of the age would not, for the
world, quote *Ainfworth* for *Proletarius*, poor, beggarly,
vulgar ; nor Johnfon for *Proletarian*, in the fame fenfe,
who gives, as an example, from *Hudibras*, " *Proleta-
" rian* tything men." Neither would you condefcend
to adopt from Afh and Cole, *Proletaneous*, a *numerous
offspring :*

In this fame confufion of the parts of fpeech, you continually fubftitute the *adjective* for the *adverb*; as I have, already, fhown, by a thoufand examples (*k*): You write, indeed, as if you thought, that true poetry can exift with grammatical inaccuracy; and genuine wit be found in palpable blunder:

" Oh, think not, mafter! more true dullnefs lies
" In Folly's cap, than Wifdom's grave difguife."

Come we now to the *verb*, which is fo fignificant in every fentence. I have already fhown, in your works avowed, and difavowed, that you feem not to know either the value, or the ufe, in conftruction, of the verb (*l*). You appear, from your practice,

to

offspring: This, then, is the fenfe of your *Proletarian*; which very properly belongs to you: But, you would rather blunder, than borrow from fuch unlearned men, as Cole, and Afh.

(*k*) In your *Purfuits*, the 7th Edit. revifed, p. 366, you have *loud* for *loudly*; *worthy* for *worthily*; and twice in the fame note (*y*), [6 Ed. p. 150] *chief* for *chiefly*.

(*l*) I will here fubjoin a few additional examples of your ungrammatical practice: " armies have fkeletons,

" and

to know nothing at all of its fubjunctive
mood, although Lowth has fully explained
its

" and fermons too." This arrangement only conveys,
that armies have both *fkeletons* and *fermons*: But, your
context required, that your *fermons* alfo fhould have
fkeletons. Again: " The life fprings iffue, and their
" force impart." Impart to what? Your active verb
impart has *no fecond object*, which that verb requires.
" When the reader *has* [fhall have] confidered."—
" Doctor Parr *will* [can] beft explain." " I could [can]
" hardly pleafe." In your *Effay on Rowley* you have
been, remarkably, inattentive to the regimen of the
verb: And I will particularize your errors, in this refpect; in order that fcholars may fee the truth of my pofitions, namely, that you cannot write at all; and that
the fame perfon, who wrote the *Effay on Rowley*, alfo
wrote the *Purfuits of Literature*. In p. 8, of *the Effay*,
" the fafety *and* well being of mankind *is*" [are]. In
the fame page, " the animofity *and* heat of any conteft *is*"
[are.] In p. 76, " the inflexion *and* orthography of
" words *is*" [are] In p. 82, " what have [has] now
" been laid before the reader." Compare with thefe
blunders, which are not accidental, the following inaccuracies in your *Purfuits*: Your fhort addrefs to the
reader, which is prefixed to your 7th edition, has four
blunders in it: It wants the article *the* in the firft line;
in the laft paragraph, the fubjunctive mood is difregarded;
when you fay, " if the poem is [be] read;" and your
intimation,

its meaning, and its value: Of this pofition,
I have already given fome incidental proofs.
I will here add a few more ftriking exam-
ples: " If Mr. Wakefield *does* [do] not

intimation, in the laft claufe, exhibits the verb in an
ungrammatical form, when you add, " that the firft
dialogue *was* firft publifhed, in May, 1794, the *fecond*
and *third* [was] in June, 1796, and the fourth in July,
1797: But, you could not grammatically apply a fingular verb, either exprefsly, or virtually, to your *fecond,
and third,* dialog*ues*, not dialogue. We thus, in an addrefs of two pages, perceive *four* blunders, which would
of themfelves fhow, that you cannot write. The mul-
titude of errors, and the irregular forms of the verb,
which, continually, occur in your introductory letter to
this corrected edition, would demonftrate that pofition,
if there were not a thoufand other proofs. In p. vii you
have, " If I *had* [had] any private end:" You fubjoin,
nonfenfically, " if I *am* believed, I *am* believed:" " It
" is neither,, Mr. Pitt, nor Lord Lanfdown, nor Mr.
" Fox, nor Mr. Gray, who *are* [is] neceffary to the
" function:" [Purf. 6 Ed. p. 208.] The disjunctive
neither requires the fingular verb. You doubt, in 7 Ed.
p. 83, " whether the drowfinefs *and* gravity of Mr. War-
" ton, and Mr. Steevens, *and* their brother-commentators
" *was* [were] in confequence:" If to write, blunderingly,
be a fign of drowfinefs, there can be no doubt, whether
you *drowfe*

" write.

" write. It is [were] devoutly to be wished.
" Whether Mr. K. underſtands [underſtand].
" If he is appointed [if he ſhould be ap-
" pointed]. Unleſs the province *is* [be] ad-
" miniſtered, it is [it were] more deſirable.
" If it terminat*es* [terminate]; if the end of
" it *is* [be] intrigue; if the girls *are* [be]
" debauched:" In theſe laſt examples we
may ſee, that the ſenſe is marred, by the
ungrammatical conſtruction. It is extremely
remarkable, that the ſame ignorance of the
ſubjunctive mood ſhews itſelf in all your
writings, acknowledged, and not acknowledged: This fact, when corroborated, as it
is, by other circumſtances, muſt induce
ſcholars to be of opinion, that the ſame pen,
which thus betrays itſelf, ſcribbled them
all (*m*).

Of thoſe important parts of ſpeech, the

(*m*) See your Purſuits, 6 Ed. 71, 72, 75, 77, 83, 107,
&c. Eſſay on Rowley, p. 7, 9, 12, 53.   Add to all the
examples in the text, the following paſſage: " If Mr.
" Pitt means [mean] that taxes ſhould be an object
" [objects] of wit." [Purſ. 6 Ed. p. 165.] We have
here, in a dozen words, *two* blunders.

Prepoſition,

Prepofition, the *Conjunction*, the *Interjec-tion*, I will here fay nothing; becaufe, I have, incidentally, marked your inaccura-cies in the ufe of them (*n*), in my notice of the other parts of fpeech of ftill greater con-fequence.

We have now feen, from a thoufand in-ftances, how far the *firft fcholar* of the age can write, with *grammatical purity:* Let us next examine, briefly, whether the *firft poet* add to his other merits, as a writer, the higher qualities of elocution, which give energy, and grace, to his poetry, and profe. In every page of your Pursuits, you affect what grammarians have denominated the *barbarifm* (*o*): Both the *term*, and the reproba-tion

---

(*n*) You frequently ufe *or* for *and*; *or* for *nor*; *nor* for *or*; *lo*, for *lo!*

(*o*) As you are a great dealer in *ftale ftuff*, fo are you an extenfive broker in *barbarifms:* You have Borgo-allegro, *Capriccio, extravaganza, meffa-baffa, armiluftrum, excurfus, ci-devant, efcopetterie, diablerie, tennanto-phobia, caninity, morofophifts, concetto, durandana,* warkworthian, thelypthoric, Switzer-ruffico-Kamtfchatcan, *Morgu, Bofs.* I will add no more from a collection of a thou-fand

tion of the thing, we borrowed of the Greeks, who preferved their language, in its native purity, for fo many centuries, by the contempt, which that learned, and elegant, people, conftantly expreffed for *the barbarifm*, and for their own writers, who prefumed to affect fuch *foreign terms*.

You abound ftill more in another grammatical fault, called the *folecifm*, which grammarians reprobate, with equal indignation; becaufe the *folecifm* fhows greater ignorance than the *barbarifm*. I have already produced a thoufand examples, which fhow, that you, continually, confound the adjective with the fubftantive, the adverb with the adjective, and the modes of the verb, the fubjunctive, and the indicative, with each other.

To the *barbarifm*, and the *folecifm*, you frequently add the fault, which grammarians

---

fand *barbarifms*:   Let Englifhmen imitate the Greeks, in making a ftand, for their language, againft the lawlefs innovation of the *grecifed* affectation of a *proletaneous* pedant, who delights to *grecife*.

reject

rians reject under the name of *the impro-priety* (*p*).

You abound, alfo, through all your writings, in a fault, not fo much againft the *purity* of grammar, as againft the grace, and energy, of ftyle : I mean a frequent repetition of unneceffary words, which is termed, by grammarians, *battology*, from a *proletarian* poet, called *Battus* (*q*). You have " *fum*, and *fubftance* (*r*) ; large, and abund-" ant, ftream (*s*) ; null, and void (*t*) ; all the " year round (*u*) ; an abyfs of darknefs, and " obfcurity (*x*) ; pleafure and fatisfac-" tion (*y*) ;" with thofe examples of batto-logy, from your *Effay on Rowley*, let us compare fome inftances, from your *Purfuits*; in order to identify the writer; " Code and

---

(*p*) You often blunder in fubftituting a wrong word for a right one ; Sympofiacks for Sympofiarchs : proletarian for proletaneous ; twang for tang ; enough for enow ; naturalift for botanift, &c.

(*q*) See Bailley, in *vo*.

(*r*) Effay on Rowley, Pref.

(*s*) Ib. p. 4. (*t*) Ib. p. 7. (*u*) Ib. p. 15. (*x*) Ib. p. 50.
(*y*) Ib. p. 117.

" volume

" volume (z); name, ftile, and title (a);
" Strawbry Horace on the hill (b); foliage
" dark, and cyprefs gloom (c); boyifh days
" at fchool:" For this practice of batto-
logy, yourfelf fhall affign an appropriate
reafon; " a mighty and majeftic river in its
" courfe through a diverfity of countries not
" only winds and murmurs in the vallies,
" but contends and foams among rocks, and
" precipices, and the confluence of torrents.
" Still its tendency is to the ocean, to which
" it pays its laft tribute, and is finally loft
" in that immenfity (d):" Herein, you
out-gilpin Gilpin himfelf, whofe appropriate ftyle of topographical defcription, you
are ftudious to reprobate (e). Let me add
to thofe remarkable fpecimens, the opening
of your *Political Dramatift* :

" *The Houfe was up*; the long debate was o'er;
" And Addington prefided now no more;
" Nor voice, nor vote along the benches crept,
" And corn committees bak'd their bread and flept;

(z) 6 Ed. p. 195. (a) Ib. p. — (b) Ib. p. 35.
(c) Ib. p. 8.
(d) Ib. p. 221. (e) Ib. p. 275.

" Somnus

" Somnus and Ceres no fage Members fcorn,

" But own the poppy grows among the corn."

Who, indeed, can refrain from fleep, when fuch genuine *battology* is fung in *lullabies divine*; " the balm of Dulnefs trickling in their " ears!" I will only add, that your readers may wake to hail thee,

" Th' immortal Battus of the prefent day,

" The laft great prophet of tautology."

It is thus apparent, that you are fufficiently acquainted with the art of multiplying words; without, indeed, knowing the meaning, or the application of them : But, you know very little of the art of arranging words, fo as to form a *fentence*. I have already fubmitted fome proofs of this pofition : I will now only add a few examples. Take, as a fingular inftance, the conclufion of " Advertife- " ment to the feventh Edition of your Pur- " fuits corrected," which is printed in the following manner : " It is remarkable : the " Speaker was William Pitt; the Reporter, " Samuel Johnfon. No more." Can there be any writing more aukward, and ungrammatical ? The laft fentence, confifting of only

two

two words, does not make any fenfe : For the
two words, *no more*, ftanding thus infulated
by themfelves, have not the leaft meaning.
Take another inftance, from the Introductory
Letter to the fame corrected edition : " I of-
" fer the poetry to thofe who are converfant
" with the ftrength, fimplicity and dignity
" of [the poetry of] Dryden and Pope, and
" [to] them alone.   I fubmit both my po-
" ems, The Purfuits of Literature, and The
" Imperial Epiftle," in this fpirit [what fpi-
" rit?] and with this confidence [what con-
" fidence?] to the public.   There are men
" (and women too) who underftand." Now;
in this laft fentence, thus infulated, by the
full point, both before, and after it, there is
not any compleat fenfe.   True : It might be
eafily made compleat fenfe, by adding but
two words : There are men, who underftand
my object.   You afterwards fay, in a feparate
fentence : " A little experience is fufficient
" for the obferving."   Here is no compleat
fenfe : The obferving what? You begin a
fubfequent paragraph thus : " I refume the
" reflections of fuffering humanity *amid the*
T t 4
" *wreck*

" *wreck of intellect.* This was not the an-
" cient character of Philofophy " I fay nothing either to the nonfenfe, or to the inco-
herence, of thefe nonfenfical, and incoherent,
fentences : But, I object to their want of any
compleat fenfe, in fupport of my pofition,
that you do not know how to arrange words,
fo as to form a fentence. (*f*)

   In forming fuch fentences, your unfkilful-

(*f*) Compare with the foregoing, the following examples from your *Effay on Rowley*; in order to eftablifh
the *univerfality* of your practice, in not forming com leat
fentences : " A fhort difquifition. It is this. Whether
fuperiority of genius, &c." [p. 97.]   There is no fenfe
in your three words, " It is this." pointed off, as they
are, into a feparate fentence.   You afterwards begin,
and end, a diftinct paragraph thus [p. 113:]   " That
" he was not ignorant of the French, Saxon and Latin
" tongues."   In this whole paragraph there is not a
compleat fentiment.   You have a dozen other paragraphs, which are all equally defective.   [p. 111-14.]
It is eafy to perceive, that the fame pen, which fcribbled
the ill-conftructed fentences, in your *Effay on Rowley,*
alfo fcribbled the illconftructed fentences in your *Purfuits,* and in your *Chinefe Epiftle.* which, in p. 9, has the
following imperfect fentence: " Perhaps *fome architects*
" might conjecture by the help of a *marine builder's*
" *dictionary.*"

                                              nefs

nefs was eafily affifted by your affectation: and your ignorance of the neceffary art of punctuation, readily effected what began in affectation, and ended in unfkilfulnefs. I have already fhewn, by examples, that you do not underftand the purpofe, and ufe of the *Comma;* becaufe you interpofe it, fometimes, between the fubject, and the verb to which it relates. You conftantly confound the femicolon [;] with the colon [:] and this laft with the period [.]: In truth, your continued blunders, in this laft refpect, have perplexed your grammatical conftruction, and have made downright nonfenfe of many of your fentences. You have, in all your writings, both in the acknowledged, and the unacknowledged, confounded the point of interrogation with the point of interjection; and, fometimes, the comma with both.

I will here clofe my Proofs, that you cannot write at all: and they are decifive; becaufe I have feldom failed to exemplify every objection by fome apt quotation from your writings. The judicious few, who may have honoured thefe proofs with their attention,

tion, will be tempted to exclaim with the poet :

"Write, then, and ftill write on, no matter why,
"Nor what, nor how ; fo Becket will but buy !"

The CONCLUSION.

I have now finifhed what I propofed to fay concerning *your* PURSUITS, under *three* feveral *Heads*. Knowing neither you, nor your writings, I did not ftep out of my way to meddle with either; but you came to me, and offered perfonal infult, in the language of defiance. I have plucked off your " vain mafk;" I have looked at your bare face ; I have examined your boaftful fcribble : But, to fuch a body of heterogeneous matter, whether imported from Bœotia, or from Botany-Bay, it is hard to give a name ; and of fuch a mingled mafs, it is ftill more difficult to give an analyfis. All mixed bodies take their names from the predominance of fome particular fubftance in them, either good, or bad : The ftandard of our gold coins is in the proportion of eleven parts of *gold*, to one part of *alloy :* Your *Blackmail* confifts, as the

the trial of *the pixe* has proved, of eleven
parts of alloy, and one part of gold; and
may well be denominated, in the language of
our affayers, " *drofs* unclean." Until, however, our Chymifts fhall have examined, by
appropriate experiments, this non-defcript
congeries, in order to afcertain its nature, and
to affign it a name, from its prevailing quality, I fhall call this vaft volume of fcribble,
by the well-known denomination of BAL-
DERDASH: For, in the anticipating couplet
of Pope:

" So all your profe, and verfe, are much the fame;
" This profe on ftilts; that, poetry fal'n lame."

Yet; as it is the boaft of modern difcoveries to find fome thing ufeful in the mean-
eft matter, fo in your balderdafh may be
found fome ufe. A volume of 444 pages,
for 8s. 6d. may appear, at firft fight, to be
rather dear; confidering that it is not illumi-
nated by *Bulmer's blaze.* But, when the
teachers of our youth fhall confider, that
they are now provided in one volume, although at a great expence, with *every poffible
fpecimen of bad writing*, which may be put
before

before their pupils, as examples of the errors of writings, that are at once fophiftical in argument, and ungrammatical in ftyle, I truft the faid teachers will be of opinion, that they have, at laft, a good bargain in *your Purfuits:*

" Yet, if by chance, you here and there impart
" Some fparks of wit, or glimmerings of art,
" If, by miftake, you blunder upon fenfe,
" Good nature will forgive the firft offence."

Amidft the vaftnefs, and variety, of your learning, you appear to have forgotten an adage of *Terence*, which, when you fat down to write lampoon, ought to have been hung up before your eyes : *Quique vult dicit, que non vult audiet;* or, in the language of our great-great-grand-mothers, " He, that fpeak-
" eth what he will, fhall hear what he will
" not." You have provided, by your af-fumed invifibility, that you fhall not be feen : Whether you have provided, equally, by *deafnefs,* that you fhall not hear, I know not. Whatever may be your *coat of darknefs,* it has not wholly concealed you from my ken : Whatever may be *your malady of not marking,* like Falftaff's, I will fay, as *the*

Chief

Chief Juſtice ſaid to the Knight, who had
playfulneſs, without malignity, " to puniſh
" you by the heels would amend the atten-
" tion of your ears :" Yet; whether you
ſpeak, or whether you be ſilent, is to me a
matter of indifference.   From *your Eſſay* on
Rowley, I have learned, that " to reaſon is
" one thing; to joke is another; that *Truth*
has at all times defied the power of ridicule (*t*) :"   Like other men, who attack
without provocation, and announce anſwers,
without any purpoſe of publiſhing them,
you may think of taking up the hard taſk of
fully anſwering unanſwerable objections.   It
may aſſiſt your determination to be told, that,
in addition to the thouſand errors, which I
have now pointed out in your poetry, and
profe, I have in reſerve a hundred pages of
manifeſt blunders, which I incidentally collected, as I went through your *Purſuits;* and
which an intimation of a wiſh from you
would induce me to ſend to the preſs, as a
warning to our youth, when they may in-

(*t*) Eſſay on Rowley, p. 51-2.

cline

cline to commence authors, not to look, for examples of good writing, into your *Pur-suits*. Meantime, I will take the liberty, at parting, of offering you Dryden's whole-fome advice,

" Learn to write well, or not to write at all;"

and of inculcating upon you the valuable maxim of Pope:

" Let fuch teach others, who themfelves excel;
" And cenfure freely, who have written well."

The End.

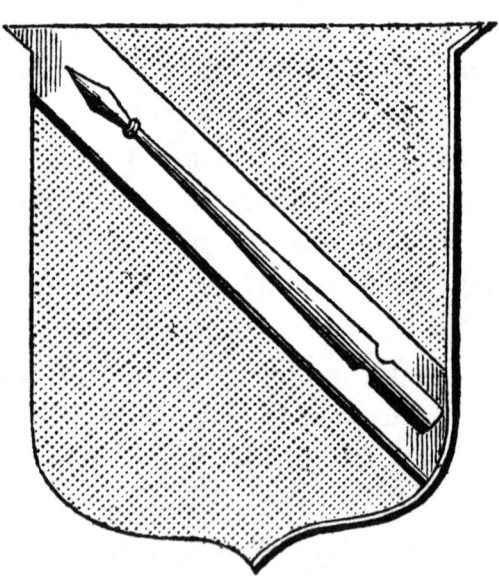

ERRATA,

In the APOLOGY:

Page 171, del. the (,) between *accuſer* and *is*.

187, the *three proper letters*, which were attributed to Spenſer, were written by Gabriel Harvey.

191, Gayarum *for* Grayarum.

—— woe *for* woo.

217, Emanuel *for* Magdalen.

252, heeps *for* keeps.

255, 1 Ed. of Camden's Rem. in 1605 *for* 1614.

259, is *for* are.

264, enough *for* enow.

286, Romeo and Juliet is quoted inſtead of *Hamlet*.

294, Underhill *for* Underwood.

318, del. the quotation of *all our bills*, from Timon of Athens.

353, a *for* an.

369, are *for* is.

—— have *for* has.

413, *Abbot* for *Lord* of Miſrule.

421, Rym. Foed. pub. in 1705 *for* 1715.

425, 1744 *for* 1742.

456, Cambrige *for* Cambridge.

470, 1763 *for* 1752.

472, belongs *for belong*.

474, ravel-rout *for* revel rout.

476, was *for* were.

523, Warwickſhire *for* Worceſterſhire.

589, Hand and hand *for* Hand in hand.

ERRATA,

In the SUPPLEMENTAL APOLOGY :

Page 52, iduuced *for* induced.

      82, may *for* many.

    153, aprentage *for* parentage.

    545, Primatif *for* Primitif.

    619, con-confiftent *for* confiftent.

PUBLISHER'S ADVERTISEMENT

EIGHTEENTH CENTURY SHAKESPEARE

During the one hundred and seven years covered by this series, the reputation of William Shakespeare as poet and dramatist rose from a controversial and highly qualified acceptance by post-Restoration critics and "improvers" to the almost idolatrous admiration of the early Romantics and their immediate precursors. Imposing its own standards and interpretations upon Shakespeare, the Eighteenth Century scrutinized his work in various lights. Certain qualities of the plays were isolated and discussed by a parade of learned, cantankerous, and above all self-assured commentators.

Thirty-five of the most important and representative books and pamphlets are here presented in twenty-six volumes; many of the works, through the very fact of their limited circulation have become extremely scarce, and when obtainable, expensive and fragile. The series will be useful not only for the student of Shakespeare's reputation in the period, but for all those interested in eighteenth century taste, taste-making, scholarship, and theatre. Within the series we may follow the arguments and counter-arguments as they appeared to contemporary playgoers and readers, and the shifting critical emphases characteristic of the whole era.

In an effort to provide responsible texts of these works, strict editorial principles have been established and followed. All relevant editions have been compared, the best selected, and the reasons for the choice given. Furthermore, at least one other copy, frequently three or more, have been collated with the copy actually reproduced, and the collations recorded. In cases where variants or cancels exist, every attempt has been made to provide both earlier and later or indifferently varying texts, as appendices. Each volume is preceded by a short preface discussing the text, the publication history, and, when necessary, critical and biographical considerations not readily available.

1. 1692 **Thomas Rymer**
A Short View of Tragedy (1693)
xvi, 184p.

2. 1693 **John Dennis**
The Impartial Critick: or, some observations upon a late book, entitled, A Short View of Tragedy, written by Mr. Rymer, and dedicated to the Right Honourable Charles Earl of Dorset, etc. (1693)
xvi, 52p.
    1712 **John Dennis**
An Essay on the Genius and Writings of Shakespear: with some Letters of Criticism to the Spectator (1712)
xxii, 68p.

3. 1694 **Charles Gildon [ed.]**
Miscellaneous Letters and Essays, on Several Subjects. Philosophical, Moral, Historical, Critical, Amorous, etc. in Prose and Verse (1694)
xvi, 132p.

4. 1710 **Charles Gildon**
The Life of Mr. Thomas Betterton, the late Eminent Tragedian. Wherein The Action and Utterance of the Stage, Bar, and Pulpit, are distinctly consider'd ... To which is added, The Amorous Widow, or the Wanton Wife ... Written by Mr. Betterton. Now first printed from the Original Copy (1710)
xvi, 176, 87p.

5. 1726 **Lewis Theobald**
Shakespeare restored: or, A Specimen of the Many Errors, As well Committed, as Unamended, by Mr. Pope in his Late Edition of this Poet (1726)
xiii, 194p. 4°

6. 1747 **William Guthrie**
An Essay upon English Tragedy with Remarks upon the Abbe de Blanc's Observations on the English Stage (?1747)
34p.
    1749 **John Holt**
An Attempte to Rescue that Aunciente, English Poet, and

Play-wrighte, Maister Williaume Shakespere, from the Maney Errours, faulsely charged on him, by Certaine New-fangled Wittes and to let him speak for Himself, as right well he wotteth, when Freede from the many Careless Mistakeings, of the Heedless first Imprinters, of his Workes (1749)
94p.

7. 1748 **Thomas Edwards**
The Canons of Criticism and Glossary. Being a Supplement to Mr. Warburton's Edition of Shakespear. Collected from the Notes in that celebrated Work, and proper to be bound up with it. To which are added, The Trial of the Letter Υ alias Y; and Sonnets (Seventh Edition, with Additions 1765)
368p.

8. 1748 **Peter Whalley**
An Enquiry into the Learning of Shakespeare (1748)
84p.
1767 **Richard Farmer**
As Essay on the Learning of Shakespeare . . . the Second Edition, with Large Additions (1767)
viii, 96p.

9. 1752 **William Dodd**
The Beauties of Shakespeare: Regularly selected from each Play, With a General Index, Digesting them under Proper Heads. Illustrated with Explanatory Notes and Similar Passages from Ancient and Modern Authors (1752)
2v., xxiv, 264; iv, 258p.

10. 1753 **Charlotte Ramsay Lennox**
Shakespear Illustrated . . . with Critical Remarks (1753-4)
3v., xiv, 292; iv, 276; iv, 312p.

11. 1765 **William Kenrick**
A Review of Doctor Johnson's New Edition of Shakespeare: In which the Ignorance, or Inattention of That Editor is exposed, and the Poet Defended from the Persecution of his Commentators (1765)
xvi, 136p.
1766 **Thomas Tyrwhitt**
Observations and Conjectures upon some Passages of

Shakespeare (1766)
ii, 56p.

12. 1769 Elizabeth Montagu
An Essay on the Writings and Genius of Shakespear, compared with the Greek and French dramatic Poets. With some
remarks upon the misrepresentations of Mons. de Voltaire
(1769)
iv, 288p.

13. 1774 William Richardson
1784 Essays on Shakespeare's Dramatic Characters: With an
1789 Illustration of Shakespeare's Representation of National
Character, in that of Fluellen (sixth edition 1812)
xii, 448p.

14. 1775 Elizabeth Griffith
The Morality of Shakespeare's Drama Illustrated (1775)
xvi, 528p.

15. 1777 Maurice Morgann
An Essay on the Dramatic Character of Sir John Falstaff
(1777)
xii, 186p.

16. 1783 Joseph Ritson
Remarks Critical and Illustrative of the last Edition of
Shakespeare [by George Steevens, 1778], (1783)
viii, 240p.
1788 Joseph Ritson
The Quip Modest; A few Words by way of Supplement to
Remarks, Critical and Illustrative on the Text and Notes of
the Last Edition of Shakespeare: occasioned by a Republication of that Edition (1788, first issue)
viii, 32p.
With the preface (revised) to the second issue of *The Quip
Modest* (1788)
viii p.

17. 1785 Thomas Whately
Remarks on some of the Characters of Shakespere, Edited

by Richard Whately (Third edition 1839)
128p.

18. 1785   **John Monck Mason**
    1797   Comments on the Several Editions of Shakespeare's Plays,
    1798   Extended to those of Malone and Steevens (1807)
            xvi, 608p.

19. 1786   **John Philip Kemble**
            Macbeth and King Richard the Third: An Essay, in answer to
            Remarks on some of the Characters of Shakespeare [by
            Thomas Whately] (1817)
            xii, 172p.

20. 1792   **Joseph Ritson**
            Cursory Criticisms on the Edition of Shakespeare published
            by Edmond Malone (1792)
            x, 104p.
            Edmond Malone
            A Letter to the Rev. Richard Farmer, D.D. Master of
            Emanuel College, Cambridge; Relative to the Edition of
            Shakespeare, published in 1790. And Some Late Criticisms
            on that work (1792)
            ii, 40p.

21. 1796   **William Henry Ireland**
            An Authentic Account of the Shakespeare Manuscripts (1796)
            ii, 44p.
    1799   **William Henry Ireland**
            Vortigern, An Historical Tragedy, In five Acts; Represented
            at the Theatre Royal, Drury Lane. And Henry the Second,
            An Historical Drama. Supposed to be written by the Author
            of Vortigern (1799)
            80, iv, 79p.

22. 1796   **Edmond Malone**
            An Inquiry into the Authenticity of Certain Miscellaneous
            Papers and Legal Instruments, published Dec. 24, 1795. And
            Attributed to Shakespeare, Queen Elizabeth, and Henry
            Earl of Southampton (1796)
            vii, 424p.

23. 1796 **Thomas Caldecott**
Mr. Ireland's Vindication of his Conduct, Respecting the
Publication of the Supposed Shakespeare Manuscripts (1796)
iv, 48p.

1800 **George Hardinge**
Chalmeriana: or a Collection of Papers ... occasioned by
reading a late Apology for the Believers in the Shakespeare
papers, by George Chalmers etc. (1800)
viii, 94p.

24. 1798 **Samuel Ireland**
An Investigation of Mr. Malone's Claim to the Character of
Scholar, or Critic, Being an Examination of his Inquiry into
the Authenticity of the Shakespeare Manuscripts, etc. (1797)
vi, 156p.

25. 1797 **George Chalmers**
An Apology for the Believers in the Shakespeare-Papers
which were exhibited in Norfolk Street (1797)
iv, 628p.

26. 1799 **George Chalmers**
A Supplemental Apology for the Believers in the Shakespeare-
Papers: Being a Reply to Mr. Malone's Answer, which was
early announced, but never published: with a Dedication to
George Steevens, and a Postscript (1799)
viii, 656 p.

For Product Safety Concerns and Information please contact our EU
representative GPSR@taylorandfrancis.com
Taylor & Francis Verlag GmbH, Kaufingerstraße 24, 80331 München, Germany

www.ingramcontent.com/pod-product-compliance
Lightning Source LLC
Chambersburg PA
CBHW070923100726
47908CB00001B/76

* 9 7 8 1 1 3 8 9 8 3 3 8 0 *